T0384018

More praise for *Jelly Roll Blues*

"Elijah Wald's latest excavation of American popular culture reminds us that music is meant to reflect life as it is, despite the genteel aspirations of commercial window dressers who seek to protect the public from itself. *Jelly Roll Blues* gives by far the most realistic and satisfying account of Morton's cultural environment to date, while also revealing the importance of cultural networks that operated beneath the commercial mainstream. Highly recommended."

—Bruce Boyd Raeburn, curator emeritus, Hogan Archive of
New Orleans Music and Jazz, Tulane University

"Elijah Wald's incisive, deeply researched, and hugely entertaining new book reminds us of the power of stories and storytelling to both shape and illuminate worlds, and what is lost when those narratives are disrupted. Using Jelly Roll Morton's fascinating 1938 Library of Congress musical memoir as a jumping-off point, and through his careful engagement with previously censored lyrics and obscured lives, Wald invites us on an important journey toward correcting incomplete historical accounts of early blues and jazz."

—Kimberly Mack, associate professor of English at the University of
Illinois Urbana-Champaign and author of *Fictional Blues:
Narrative Self-Invention from Bessie Smith to Jack White*

"I enjoyed *Jelly Roll Blues* immensely. Whatever one's estimate of Morton's importance and credibility, there is no doubt about his ability to be in interesting places at interesting times, doing interesting things. Wald guides the reader round that world with admirable clarity. For blues enthusiasts, some of his observations about the history and origins of the form will be required reading."

—Tony Russell, author of *The Blues: From Robert Johnson to
Robert Cray* and *Rural Rhythm*

Jelly Roll Blues

ALSO BY ELIJAH WALD

Dylan Goes Electric! Newport, Seeger, Dylan, and the Night That Split the Sixties

The Dozens: A History of Rap's Mama

The Blues: A Very Short Introduction

How the Beatles Destroyed Rock 'n' Roll: An Alternative History of American Popular Music

Global Minstrels: Voices of World Music

Riding with Strangers: A Hitchhiker's Journey

Dave Van Ronk: The Mayor of MacDougal Street (with Van Ronk)

Escaping the Delta: Robert Johnson and the Invention of the Blues

Narcocorrido: A Journey into the Music of Drugs, Guns, and Guerrillas

Josh White: Society Blues

River of Song: A Musical Journey Down the Mississippi (coauthored with John Junkerman)

Jelly Roll Blues

Censored Songs & Hidden Histories

ELIJAH WALD

New York

Jacket design by Terri Sirma
Jacket photograph © Historical/Getty Images
Jacket illustration © Douglas Miller
Jacket copyright © 2024 by Hachette Book Group, Inc.

Hachette Books
Hachette Book Group
1290 Avenue of the Americas
New York, NY 10104
HachetteBooks.com
Twitter.com/HachetteBooks
Instagram.com/HachetteBooks

First Edition: April 2024

Published by Hachette Books, an imprint of Hachette Book Group, Inc. The Hachette Books name and logo is a trademark of the Hachette Book Group.

The Hachette Speakers Bureau provides a wide range of authors for speaking events. To find out more, go to hachettespeakersbureau.com or email HachetteSpeakers@hbgusa.com.

Books by Hachette Books may be purchased in bulk for business, educational, or promotional use. For information, please contact your local bookseller or Hachette Book Group Special Markets Department at: special.markets@hbgusa.com.

The publisher is not responsible for websites (or their content) that are not owned by the publisher.

Print book interior design by Amy Quinn

Photo insert design by Sandrine Sheon

Library of Congress Control Number: 2023951166

ISBNs: 9780306831409 (hardcover); 9780306831423 (ebook)

Printed in the United States of America

LSC-C

Printing 1, 2024

To David and Roselyn, my first and dearest friends in New Orleans

Contents

We had plenty of fun, the kind of a fun I don't think I've ever seen any other place. Of course, there may be nicer fun, but that particular kind—there was never that kind of fun anyplace, I think, on the face of the globe but New Orleans.

—Jelly Roll Morton, Library of Congress Recordings

It was the music. The dirty, get-on-down music the women sang and the men played and both danced to, close and shameless or apart and wild. . . . Just hearing it was like violating the law.

—Toni Morrison, *Jazz*

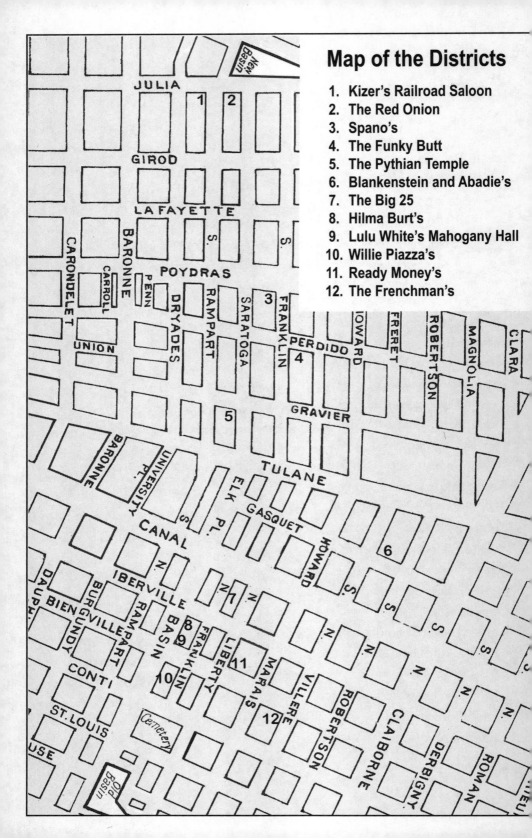

Map of the Districts

1. Kizer's Railroad Saloon
2. The Red Onion
3. Spano's
4. The Funky Butt
5. The Pythian Temple
6. Blankenstein and Abadie's
7. The Big 25
8. Hilma Burt's
9. Lulu White's Mahogany Hall
10. Willie Piazza's
11. Ready Money's
12. The Frenchman's

A Note on Language,
Offensive and Otherwise

THIS IS A BOOK OF QUESTIONS, JOURNEYS, AND DISCOVERIES, EXPLORING some rarely traveled paths of American music and culture. Much of it involves sex, often in explicit language. Much of it involves race, often in complicated ways. All of it involves history: how history is constructed, and by whom, and how much is left out, and why, and how wary we should be about how other people tell our stories and how we tell other people's stories.

I was inspired by some blues recordings Jelly Roll Morton made in 1938 at the Library of Congress, recalling the Gulf Coast styles of the early 1900s, but unissued until the 1990s because they were considered obscene. If a significant body of work by one of the most celebrated figures in American music was buried for sixty years because of prudery and censorship, I wondered how much else had been buried for similar reasons and what might be learned from that material. Searching through the papers of early folk, blues, and jazz researchers, I found that many had preserved lyrics they considered unpublishable—or, tantalizingly, wrote about songs they did not collect or preserve for that reason. This book is largely based on that research and the ways those discoveries connected to other music and culture that has been omitted, obscured, and misunderstood over the years, voices that have been suppressed or ignored, and the stories they tell.

I have tried to present this material and my exploration of it as transparently as possible. When working from written sources, I have preserved the original orthography, for example spelling the name of the mythic bad man inspired by the historical figure of Lee Shelton variously as *Stackalee, Stack O'Lee, Stagolee*, and so on, because people wrote it all those ways, and as a reminder that writing is a questionable means of preserving oral culture. Official documents were often equally inconsistent, and if I sometimes settled on a particular spelling—Desdunes for the name sometimes written as Desdume or Desdoumes, or Connor for the name often written as Connors—I do not mean to suggest those spellings are uniquely correct.

When working from recordings, I have used standard dictionary spellings for standard dictionary words. There is a long tradition of transcribing the speech of middle-class, formally educated white people with standard spelling while transcribing Black and working-class speech phonetically, but that is a choice to mark one group's speech as standard and others' as divergent. I choose instead to treat normal speech as normal; I have not altered anyone's syntax, but, for example, write "They was going" rather than "They was goin'," regardless of whether a speaker sounded the final *g*.

That choice reflects my own preferences, politics, and time, as previous writers' choices reflect theirs. Since this book is an effort to explore that process, when I quote other people's writing I have preserved details like the choice to write *negro* with a small *N* or to elide some words while treating others as acceptable: if someone wrote "mother—er," I don't fill in the missing letters, and if they wrote the n-word in full, I don't censor it. This book includes many quotations and lyrics that some readers will find offensive. I find some of them offensive myself. I was tempted to censor some passages, but in a book that criticizes other writers for censorship and examines the ways their viewpoints and prejudices affected their work, I have no business shielding myself. In some passages, I have tried to distance myself by highlighting the racism or misogyny of a quotation, and I was tempted to do so more often, but there are so many such passages that it felt repetitive and condescending to highlight each of them. So, caveat lector.

In the end I removed one verse, because it kept ricocheting around my brain in disturbing ways and I didn't want to put it in other people's brains—it is in Vance Randolph's collection of "unprintable" Ozark folklore for anyone who wants to explore this field more thoroughly. Some readers may find other rhymes and quotations similarly disturbing and wish I had omitted them, and I expect this book to prompt some uncomfortable conversations—but I think we should be aware of this material, and having those conversations. I learned a great deal on this journey but always found more questions than answers, and I do not necessarily trust the answers I found or the ways I have understood them. I hope this book will prompt more questions, spur more exploration, and lead other people to find more and different answers.

A few words require additional explanation: *sporting*, as in "the sporting world," "sporting life," and "sporting folk," was a common term in the nineteenth century for the world of boxing, racing, and gambling, and by the later nineteenth century it had become a standard euphemism for prostitution, as in "sporting house" and "sporting women." Those meanings overlapped, along with the worlds and people they described: it was common for boxers and gamblers to be romantically involved with women who did sex work; for those women to frequent races and boxing matches; and for all of them to favor rowdy new musical styles like ragtime, jazz, and blues.

The word *toast* underwent a somewhat similar evolution. In many areas and situations, it was common to recite elaborate, rhymed toasts before downing a round of drinks, and in African American culture the term became standard for any long, rhymed recitation, whether poems learned from books or vernacular epics like "Stackolee," "Shine and the *Titanic*," and "The Signifying Monkey."

Finally, through much of the twentieth century *cock* was used by Black southerners—as well as many white southerners and some people in other regions—to mean *vulva* rather than *penis*. This seems to be a

variant of *cockle*, from the French *coquille* (shell), a derivation that survived in lyrics like *"her cock flew open like a mussel shell."* Cockle or scal-
lop shells have been used for millennia to represent female genitalia,
and hence female creation; images of the Egyptian goddess Isis and the
Roman goddess Venus often showed them nestled in a half shell, and this
iconography is maintained in modern statues of the Virgin Mary.[1]

Songs and Silences

In the spring of 1938, Jelly Roll Morton sat at a grand piano in a concert hall of the Library of Congress and sang an epic ballad of sporting life in turn-of-the-century New Orleans. The beginning of the song was not preserved, but what remains lasts half an hour, filling seven sides of four 78-rpm discs. We first hear a woman warning a rival about messing with her man, then she shoots the other woman, stands trial for murder, is sent to prison, and eventually dies, commending herself to heaven and warning other women not to make her mistakes.

There are fifty-nine verses in all, most using the standard twelve-bar blues form: two repeated lines and a third that completes the thought and caps it with a rhyme. The recording begins in mid-conversation:

"I know you've got my man.
I know you've got my man.
Try to hold him if you can."

Some verses are in the woman's voice, some in the voices of other characters, some shift to a third-person narration:

Policeman grabbed her and took her to jail,
Policeman grabbed her and took her to jail,
There was no one to go that poor gal's bail.

Toward the end of the fourth side, as the heroine adjusts to prison life, the story takes a new twist:

"I can't have a man, so a woman is my next bet,
I can't have a man in here, a woman is my next bet,"
She said to a good-looking mama, "Baby, I'll get you yet."

The fifth side develops the romance; the sixth and seventh express the woman's regrets and prayers, foretell a lonely death, and end with a warning to her fellow prisoners:

"If you get out of here, try to be a good girl."
(Spoken: "Oh, I had to tell 'em.")
"Girls, if you get out of here, try to be a good girl,
That's the only way you gonna wear your diamonds and pearls."

Morton's voice is warm and conversational, his piano relaxed and swinging. He was revisiting a familiar style from his youth, and neither he nor Alan Lomax, the folklorist who made the recording and titled it "The Murder Ballad," seems to have regarded this performance as unusual. That surprised me the first time I heard it, because I have spent much of my life listening to early blues and there is nothing else like this on record, nor any mention of half-hour-long narrative ballads in the standard twelve-bar form. The most famous African American murder ballad, "Frankie and Johnny," and the most popular ballad of New Orleans nightlife, "House of the Rising Sun," trace somewhat similar arcs, but the recorded versions of ballads like "Frankie" and "Stackolee" last at most five or six minutes, and although some collectors preserved longer lyrics in print, none comes close to Morton's half-hour epic and most are set in the ragtime-flavored forms of the 1890s rather than what we now think of as blues.

If researchers had asked other performers of Morton's generation for similarly lengthy narratives in blues form, we might have a quite different picture of the Black lyrical tradition, but none did, in part because they didn't know this song existed. Morton's Library of Congress recordings were issued on a series of 78-rpm albums in the 1940s and on LPs in the 1950s, but the seven sides with "The Murder Ballad"—along with four sides with a similarly unique and extensive version of "Make Me a Pallet on the Floor"; two versions of his early theme song, "Winding Ball"; and several shorter performances—were not included, because they were considered obscene. One of the "Winding Ball" sides was released in the 1970s, but the other censored performances were not made available until 1993, and a full set of Morton's Library recordings was not issued until 2005.[1]

When the censored songs finally appeared, many listeners were startled to hear Morton using language as rough as anything in gangsta rap. Some were shocked, some thrilled, but few noted the novelistic way he employed that language. Unlike most "bawdy" songs—the coy term folklorists use for songs about sex—Morton's ballad consistently matches the characters' speech with their situations. In the scene leading up to the killing, the woman warns her rival, *"If you don't leave my fucking man alone . . . I'll cut your throat and drink your fucking blood like wine,"* and immediately afterward explains, *"I killed that bitch because she fucked my man,"* but in court she is appropriately circumspect, saying she killed the woman *"because she had my man."* In the jailhouse sex vignette, she tells her prospective lover, *"I want you to give me some of this good cunt you've got,"* but when she is reflecting on her past, meditating on her mistakes, or expressing regrets, her language matches those moods.

Morton's other censored performances were closer to familiar "party song" traditions. "Pallet on the Floor" is an exuberantly filthy sketch of an afternoon tryst between a hustling man and a workingman's wife, played as raw comedy. As with "The Murder Ballad," there is nothing else like it on record; the melody and opening verse were known throughout the South and recorded numerous times, but Morton's version lasts fifteen minutes and is the only one with an extended, cohesive

narrative. Once again, he did not present it as anything special, just saying it was "one of the early blues that was in New Orleans, I guess, many
years before I was born."

Morton began working as a pianist and singer in the first decade of the
twentieth century and spent his teens playing in honky-tonks and houses
of prostitution around New Orleans and the Gulf Coast states. Those were
the formative years of blues and several of his contemporaries remembered
him as specializing in that style, but by 1912, when blues swept the country as a hot new craze, he had moved on to other venues and music. Over
the next quarter century, thousands of blues songs were published in sheet
music and issued on records, but he was working as a musical comedian in
vaudeville theaters, then began leading dance bands and reached national
prominence in the 1920s with a series of recordings that established him
as a foundational composer and arranger of instrumental jazz. His period
as a blues singer was over before W. C. Handy, Ma Rainey, Blind Lemon
Jefferson, and thousands of other artists reshaped that style to fit the
strictures of commercial publication and the limitations of three-minute
78-rpm discs—and, as a result, his blues recordings for the Library of
Congress provide a unique glimpse of an earlier world.

If that glimpse is accurate, then what was preserved on commercial
recordings and in published folklore collections is a truncated, censored revision of the vernacular style; the familiar history of blues is
censored history; and the censorship not only cleaned up language but
obscured entire lyrical forms, erasing complex modes of storytelling and
the stories that were told. The erasure did not happen all at once, but as
blues was increasingly marketed in print and on recordings, performers learned that some words, styles, and approaches were not appropriate to professional performance. It was a circular and ongoing process:
singers reshaped and edited songs to fit the demands of publishers and
record companies, and the commercial products shaped the standards
and repertoires of later singers. In the 1930s, a Federal Writers' Project
fieldworker in the Florida turpentine and logging camps wrote, "When
the nickel phonograph made its appearance, the change was immediately noticeable . . . songs that had formerly been more or less peculiar

to the particular section in which they were sung began giving way to the 'Pine-top's Boogie-Woogie,' the 'Mistreating Blues,' and other favorites of the machines." He added that these songs continued to evolve in live performance "to satisfy the tastes of the community's own singers," who added "unprintably vulgar" lyrics, and "men and women alike were laughingly singing their changed edition."[2] Vernacular traditions did not disappear overnight, but the new technology drastically altered the ways people experienced and understood music. By the 1960s, when a wave of researchers began combing the South for musicians who could tell them about the early days of blues, everyone they met was familiar with records by Bessie Smith, Lemon Jefferson, and their many successors, and most would never have heard anything like "The Murder Ballad," much less performed it.

The shift to censored, mass-market forms obscured more than dirty words and phrases, but if it had been limited to details of language, that is not a small thing. The way people talk is basic to their identity and culture, and if their speech is considered unacceptable, that implies they and their culture are unacceptable. In the case of blues, those judgments went along with a deep history of racism, but other working-class cultures were similarly censored, and by exploring what was suppressed we can not only get a deeper sense of blues but also find connections to other traditions, other kinds of songs, and the varied and intersecting cultures of people whose voices were rarely and selectively preserved.

History is not simply what happened in the past; it is an active process and the Haitian historian Michel-Rolph Trouillot noted that it "is always also the creation of silences." He wrote that those silences "enter the process of historical production at four crucial moments: the moment of fact creation (the making of *sources*); the moment of fact assembly (the making of *archives*); the moment of fact retrieval (the making of *narratives*); and the moment of retrospective significance (the making of *history* in the final instance)." Thus, he added: "Power does not enter the story once and for all, but at different times and from different angles. It precedes the narrative proper, contributes to its creation and to its interpretation."[3]

If we want to understand the past, we must not only study what survives, but also think about what does not survive, and why, and make an effort to explore those silences. Paradoxically, a consistent pattern of censorship can make this easier, because by looking at what was censored we get a better understanding of what we don't know and why we don't know it; of what was obscured, and why, and by whom. Early blues songs were overwhelmingly performed by Black, working-class people in their own communities, but recording, preservation, and history were overwhelmingly the domain of white middle-class men, some white middle-class women, and a few Black scholars who also tended to be middle-class and university educated. Those groups had different tastes and customs, and the individual singers and collectors also had personal quirks and interests and did their work with varying audiences in mind.

Folklorists tended to assume their readers were more innocent or prudish than their informants: The ballad scholar Cecil Sharp explained that English rural singers traditionally treated "'the way of a man with a maid' simply and directly," but collectors and editors had to "undertake the distasteful task of modifying noble and beautiful sentiments in order that they may suit the minds and conform to the conventions of another age, where such things would not be understood in the primitive, direct, and healthy sense."[4] John A. Lomax, Alan's father, similarly wrote that the "profanity and vulgarity" of the cowboy songs he heard in his Texas youth had "a Homeric quality," reflecting "the big, open, free life lived near to Nature's breast," but had to be toned down for "so-called polite society."[5]

Some blues scholars struck a similar tone: Alain Locke praised the "healthy and earthy expression in the original peasant paganism" of the first generation of blues and jazz artists, whose "deadly effective folk speech was clean and racy by contrast with the mawkish sentimentality and concocted lascivity of the contemporary cabaret songs."[6] Others were less appreciative: Howard Odum, who pioneered the use of a phonograph to collect Black folklore in the first decade of the twentieth century, was working toward a degree in psychology and wrote that the material he recorded in rural Mississippi exhibited "every phase of immorality and filth" and showed how "the vivid imagination of the negro makes his constant thought a putrid bed of rottenness and intensifies his already depraved nature."[7] Most folklorists were less judgmental, or at least more careful about how they phrased their judgments—and Odum took a different tone in his later writing—but all understood that many lyrics sung in working-class environments could not be published without editing and expurgation, and that some songs were unredeemable.

The more conscientious collectors knew they were producing a distorted picture and tried to preserve unexpurgated texts for the use of serious scholars. In 1907 John Lomax circulated a letter to newspapers around the Southwest requesting examples of "frontier songs," and its final paragraph specified that readers should send lyrics "in the precise form which they have popularly assumed . . . [since] ballads and the like which, because of crudity, incompleteness, coarseness, or for any other reason are unavailable for publication, will be as interesting and as useful for my purposes as others of more merit."[8]

DINK'S BLUES

LOMAX WAS PARTICULARLY INTERESTED IN COWBOY BALLADS, WHICH could be framed as extending a respected British tradition and celebrating the brave, independent spirit of the Western pioneers. However, he was also planning a collection of Black folklore and was pleased to receive a letter from eastern Texas with what the writer described as "the words to some old nigger songs" and a recommendation that he visit the Brazos River bottoms, where such songs were still common. His informant added a note of warning: "Most of those old backwoods niggers are still singing the old songs they sang fifty years ago. A good many of their songs are too smutty to send through the mail. I left off several verses from the songs I enclosed on that account."[9]

A year or two later, in a land reclamation camp on the banks of the Brazos, Lomax made the first documented recording of what we now would recognize as a twelve-bar blues.[10] The singer was a woman named

Dink, and all we know of her is from Lomax's writings. In his 1947 memoir, *Adventures of a Ballad Hunter*, he recalled that a crew of levee builders had been brought from Vicksburg, Mississippi, and their supplies included several dozen women who were "shipped from Memphis along with the mules and the iron scrapers."

> The two groups of men and women had never seen each other until they met on the river bank in Texas where the white levee contractor gave them the opportunity presented to Adam and Eve—they were left alone to mate after looking each other over. While her man built the levee, each woman kept his tent, toted the water, cut the firewood, cooked, washed his clothes and warmed his bed.

Lomax wrote that Dink first brushed him off, saying, "Today ain't my singin' day," but he stuck around and "finally a bottle of gin, bought at a nearby plantation commissary, loosed her muse."

> She sang, as she scrubbed her man's dirty clothes . . . her little two-year-old nameless son played in the sand at her feet. "He ain't got no daddy, an' I ain't had no time to hunt up a name for him," she explained.[11]

Did it really happen that way? Lomax's files include a handwritten transcript of Dink's blues and what seems to be a contemporary typescript, but his notes on the typescript say only that she was from Mississippi; she used some unusual phrases, referring to steamboats "on us river" and to the antebellum period as "befo' reb times"; and "she says there are hundreds of verses to this song." His first published report of their meeting did not mention a child and described her as "a lithe, chocolate-colored woman with a reckless glint in her eye," who told him:

> "You're jes' lucky I happened to want to sing this mornin'. Maybe to-morrow I wouldn't 'a' sung you nothin'. Anyhow, maybe tomorrow I won't be here. I'm likely to git tired, or mad, an' go. Say, if I got mad, I'd

about dump that tub o' wet clo's there in that bed, an' I wouldn't be here by night."[12]

Alan provided yet another version of the meeting, saying his mother, Bess Brown Lomax, was there as well and Dink said she knew a song, but "would only sing it for my mother. So the ladies went off into Dink's little hut."[13] Women were often hesitant to sing for male collectors—another source of historical silences—and were likely to be circumspect about their conversation and repertoires when they did. If that memory is accurate, John's colorful descriptions may likewise be secondhand, with modifications for literary effect.

Whatever the surrounding details, Dink recorded two songs on wax cylinders and Lomax took them home and transcribed the lyrics. He continued to play the recordings for friends and visitors until the grooves were worn down and Dink's voice was no longer intelligible, then discarded them—in those early years, it was common for folklorists to use recording as an aid to transcription rather than as a permanent form of documentation. He published both lyrics in a 1917 article titled "Self-pity in Negro Folk-Songs," and again in *American Ballads and Folk Songs*, a 1934 collection co-edited with Alan, as "Dink's Song" and "Dink's Blues."

More accurately, he published adaptations of the lyrics. Although the blues was presented in both publications as what Dink sang on the banks of the Brazos, half the verses in the 1917 version were from other sources and Lomax reworked several of Dink's lines, in one case substituting a minstrel-show "mammy" where the transcript had "mother." The 1934 version was closer to the original but omitted several verses, and neither included her fifth verse:

Jest as soon as the big boat git way round the curve, [2x]
O Lordy the fuckin old pilot lookin all round the world.

As with the verses I quoted from Morton's "Murder Ballad," there is nothing sexy about that couplet, but it includes a word that could not be published or sent through the mail. Other verses were sexier:

My chuck grindin' every hole but mine. ⌈3x⌉

My man is a jockey and he learned me how to ride ⌈2x⌉
An' he learned me how to cock it on the side.[14]

The Lomaxes printed the first of those verses in their book and omitted the second—perhaps because it had the word *cock*, but there is no way
to be sure, since they also omitted several verses that had no offensive
language. Nor do I have any idea why they left off the verse about the
pilot rather than simply removing the unacceptable word.

By most standards, that word is an insignificant detail, but I was
excited when I found it. For one thing, it confirmed my assumption that
before the era of commercial distribution, blues lyrics were extensions
of normal vernacular speech and used words like *fuck*, not to shock or
titillate, but because that was the way people talked in the venues and
situations where the songs were performed.[15] For another, I took it as
evidence of the transcript's authenticity: since Lomax knew he could not
print the word, its inclusion suggests the transcript was uncensored and,
aside from possible mishearings, is an accurate record of what Dink sang.
If so, it is the earliest reliable transcript of a fully formed blues lyric—and
although I doubt either Lomax or Dink would have called it blues at that
time, I could be wrong. The first page of the original, handwritten transcript has been lost, but the earliest typescript (which elides "fuckin" as
"F—in") is headed "THE BLUES."

Whenever he added that title, Lomax did not yet consider blues to be
a style or genre. He thought of it as one infinitely long and variable song,
which people—especially Black women—sang all over the South, "called
variously 'The Railroad Blues,' 'The Cincinnati Blues,' 'The Graveyard
Blues,' 'The Waco Blues,' 'The Dallas Blues,' 'The Galveston Blues,' or
simply 'The Blues.'"[16] By 1917 dozens of distinct compositions with set
verses and choruses were also being marketed as blues and some had
become popular hits, but Lomax's interpretation was not unusual. James
P. Johnson recalled that when he played for Ethel Waters in New York

nightclubs around 1919, she often just sang "the blues, with no special tune and with words she made up herself."[17]

Though it is reasonable to describe "Dink's Blues" as the first surviving example of a twelve-bar blues song, it makes equal sense to think of it as a random sample of possible verses. Dink would have been unlikely to sing the same set of lyrics even five minutes later, and many of her couplets were collected or recorded over the next few years from other singers and had presumably been circulating with regional and personal variations throughout the southern United States:

Some folks say that the worry blues ain't bad,
It's the worst old feelin' ever I had.

Want to lay my head on the Southern Railroad line,
Let some east bound train come and ease my troubled mind.

If I feel tomorrow like I feel today,
Stand right here look a thousand miles away.

Dink's lyric is evidence that the twelve-bar blues form and some standard verses were already common in the first decade of the twentieth century, and her story shows one way the music spread: Black southerners were traveling widely, some for work, some to get away from oppressive or unpleasant situations, and some just because they could. As she sang in another verse, *"If I leave here walkin' it's chances I might ride."*

Given the breadth and richness of Dink's lyrics, it may seem perverse to fixate on one little "fuckin," but that was why I was going through Lomax's transcripts. The censorship of Morton's recordings made me wonder what other songs had been similarly censored and what uncensored scraps might survive, so I went looking for them. Finding that word in Lomax's files was like finding a distinctive potsherd in an archaeological dig; it suggested there were more fragments to be found and, if I kept looking, I might even find some whole pots and learn more about the

worlds and people that produced them—as well as getting a better sense
of how those worlds and people have been obscured and overlooked.

To a great extent, that meant exploring how African American music
was collected, preserved, altered, censored, and disseminated by white
scholars, record scouts, and enthusiasts, but any exploration of race and
racism inevitably becomes complicated and even the most accurate gen-
eralizations are inevitably misleading. Along with the choices made by
collectors, every text and recording reflects the choices of singers who
routinely adapted and censored their performances, whether to reach
a broader public, because they did not know a particular audience well
enough to be sure a verse would be acceptable, or because they knew
very well that an audience would not like a verse. Mary Wheeler, a white
woman who collected Mississippi riverfront songs in the late 1930s,
described singers beginning a verse, then hesitating and whispering
to each other before leaving it unfinished, and a man telling her, "No,
honey . . . I don't know no rouster songs fittin' fo' a nice lady to write
down."[18]

Professional performers were more likely to come up with
work-arounds. The Chicago singer Arvella Gray explained to a folklorist
named Donald Winkelman that a lot of words in his blues would have to
be changed for recording because they were "on the blue side," and when
Winkelman pressed him for examples, sang:

> *There ain't no telling what the poor girl doing,*
> *There ain't no telling what the poor girl doing*
> *Say she may be cooking and she may be screwing.*

He suggested if they made a record, "Maybe you'd say, 'might be sew-
ing,'" then provided another example that referred to the miseries of
gonorrhea:

> *Now when your peter gets sore, partner, and begin to run,*
> *Say, when your peter gets sore, partner, and begin to run,*
> *Said, hot boiling water, partner, will not help you none.*[19]

Gray did not come up with alternate language for that verse, but a couple of commercial records show how other singers dealt with it. In 1929, the Virginia guitarist Luke Jordan sang:

If I call you, woman, doggone, you refuse to come
If I call you, woman, doggone, you refuse to come
Hot boiling water, I swear, won't help you none.

That couplet makes no sense, but many listeners may have filled in the censored line for themselves; it was clearly familiar in oral tradition, since seven years later Robert Johnson coupled Jordan's substitute with a reference to the Arkansas resort whose waters were famed for curing venereal disease: *"All the doctors in Hot Springs sure can't help her none."* [20]

In the early days of blues recording, it was common knowledge that singers were censoring themselves. The white folklorist Guy Johnson wrote in the 1920s that he "frequently met the remark, after repeating the words of some late blues to a Negro laborer, 'Why I've known a song like that for ten years—except mine wouldn't do to put on a record.'" [21] A Black researcher, Sam Adams, managed to collect a dirty version of "Casey Jones" from a Mississippi singer named Joe Cal, but only after Cal explained, "I know lots of them old tales and songs, and when I'm by myself I sings them, but I just don't like to do that kind of stuff among folks that ain't like me." [22] Nor was that just a matter of propriety: a woman named Ruth Shays told the Black sociologist John Langston Gwaltney, "Our foreparents had sense enough not to spill their in-gut to whitefolks, or blackfolks, either, if they didn' know them." [23]

What survives from the past has been shaped by choices made by all sorts of people, in all sorts of situations, and censorship is far from the only problem. Lomax's handwritten transcript of Dink's blues includes a false start to one verse, the crossed-out phrase *"Open my leg..."* My first thought was that she started to sing a dirty verse but thought better of it, or possibly she sang the whole verse and Lomax decided not to transcribe it. Both of those explanations fit my agenda by showing how censorship affected the historical record, and I wrote and revised an analysis of this omission several times before a third explanation occurred to me: Dink had previously sung several sexy verses and those three crossed-out words are followed by a verse beginning, *"Want to lay my head on the Southern Railroad line . . ."* So maybe Lomax was primed to expect something dirty and misheard *"Wan' lay my head"* as *"Open my leg,"* then realized his mistake and corrected it. Or maybe not.

History and its silences are shaped not only by human choices but by human errors and ignorance. White collectors misunderstood what they heard from Black singers, singers misunderstood or misinterpreted each other's lyrics, and it is not always easy to distinguish misunderstandings from intentional changes or to know when one is introducing new mistakes. The same words and phrases often have different meanings or nuances in different communities, and in some cases are meant to have multiple meanings and to be obscure to outsiders—especially when it comes to private or secret language. An amusing sideline to studying censorship is finding things censors missed because they didn't understand what they were hearing.[24]

HOG-EYE

Most of this book is about blues and African American vernacular culture, but the practices and prejudices of collectors and archivists—whether academic outsiders or community members—have similarly affected what was preserved in all sorts of situations. Any collection of cowboy, sailor, or army songs that does not include words like *fuck* and *cunt* is a censored collection, and if those words tended to be more common in all-male environments, plenty of women used them as well and sang songs that used them; one of the reasons I am interested in dirty blues is that the rawest blues lyrics have often been performed by and for women and reflect female tastes and experiences. When I began exploring the censorship of early blues, I kept stumbling across similar lyrics in other songs and communities and finding connections that censorship had obscured—for example between sea shanties, which are often considered white culture, and the songs of Black farmhands and railroad workers, or the Euro-Afro-Hispanic-Native culture of southwestern ranches.

John Lomax grew up on a farm in Texas, immersed in cowboy traditions, and he preserved some notably uncensored cowboy songs. His most prolific source was a man named Tom Hight, who "knew more cowboy melodies than any other person I have ever found." He met Hight around the same time he recorded Dink, and described a two-day session in an Oklahoma City hotel where Hight's muse was aided by "two quart bottles of rye which he consulted frequently between songs."[25] Lomax published one of those songs as "The Bull Whacker" in his first book, *Cowboy Songs and Other Frontier Ballads*, in 1910, and in *American Ballads and Folk Songs*, the collection he co-edited with Alan in 1934; and Alan included it in his 1960 collection, *Folk Songs of North America*. The printed texts varied a bit, but the penultimate verse was consistent:

There was good old times in Salt Lake
That never can pass by,
It was there I first spied
My China girl called Wi.
She could smile, she could chuckle,
She could roll her hog eye;
Then it's whack the cattle on, boys,—
Root hog or die.[26]

What Hight actually sang was rather different. Lomax's unpublished transcript had "pass o'er" rather than "pass by," a poetic flourish that rhymed with "my little China hoar" (an archaic spelling of *whore*) and continued: "*She could fuck and she could suck, and she could roll her hog eyes.*"

That sort of bowdlerization was standard in collections of cowboy and sailor songs, and Lomax's excisions are in some ways less interesting than what he retained. I assume he originally wrote "hog eyes" in the plural because he imagined a woman rolling her eyes flirtatiously, and corrected it to "hog eye" because he realized that was what Hight sang, but I wonder what he thought it meant; specifically, whether he knew it was used variously as slang for *anus* or *vulva* and printed it anyway because he assumed most of his readers would not. He was a circumspect editor but not entirely prudish or humorless, and the term was known throughout the United States and formed the burden of one of the most popular sea shanties. A collector named Annie Gilchrist mentioned it in 1906 in the British *Journal of the Folk-Song Society*, noting: "This shanty was not allowed so long as any passengers were aboard; directly they were landed this was the only shanty that would suit sailor John. The words cannot be given, but the tune is characteristic. It is of negro origin, from the slave states."[27]

Many sea shanties were drawn from African American work-song traditions and could reasonably be considered a subset of those traditions. By the early nineteenth century about a fifth of the men working on American ships had African ancestry, and they were often favored as song leaders. Frank T. Bullen, who worked on British sailing ships for twenty years, wrote that shanties tended to be picked up in the West Indies and the southern United States and noted the particular facility of Black seamen—adding, in an aside that has obvious relevance to blues and jazz, "Many a Chantyman was prized in spite of his poor voice because of his improvisations." Bullen did not print lyrics for most of the songs he collected, writing: "The stubborn fact is that they had no set words beyond a starting verse or two and the fixed phrases of the chorus . . . Poor doggerel they were mostly and often very lewd and filthy, but they gave the knowing and appreciative shipmates, who roared the refrain, much opportunity for laughter."[28]

In 1921 Richard Runciman Terry devoted a couple of paragraphs in his *Shanty Book* to "The Hog-Eye Man," writing: "Every old sailor knew the meaning of the term" and "as a boy my curiosity was piqued by reticence, evasion, or declarations of ignorance whenever I asked the meaning." He added that although he eventually solved the mystery and it "had nothing whatever to do with the optic of the 'man' who was sung about . . . that is all the explanation I am at liberty to give in print."[29]

A century later, no one has published or recorded a "Hog Eye Man" lyric that justifies those descriptions.[30] However, Stan Hugill, whose voluminous *Shanties from the Seven Seas* made the usual evasions and apologies, sent a manuscript of uncensored sailor songs to Gershon Legman, a scholar of dirty folklore, which included a set of verses with a note that they were also used for another shanty, "Johnny Come Down to Hilo." He noted that some collectors believed *hog-eye* had a "filthy meaning," but "my contention is that they have got the word mixed up with 'deadeye' meaning 'anus.'"[31]

The lyric Hugill provided for "Johnny Come Down to Hilo" included the latter term:

> *He travelled all around till he came to the shack*
> *Where his Sally made a livin' oh, a-layin' on her back. . . .*
> *He opened the door—she gave a little cry,*
> *An' then he stove his toggle up her old deadeye.*

If this was also sung in "The Hog-Eye Man," it would have been followed by the crew lustily chorusing:

> *Oh, the hog-eye o! Row the boat ashore for her hog-eye,*
> *Row the boat ashore for her hog-eye O,*
> *She wants the hog-eye man!*[32]

Which, despite his protestations, suggests the terms could overlap.

One of the tricky things about understanding the past is that words and phrases do not have fixed or universal meanings and are used or understood differently from setting to setting and person to person. There is a port called Hilo in Hawaii, and sailors may have been thinking of it when they sang "Johnny Come Down to Hilo," but before that port existed, enslaved Black laborers in South Carolina were singing *"Johnny come down de hollow,"* in a song about a man being sold away to Georgia.[33] The shift from "hollow" to "Hilo" may have begun as a misunderstanding, but became standard as the song acclimated to a new environment with different landmarks—and if such shifts are sometimes confusing, they can alert us to other shifts and evolutions.

The earliest surviving "Hog-Eye" lyric seems to have been published in Solomon Northup's 1853 memoir of kidnapping, enslavement, and rescue, *Twelve Years a Slave*. Northup was a fiddler and recalled playing for dances on a Louisiana plantation where, when he paused to rest, the frolic continued to the accompaniment of "unmeaning songs, composed rather to a certain tune or measure, than for the purpose of expressing any distinct idea." As an example, he quoted some lyrics of "'Old Hog Eye . . .' a rather solemn and startling specimen of versification":

> *Who's been here since I've been gone?*
> *Pretty little gal wid a josey on.*
> *Hog Eye!*
> *Old Hog Eye,*
> *And Hosey too!*[34]

Although this has a shorter chorus than the "Hog Eye" shanties, a common sailor verse—often reworded in modern collections—was "*Who's been here since I been gone? / A big buck nigger with his sea-boots on.*" Hugill's unpublished version had "hard-on" instead of "sea-boots," and he suggested the song was "possibly from Negro railroad gangs, or Negro crews of barges known as 'Hogeyes' used in America about 1850."[35] That suggests an innocent definition for the title term, but the only references to hog-eye barges I have found are in discussions of this song and, although they may have existed, I would suggest they are mentioned in this context to distract readers from other etymologies.

However people understood it, the song was known throughout the United States. The same year Northup published the verse from Louisiana, a white violinist named Septimus Winner published a melody for "Hog Eye" in Philadelphia, and in 1855 it was mentioned as the favorite tune of the Monte Valley, outside Los Angeles.[36] In 1868 it turned up in a scurrilous satire on the North Carolina Constitutional Convention, which met for two months following the Civil War and composed laws forbidding slavery, removing property qualifications for voting, and introducing universal male suffrage and public education regardless of race. The delegates included 105 white and 15 Black men, and on the final day they celebrated by joining hands and singing "John Brown's Body." The *Raleigh Sentinel* decried the performance of this "disgusting melody," and other newspapers expanded the story into a burlesque on the dangers of "re-destruction," the *Daily North Carolinian* reporting that "the whole mongrel delegation" followed with "O! say yeller gal can't yer come out to-night," and "the roaring air of 'Hog Eye,' a favorite negro corn-shucking melody which begins 'Sal's in the garden siftin' sand' and has for its second line a rhyme too indecent to repeat."[37] Versions of that line were recorded by several white country bands in the 1920s and are still sung at bluegrass shows: "Sally's upstairs [or "in bed"] with the hog-eye man."

I have wandered far afield from Tom Hight's cowboy song and further still from Jelly Roll Morton, but that is the point: the varied sightings of *hog-eye*, a term that seems to have been documented exclusively in song lyrics, suggest a striking range of cultural connections and overlaps, and the absence of fuller texts reveals a consistent pattern of censorship and bowdlerization. There is also some honest confusion: despite Hugill's demurral, I have the sense that *hog-eye* was generally understood by sailors and a lot of other people to mean *anus*—the Spanish equivalent, *ojo de puerco*, is still current in Mexican slang, often with a connection to homosexual intercourse[38]—and I was primed for that definition by Ernest Hemingway's recollection of "wolves" on the Great Lakes who expressed their preference for sex with boys rather than women with the rhyming phrase, "gash may be fine but one-eye for mine."[39] But some people clearly used it to mean *vulva*. Jennie Devlin, a white woman born in 1865 and raised in upstate New York, recalled a verse that went:

Some for the girl that dresses neat,
Some for the girl that kisses sweet,
But I'm for the girl with the lily-white thighs
With a hole in her belly like a dead hog's eye.

The form of this verse suggests it was a drinking toast, many of which were obscene and began "Here's to the girl. . . . "[40] Such toasts were typically preserved as white male culture but often crossed racial lines.[41] Alger "Texas" Alexander, who was born sixty miles north of Dink's levee camp and became a popular recording artist in the 1920s, sang a "Boe Hog Blues" that echoed the second couplet of Devlin's toast:

> *She got little bitty legs, gee, but them noble thighs.*
> *She got little bitty legs, gee, but them noble thighs.*
> *She's got something under yonder, works like a boar hog's eye.*

Alexander's opening verse hinted at the term's alternate meaning:

> *Oh, tell me, mama, how you want your rolling done.*
> *Oh, tell me, mama, how you want your rolling done.*
> *Said, your face to the ground and your noodle up to the sun.*[42]

Whatever the anatomical specificities, the juxtaposition of Devlin's and Alexander's lyrics suggests a significant way dirty blues diverged from dirty white culture. Devlin's toast was framed for a male speaker and audience, with a strong flavor of misogyny; Alexander's song was addressed to a woman and treated her as an active participant, asking what she wanted and describing her as working together with him. Unlike the songs of sailors, cowboys, soldiers, and men's clubs, which are often openly hostile to women, blues was typically performed in venues where women were present, often sung by women and with women as the most active and enthusiastic audience. Two years after Alexander's recording, a female guitarist in Houston reframed his title verse as an expression of her own sexual power:

> *I've got little bitty legs, gee, but these noble thighs.*
> *I've got little bitty legs, gee, but these noble thighs.*
> *Eyyy, gee, but these noble thighs.*
> *I've got something underneath them that works like a boar hog's eye.*[43]

SPORTING LIFE AND SPORTING LANGUAGE

LILLIE MAE "GEESHIE" WILEY AND HER FREQUENT PARTNER, L.V. "ELVIE" Thomas, recorded only six songs but have become hallowed figures in the blues pantheon, their instrumental and vocal skills supplemented by stories of their fierce independence. Thomas's friends recalled her masculine demeanor and style of dress, one remarking, "You know how some women gotta have some help, have a man around? She didn't have to have one."[44] It seems likely that she and Wiley were lovers, and Wiley did not specify a gender when she sang,

> *But when you see me coming, pull down your window blind.*
> *But when you see me coming, pull down your window blind.*
> *You see me coming, pull down your window blind.*
> *So your next door neighbor sure can hear you whine.*

Nor did she specify the gender of the person addressed in her final verse:

> *I'm gonna cut your throat, baby, gonna look down in your face.*
> *I'm gonna cut your throat, babe, gon' look down in your face.*
> *Ehhh, gon' look down in your face.*
> *I'm gonna let some lonesome graveyard be your resting place.*

That verse is exceptional not for its violent imagery, which was fairly common, but because in 1931 Wiley killed her husband by stabbing him in the neck.[45] There is no indication that she was arrested or charged; maybe the authorities dismissed the killing as self-defense; maybe they didn't care about domestic violence in Black neighborhoods; or maybe she was tried and the court papers were lost or destroyed.

Wiley's story is a reminder that songs like Morton's "Murder Ballad" were performed for audiences that heard them as neighborhood gossip, perhaps exaggerated for dramatic effect but reflecting their daily lives and concerns. In Black honky-tonks and sporting districts, men and

women sang about the power, pleasures, and complications of sexual relationships, often in language that middle-class, respectable folk considered
dangerous and unprintable. I tend to refer to that language as *dirty*, a
term that can be pejorative but is also a reminder that dirt was a basic
element of working-class life. New Orleans, with its low elevation and
frequent flooding, was one of the last major urban areas to have a universal sewer system and only got clean running water in 1909.[46] That was
an obvious issue for anyone doing manual labor, the only labor available
to most Black people, as well as for people doing sex work or enjoying
sexual pleasure, and blues songs often dealt with the smell—the *funk*—of
heated bodies. Early blues and jazz musicians routinely referred to their
songs and styles as "dirty," "smelly," "nasty," or "ratty," with the understanding that the results might offend outsiders but suited their audience's tastes and experiences.[47]

Since language is basic to the way people define themselves, it is
important to be attentive to their terminology. White tourists and boost-
ers called New Orleans's downtown prostitution district "Storyville," in
mocking reference to Sidney Story, the alderman who wrote the legisla-
tion limiting sex workers to a twenty-block area near the Southern Railway Terminal on Basin Street, and by now most historians have adopted
that term. But Black New Orleanians almost never used it; they called
that area the Red Light District, the Tenderloin District, or most often
just "the District." Louis Armstrong dismissed "Storyville" as "a phony
name," and Pops Foster recalled that when northern jazz fans began asking him about it, "I thought it was some kind of little town we played
around there that I couldn't remember. When I found out they were
talking about the Red Light District, I sure was surprised."[48] Nor was
everyone talking about the same District; along with the downtown section, which catered exclusively to white customers, there was an uptown
District on the other side of Canal Street that served a racially mixed clientele and was where blues and the rougher jazz styles flourished.

At the turn of the twentieth century every town of any size had a red
light or tenderloin district where sex was the primary business, along
with gambling, alcohol, and other drugs and hustles. The language of

those businesses was rarely circumspect, nor was the language of many country folk. Zora Neale Hurston wrote that Black laborers in Florida "do not say embrace when they mean that they slept with a woman"—and although she phrased that comment for delicate readers, she applauded not only the men's speech but their attitude, writing that "love-making is a biological necessity the world over and an art among Negroes. . . . a man or woman who is proficient sees no reason why the fact should not be moot. He swaggers. She struts happily about. Songs are built on the power to charm beneath the bed-clothes."[49]

Morton blazoned that power in his nicknames—first "Winding Ball," then "Jelly Roll"—and the diamond that glittered from his front tooth, the mark of a successful pimp. In his world, that was a source of pride. James P. Johnson, the dean of Harlem stride pianists, recalled that all the top ragtime players of his youth "were big-time pimps or at least did a little hustling," and Willie "The Lion" Smith said that when Morton first came through New York in 1911 he was "pimpin' for a stable of women [and] the east coast pianists were more impressed by his attitude than they were by his playing."[50] Eubie Blake, who was noted for the refinement of his music and speech, recalled:

Jelly knew all the—I hate the word; I'll call them "gentlemen of leisure". . . . I did, too; you see, we didn't have any other place to play but in the sporting houses. . . . And you know about the diamond in his teeth. All the big gentlemen of leisure—the *big* ones—had them in their teeth. They represented prosperity.

Some devotees of early ragtime, jazz, and blues prefer to gloss over those associations and the racist stereotypes that go along with them, but for the musicians of that time they were inescapable. Blake continued:

I have to say the word now, because people don't know what I'm—they're pimps. I hate that word. I never use it around women. I never say "jazz" around women, either. "Jazz" is a dirty word—you people don't know that.[51]

Sidney Bechet similarly insisted his music should be called ragtime rather than jazz because "Jazz could mean any damn' thing: high times, screwing, ballroom. It used to be spelled *Jass*, which *was* screwing."[52]

In Morton's world, male musicians routinely lived, partied, and slept with women who did sex work—some, like Louis Armstrong and Richard M. Jones, were children of women who did sex work—and often got money from them, and some female musicians doubled in sex work, and sang about sex work as well as sex play. Angela Davis suggests that the songs recorded by artists like Ma Rainey and Bessie Smith in the 1920s are important in part because they "point the way toward a consideration of the historical politics of black sexuality," and applauds the "provocative and pervasive sexual—including homosexual—imagery" of blues lyrics as declarations of independence:

> For the first time in the history of the African presence in North America, masses of black women and men were in a position to make autonomous decisions regarding the sexual partnerships into which they entered. Sexuality thus was one of the most tangible domains in which emancipation was acted upon and through which its meanings were expressed. Sovereignty in sexual matters marked an important divide between life during slavery and life after emancipation.[53]

Davis focused on the ways recordings spoke to and for the mass of Black female record buyers and barely mentioned the connection of blues to the sporting world and sex work. But along with the freedom to choose one's sexual partners, emancipation brought the opportunity to get paid for what had previously been a system of pervasive, socially sanctioned rape. Sex work was often demeaning, unpleasant, and dangerous, but that did not differentiate it from much of the other work available to Black women; even in terms of sexual exploitation, domestic workers were often forced to choose between submitting to sexual harassment and rape or losing their jobs. Along with misery and danger, sex work could provide a rare degree of independence and a sense of superiority: in the sporting world, some Black women built substantial businesses and white men were anonymous, ineffectual tricks.

White women and Black men were also involved in this story, as were issues of who was Black and who was white, and to what degree, and in which situations or neighborhoods. Historians often emphasize the extent to which US laws and attitudes imposed a racial binary, but no one in New Orleans saw race in purely binary terms. Racial groupings included the ternary of white, Black, and Creole, along with Italians and Jews, who were not Black but not quite white—the uptown District was populated by a mix of Blacks and Italians, and the downtown houses of prostitution included separate establishments offering White, Black, Octoroon, and Jewish women—and there were also intermediate categories like Quadroon and Griffe, for people who were darker than Octoroon but lighter than Black. New Orleans was famous for its international flavor and racial complexities, but those social codes and variations had echoes and parallels throughout the United States. The patterns of racial segregation and exploitation were shifting and capricious, and there was always far more mixing than white people cared to notice or admit.

Morton's recordings for the Library of Congress range from the rough songs of Gulf Coast sawmill camps to pop tunes, Italian opera, original compositions he published to national acclaim, and lyrics improvised in the moment and forgotten a moment later. His blues repertoire is of particular interest because he abandoned that style so early and seems to have paid little or no attention to later trends; his performances give the clearest sense on record of how blues was performed by urban professionals in the first decade of the twentieth century, when the style was more a process than a product, a way of shaping lyrics to fit varying audiences and occasions. Alan Lomax labeled most of Morton's blues performances generically—"New Orleans Blues," "Honky Tonk Blues," "Low Down Blues"—and it is a matter of choice whether we consider them separate songs or examples of a single, infinitely variable framework. Even when he played a familiar favorite like "Alabama Bound" or "Pallet on the Floor," or a song he credited to Tony Jackson or Mamie Desdunes, he was recalling not static compositions but themes and patterns. He censored himself at the first sessions, but on the later recordings his blues consistently used the raw language of streets and honky-tonks, preserving voices that are long gone but often feel startlingly modern.

Morton's improvisational skills were not limited to music; he was an indefatigable raconteur, hustler, and promoter of bands, nightclubs, business schemes, and his personal legend, and his recollections were another sort of performance. They do not always fit the strictures of academic history, but if we want to explore the world that produced early blues and jazz and the ways those styles were heard and performed in the years before they were packaged for mass consumption, he is a matchless guide. Many of his stories are supported by written documents and the reports of his contemporaries, and if others were exaggerations or fabrications, that makes them no less valuable or even necessarily less accurate. He was a leading figure in a generation of brilliant innovators who were creating new music, new lyrical forms, and new identities, reshaping the world around them in ways that continue to resonate today. If their times and customs seem distant to us, that is in part because we have been separated by a century of intermediaries, with later tastes and agendas. The eight hours of songs and stories Morton recorded at the Library provide a direct connection to that world, and challenge us to look for other voices that have been censored and suppressed, exploring what they can tell us about their times and ours.

~ one ~

Alabama Bound

Ferdinand **"Jelly Roll"** Morton recorded the first session of his musical memoir on May 23, 1938, seated at a Steinway grand piano on the stage of Coolidge Auditorium at the Library of Congress. Alan Lomax sat on the floor nearby, with two battery-powered phonographs, flipping and changing the discs and occasionally asking a question. The first side begins with Morton playing a slow, lightly fingered melody and talking about his early travels along the Gulf Coast:

> I was down in Biloxi, Mississippi, during the time. I used to often frequent the Flat Top, which was nothing but a old honky-tonk, where nothing but the blues were played. There was fellows around played the blues like Brocky Johnny, Skinny Head Pete, old Florida Sam, and Tricky Sam, and that bunch.

Lomax's voice comes faintly from the floor: "What did they play?"

"Well, they just played just ordinary blues; the real, lowdown blues, honky-tonk blues."

"What were the names of some of them?"

"Well, for an instant, Brocky Johnny used to say—sing a tune something like this. The title was, uh, 'All you gals better get out and walk, because he's gonna start his dirty talk.'"[1]

FERDINAND LAMOTHE—OR LAMENTHE, OR LAMOTTE, DEPENDING ON THE source—was born sometime between 1885 and 1890; most likely the later date, though he usually claimed the former.[2] His parents separated a few years later and his mother married a man named William Mouton, which he anglicized to Morton. New Orleans was a famously musical city, and young Ferd absorbed everything from the melodic calls of pushcart peddlers to French opera, local songs that might have circulated for years with no discernible author, national hits like Harry Von Tilzer's "A Bird in a Gilded Cage" and Paul Dresser's "My Gal Sal," and snatches of verse and melody improvised by barroom entertainers to suit whatever the audience, situation, or mood demanded. Dance bands mixed European waltzes, polkas, schottisches, mazurkas, and quadrilles with styles from West and Central Africa and fusions developed over centuries in the Americas. Ragtime was the current hot rhythm, but by 1900 a lot of Black dancers in the South were also grinding and belly-rubbing to the slow drag and what Morton called "ordinary blues." It was not necessarily what later fans would call blues; in the first decade of the twentieth century, that term was not associated with a specific chord pattern but with a rhythm and feel, with people who played or sang in certain ways and the places they worked. Richard M. Jones, the Louisiana pianist and songwriter who composed "Trouble in Mind," was born around the same time as Morton and said "the real blues" tended to be played by people who couldn't play anything else: "The guy only knew the one blues. They would say, 'play something else,' and he would play it faster. That's all. They would all start dancing faster and then alternate with a slow one."[3]

Morton concurred, writing: "Blues just wasn't considered music—there were hundreds, maybe thousands who could play blues and not another single tune."[4] The style was associated with low dives, rough bands, and illiterate piano pounders or guitar strummers. The melodies were simple and repetitive, the lyrics a mix of verses picked up here and there or made up on the spot, some unique and personal, some familiar to everyone because everyone sang them.

Those early blues were not songs in the sense that someone born in 1915—someone like Alan Lomax—grew up thinking of a song. Before songs were regularly marketed on sheet music or records, they were often just a musical equivalent of stories. People have always told stories about their experiences and adventures, their relatives, their friends, and all sorts of fabulous or funny characters. Some have favorite stories they tell regularly; some, especially in situations where storytelling is a valued art, are known for being able to spin a story to fit any topic or occasion. Stories are also printed in books and magazines and performed in theaters, and sometimes people tell those as well, but if you ask someone for the title of a story they just told, they will tend to be puzzled by the question: "That was just something that happened to a friend of mine—it doesn't have a title." A lot of songs used to be like that; Manuel Manetta recalled that when people would ask King Oliver for the name of a piece his band played, he would indiscriminately reply, "Don't Hit John," and when he made records, "he wouldn't know what title to say to a song—'Black Rag,' or anything."[5] Manuel Perez, born in 1873 and one of the top cornet players in turn-of-the-century New Orleans, recalled, "Many of the pieces didn't have any titles. We knew them as the number two or the number five or the march in E flat."[6] Most listeners didn't even know those designations; when they wanted to hear a particular song or tune, they might ask for "that waltz you played on Saturday" or "that piece Susie likes," or "the song about the man who came home drunk," or about Stackolee, Barbara Allen, or the woman who killed the pimp. Dancers would not even be that specific, just requesting a waltz, a polka, something upbeat, or some blues.

As the Library sessions continued and Morton settled into his role as a historical authority, he similarly explained that "the honky-tonk tunes didn't have any names," but at the outset he was trying to be cooperative and provide answers, hence the "title" he attributed to Brocky Johnny's performance. He was also being polite about his language; when he repeated the line about "All you gals better get out and walk," he added: "Only they didn't say 'gals'—a lot of them were dirty songs."[7] He was speaking to a government functionary in a formal concert hall and, while trying to give an accurate picture of the Gulf Coast scene, was circumspect about some specifics.

By 1938 there was already a long tradition of censoring blues lyrics on records. Memphis Minnie recorded a song in 1930 that began with a variant of Brocky Johnny's line: *"Come all you folks and start to walk / I'm fitting to start my dozen talk."*[8] Her record was issued as "New Dirty Dozen," capitalizing on a "Dirty Dozen" recorded the previous year by Speckled Red, and both were bowdlerized versions of a barrelhouse standard known all over the South and Midwest. The words and music varied from performer to performer but the basic theme was a mix of dirty insult rhymes, typically directed at parents or relatives. A common verse was recalled by Will Shade, the leader of the Memphis Jug Band:

> *Clock on the mantelpiece going tick, tick, tick,*
> *Little sister's in the henhouse, sucking her grandpa's dick.*[9]

Mance Lipscomb sang a Texas variant:

> *Your mama's in the backyard, picking up sticks*
> *Your sister's in the alley just sucking off dicks.*[10]

Brocky Johnny may have sung something like that in Biloxi—we have Shade's and Lipscomb's versions because they lived into the 1960s, but no one was recording Black honky-tonk songs in 1908 and, if they had, they would not have included those lines. Morton said he heard "The Dirty Dozens" for the first time in Chicago, so Johnny presumably used a different theme, but blues was an infinitely adaptable form and favorite verses routinely turned up in new settings and situations.

Morton picked up a broad repertoire of floating verses and melodies in his travels around the South. New Orleans and Biloxi were his main bases but at some point he "happened to truck down to Mobile," where he met a local pianist named Porter King, whom he memorialized with a composition called "King Porter Stomp," and other players, some of them known only from his recollections: a local named Charlie King; Baby Grice and Frazier Davis from Florida; and Frank Rachel, who "was supposed to be the tops when it came down around Georgia."

Songs traveled because singers were traveling. The Great Migration of Black southerners to northern cities was part of a larger story: with emancipation, people who had been forced to stay or go at someone else's whim asserted their freedom by moving as they chose. When the Federal Writers' Project interviewed a man named Austin Grant about his memories of slavery, he said only one Black family stayed on the Texas plantation where he was born: "The rest was just like birds, they jes' flew."[11] Some went north, some west, some east or south. Some traveled to distant states or territories; some just moved a few miles down the road. Many left rural areas for cities where they hoped to find better opportunities for themselves and their children and to become part of a different, modern world. Between 1880 and 1910, forty thousand African Americans moved to New Orleans, and there were similar inflows to Memphis, Atlanta, Birmingham, and smaller centers like Biloxi and Mobile.[12] The new urbanites were mostly young and adventurous, and the new styles of ragtime, blues, and jazz were their music, accompanying and chronicling their lives and desires.

Morton introduced his first song at the Library sessions as a memento of that trip to Mobile:

The frequent saying was, any place that you was going, why, you was supposed to be "bound" for that place. So in fact we was Alabama bound, and when I got there I wrote this tune called "Alabama Bound." It goes this way:

I'm Alabama bound, Alabama bound,
If you like me, sweet baby, you've got to leave this town.

When that rooster crowed, when the hen ran around,
"If you want my love, sweet babe, you've got to run me down."

She said, "Don't you leave me here. Don't leave me here.
But, sweet papa, if you just must go, leave a dime for beer."

If Morton was the original composer of "Alabama Bound," that would be a significant item in his legacy, since it circulated throughout the South and was one of the first songs marketed as a blues. A few previous publications used "blues" in their titles, but always in ways that suggested it meant sadness or depression rather denoting a musical style.[13] The first evidence of the word being used for a kind of song rather than an emotion was on sheet music of "I'm Alabama Bound," published as a piano instrumental in 1909 by a New Orleanian named Robert Hoffman, with the subheading "A Rag Time Two Step (Also known as the Alabama Blues)." The verse of Hoffman's song used the tune Morton played, and when it was republished in 1910 with a lyric credited to a music store owner named John J. Puderer, the words were similar to Morton's, though supplemented with a racially demeaning tag line:

I'm Alabama bound, I'm Alabama bound,
I've tried you out, I've got to turn you down,
You're a dog gone low down measly coon.

Hoffman and Puderer were white, but another version of the song was published around the same time in Columbia, Missouri, by Blind Boone, a Black piano virtuoso born in 1864 and famous for playing everything from formal classical compositions to parlor ballads and early ragtime. He began touring with his own company in the 1880s, and in 1908 and 1909 he published a pair of "Southern Rag" medleys that were time capsules of the music African Americans were singing in that region around the turn of the century. In a vernacular continuum that songwriters and record companies would keep mining over the next few decades, they were not exactly rags, not quite blues, and would be reworked and filed in different marketing categories to suit evolving fashions. Medley number one was subtitled "Strains from the Alleys" and included the first publication of "Make Me a Pallet on the Floor" and a song that probably reached back to slavery times and would be recorded in later years as "Pay Day," "Reuben," and various other names. Boone's version might have doubled as a minstrel or "coon song," with a stereotyped verse about chicken-stealing:

> *I got a chicken on my back, there's a bull dog on my track,*
> *But I'll make it to my shack 'fore day.*

Other versions did not mention chickens—Mississippi John Hurt sang, "*The hounds is on my track, and the knapsack on my back,*" suggesting a more serious theme.[14] At an abolitionist meeting in Indiana around 1854, a woman sang a song with the verse:

> *The baying hounds are on my track,*
> *Old massa's close behind,*
> *And he's resolved to take me back,*
> *Across the Dixon line.*[15]

The theme continued to be reworked over the years; in 1929, the Texas blues singer and pianist Victoria Spivey sang:

> *Blood hounds, blood hounds, blood hounds are on my trail.*
> *Blood hounds, blood hounds, blood hounds are on my trail.*
> *They want to take me back to that cold, cold lonesome jail.*[16]

Spivey's song was a twelve-bar blues and she claimed it as an original composition, which made sense, since she had adapted it to fit her style and the current market, and by that time songwriter credits could bring royalties. In earlier ages, few people bothered to make those distinctions; if you sang a song regularly and people associated it with you, it was yours. Morton recorded a uniquely long version of "Pallet on the Floor," tracing an illicit sexual encounter, and could justifiably have claimed it as his own; other people used the same tag line and melody for another lyric about fleeing capture: *"Sheriff's on my trail with a big forty-four, won't you make me a pallet on your floor."*

Boone's second "Southern Rag" medley was subtitled "Strains from Flat Branch,"[17] referring to a Black neighborhood on the outskirts of Columbia, and used "I'm Alabama Bound" for its second section. The only lyric in the sheet music was that three-word phrase, repeated at the beginning and end of the strain—which may mean his troupe sang only those words or that they sang various lines in between and used that phrase as a tag or chorus. Huddie "Lead Belly" Ledbetter, born in the Texas-Louisiana border region in 1888, recorded the song several times in later years, varying the lyrics but always starting with a verse that fit Boone's pattern:

> *I'm Alabama bound, I'm Alabama bound*
> *If the train don't stop and turn around,*
> *I'm Alabama bound.*

In 1909 it was normal to label songs like this as "rags" if they were published in sheet music. In other contexts they could be called min-strel songs, folk songs, corn songs, hollers, reels, ditties, or blues. Albert Glenny, a New Orleans bass player born in 1870, said local bands started playing blues around the turn of the century, adding: "They used to play the *real* blues; they don't play no blues now."

That was in 1957, and Glenny's interviewers included Nesuhi Ertegun, the Turkish co-founder of Atlantic Records, which was leading the R&B field with Big Joe Turner, Ruth Brown, Ray Charles, and other up-to-date blues singers. Obviously intrigued, he asked, "What was it like, the real blues?"

"I can show you," Glenny said, and began to clap a slow, irregular beat that merged into a more lively, syncopated rhythm as he hummed the tune of "Alabama Bound."

It was just a brief snatch of melody, and Ertegun asked, "Does that have a name, this song you just sang?"

"That's the *blues!*" Glenny replied. "That's the *real* blues."

Later in the interview, Glenny recalled playing at the Pig Ankle, a cabaret and dance hall on the corner of Franklin and Custom House (now Iberville) Streets in the downtown Red Light District. "We played all dancing music," he said: "Waltz, schottische, and slow drag and all that." Ertegun asked what a slow drag was, and Glenny responded by singing the same melody, this time with words:

I'm Alabamy bound, I'm Alabamy bound,
And if you want me, my baby—you got to kiss me right.

Glenny was vague about dates, at one point saying he played that music during the Spanish-American War, which would be 1898, and later that bands started playing "the old time blues" in 1904. Nor did he necessarily think of that melody as "Alabama Bound." He shortly recalled another song that used the same tune but had Creole French words:

C'etait un autre cancan, c'etait un autre cancan.
Si vouv leme mwen, m'ape vou, bo mwen deux ou trois fois.[18]

Although he called this a different song, I am inclined to think of it as the same verse in a different language; the second line of the Creole lyric is a paraphrase of what he sang in English—or vice versa—meaning "If you love me . . . kiss me two or three times."

If I had read that lyric rather than hearing it, I would not have associated it with blues, since one of the most popular Creole songs had the same opening phrase and was set to a perky dance melody. Morton sang it at the Library of Congress:

C'est un autre cancan, paix donc,
C'est un autre cancan, paix donc.[19]

Morton was puzzled by this lyric, saying, "There seemed to be some vulgar meaning to it that I have never understood . . . I can't understand the can-can business. But I'll tell you, everybody got hot and they threw their hats away when they would start to playing this thing." *Cancan* is a French term for malicious gossip or brouhaha—some etymologies suggest it was onomatopoeia for the quacking of ducks—and is not generally considered to have a hidden or dirty meaning, but the same word was used for a famously naughty dance and Morton might have been making that association, since the high kicks of the cancan were a standard late-night entertainment in New Orleans cabarets: many musicians recalled bar owners hanging a ham from the ceiling and women competing to kick it.[20]

The trombonist Kid Ory recorded a longer version of this piece as "Creole Song (C'est L'Autre Cancan)," and although none of the verses were salacious, he may have cleaned them up or avoided naughtier alternatives. Morton followed it with an English-language variant, using a slightly different melody and the lyric:

> *If you don't shake, you don't get no cake,*
> *If you don't rock, you don't get no cock.*

And, after an instrumental chorus:

> *If you don't fuck, you gonna have no luck,*
> *If you don't fuck, you don't have no luck.*

In oral culture it is common for the same lyrics to turn up with different tunes, tunes to turn up with different lyrics, lines to migrate from one song to another, and, in communities where multiple languages are spoken, for songs in one language to merge or evolve into songs in another. Throughout the Library sessions, Morton wove stories and songs in a flowing narrative, and although Lomax likened this to a French *cantefable*—a term from the thirteenth century for romances alternating sections of prose and verse—there is no need to cite arcane literary models. People have been merging songs with stories for millennia, and many have not made distinctions between those forms, or between poetry and song, or poetry and prose.[21]

The first verses Morton sang for "Alabama Bound" were standard throughout the South, but as he continued his story about the trip to Mobile, he returned to the song as commentary. He talked about playing "for the girls who'd do the high kicks," saying, "that's just the way they used to act down in Mobile in those days." He was making most of his money as a pool shark and did pretty well until he ran into a sore loser:

The guy was gonna knife me right in the back . . . He said that I only used the piano for a decoy—which he was right. And of course he had it in his mind that I was kind of nice-looking. Imagine that, huh. . . . He was kind of jealous of me—I suppose he was, anyhow. *But I said—*

Alabama bound, yes, Alabama bound,
One of them good-looking gals told me,
"Come on, baby, and leave this town."

I got put in jail, I got put in jail.
There wasn't nobody in town wouldn't go my bail.

Morton said the arrest was due to another case of jealousy: a sporting woman had fallen for him, her boyfriend called the police, and a "copper came, said, 'You come around here and try to take the town, you big pimp! We'll show you what we'll do with guys like you.'" Sentenced to pay a hundred-dollar fine and serve a hundred days cutting grass on a chain gang, he escaped after a couple of days, but there were other incidents: he was arrested on suspicion of train robbery while hoboing through southern Mississippi, and in Moss Point, outside Pascagoula, he was accused of stealing some clothes and spent eighteen days shackled and shoveling dirt.[22] Jail was always a danger if you were a Black man, especially if you associated with the sporting crowd. Louis Armstrong recalled:

We used to get raided in them honky-tonks all the time . . . because of
gamblin' and all that goin' on . . . Everybody's a bum when the wagon
comes. I got that experience being in the yard with all them bad characters, they all know me. Everybody goes to jail in New Orleans.[23]

Morton was locked up for the first time as a baby, when his grandmother left him in the care of "some type of sporting woman" who got in
a fracas,[24] and decades later he was briefly jailed while running a nightclub in California. Along with official harassment, there were the constant threats faced by any Black person in the South: in Biloxi, Morton
was playing piano for a white madam named Mattie Bailey and had to
make a hasty departure when a rumor started that they were intimate
and "some of the bums and low riff-raff decided to lynch me." He had several stories about lynch mobs, in one of which a touring vaudeville troupe
had to slide out a window on a rope he made from bedclothes.

There is no way to know if all those stories were true. Morton was
more reliable than some of his critics have claimed, but he was a prac-
ticed raconteur and shape-shifter. He boasted of his French ancestry and refined upbringing and also of his familiarity with the most
"notoriety" prostitutes, the hottest jazz players, and an array of gamblers, hustlers, thieves, and tough guys. He identified at various times
as French, Creole, Negro, and on a couple of occasions as Cuban or
Mexican. Sometimes he presented himself as a serious musician, other
times as a pool shark, pimp, or hustler who only used music as a front.
He spent a fortune on his wardrobe and many people recalled his styl-
ishly tailored suits, but the pianist Lovie Austin recalled him arriving
in Chicago from the West Coast in garish bell-bottom pants and a big
cowboy hat: "He was kind of a clown," she said. "But a very, very talented musician." Austin was working for Will Rossiter, who published
Morton's "Jelly Roll Blues" in 1915, and said she had to transcribe the
piece for him because "he couldn't read no music. He wouldn't know a
note if he's to get it on a telegraph." Other people remembered Morton as a superlatively literate musician, one saying he could sight-read
a score upside down—which seems astonishing until one balances it

with his story of impressing a bunch of musicians by pretending to sight-read tunes he had previously memorized.[25]

TRAVELING NAMES

It is tempting to cap a litany of Morton's contradictions by saying even his name is disputed, but that was mostly a matter of changing customs. His family name is often given as Lamothe or LaMothe; on his baptismal certificate it is Lemott; his great-grandfather's name was documented as Lamotte; Lomax wrote it La Menthe, which some historians call a mistake, but Morton sometimes wrote it Lamenthe and in the Library sessions pronounced it "Lamont"—the French pronunciation of that spelling. Though confusing to modern chroniclers, such multiple orthographies were common as long as writing was simply considered a way of preserving speech. Shakespeare famously wrote his name at least four different ways, none of them the familiar modern spelling, and all were equally correct in his time, because all represented the way he said it.[26] Likewise, the shift from Mouton to Morton may have been more a linguistic evolution and bureaucratic accident than a decision; speakers' accents shifted and writers took down the names they heard: Müller was written as Miller, Abadie as Aberdeen, and in the streets of New Orleans the change might not be noticed: "You remember Louise Abadie?" "Sure, everybody knew the Aberdeens."

People also adopted colorful cognomens. Beginning a story about a friend called Jack the Bear, Morton explained: "Very often, the boys, to be recognized as somebody, would use alias names." That was common in show business, in the underworld, and among hoboes, sailors, cowboys, and other groups that lived outside the respectably ordered bounds of property and paperwork. In the 1800s, people in the Western territories sang:

What was your name in the States?
Was it Thomson, or Johnson, or Bates?

Did you murder your wife,
And then flee for your life?
Oh, what was your name in the States?[27]

For African Americans whose previous names had been assigned by kidnappers and slavemasters, choosing a new one was also a form of protest and liberation. Emancipation came barely a quarter century before Morton's birth, and many people celebrated by claiming new identities: in Texas, Austin Grant's family had been known by the last name Harper, for the man who enslaved them; with emancipation, his father took the name Grant—presumably after the Union general—while his uncle chose the name Glover and their father chose Filmore.[28] In the early twentieth century, Black family names were often younger than the people who bore them and could easily be discarded or replaced at a bearer's whim.

When Morton and his contemporaries recalled notorious characters of that time, many of the names had a mythic quality. Responding to a question about famous New Orleans "bad men," Morton first mentioned a hardbitten killer named Aaron Harris, then a couple named Toodlum and Boar Hog, who were responsible for Harris's death, and "another tough guy by the name of Sheep Bite." The trumpeter Lee Collins recalled a saloon called Sweet Child's on the corner of Franklin and Gravier Streets in the uptown District, a block from the spot where Harris was killed, where the blues singer Ann Cook performed for regulars named Gold Tooth Irene, Mary Jack the Bear, One-Leg Horace, and Good Pussy Virginia; contemporary police records list Jack the Rabbit, Jack the Ripper, Willy the Pleaser, Ratty Kate, Mary Meathouse, Drop a Sack, Hit 'Em Quick, Diamond Dick, Lead Pencil, Cinderella, Two Rooms and a Kitchen, and Baggage Car Shorty.[29]

James P. Johnson recalled that the top pianists of his youth were "real celebrities" who "had lots of girlfriends, led a sporting life and were invited everywhere there was a piano." In those days, that included pretty much any bar, club, lodge, community hall, bordello, or party flat, and plenty of private homes: "Most people who had pianos couldn't play them, so a piano player was important socially."[30] In the high-class houses of prostitution that lined Basin Street in New Orleans, the top pianists were known as "professors" and most used normal, respectable names: Alfred Wilson, Albert Carroll, Sam Davis, and the acknowledged master, Tony Jackson. Honky-tonk ticklers in the uptown District chose more evocative aliases: Black Pete, Birmingham, Boogers, Drag Nasty, and Sore Dick.

Eurreal "Little Brother" Montgomery learned piano by imitating the itinerant players who came through his father's barrelhouse in Kentwood, Louisiana, and remembered Morton visiting for several days, as well as Skinny Head Pete and dozens of others who worked the circuit from New Orleans to Memphis: Rip Tops, Son Framion, Loomis Gibson, Cooney Vaughn, Charlie Mahana, No-leg Kenny, Red Caillou, Fats Pichon, Udell Wilson, Burnell Santiago, Mean Little Dooky, Cracking Kid, Ernest "Flunkey" Johnson, Varnado Anderson, Leon Bromfield, Friday Ford, Sudan Washington, Blind Homer, Blind Jug, Burnt Face Jake, Papa Lord God, and Gus Pevsner, who stood out on the barrelhouse circuit because "he was a musicianer . . . you know, musical, played by notes and things."[31]

Any traveling musician could have produced a similar list, varying from region to region, and many of the names would be unfamiliar to even the most assiduous modern researchers. Some players specialized in styles we would now call blues, some played varieties of backwoods ragtime, and most could fill requests for a basic repertoire of current pop songs. We can get some sense of their range and styles from old interviews and the few who made records, but the earliest recordings are from the 1920s, reflect the tastes of the people who supervised the sessions rather than what the musicians or their local audiences preferred, and may not be typical of what they were playing ten years earlier or even previous night. Robert Shaw, a master of the Texas barrelhouse style, described the "hard knockers" who worked that circuit, in particular one named Roadside. "Oh, man—he's a salty papa," Shaw recalled, and I assumed he was talking about a rough bluesman until he listed Roadside's big numbers: "Five Foot Two, Eyes of Blue," "Sweet Georgia Brown," and "I Can't Give You Anything but Love."[32]

Some of the men on Montgomery's list were known beyond the back-country tonks: Udell Wilson was well remembered in New Orleans;

Joseph "Red" Caillou worked regularly around that city and later led combos in California; Papa Lord God was an important influence on the St. Louis pianist James Crutchfield. A few made recordings: Cooney Vaughn was probably the pianist on the Mississippi Jook Band's records; Ernest "44" Johnson recorded as accompanist to a singer named Tommy Griffin; Walter "Fats" Pichon worked with numerous bands, lived for a while in New York and Boston, and even played a character on the popular *Duffy's Tavern* radio program.

Those artists were ten or fifteen years younger than Morton, born after the turn of the century, and most earlier players are not even remembered as stray names. When names survive, we often do not know if they were remembered correctly, if an interviewer heard and wrote them accurately, or if the musician was using that name a year earlier or later. Official records can be helpful but also misleading, since multiple people shared the same names. There were lots of Robert Johnsons in rural Mississippi, and the one who recorded two spectacular sessions in the 1930s often called himself Robert Spencer. Huddie Ledbetter lived for ten or fifteen years as Walter Boyd. Memphis Minnie was also known as Kid Douglas. In *American Ballads and Folk Songs*, John and Alan Lomax credited a version of "Stackolee" they recorded in 1933 to a Texas pianist named Ivy Joe White; fifteen years later, he was a national star named Ivory Joe Hunter.[33] In 1942 Alan Lomax interviewed a guitarist in Mississippi who introduced himself as Joe Williams, a well-known blues recording artist; he was actually David "Honeyboy" Edwards, who traveled and played with Williams and recalled fifty years later how he pretended to be his famous friend when he was hustling around the Delta.

MEMPHIS BOUND

EDWARDS TOLD LOMAX HE WOULD HIT SMALL TOWNS ON PAYDAY, PLAY A little music to work up a stake, then put his guitar aside and make the real money shooting dice. Roosevelt Sykes, who worked the Mississippi barrelhouse circuit for many years, said Memphis Slim and Sunnyland

Slim were the same way: "All them guys, they just would only play if they get broke. Then they'd say, 'I'm going to play the blues,' start playing because somebody'd give 'em a stake to get back in the game. . . . Then, too, they could get the women—lots of girls'd fall for blues players . . . He go to playing the blues; somebody come up, some girl'll give him five dollars, and he go and get back in the game."[34]

Lomax's field notes quote "Joe Williams" saying women liked musicians "better than a man that's working—Joe gets for nothing what it costs other guys $2 to get."[35] Fifty years later, he wrote that Edwards capped this conversation with a rhyming toast:

> *My back is made of whalebone, my belly is made of brass,*
> *I save my good stuff for the working women, and the rest can kiss my*
> *ass.*[36]

This toast is not in the original notes, and I suspect Lomax added it later to improve the anecdote. It was an old rhyme he might have picked up elsewhere on his travels or learned from Lucille Bogan's "Shave Me Dry," a rare example of uncensored blues recorded in the early 1930s, which has a verse that is virtually identical, though from a woman's point of view and with a straightforward "fucking" instead of the euphemistic "good stuff."[37]

The relationship of sporting folk to working men and women was a frequent subject of humor and resentment. Big Bill Broonzy—born Lee Bradley in rural Arkansas in 1903, though he claimed to have been born ten years earlier in Mississippi—grew up on a farm and contrasted hardworking country people like himself with the "big town blues players" in "places like New Orleans, Memphis, Saint Louis, Kansas City, Atlanta, Houston, Little Rock, Jackson, Vicksburg":

These musicians was not seen in the day. They came out at night. . . . We called them kind of men "sweet back papas." Them men didn't know how cotton and corn and rice and sugarcane grows and they didn't care. They went out, dressed up every night and some of them had three and four

women. One fed him and the other bought his clothes and shoes. These is
the men that wear ten-dollar Stetson hats and twenty-dollar gold pieces at
their watch and diamonds in their teeth.[38]

Morton fit that description precisely and boasted that he "never did
no manual labor." When he mentioned an early job in a cooperage, he
quickly added that he only took it to hang out with friends who had jobs
there, and likewise said he sometimes helped his godfather do caulking,
but just "for sport." He sometimes talked about music the same way, saying he only took piano jobs to rope in the suckers.

The free-living hustler image was a fantasy that mirrored brutal
realities. Black Americans had been worked to death for centuries while
the white men who enslaved or employed them enjoyed lives of leisure:
playing cards, sipping whiskey, and—secretly for white society but very
obviously for Black society—slipping out to have sex with Black women.
Those relationships continued long after emancipation: Black southerners
were still slaving on farms, trapped in debt peonage, at times in chains;
well into the twentieth century, a Black man or woman who could not
prove they had a white employer was liable to be arrested at harvest time
and leased out to pick cotton.

It was easy for someone in that situation to regard the society as
rigged and its laws and strictures as traps and hustles. Most people nonetheless tried to build respectable lives through hard work and
proper behavior, but some chose to ignore or break the rules and live
off the whites and the working folk, in a sporting world where at least
the hustle was in the open. Morton and his cronies tended to say "working man" in the same tone they might have said "farmer," "rube," or a
couple of decades later, "square." He recalled apprenticing with a card
sharp in Biloxi and almost getting killed when he tried his new skills
in a back-country lumber camp, with the wry laughter of a fox who was
almost pecked to death by angry chickens.

In the longest nonmusical section of the Library recordings, Morton
spun a trip to Memphis with Jack the Bear into a hustler's odyssey that
took up five disc sides. Jack suggested hoboing on trains, but Morton

had ruined a sixty-dollar suit hopping off a freight car and insisted they finance their journey by other means. Their first stop was Yazoo City, where Morton got a job playing in a sporting house and "made the landlady," who lodged and fed them until his success irritated some local guys and they had to move on. In Clarksdale, he won a couple of bucks shooting pool and Jack used the stake to buy some Coca-Cola, which they doctored with salt and sold as a cure for tuberculosis. Morton was the front man: "I've always been known to be a fair talker, so I went around from door to door to some of those poor old people, white and colored. Consumption, then, they had a lot of it in this country, and anybody said that they could cure consumption, boy, you could really reap a fortune." Their concoction was not a cure, but he assured Lomax, "There was nothing in it to hurt anybody." Nonetheless, "somehow or another we sold one of these bottles to a poor family and the child died. So we caught the next train."

On the train, Jack singled out some "real simple-looking colored people" who were wearing lodge pins on their jackets, pretended to be an official of the lodge, and fined them for violating invented regulations. When they reached Helena, Arkansas, they had a small stake and Morton hustled the local pool players until one chalked the back of his jacket, marking him for the police, who ran them out of town, so they caught a steamboat to Memphis.

Memphis was the capital of the Delta region and Morton headed for Beale Street, the main Black business and entertainment center. He set his sights on the Monarch Saloon, an impressive establishment with a bar downstairs that was open around the clock and a hall upstairs for dancing on busy nights. "Nothing went into that saloon but pimps, robbers, gamblers," he recalled, adding: "It's a shame to think about those environments that I really just drifted into."

The Monarch was owned by a white ward boss named Jim Kinnane and the daytime floor manager was a Black man named Bad Sam, whom Morton recalled as "the toughest man around that whole section of the world." The regular pianist was Benny French, a local favorite whose playing would be a model for W. C. Handy's arrangement of "Beale Street

Blues."[39] Morton said French was especially popular with the Monarch's "low-class whores" and "some of them that was a little better class," and described a special dance they did to his playing: "I had never seen it before or since. . . . They would run right directly up to the wall with a kind of a little bit of a shuffle, and slap their hands together, and kick back their right legs and say, 'Oh, play it, Benny, play it!'"

Morton demonstrated French's style as a thumping, rudimentary sort of ragtime, and said he listened for a couple of days, then told Bad Sam, "That damned fool can't hit a piano with a brick. . . . I'm not supposed to be good, but if that's playing I can beat all them kind of suckers." Sam told him to prove it, so he sat down at the keyboard, led off with a fast stomp, then sang a current pop hit, "All That I Ask Is Love."

> *All that I ask is love,*
> *All that I want is you,*
> *And I swear by all the stars,*
> *I'll be forever true.*

He sang the sentimental lyric in a reedy tenor, accompanied with flowery arpeggios and ending on a high note in lingering falsetto. It seems an odd choice for a rough dance hall on Beale Street, which was home to some of the rowdiest clubs in the urban South and is widely remembered as "the home of the blues." But he capped the performance with a firm chord and declared: "I brought the house down with that thing—now, don't believe me, think I'm kidding you, I brought it *down!*"

MORTON MOVES ON

MORTON DATED THIS TRIP TO 1908, BUT "ALL THAT I ASK IS LOVE" WAS published in 1910 and other reports suggest that was a likelier year for his Memphis sojourn.[40] By then he had finished his apprenticeship as a honky-tonk and sporting house entertainer, which was also his relatively brief period as a blues singer. The chronology is somewhat conjectural, but he seems to have entered that life around 1907, after an earlier period playing guitar with a male quartet that performed religious songs at wakes and serenades in private homes, and with a small string band in the "wine rooms" of New Orleans saloons. He recalled the band's repertoire as a mix of parlor ballads like "A Bird in a Gilded Cage," "I'm Wearing My Heart Away for You," and "The Old Oaken Bucket" and upbeat ragtime numbers like "Hot Time in the Old Town Tonight" and "Mr. Johnson Turn Me Loose."

Morton came from a relatively middle-class background and had some early piano lessons with formal music teachers, though he dismissed their instruction as worthless. He credited a slightly older lad named Frank Richards with giving him pointers in ragtime and blues, adding that they could not play the latter style in his neighborhood, "blues being considered extremely vulgar in the more respectable parts of town, where people would be insulted if they heard the blues being played."[41] For that music they went uptown to the Garden District and Central City, where pianists like Game Kid and Buddy Carter entertained a public that had arrived in the city more recently and had less urbane tastes. By his mid-teens, Morton was playing in the downtown tenderloin district, and Manuel Manetta, who was born in 1889 and met him when they were both teenagers playing in District saloons and sporting houses, said at that point he was strictly a bluesman. Another District pianist, Rosalind "Rose" Johnson, recalled him playing "Sugar Moon," "Mandy Lane," and "That Barbershop Chord," all of which date from 1909 or 1910 and suggest how his repertoire evolved.[42] A key inspiration was Tony Jackson, a versatile pianist and singer whom Morton described as "the greatest single-hand entertainer in the world." It was a gradual evolution: first singing quartet harmonies and playing string-band ragtime; then an immersion in the piano styles of the barrelhouses and honky-tonks; then mastering the more high-toned fare favored by white clients in the opulent mansions on Basin Street.

By 1911 Morton was touring with William Benbow's vaudeville troupe, playing in theaters and traveling to Washington, Philadelphia, and New York. That was his first trip to the Northeast, and James P.

Johnson recalled his entrance in a New York nightclub as the apotheosis of musical cool: doffing his overcoat and turning it inside out to show the expensive lining, laying it along the top of the piano, taking a silk handkerchief from his pocket and dusting the stool, then sitting down and hitting a trademark chord.[43]

Benbow's show featured Butler "String Beans" May, a comedian and singer who set a pattern for the vaudeville blues acts of the teens and twenties—by some accounts he was the first star to be regularly associated with blues, and his followers included Jodie "Butterbeans" Edwards, whose team of Butterbeans and Susie was still entertaining Black theater audiences in the 1960s. Morton remembered May as "the greatest comedian I ever knew and a very, very sweet fellow," and he emulated the star's comic routines and blackface makeup. In the process he acquired a new nickname: as he told the story, he was ad-libbing a skit with a partner named Sammie Russell and Russell got a big laugh by introducing himself as "Sweet Papa Cream Puff, right out of the bakery shop." Not to be outdone, Morton responded that he was "Sweet Papa Jelly Roll, with the stovepipes in my hips, and all the women in town was dying to turn my damper down."

There is an element of folklore to that anecdote: Dewey "Pigmeat" Markham, a popular comedian of a later generation, similarly explained that he got his name from a routine where he introduced himself as "Sweet Papa Pigmeat, with the River Jordan in my hips, and all the women ran to be baptized."[44] Richard M. Jones said there was a previous pianist named Jelly Roll, who came through New Orleans from Atlanta and "was so popular with the women of the district, Morton latched onto the nickname after the Atlanta cat pulled up stakes and left town."[45] However Morton chose it, the alias was only tangentially related to baked goods. In a 1927 study of "Double Meaning in the Popular Negro Blues," Guy Johnson described *jelly roll* as "by far the most common" sexual euphemism in blues lyrics, writing, "it stands for the vagina, or for the female genitalia in general, and sometimes for sexual intercourse."[46]

In keeping with the theme of variable orthographies, the first surviving mention of Morton's new sobriquet was in a 1913 publicity post to the

Indianapolis Freeman by S. L. Jenkins of the vaudeville team Jenkins and Jenkins, which boasted: "Jelly Rool, our piano player, is there on the piano like a ship at sea. He don't bar no rag time piano player, and when he plays the rag they calls the New York Rool, he makes the audience stand up and take notice, believe me pa."[47]

By that time, Morton had left New Orleans for good. In 1912 he relocated to Houston, playing in sporting houses while trying to start a theatrical stock company and buying a tailor shop with the idea of "going after the tenderloin trade." He shortly was back on the road in a double act with a woman named Rosa Brown—there is no record of a marriage, but they were billed as Morton and Morton (or sometimes Moton and Moton, or Moten and Moten). A review from 1914 described Brown as a "wideawake performer" who "puts over the 'Blues' to the satisfaction of the audience, who for some reason take very kindly to that kind of singing." Morton was described as "a slight reminder of 'String Beans,'" who composed his own comic songs and could play "classics and rags with equal ease," including a classical selection played only with his left hand. The reviewer noted his "grotesque" makeup, and a photograph showed him in blackface and a ragged tramp costume, hunched over sideways, with one hand supporting his sagging pants.[48] By the end of that year he had settled in Chicago and was leading a seven-piece orchestra at the Deluxe Café, and in 1915 he assumed management of the popular Elite Café and his "Jelly Roll Blues" was published and became a substantial hit.

It would be another eight years before Morton made his first recordings and eleven before the Red Hot Peppers sessions established him as one of the defining bandleaders and arrangers in early jazz. That music was very different from what he sang as an itinerant honky-tonker working "the worst dives" of the Gulf Coast and "every pig pen from Orange to El Paso." When he graduated to theater performances and dance band orchestrations and shifted his bases of operation to Chicago, Los Angeles, and New York, he left that character behind, and he seems to have paid minimal attention to the later blues singers who dominated the "Race record" business in the 1920s. He played piano on a couple of recordings by minor blues queens, but none of his interviews, letters, or writings mention Bessie Smith, Ma Rainey, or any of their peers, much less the wave of male singer-guitarists who became big sellers later in the decade. Nor does he mention any blues hits of that later era; other artists of his generation sometimes slipped into anachronism, saying they heard late-1920s hits like "How Long Blues" or "It's Tight Like That" in their youth, but once he moved on, he seems to have paid no attention to blues, except as a flavor for jazz band orchestrations.

We only know about Morton's earlier incarnation because he fell on hard times in the late 1930s, happened to be managing a nightclub in Washington, happened to be introduced to Alan Lomax, and saw a chance to establish his place in history. Their recording project seems to have been his idea, and two months before it got under way he told a reporter they would need more than a hundred records to preserve his memories of "the trend of popular American music from the standard sentimental songs, thru ragtime and up to jazz," including religious sermons, funeral marches, his own compositions, and the "old song legends of the South."[49] The range and direction evolved over the course of the sessions, but the intention was always to use his personal experiences as a narrative thread to explore and preserve the music and customs of a vanished world—before moralizers abolished the tenderloin districts and Prohibition closed the saloons, before *blues* and *jazz* had become familiar marketing terms, and before sheet music and recording turned improvisatory traditions into a fixed canon of printed lyrics and discrete sonic objects that remain unchanged a century later. It was not yet the world of Jelly Roll Morton, the composer and bandleader whose records are revered as pioneering masterpieces and continue to influence musicians in a new millenium; it was the world of the hustler, honky-tonk singer, and barrelhouse pianist known as Winding Ball.

~ two ~

Hesitation Blues

Morton followed **"Alabama** Bound" with a sprightly ragtime instrumental, "King Porter Stomp." He explained that the title was a tribute to Porter King, a musician he met in Mobile, "a very dear friend of mine and a marvelous pianist, now in the cold, cold ground; a gentleman from Florida, an educated gentleman with a wonderful musical education, far much better than mine." Following those clues, researchers have found traces of King in census and city records, but if Morton had not titled a piece in his honor, we would have no way of knowing he existed.[1]

By the late 1930s, Fletcher Henderson and Benny Goodman had established "King Porter Stomp" as a big band swing standard. Morton had mixed feelings about that; he was pleased that his compositions were being featured by the country's most popular bands but regarded the current stars as pale imitators of the New Orleans masters and was sure if he could get some financial backing he would be bigger and better than any of them. He saw the Library sessions as a way of reasserting his reputation and making new contacts, and mingled his memories with performances of his most popular and intricate compositions and disquisitions on the rhythmic and harmonic approaches necessary for playing jazz correctly.

Lomax had always regarded jazz as a debased mass-media style that was "wiping out the music that I cared about—American traditional folk music." When Morton showed up at the Library, he recalled, "I looked at him with considerable suspicion. But I thought . . . I'll see how much folk music a jazz musician knows."[2] If a jazz fan had been at the helm, the Library recordings would presumably have focused on Morton's interactions with other early jazz players and his development as a composer, arranger, and bandleader, but Lomax steered the conversation in other directions. Morton talked about his family history, his childhood, his travels, his first experiments with guitar and piano, the variety of music he heard in his youth, from hymns, street chants, and ballads to opera—he mentioned *Faust* and *Lucia di Lammermoor* and played the "Miserere" from Giuseppe Verdi's *Il Trovatore*—and his immersion in blues, honky-tonk, and sporting house styles. He described the saloon that served as his musical proving ground, on the corner of Villere and Bienville Streets in the downtown Red Light District:

> It was only a back room, where all the greatest pianists frequented after they got off from work. All the pianists got off from work in the sporting houses at around four or after unless they had plenty of money involved. And they would go to this Frenchman's—that was the name of the place—saloon, and there would be everything in the line of hilarity there. They would have even millionaires that come to listen to the different great pianists. . . . All the girls that could get out of the houses, they were there. There weren't any discrimination of any kind. They all sat at different tables at any place that they felt like sitting. They all mingled together as they wished to, and everyone was just like one big happy family.

Morton named Sam Davis and Tony Jackson as the best players in that period, demonstrating Davis's supple ragtime style and singing Jackson's most popular hit, "Pretty Baby." Jackson was openly gay and apparently composed the song about a male lover, but the published lyric was rewritten by a white songwriter, Gus Kahn. Kahn's chorus began *"Ev'rybody loves a baby, that's why I'm in love with you, Pretty Baby."* Jackson's had been *"You can talk about your jelly rolls, but none of them compare, with my baby."*[3]

Morton admired Jackson's vast repertoire and mastery of disparate styles: "His range on a blues tune would be just exactly like a blues singer. On an opera tune would be just exactly as an opera singer. And he was always one of the first with the latest tunes." After singing a version of "Pretty Baby," Morton demonstrated one of Jackson's "fast speed tunes," explaining that it would be played to accompany "naked dances," a common entertainment for big spenders in the Basin Street mansions. He recalled that environment with pride, saying the New Orleans Red Light District was "second to France, meaning the second greatest in the world, with extensions for blocks and blocks." The downtown section was "supposed to be the highest class, although . . . [it] ran from the lowest to the highest, meaning in price and caliber alike." That section catered to an exclusively white clientele and its more prominent houses were listed in an annually updated *Blue Book*, which designated the races of "entertainers" available in each, marking them with a *W*, *O*, or *C* for *White*, *Octoroon*, or *Colored*, and in some editions with a *J* for Jewish women—there was a section of Jewish cribs along Iberville Street, identified in the 1903 guide as "Sheenie Town"—and a *69* for "French houses."[4] The *Blue Books* did not include the uptown section across Canal Street, where both Black and white customers were accommodated and virtually all the workers were Black. Morton explained that the uptown District provided work for many musicians, "but never the first-class artist, because the money wasn't there."

Lomax was primarily interested in vernacular and working-class styles and immediately asked what tunes were played in "the lower class districts"—in these first interviews he does not seem to have understood that Morton was using *District* in a specific sense. Morton started by explaining that the uptown saloons were "honky-tonks . . . , dirty, filthy places where they gambled and they had a lot of rough people that would fight and do anything else. . . . It was really dangerous to anybody that would go in there that didn't know what it was all about." He mentioned

Kizer's and the Red Onion, on Julia Street at the turnaround of the New Basin Canal, and Spano's, a few blocks downriver, all notorious criminal hangouts. Kizer's was owned by a disgraced police detective, Marshall A. Kizer, and the New Orleans *Times-Democrat* described it as a "negro saloon . . . with obscene pictures of white women displayed around the bar"; a lodging house upstairs; and a back section housing the Ivory Social Club, "an institution for the benefit of negroes of the lowest type," from which "stick-up men and thieves emanate to prey upon the defenseless and unarmed."[5]

FREESTYLING THE BLUES

MORTON RECALLED THE UPTOWN HONKY-TONKS WITH A MIX OF NOSTALGIA and scorn: "They always had an old broke-down piano with some inferior pianist. . . . The girls'd start, 'Play me something there, boy, play me some blues.' So they'd start playing in this way." He demonstrated a slow, twelve-bar accompaniment, his left hand keeping a steady beat and his right picking out a simple melody, and sang a meditative lyric:

> *I could sit right here, think a thousand miles away,*
> *Sit right here, think a thousand miles away.*
> *Since I had the blues this bad, cannot remember the day.*

That verse was Morton's standard way of starting a blues. He used it to begin four songs over the course of the Library sessions, and it served as a lyrical overture, setting the mood and giving him time to think of how he would continue. Lomax titled this performance generically as "Honky Tonk Blues," and it was made up of stock verses, including a typical male boast Morton would repeat later in the sessions:

> *I never believed in having one woman at a time,*
> *I never believed in having one woman at a time,*
> *I always have six, seven, eight or nine.*

Morton said the uptown District drew a notably varied crowd: "They'd have good-looking women of all kind, beautiful women; some was ugly, very ugly.... They had all kind of men, dressed up—rags looked like ribbons on some of them. Some of them with big guns in their bosoms." Wealthy white men showed up as well: "they called theirselves slumming, I guess, but they was there, just the same, nudging elbows with all the big bums." Morton laughed as he remembered a "lousy" bum, in the literal sense of being infested with lice, throwing a bug onto the collar of a well-dressed customer "to get him in the same fix."

Morton said the Black laborers who frequented those saloons mostly worked on the waterfront, as longshoremen, roustabouts, or screwmen— operators of the screwjacks that compressed cotton bails for shipping— and Lomax asked if he remembered any of their songs. A couple of weeks earlier, Lomax had asked W. C. Handy a similar question and Handy responded by singing a traditional a cappella "holler," in the West African style Lomax and his father had recorded from rural laborers in Texas and the Mississippi Delta. Morton had no interest in country hollering, so he complied with the request by improvising a mellow eight-bar blues about levee life:

I'm a levee man, I'm a levee man,
I'm a levee man, yes, I'm a levee man.

I said, "Captain, captain, let me make this trip,"
I said, "Captain, captain, let me make this trip."

If you do, captain, I will get my grip,
If you do, my captain, let me go home and get my grip.

'Cause I need the money, oh, the money, babe, and I need it bad,
I need the money, and I need it bad.

Because I want lot of money, 'cause I never had,
I want a lot of money, 'cause I never had.

Lomax interrupted at that point—he had been hoping for a traditional work song, not a bespoke barroom blues, and Morton's lyrics were not particularly compelling—but it is a good example of how Morton treated a request for a song or style he didn't know. In those situations, he typically turned to blues, a form ideally suited to the sort of impromptu flights that rappers call freestyling. The New Orleans bass player Pops Foster said Morton was famous in the District for improvising verses about anything and anybody: "That's where he was great. When a customer would come in the door, Jelly would make up a dirty rhyme on your name and play it to his piano playing. Even if you'd walk by the place, he'd get off a rhyme."[6]

It had been almost thirty years since Morton exercised those skills, and he was rusty, but throughout the Library sessions, when he did not know a song that fit Lomax's queries, he tended to make up a blues on the subject. Lomax next asked about Stackolee, the hero of a widespread African American ballad. Morton was aware of the song and correctly connected it with St. Louis—Lomax thought it was from Memphis—but the disc ran out before he could say more and he apparently did not know or care to sing it, since Lomax began the next side by asking about "bad men they had down in New Orleans." Morton responded with a story about shooting pool with Aaron Harris, "a ready killer" and "the most heartless man I've ever heard of or seen." This took up a full side, and I'm guessing Lomax then asked if there were any songs about Harris, since the next disc began with a twelve-bar blues that Morton introduced as "a song they wrote about him." Harris was killed in 1915, several years after Morton left New Orleans, and this song was clearly another improvisation, starting with a generic stopgap:

> *Aaron Harris was a bad, bad man,*
> *Aaron Harris was a bad, bad man,*
> *He is the baddest man that ever was in this land.*

Four verses told about Harris murdering his "sweet little sister and his brother-in-law," being protected by "a hoodoo woman," the police fearing him, and his end:

He pawned his pistol one night to play in a gambling game,
He pawned his pistol one night to play in a gambling game,
When old Boar Hog shot him, that blotted out his name.[7]

Like the levee blues, it was a competent but unexceptional performance, and Morton easily topped it in a spoken coda, saying: "That man
would chew pig iron and spit it out into razor blades."

HESITATION

THEY WERE AN ODD PAIR: MORTON WAS ALMOST FIFTY YEARS OLD—OR, IF
one accepts the date he usually claimed, would turn fifty-three in the
course of the Library sessions. He had lived a rich and varied life, experienced multiple careers, and been a nationally successful composer and
recording artist in the most fertile period of early jazz. However, by 1938
most musicians and listeners regarded him—if they thought of him at
all—as an aging has-been, out of step with current trends.

Lomax was twenty-three years old, an enthusiastic collector and
proselytizer of American vernacular music who had assisted his father
on song-gathering expeditions since his teens and was now in his first
year as assistant in charge of the Archive of American Folk Song at the
Library of Congress. Though less than half Morton's age, he had a position with the US government and the confidence of a bright young white
man who believed he was preserving the hopes, dreams, history, and philosophy of the peasant or working classes—the mass of humanity—and
could be a translator and ambassador for communities whose voices had
been disrespected and ignored.

For Lomax, the sessions with Morton were a unique opportunity
to record the personal and artistic statement of an important figure in
American music and demonstrate the deep traditions underlying current
pop styles—as well as to prove he was the right man for his new position
and more than just his father's son. He was inspired by Morton's skill as
a raconteur and imagined a new sort of historical document, a long-form

recorded memoir, pioneering the form that would come to be known as *oral history*. He wrote and spoke about those sessions many times over the years, most prominently in the book he shaped from Morton's narrative, *Mister Jelly Roll*, and he went on to document the stories and music of numerous other singers and performers.

Morton wanted his words and music recorded for posterity, but also to reinvigorate his career and prove he was an active, innovative artist who could be leading bands and getting hits. He instigated the project and mentioned it with pride in several interviews, but was not entirely satisfied with the result, and in later letters he expressed mixed feelings about the young man who asked the questions, ran the disc cutters, and provided a bottle of whiskey to relax him in the stiff and unfamiliar setting.

Most of the sessions were recorded in late May and early June of 1938, with a further session in December. All but the last were recorded on lacquer-coated twelve-inch 78-rpm discs, which held about four and a half minutes of conversation and music on each side. For some sequences, Lomax changed discs as fast as he could, switching between two machines so as not to interrupt Morton's train of thought; others were more organized, with one side per song, and at times Lomax seems to have paused the process to give Morton a break or discuss what to do next. Most of the discs are not dated, so we cannot know for sure when one session ended and the next began, but changes of theme or approach suggest they preserved between an hour and an hour and a half of music and monologues at each session. If I have figured the breaks correctly, the first session ended with Morton demonstrating the styles of a couple of uptown pianists, some proto-boogie-woogie from a player called Game Kid and a heavy-handed ragtime piece from Buddy Carter, who "played blues as well as . . . hot honky-tonk numbers." He concluded: "That was when I was a little bitty fellow there. I guess times has changed considerable."[8]

The second session began with Morton talking about New Orleans funeral traditions and demonstrating two spirituals he performed with his teenaged vocal quartet at wakes, then playing a pair of funeral marches: first the slow "Flee as a Bird," which brass bands would play on the way to the cemetery, then the rousing "Didn't He Ramble," played on the return journey. He explained that band musicians might be paid two dollars for a funeral and that was good money for them: "Band men didn't make very much in New Orleans. The only musicians that made real money was the piano players." The recording paused at that point, and resumed with Morton explaining how he composed "Tiger Rag," a multi-section New Orleans standard that was popularized and copyrighted by the white Original Dixieland Jass Band in 1917, though he claimed to have assembled it "many years before the Dixieland had ever started" by reworking a set of French quadrilles. This claim has generally been disputed, but he made a compelling case, demonstrating how each section had originally sounded and how he transformed them in jazz style. He moved on to a general discussion of the shift from ragtime to jazz, expounding his theories of appropriate and misguided approaches to tempo and harmony, and showing how the jazz approach could be applied to any type of tune depending on "your ability for transformation." He ended the disquisition by playing a sprightly snatch of "Salty Dog" in the style of his brother-in-law, the bass player Bill Johnson, and explaining how Johnson formed the first touring group playing "what is known now as the Dixieland combination"—the Original Creole Band—and brought the style to California, Chicago, and New York.

At that point Lomax seems to have had enough of jazz, since the disc ends with Morton in mid-sentence and the next begins with him introducing a ragtime-flavored blues hit of the midteens, "Hesitation Blues." This was a foundational song in the evolution of blues as a popular style, establishing a new variant of the twelve-bar form—a two-line, four-bar verse with an eight-bar chorus—which became a standard framework for naughty novelties like "Shake That Thing," "Tight Like That," and dozens of similar efforts. Morton opened with a common verse:

If the river was whiskey and I was a duck,
I'd dive to the bottom and I'd never come up.
*   Oh, how long do I have to wait?*
*   Can I get you now, or do I have to hesitate?*[9]

Morton garbled the first line, singing, *"If I was whiskey and you was a duck,"* but otherwise it was familiar fare, and the next five verses used a fairly common mix of couplets that were floating around the South. Then things went a bit astray. Morton sang, *"There's a girl sitting on a stump—"* but caught himself and, instead of providing a rhyming second line, echoed, *"I know, know she's on the stump,"* and explained: "This is a dirty little verse . . . couldn't say that."

Lomax responded, "Say it," but Morton laughed and murmured, "No, can't do that." At least, I think that is what he said; it is hard to make out his words, since an unidentified woman was simultaneously saying, "Don't mind me." In any case, he demurred and sang an innocuous closing couplet he had used in a previous song: *"Tell me babe what you've got on your mind / I'm eating and drinking, having a lovely time."*

"Hesitation Blues" was popular throughout the country, sung and played by professionals and amateurs alike. In 1916, the first reviews to mention Bessie Smith in a blues context described her as "a riot singing the 'Hesitation,' 'St. Louis,' and 'Yellow Dog Blues'," and "singing the Hesitation Blues and St. Louis Blues to three and four encores every night."[10] Many people regarded the song as dangerously naughty, with its nudging question, "Can I get you now?," and when W. C. Handy published a version in 1915—presumably the one Smith performed, since her other selections were his compositions—he carefully omitted that phrase. An article from 1917 said his "Hesitating Blues" had nonetheless been banned after being "confounded with another Blues with almost the same title. It was claimed that it carried suggestion or smut. This is not true."[11]

Handy included "Hesitating Blues" in his 1926 collection, *Blues: An Anthology*, and the introduction explained that he had learned it from a "wandering musician" and it "may be the only blues with a refrain." This section was written by a white lawyer named Abbe Niles, and provided some common verses—*"Silk stockin's an' ruffled drawers, / Got many-a po' man wearin' overalls"*; *"Ashes to ashes, an' a-dus' to dus', / Ef de whisky don't git you, den de cocaine mus'"*; and the diving duck couplet—with a note that others were omitted because "most of them are too powerful for these pages."[12]

Handy's publishing company promoted the song in 1915 as "The Bluest Blues ever published by 'The Home of the Blues,'"[13] but if some customers understood that to mean it was sexy, the title change from "Hesitation" to "Hesitating" went along with a new lyric that was blue only in the mournful sense. Rather than the usual assemblage of floating verses, it had a cohesive lyric about a man trying to propose marriage over the telephone and a woman hesitating to respond and regretting her indecision. It was not at all smutty, and although it was recorded by a couple of professional singers, it did not enter the vernacular tradition and is rarely remembered.[14]

A more familiar version of "Hesitation" was published around the same time in Louisville, Kentucky, with the music credited to a white songwriter named Billy Smythe and the lyrics to two other white men; Scott Middleton and, in later printings, Art Gillham. Gillham explained that their version was based on "an old black folk song,"[15] and although the sheet music included an introductory verse with another melody, most people seem only to have sung the twelve-bar couplet-and-chorus section and took the published lyrics as suggestions rather than requirements. When Gillham recorded a version in 1925, he sang a mix of floating verses, keeping only the opening couplet from the sheet music—which, like the diving duck verse, was known throughout the South and not specific to this song:

I'm going down to the levee, take a rocking chair,
If the blues don't leave, I'm gonna rock away from there.[16]

"Hesitation Blues" perfectly bridged the transition from oral culture to print and phonograph recordings: over the next couple of years there were reports of it being sung in vaudeville theaters and honky-tonks, in minstrel shows, at college and community functions, and on army bases as troops mustered for the European war—and everyone, whatever the region or setting, seems to have added or improvised verses to suit their tastes and the occasion.

That kind of improvisation was standard in most African singing traditions and many European cultures. One of the most popular cowboy songs, "The Old Chisholm Trail," was notoriously polymorphous and obscene. John Lomax recalled a veteran ranch hand who claimed to know eighty-nine verses but refused to record them because they "would burn up his old horn"—the acoustic megaphone of the phonograph—and Philip Ashton Rollins, a cowboy chronicler born in 1869, said his father had a ranch near the Texas section of the Chisholm Trail and kept a ledger in which passing cowpokes wrote down favorite stanzas, eventually including "1042 verses . . . of which 1040 weren't fit to print."[17]

What was different about "Hesitation Blues" was that, unlike "Old Chisholm Trail" or "Alabama Bound," it was hailed as a trendy new creation and spread through print publication and professional performance. Lead Belly recalled hearing it around 1907, but his dating was erratic and the earliest reliable sighting—assuming it was the same song—is a newspaper item from 1913 about a pair of Black vaudevillians, George and Nana Coleman, who were featuring a number called "How Long Must I Wait" at the Dreamland Theater in Waco, Texas.[18] It may have been circulating a couple of years before that, but when it became widely popular everyone seems to have treated it as a modern twist on the blues form, tacking comical verses onto a suggestive chorus.

BACK ROOMS AND SALOON SINGERS

THE CHORUS MADE "HESITATION" PARTICULARLY ATTRACTIVE FOR GROUP SINGing, and the suggestiveness made it a favorite for barroom singing. Before Prohibition reshaped public life, saloons were exclusive male preserves—in Morton's words, "where men put their feet up on the rails and drank what they wanted." In many parts of the world, they still are: traveling around Mexico, I have never seen a woman in a working-class cantina, and often the walls are papered with nude centerfolds, a modern equivalent of the painted nudes that adorned saloons throughout the United States. Along with the main barroom, some urban saloons had a back room that could be used for noisier parties, meetings of men's clubs, gambling, musical get-togethers, and sometimes for socializing with women.

Nostalgic recollections of the "gay nineties" and the era before Prohibition often include men harmonizing around a back-room piano, and for white, middle-class men, singing rough lyrics about Black barrelhouse life provided the same vicarious pleasure their great-grandsons would get from bumping gangsta rap. In 1917, one of the first articles on the new style of music "variously spelled Jas, Jass, Jaz, Jazz, Jasz and Jascz" explained that it originated in New Orleans and "crept slowly up the Mississippi" to Chicago, "whence it had been preceded by the various stanzas of 'Must I Hesitate,' 'The Blues,' 'Frankie and Johnny,' and other classics of the levee underworld that stir the savage in us with a pleasant tickle."[19]

Some saloons permitted women to drink in their back rooms, which were designated "family rooms" or "wine rooms" to suggest a more sedate or refined atmosphere, but an early piece about the ragtime songwriter Ben Harney gives a sense of how those women were regarded:

> Harney began as a "back-room entertainer," playing for throw money or a meager straight salary in the back rooms of saloons. These were furnished with chairs, tables, and a piano, and in them ladies, with or without escorts, could order refreshments, enjoy the music, and make social contacts often to their financial advantage.[20]

Ada "Bricktop" Smith, a friend and business associate of Morton's who later ran nightclubs in Paris, Rome, and Mexico City, got her start in Chicago around 1911 singing in establishments like Jack Johnson's Café du Champion. She recalled the clientele as including plenty of women and was similarly cute about their reasons for being there: "Some were ladies with husbands; some were with other ladies' husbands, offering companionship for the night."[21]

In smaller saloons, the musical entertainment might be limited to customers harmonizing for their own amusement and occasional buskers singing for drinks and tips, but the larger or more profitable establishments often employed professionals, at least on weekends. Smith started as a dancer in vaudeville troupes and switched to singing in back rooms because she was tired of traveling and could earn more in tips from well-heeled patrons. Some saloonkeepers paid entertainers a small salary, but tips were the main source of income; the singers would stroll from table to table and were supposed to pool and divide their earnings, with an extra share for the piano player, who functioned as both accompanist and musical director, watching the crowd and deciding who would perform next and what they should sing.

In Smith's recollection, the "saloon customers cut right through American life—on any given night you could find the steady family man, the politician, the gambler, the pimp." However, she added that her mother never came to see her perform, and the respectable women in her neighborhood, if they drank alcohol at all, sent a child to fetch a bucket of beer at the back-room door rather than going themselves. She described the early teens as a boom period: "The city was on a big crusade against vice and had shut down all the whorehouses . . . [so] the girls simply moved into the saloons, picked up their tricks there . . . and the pimps and madams moved into the saloons to keep an eye on what was going on." She added that none of the pimps tried to rope her into their "stables," but on the contrary recommended her for singing jobs and "went out of their way to protect me." Ethel Waters similarly recalled the pimps in her Philadelphia neighborhood steering her away from their line of work, and contrasted them with the sleazy johns who considered any young Black woman potential prey. Smith and Waters were exceptional figures, and their memories may have been colored by nostalgia for the youthful haunts they left when they became stars, but suggest some of the more nuanced aspects of saloon and tenderloin society.

A 1915 court case from Albany, New York, provides a less cheerful picture. Excise agents working undercover to detect illegal vice described "a public sitting room adjoining the barroom," where customers were entertained by "three colored men playing a piano, banjo and drums" on a small stage surrounded by a wooden rail, and a half-dozen singers—four men who doubled as waiters and two women, all apparently white—performing from the floor in cabaret style. The agents sat at an empty table and were shortly approached by a pair of women named Doris and

Goldie, who chatted for a few minutes, then propositioned them, explaining, "The rooms will only cost you one dollar each, and we will screw you and do it right for two dollars each." Goldie was talkative, criticizing one of the singers—"That lousy bastard of a cunt thinks she is a coon shouter, but she would not be able to shout if she sucked a prick from now until next Monday"—and complaining about the low standards in her line of work:

> These cock-sucking cunts who never had a bit of education can make more than the girls with an education. Now take me for instance. My father gave me a fine education. I am a good conversationalist . . . but for all the good it does me, I can stick the education up my ass and grow hair on it.[22]

Those quotations are noteworthy because so few women's voices have been preserved from that world, even in books and articles purporting to give uncensored pictures of saloon life. This was a cabaret in upstate New York, prosperous enough to support a staff of singing waiters and a three-piece band. It was not in a red light district and there is no reason to think the women were full-time sex workers; in an era when they were increasingly expected to be financially independent but the available jobs were mostly unpleasant and poorly paid, many young women shared small apartments or lived at home with their parents and picked up some extra money doing "sporting" work. Goldie's comments were bitter, but also fierce and funny; she was talking to a couple of square-looking men who were taking her time and declining to employ her, and may in part have been amusing herself by shocking them.

The agents said nothing more about the "coon shouter" Goldie disparaged, and she could have sung "Hesitation Blues" with verses appropriate to the setting. Presumably none of her lyrics included outright obscenities, since the agents would have mentioned that, but Morton's second verse would have done nicely:

If I had a woman, she was tall,
She'd make me think about my parasol.

> *Oh, how long do I have to wait?*
> *Can I get it now? Do I have to hesitate?*

Since men did not carry parasols, that word may have been a double entendre for a penis, likewise long, pointed, and expanding for use, or for the opening folds of a woman's vulva. In 1934, the Lomaxes transcribed a verse of "Staving Chain," a song that routinely shared lyrics with "Hesitation," sung by a man named Fred Fields in Waco, Texas, "who learned it in a whore house":

> *Spread your legs from wall to wall,*
> *Tooty flew open like a parasol.*[23]

Hubert Canfield, a printer in Rochester, New York, preserved a more aggressive variant in the mid-1920s:

> *I pushed her back against the wall,*
> *And her coozie flew open like a red parasol.*[24]

Canfield was compiling a collection of bawdy lyrics for private publication and placed requests in the *Nation* and *New Yorker* magazines, concealing his identity with a pseudonym and asking that people send him "hidden and forbidden" songs. He did not specify who sent this verse, but its appearance in various forms, regions, and decades suggests it had wide circulation and Morton's less explicit version would have elicited some knowing chuckles.

All of Canfield's correspondents seem to have been white and, although the Lomaxes' other versions of "Staving Chain" were collected from Black singers, all they noted about Fred Fields were his name and location, so perhaps I should be wary about assuming this verse was current in Black as well as white tradition—especially since the white tradition had a tendency to ascribe dirty verses to Black tradition.[25] Canfield grouped forty-six couplets with the "Hesitation Blues" chorus, first as "Chicago Blues (Hesitation Blues)," then retitled "Nigger Blues."

Most of the African American songs preserved in the nineteenth and early twentieth centuries were transcribed by white chroniclers or recorded by white collectors, and it is always worth considering how much of this material—even if genuinely heard from Black artists and accurately transmitted—may have been created to entertain white listeners and give them that "pleasant tickle" of savagery. Ragtime made Black bands fashionable at white dances, and there were plenty of places like the cabaret in Albany with white "coon shouters"—a common term for singers who specialized in ragtime or blues, regardless of race—backed by Black musicians who were kept explicitly separate: the court testimony included several questions clarifying that there was a railing between the band and the singers.

When Morton declined to sing a particularly raw verse for Lomax and the unidentified woman in Coolidge Auditorium, that might have been out of respect for their sensibilities, but it could also have been because he did not choose to be cast in a role he knew all too well. Many people think of blues as a Black community style that was only later discovered by whites, and if one goes back far enough that was undoubtedly true; but when the Mississippi guitarist Robert Lockwood talked about his early days—he was born in 1915, so this would have been the 1930s—he said he mostly played for picnics and house parties and, when the interviewer asked if some of those events were for white people, he laughed and said, "That's what we was hired by most times, white. You didn't know that? My clientele's been white damn near all my life!"[26]

Likewise, the voices of women doing sex work have almost always been filtered through chroniclers who were not from their community, and frequently through men—the witnesses in the Albany court case included the excise agents, the cabaret owner, and a couple of waiters, but no women—and much of what was preserved may have been tailored to entertain those men rather than reflecting the women's own views or how they spoke to one another. Women who did sex work used raw language among themselves and Black people sang dirty blues songs to amuse one another, not just to tickle white customers, but white male customers and voyeurs were not invisible bystanders; their presence affected what was said and sung in their company, and their tastes and standards affected what was preserved.

VARIATIONS OF HESITATION

CANFIELD'S COMPILATION SUGGESTS THE EXTENT TO WHICH WHITE SOCIETY embraced "Hesitation Blues" as a touchstone for blues in general, and the song was adopted in all sorts of situations as a framework for constructing new variations. When the United States entered World War I, a newspaper in Enid, Oklahoma, printed a letter from a soldier headed to Europe, ending: "We're going to Germany, and we ain't coming back, until we make the Kaiser 'ball the jack.' (Baby, tell me how long must I hesitate.)"[27] An Atlanta newspaper found "a corpulent and jovial" young sergeant in a local mobilization camp singing "The Guardhouse Blues," with topical verses including:

> *Votes for the women, don't fall for that stuff;*
> *You can't pet a woman, gotta treat 'em rough.*
> *Oh May Belle, how long must I wait—*
> *Will you kiss me now, or must I hesitate?*[28]

As with gangsta rap, the song's mass appeal was in part a matter of white projection and theatrical posing for white consumers, but it was also popular in Black venues and reflected the attitudes and humor of Black singers. One of the verses Canfield collected was:

> *There's two kinds of people I can't understand,*
> *That's the cock-suckin woman and the cunt-lapping man.*

Variants of that verse turned up in numerous songs, venues, and regions, often with a homophobic twist: Bessie Smith sang about her inability to understand "a mannish-acting woman, and a skipping, twisting, woman-acting man," and Creole George Guesnon sang the same lines about "a bulldagging woman and a morphodite man"—a slang adaptation of *hermaphrodite*. The novelist Claude McKay wrote that when he returned to Harlem in 1919, after spending the war years in Europe, he heard "a wonderful drag 'blues' that was the favorite of all the low-down dance halls," though "in all the better places it was banned." It was "an old tune, as far as popular tunes go," but "everyone there was giggling and wriggling to it," and he quoted a sample:

> *There is two things in Harlem I don't understan'*
> *It is a bulldycking woman and a faggotty man . . .*
> *Oh, baby, how are you?*
> *Oh, baby, what are you?*
> *Oh, can I have you now,*
> *Or have I got to wait?*
> *Oh, let me have a date,*
> *Why do you hesitate?*[29]

Though routinely cleaned up for recording, explicit versions of "Hesitation" remained popular in oral tradition. In 1968, civil rights activists established a tent encampment called Resurrection City on the Capitol Mall in Washington, D.C., and stayed for six weeks, pelted by rain and slogging through mud until police eventually evicted them. They listened to speeches, sang freedom songs, and sometimes at night, after the older and more respectable folk had gone to bed, a song leader from the northwest corner of Louisiana named Frederick Douglass Kirkpatrick—a minister, but aware that the tired, wet campers needed comic relief—sang verses including:

> *Woman got a pussy that can cut you to the bone,*
> *You can fuck it, you can suck it, you can leave it alone,*
> *Tell me how long must I wait,*
> *Can I get it now, or must I hesitate?*[30]

Dave Van Ronk, an Irish American working-class musician from Queens, New York, who became the dean of Greenwich Village folk-blues guitarists in the late 1950s, sang a variant of that verse with the first line *"Pussy ain't nothing but meat on a bone."* I have no idea where he learned it, but the fact that he and Kirkpatrick both sang it in "Hesitation Blues" suggests a deep and widespread tradition, and it held on long enough for the pioneering southern party-rap group 2 Live Crew to use the same couplet as a shout-along chant in their 1990 recording "Face Down, Ass Up."

Along with myriad improvised and floating verses, the "Hesitation Blues" chorus was linked to a particular lyrical pattern that was ideally suited to comic improvisation. The earliest printed example was published in Louisville in 1916, a year after "Hesitation," in an obscure song titled "The German Blues." At that point the United States was staying out of the European war, and the sheet music cover showed a trench of German soldiers firing through barbed wire at the French and English, with the subtitle "It's Neutral." An introductory verse was written from the point of view of a soldier "singing those good old German Blues," but the stanzas that followed had no relationship to that theme. The first was:

> *I ain't no plumber Honey. I ain't no plumber's son,*
> *I said I ain't no plumber, I ain't no plumber's son.*
> *But I'll stop your leak,*
> *Until the plumber comes, until the plumber comes.*

The rest fit the same pattern: *"I ain't no butcher, no butcher's son, / But I'll chop your meat . . . ";* *"I ain't no ashman, no ashman's son, / But I'll haul your ashes . . . ."*[31] This was a variant of the basic three-line blues—the first two repeating, with a rhyming third—but around the same time an amateur collector in Auburn, Alabama, preserved a version of "Hesitation" that combined a two-line *"I ain't no miller no miller's son, / But I can do your grinding till the miller comes"* with the standard chorus, and that combination was common throughout the country.[32] Canfield's "Hesitation" verses included *"I ain't no jockey, no jockey's son / But I'll do your easy riding . . . "*; *"I ain't no iceman . . . but I'll fill your box"*; and *"I ain't the lieutenant . . . but I'll handle your privates,"* with the note "and so on through countless occupations." The pattern showed up on numerous Race records in the 1920s and 1930s, sometimes substituting other choruses for "Hesitation," with pairings including *miller/grinding, butcher/cutting, coal man/keep you warm, doctor/ease your pain, milkman/furnish your cream,* and, from the notoriously naughty Bo Carter, *milkman/pull your titties.*[33]

This formula was an easy framework for round-robin improvisation: men singing around back-room pianos could take turns coming up with couplets and everyone could harmonize on the "Hesitation" chorus. The song could also be spun into extended comic performances: The Reverend Gary Davis was born in 1896 and spent several decades playing guitar and singing around the Carolinas, at house parties and picnics, on city streets, and for the crowds that came to Durham for tobacco auctions. He was adept at entertaining Black, white, and mixed audiences, and although by the 1930s he was an ordained minister, he retained a deep repertoire of ragtime and blues songs, some of which were far from genteel. He moved to New York in the 1940s and by the 1960s was a popular figure on the burgeoning folk circuit, mentoring a generation of young guitarists and generally sticking to gospel, but occasionally he would recite racier lyrics—he made a moral distinction between singing worldly songs and reciting the words—and at a college concert in 1968 he extended "Hesitation Blues" into a twelve-minute comedy routine, beginning with a standard verse and some explanation:[34]

> *Ain't no use in me working so hard,*
> *I got me two good women working in the rich folks' yard.*
> *Tell me how long—*

He's a pie-back, you understand? Trying to break up every home . . . Some of you women quit a good man for an old pie-back man, ain't done nothing but wander from town to town . . . Say:

I ain't your good man, neither your good man's son,
But I'll get in the place of your good man till your good man comes.
    Tell me how long—

"Pie-back" was a variant of "sweet-back," a common term for *pimp*. Zora Neale Hurston explained that for many Black urbanites *pimp* had "a different meaning than its ordinary definition as a procurer for immoral purposes. The Harlem pimp is a man whose amatory talents are for sale to any woman who will support him, either with a free meal or on a common law basis; in this sense, he is actually a male prostitute."[35] I would say he was more the male equivalent of a kept woman, since prostitutes work for many customers and work hard, while "sweet-back" implies a life of indolent pleasure, and that analogy is still a bit off, since mistresses and kept women are thought of as sexual servants to wealthy men, while sweet men were thought to wield sexual power over working women. The parallel term in white society was "cake-eater," expressing a similar mix of contempt and envy.[36]

Musicians were routinely typed as sweet-backs—Morton talked about "sweet papas" going around to see lady friends who "worked out in the white people's yards" and eating pans of the choicest morsels from the white folks' kitchens, adding: "Sometimes in fact I've tried those pans myself. Some of those pans were marvelous, I'm telling you."

A century later, there is still a popular riddle:

"What do you call a musician without a girlfriend?"
"Homeless."

In the early twentieth century the Black sweet-back man was a frequent figure of comedy, an updated version of Zip Coon, the caricatured fancy-man of blackface minstrelsy. This stereotype got laughs from all kinds of audiences, but Black men might laugh for different reasons than Black women, and white men and women for still other reasons—some with knowing familiarity, some carefully preserving their distance, all prompted by different desires, prejudices, fears, and myths.

I don't know how closely Davis's performance of "Hesitation" for a group of white college students in the late 1960s resembled the performances he gave for white auctioneers and traders in Durham tobacco barns fifty years earlier, or in Black barbershops, but the verses and themes would have been universally familiar:

Well, I ain't no miller, neither no miller's son,
But I can grind a little corn for you till the miller comes.
    You know, how long—

He's offering himself to her, you know? She got sense enough to talk to herself, you know, 'cause she knows she got a good man. But he looks all right to her, you understand? She might not but to be persuaded. . . . She say, "I got me a good man." He say:

Well, I ain't no wine presser, neither no wine presser's son,
But I can press out a little juice for you till the wine presser comes.
    Can I get you now, baby . . . ?

He just wants somewhere to lay his head, you know?

Further verses limned a panoply of characters: Grocery man, Doctor, Bookkeeper, Milkman, Chauffeur, Cradle-rocker, Backbreaker, Rent-payer. Davis also tossed in some floating and proverbial verses:

Well, I ain't been to heaven, but I been told,
They say Saint Peter learned the angels how to do the jelly roll.
    Can I get you now baby? Do I have to hesitate . . . ?

Blacker the berry and the sweeter the juice,
I'd be a fool if I quit the woman I got, 'cause it ain't no use.
    Tell me how long—

Men in the country hollering "Whoa, haw, gee!"

> *Women in the city flying around, asking the question, "Who*
>   *wants me?"*
>   *Can I get you now, baby? Do I have to hesitate . . . ?*

As usual, those couplets were found all over the country. A farmer in
Alabama heard field hands singing, *"The men on the levee hollowing 'woo,*
ha, gee,' / And the women in the hoar house hollowing 'who wants me?'" In
Chicago, Sam Theard sang, *"Women in Georgia hollering 'Whoa, haw,*
gee,' / Women on State Street hollering, 'Who wants me?'" And a man named
John "Big Nig" Bray, near Morgan City, Louisiana, sang a blues about
fighting in the trenches in World War I with the verse *"The women in*
France hollerin', 'I no compris,'/ Women in America hollerin', 'Who wants
me?'"[37]

It is hard to say how typical Davis's version of "Hesitation" may have
been. Most folk song collectors would have edited this kind of performance, omitting the spoken passages and just preserving the rhymed
verses. I have tried to give a fuller sense of the performance by including both speech and rhymes, but differentiated the sections I considered
to be verse by printing them in italics, which likewise imposes my own
standards. In social settings, and generally in oral culture, there was no
need to distinguish song from speech, or performance from commentary.
Davis was using a range of techniques common in churches and camp
meetings, where preachers interweave snatches of gospel songs and spirituals with homilies, parables, and exhortations. When outsiders describe
those events, we often present the songs as discrete, separate elements—
sometimes in collections that make no mention of the circumstances in
which a song was found—but in the original congregations and communities, everything said, sung, and experienced is part of a shared and
seamless whole and includes not only what happens on the stage or in the
pulpit but the responses of everyone present.

If Davis had performed his version of "Hesitation" for a Black,
church-raised audience, it would have been an interactive experience:
people would have talked back to him, commending and correcting
according to their mood and inclinations; he would have reacted to their

comments; and the routine might have lasted twice as long or evolved into something completely different. If he had performed it in a barbershop or the back room of a saloon, other men might have added their own verses—sung or recited, depending on their tastes and talents. There were always more professions to be joked about: *"I ain't no guitar player, no guitar player's son, but I can stroke your box . . ."* Some might add verses they picked up in other contexts. Singing at home for a couple of friends, Davis ended another performance of the song with a pair of country couplets:

> *Corn in the crib, and it's got to be shucked,*
> *Well, the women in the bed, I swear they got to be fucked.*
> > *Tell me, how long—*
> > *Can I get you now?*

Here what a kind of a man a woman call for:

> *If you want to be a man, be a man in full,*
> *Let your nuts hang down, just like a Jersey bull.*
> > *Tell me, how long do I have to wait?*
> > *Can I get you now? Do you have to hesitate?*[38]

UNCLE BUD

THOSE VERSES WERE TYPICALLY ASSOCIATED WITH A DIFFERENT SONG, celebrating a legendary character named Uncle Bud. Zora Neale Hurston sang a version she learned in Florida, starting with another standard verse:

> *Uncle Bud's a man, a man like this,*
> *He can't get a woman, gonna use his fist.*

Her chorus just repeated the name—*"Uncle Bud; Uncle Bud; Uncle Bud, Uncle Bud, Uncle Bud"*—and she sang about him being a man in full, whose *"nuts hang down like a George-ay bull,"* and having corn *"that*

sure needs shucking" and gals *"that sure need fucking."* Other verses were
scatological:

> *Little cat, big cat, little bittle kitten,*
> *Gonna whup their tails if they don't stop shittin'* . . .

> *Who in the hell, the goddamn nation,*
> *Shit this turd on Pa's plantation?*
>> *Uncle Bud! Uncle Bud! Uncle Bud, Uncle Bud, Uncle Bud.*

Hurston explained that this was "a sort of social song for amusement":

> It's so widely distributed, it's growing all the time by incremental repe-
> tition. And it is known all over the South. No matter where you go, you
> can find verses of "Uncle Bud." And it's the favorite song, and the men get
> to working in every kind of work and they just yell down on "Uncle Bud."
> And nobody particular leads it; everybody puts in his verse when he gets
> ready.

A member of her folklore team asked if the song was ever performed
in the presence of "respectable ladies," and Hurston's reply was emphatic:
"Never! It's one of those jook songs, and the woman that they sing 'Uncle
Bud' in front of is a jook woman."

The questioner seemed puzzled, saying: "I thought you heard it from
women."

Hurston laughed and replied: "Yes, I heard it from women."[39]

Six years earlier and a thousand miles west, a man imprisoned on
the state farm in Sugar Land, Texas, sang an almost identical version of
"Uncle Bud" for John Lomax. James "Iron Head" Baker was apparently
born around 1884, though he told Lomax he was fifteen years older, and
it seems likely that "Uncle Bud" had been circulating since the nineteenth
century. A typescript in the Library of Congress has some relatively clean
verses collected from men picking cotton near Atlanta in 1908; Gates
Thomas printed a version dated to World War I with a bowdlerized Jersey

bull couplet and the note "other stanzas not printable"; and when some cleaned-up versions surfaced on records in the 1920s, the dirty verses were so familiar that Frankie "Half Pint" Jaxon could sing the meaningless *"Who in the world, this tarnation / Broke all these jugs on my plantation?"* and expect listeners to be amused by his evasion.[40]

Unlike "Hesitation Blues," with its jaunty melody and catchy chorus, "Uncle Bud" was almost tuneless. Some performances were more melodic than others, but there was no tune people would have recognized as specific to this song, and the chorus could just be the words "Uncle Bud," or variations like, *"Uncle Bud, Uncle Bud, who in the hell's Uncle Bud?"*[41] Simple as it was, the versions collected from Black singers across the South were notably consistent: many added extra verses—*"Uncle Bud got this, Uncle Bud got that / Uncle Bud got a dick like a baseball bat"*—but the stanzas Hurston sang were standard everywhere, with minor variations: in New Orleans, where sore feet were more common than corn cribs, George Guesnon sang the couplet about *"corn that never been shucked"* as *"corns that never been cut."*[42] In the late 1950s Roger Abrahams transcribed a version from a teenager in Philadelphia that retained Hurston's basic verses and had a strikingly monotonous melody—a single repeated note, except when he dropped down a tone for the *Un* of *Uncle*—and in the 1990s, when rap made explicit language and rhythmic rhyming marketable on commercial recordings, the Louisiana zydeco accordionist Boozoo Chavis and the Texas blues guitarist Gary B. B. Coleman released versions that, aside from the instrumentation, could easily have been sung by their grandparents.

The same elements that prevented "Uncle Bud" from being issued on sheet music or catching on with white audiences in the teens and twenties kept it from sounding dated as musical styles evolved from ragtime to rap, and made it a touchstone for underground Black culture. When Ralph Ellison recalled the sounds drifting through his Harlem window in 1949, he mentioned drunks singing "a fair barbershop style 'Bill Bailey,' free-wheeling versions of 'The Bastard King of England,' the saga of Uncle Bud, or a deeply felt rendition of Leroy Carr's 'How Long Blues'"; and when Richard Wright evoked the Mississippi of his youth in his final novel, he had the protagonist sing, *"Old man Bud / Was a man like this / He saved his money / By loving his fis'."*[43] Passed from generation to generation outside the commercial mainstream, it remained something teenagers shared when no adults were around or that older folks sang to recapture the thrills and pleasures of their youth.

In some communities, "Uncle Bud" had a further, subversive meaning. Black Texans sang it about Bud Russell, the "transfer agent" who supervised the movement of convicted prisoners between the state penitentiaries and prison farms, and a Mississippi Delta singer named Houston Bacon performed it as a "yahoo song," mocking rural whites. Framing Uncle Bud as white gave extra flavor to the lines about him masturbating because he couldn't get a woman, wondering who *"shit that turd on my plantation,"* and the verses about his daughters—Bacon sang an updated couplet about a daughter named Kate, who *"Got a cut-out on her pussy like a Cadillac eight."*

Bacon followed "Uncle Bud" with a song that mixed similar verses with a chorus in the character of a white yahoo:

> *I'm a rowdy soul, I'm a rowdy soul,*
> *I'm rowdy all 'round my red asshole.*

Or, sometimes:

> *I'm a rowdy soul, I'm a rowdy soul,*
> *I don't see a nigger in a mile o' mo'*

He told Alan Lomax, whose field notes are the source for those verses, that he had to watch out where he sang them: "If you sing one of 'em around the peckerwoods, you got to run—they don't like em ... if you want to stay in this country, you can't fool with songs like that." Lomax noted the fidelity of Bacon's imitation of white country hollering, writing that after each chorus he would "give a sort of throaty falsetto yell, much like the yells that father gives as typical country boy yells from Bosque Co. [Texas]."

The effect of the whole is to double him up with laughter after each stanza. The pleasure and wickedness of imitating the aggressor, who is a clumsy and harsh voiced singer. He has no understanding for nor sympathy with the "peckerwood."[44]

I would concur about the lack of sympathy, but am not sure there was a lack of understanding. Black traditions of mocking white people were rarely documented, for obvious reasons, but the Lomaxes preserved a handful of examples, some apparently harking back to slavery times. A man named Will Petterweight, who had been imprisoned for fourteen years in Texas, sang a song called "Johnny Woncha Ramble" with verses about "old master" riding with *a bull-whip in one hand, a cowhide in the other . . . / Pocket full of leather strings to tie your hands together.*" Those verses have been reprinted in numerous books as testimony to the horrors of slavery, but Petterweight's further couplets have been omitted—perhaps because they were considered less relevant, but also because they were obscene—with the result that the singer appears purely as a victim. The missing verses provide his wry counterthrust:

Old mistis had a peacock,
But she could not rule her own cock
Old Master had a jackass,
And could not rule his own ass.[45]

Black singers were understandably discreet about performing verses like that for white collectors, and since there were few Black folklorists—and those few tended likewise to be outsiders in the communities where they were collecting—I assume there were many more lines and rhymes on this theme that failed to be preserved. The absence of songs mocking whites is especially striking when compared with the white tradition of blackface minstrel comedy, which was disseminated internationally in print, on recordings, in films, and later on radio and television, and still shapes performances and reactions in the twenty-first century. Some Black mockery survived in commercial culture: the cakewalks that were popular at the turn of the twentieth century seem to have started as Black burlesques of white ballroom styles, and some Black vaudeville comedians did comical whiteface routines—though in general they mocked specific categories of white ethnics, performing "Hebrew," "Wop," and "Paddy" acts, along with some tramps and "rubes." There are also some subtle digs at white supremacy on early Race recordings: in 1933 a Chicago cabaret entertainer named Whistlin' Rufus recorded a risqué song with a variant of a standard Uncle Bud verse kidding the Confederate anthem:

> *In Dixieland I'll take my stand,*
> *Can't get the woman I want, I'm gonna use my—*
> > *Who's gonna do your sweet jelly rolling,*
> > *Sweet jelly rolling, when I'm gone.*[46]

STAVING CHAIN

FROM SLAVERY TIMES TO HIP-HOP AND BEYOND, THERE IS A RICH TRADI-tion of songs and stories in which Black men outsmart, outshoot, out-work, and, in underground culture, outfuck white bosses, authorities, and whoever else needs schooling: Stackolee, Railroad Bill, John Henry, Shine, Jody, Jack—some names are mythic, some are everyman. Morton boasted in his early theme song, "Winding Ball," that he could *"take it up and shake it like Staving Chain,"* and every barrelhouse singer seems to have had a Staving Chain song. There was even a minor pop hit in the early 1920s, "Stavin Change (The Meanest Man in New Orleans)," credited to Al Bernard, a white singer who specialized in blues and "coon song" material, which described its hero carrying *"a knife long enough to row a boat, a big forty-four underneath his coat"* and making *"the sweet mammas glad—and sad."*[47]

Most of the Staving Chain songs were simpler and nastier. Mance Lipscomb sang one that began with a couplet familiar from "Uncle Bud" and graphically extended the image:

Staving Chain was a man like this,
Couldn't get a woman, he'd fuck his fist;
Fuck his fist, he would sling his slime,
Save his money for hard times.
    Somebody gonna do like Staving Chain,
    Somebody gonna do like Mister Staving Chain.[48]

In the 1930s, Jazz Gillum and Lil Johnson recorded cleaned-up versions of this song, using the same melody Lipscomb played. Johnson's opened with *"If you don't shake, you won't get no cake,"* though instead of Morton's *"If you don't fuck"* couplet, she followed with the relatively innocuous *"If you don't hum I ain't gonna give you none"*—which could possibly be a reference to oral sex, but more likely was just a convenient rhyme. Her title verse portrayed a powerful character and potentially a good customer—*"Staving Chain was a man of might, / He'd save up his money just to ride all night"*—while the chorus showed she was equally tough and fully in control: *"You can't ride, honey, you can't ride this train, / I'm the chief engineer, I'm gonna run it like Staving Chain."*[49]

John Lomax described Staving Chain as "a sort of sexy Paul Bunyan," telling an interviewer: "When it comes to negro heroes, John Henry isn't in it beside Stavin Chain, but you'd better not mention his particular prowess in the paper."[50] He regularly asked Black singers if they knew the song, and his prompting led to versions being recorded by some people who might not have come up with it spontaneously—another reminder that what survives depended first on what interested folklorists and only secondarily on what was sung by folk, and that singers at times reworked or invented material to please collectors. Lomax recorded three versions of "Staving Chain" from a man named Homer "Tricky Sam" Roberson during two visits to the Texas State Penitentiary at Huntsville, and noted that one was particularly long because Roberson was joined by another prisoner and they "got interested in rhyming up a long song," adding: "Most of the following text is, therefore, improvised."

Roberson's lyrics were standard blues fare:

Staving Chain is dead and gone,
Left me here to carry his good works on.
   I'm making it down, baby, like Staving Chain, oh, Staving Chain,
   I'm making it down, just like Staving Chain. . . .

I went home last night, went walking through my hall,
Spied another rounder kicking in my stall,
   He was making it down like Staving Chain . . . [51]

Lomax assumed Roberson knew naughtier verses, and when he and
Alan included the song in *Our Singing Country*, they wrote that it was
"sung and censored for us by Tricky Sam." They credited this version to a
recording they made of Roberson in 1934, but in fact it was compiled from
multiple sources—since singers routinely borrowed verses from one song
for another, the Lomaxes gave themselves the same freedom. The notes
positioned them as experienced wanderers in romantic worlds, outsiders
who knew the score: "We have encountered a number of guitar players
nicknamed Stavin' Chain—Little Stavin' Chain, Big Stavin' Chain, etc.—
none of whom could or would tell us what his nickname meant. Guitar
players, however, have the reputation of being midnight creepers."[52]

   Mack McCormick, a brilliant eccentric who spent decades researching
Texas blues, suggested that the name was inspired by Exodus 25:14, which
instructed the builders of the Ark of the Covenant, "thou shalt put the
staves into the rings by the sides of the ark." He explained: "For the laborer
who spikes down or hammers staves, the act of driving a stave through the
ring of a chain suggests to his active imagination the same familiar sym-
bolism as in slipping a wedding ring over a girl's finger."[53] The Mississippi
guitarist Johnny Temple recorded a verse that fits this interpretation: *"My
staving chain been all right, till my baby wanted it every night."*[54] Morton, by
contrast, said "Stavin' Chain don't mean a thing," and some singers implied
it was just a proper name, Willie McTell singing about a character named
"Chainey," Furry Lewis about someone who was *"Naturally gonna shake it
like Chaney did,"* and Zora Neale Hurston writing of men who would "strut
like Stavin' Cheney."[55]

Whatever its source, by the early twentieth century the name was familiar throughout the Black sporting world. Richard M. Jones recalled a pianist named Stavin Chain who came through his hometown of Donaldsonville, Louisiana, in 1904 playing what was later known as boogie-woogie:

> Chain walked into that saloon one night . . . and sat down at an old piano. I was a youngster, but I remember him. He started rambling around on the keyboard, then he told some onlookers he was going to play a tune he called *Lazy Rags* which featured a lot of walking bass. I'm telling you, customers started coming into that saloon like gangbusters . . . "Roll that walkin' bass, Papa Stavin Chain. Roll it a week," I remember them all shouting. . . . I was in knee britches, and the cops more than once chased me away from the windows where I was peeking in, watching Stavin and the girls.[56]

Johnny St. Cyr said the song was popular in New Orleans around 1908 and celebrated a local character:

> He was supposed to have more women in the District than any other pimp. . . . Women were supposed to be crazy about him . . . I think the song was composed when he was alive, because I think I remember some of the words was, "Nobody in town can—[he paused to think of an appropriate euphemism]—*love* like Staving Chain."[57]

Morton's recollection was less complimentary:

> Stavin' Chain didn't amount to very much. There was just a song around him. He was a very low class guy, belonged to the honky-tonk gang. Just a ladies' man. Was an ugly, gawky fellow. Nothing to make nobody think about him the second time.[58]

In 1907 the New Orleans *Times-Democrat* reported that a man named William Franklin, alias Staving Chain—described as "a light griff," a

French term for the child of a Negro and a Mulatto—had shot two people in the Bayou town of Franklin, but there is no reason to think he
was the same person St. Cyr or Morton recalled, since six months later
the *Daily Picayune* reported that police had arrested a man for this crime
in an uptown saloon, the Red Onion, and when they dragged him back
to Franklin he turned out to be another Staving Chain named Frank
Shields.[59] Newspapers throughout the South and Midwest had stories
about Black Staving Chains, usually mentioned in connection with killings or other criminal incidents—which may say less about who used
the nickname than how Black men got mentioned in newspapers—
including a man with the given name Wallace Chains, whom John and
Ruby Lomax recorded in a Texas prison, along with another prisoner
who claimed the same nickname.[60]

John and Alan Lomax recorded a guitarist and singer named Wilson
Jones in Lafayette, Louisiana, who called himself Stavin' Chain and sang
three versions of the song accompanied by a fiddler. Only one survives
on record, but they preserved the others as texts, and one neatly comple-
ments Morton's self-referential verse about being the Winding Ball, who
could "shake it like Staving Chain":

> *Stavin' Chain was a man like dis,*
> *Stood on the corner an' wind his fist,*
> > *No, you can't wind, like Stavin' Chain,*
> > *No you can't wind, wind like the bully,*
> > *Mister Stavin' Chain.*[61]

~ three ~

Winding Ball

I'm the Winding Ball, don't deny my fucking name.

—Jelly Roll Morton, Library of Congress recordings

Morton followed "Hesitation Blues" with "My Gal Sal," a nostalgic ballad published in 1905 by Paul Dresser. Dresser's younger brother, the novelist Theodore Dreiser—another evolving name—wrote that the song was a tribute to Sallie Walker, who ran a "house of ill repute" in their native Evansville, Indiana.[1] Morton recalled it as "a real favorite in the city of New Orleans" around 1906 or 1907, and sang it first in the sentimental pop style of that time, then as an upbeat jazz number. He followed with a story about his first visit to St. Louis as a member of McCabe's Minstrels, saying he impressed the local musicians with his ability to execute intricate ragtime compositions and classical pieces like Antonín Dvořák's "Humoresque" and Franz von Suppé's *Poet and Peasant* overture, and demonstrated how he would rework those styles "on the version of my creation, of jazz music," playing Scott

Joplin's "Maple Leaf Rag" in the fast ragtime style, then with a slower Afro-Caribbean lilt, and swinging a medley of the "Miserere" and "Anvil Chorus" from *Il Trovatore*.

This was not Lomax's kind of music, though he dutifully recorded it, and Morton reciprocally provided some examples of vernacular folklore. They had disparate interests but tried to satisfy one another, and blues provided an obvious meeting ground, since it merged old rural traditions with evolving urban trends. Count Basie's orchestra was getting national hits playing a cleaned-up, orchestrated version of styles Morton had learned in Gulf Coast honky-tonks when Basie was in diapers, and if Morton had mixed feelings about that evolution, he could still improvise a blues to fit any situation and was happy to prove his mastery of the form. Lomax had the opposite attitude: he was always going to be more excited by what was played by a juke joint piano-pounder or backwoods guitar-picker than by anything a popular orchestra played on the radio. So, following the St. Louis segment, he apparently asked Morton for a real "lowdown" blues. Morton complied, as he had when Lomax asked for levee songs and bad man ballads, singing a blues that began with his usual *"I could sit right here and think a thousand miles away"* and continued with some standard twelve-bar verses and an impromptu stanza tailored to the request, which he repeated twice.

> *I've got a sweet woman, she lives right back of the jail.*
> *I've got a sweet woman, lives right back of the jail.*
> *She's got a sign on her window: "Good cabbage for sale."*
>
> *My gal's got a Hudson, her pal's got a diamond ring.*
> *My gal's got a Hudson, her pal's got a diamond ring.*
> *Her sister's got a baby from shaking that thing.*
>
> *Aw, got the lowdown blues; got 'em lowdown blues.*
> *Aw, lowdown blues, yes, lowdown blues.*
> *I've got the lowdown blues, too doggone mean to cry.*

It was an upbeat, entertaining performance, but Lomax was not just asking for a blues with the word "lowdown" in it. He had urged Morton to complete the verse in "Hesitation Blues" about "a girl sitting on a stump," and was trying to get past that kind of self-censorship and hear what Black performers sang in lowdown honky-tonks when respectable white folks were not listening. He and his father had regularly been thwarted in that mission: they asked multiple singers for versions of "Staving Chain," but Fred Fields was the only one to give them an uncensored lyric—which happened to include the verse about a woman who lived back of the jail, in that case with a sign reading "good booty for sale."[2] Now he had the time and resources to plumb the repertoire of a major figure from a famously rowdy region at the dawn of the blues era, and was determined to get some of the real stuff.

The conversation surrounding "Low Down Blues"—as Lomax titled it on the Library's file card—was not preserved, so I am guessing about some of this, but my guesses fit the sequence of recording and the men involved. Lomax was always looking for material other collectors had missed, and was proud of his ability to ferret it out. Katharine Newman, who collected the songs and memories of Jennie Devlin, an elderly white woman in upstate New York, recalled that in 1938 she brought Lomax to record Devlin and privately told him, "She knows more naughty songs than I have been able to get."

Lomax said, "Give me half an hour alone with her. I bet you a dollar I'll get them." Newman was sure Devlin would never sing those songs for a stranger, much less a male stranger, but she went off for a while and came back to find Lomax grinning and demanding the dollar.[3]

The Library setting made it easy for Lomax to argue that he was recording for historical purposes and any questionable material would be restricted for the perusal of serious scholars. He may have demonstrated his comfort with obscenity by quoting naughtier versions of the "cabbage" verse or a dirty toast. He may have asked Morton to finish the verse about the girl on the stump, and may have known from earlier conversations that there was a song that went with Morton's youthful nickname. Whatever the specifics of their discussion, Morton followed his generic "lowdown blues" with an uncensored version of "Winding Ball," starting with two choruses of the title verse, then the verse he had previously censored:

> I'm the Winding Boy, don't deny my name.
> I'm the Winding Boy, don't deny my name.
> Winding Boy, don't deny my name,
> Pick it up and shake it like Staving Chain,
> I'm the Winding Boy, don't deny my name. . . .

> I seen that gal, she's sitting on the stump.
> I seen that gal, she was sitting on the stump.
> I seen the gal, sitting on the stump,
> I screwed her till her pussy stunk.
> I'm the Winding Boy, don't deny my name.

It is easy to understand why Morton was hesitant about singing that verse, especially in front of a respectable young woman. Many listeners would have found it shocking or disgusting, and if some women accepted or enjoyed dirty language, they might nonetheless be offended by the implied misogyny. One of the distinguishing features of dirty blues, as compared with the dirty ditties popular in white culture, was the acknowledgment that sex is messy and pungent, but there was nothing distinctive about portraying the messiness and smell as inherently female. White and Black culture alike have jokes, rhymes, and insults about the unpleasant or "fishy" smell of female genitalia, and there is no parallel folklore about nasty or stinky penises. Fred Fields sang, *"I went down to Mr. Shankel's trough, / Washed my dinger till the head came off,"* but that was about his fear of being contaminated during sex and imputed the nastiness and contagion to a woman.[4] Mance Lipscomb explained that gonorrhea came from women who had "filth" inside them from previous partners, singing, *"Every time I go to pee / Think about the gal give this to me,"* and there are similar verses in dozens of cowboy, sailor, and army songs.[5]

The stump verse was apparently one of Morton's favorites, since he almost sang it in "Hesitation," repeated it in two performances of his theme song, and used it again in "Make Me a Pallet on the Floor." If one imagines it as something he sang for male audiences, and in particular for white men buying the sexual services of Black women, its misogyny is brutally obvious: the man gets his pleasure and leaves the woman stinking. But what if he sang it for after-hours audiences of women who did sex work? He made his reputation in a world where running water was a luxury and those women were constantly dealing with the mess and smells of sexual encounters, trying to protect themselves from disease, preparing for the next client, and simply trying to keep clean. They could have heard this verse as a joke about country girls—urban women don't have sex on stumps, and Morton's next verse was about having sex on the grass, with the rhyming line *One day she got scared and a snake ran up her big ass.*[6] The snake could represent a penis, but it could also recall a rural world that much of his audience had recently escaped, or be heard as a comical exaggeration of the sexual experimentation Morton labeled "freakishness." He later described Chicago as "a freakish center" and sang a version of "The Dirty Dozens" he heard there that also had a snake verse: *"I went one day, out to the lake, / I seen your mammy fucking a snake."*

Although many writers have assumed Morton performed his sexually explicit material for the customers in Basin Street brothels, all his references to early blues—like most recollections of blues among New Orleans musicians of his generation—framed the style as specific to Black honky-tonks, after-hours joints, and dance halls, and particularly favored by sporting women. William Russell recalled Morton's brother-in-law, Dink Johnson, singing a version of "Winding Boy" that was "much more vulgar and obscene than any of Jelly's," for a couple of women who wandered into the bar he ran in Los Angeles:

He started, "Now all you ladies better take a walk, 'cause Mr. Johnson's gonna start some of his nasty talk." Then he began. "I'm the Windin' Boy and I don't deny my name. . . . " Dink described explicitly all the activities of a whorehouse—everything from "little sister at the door . . . "

(She was only eight years old but was a very smart girl and didn't deny
her name) . . . and "little brother who swept up the floor," to big sister
upstairs.[7]

Dink's Place was a small barroom behind Wrigley Field—the original ballpark with that name, predating the more famous Chicago
location—and served a late-night crowd of "panhandlers, hustlers," and
other sporting riffraff. There were plenty of places like that in turn-of-
the-century New Orleans, and songs like "Winding Ball" suited their
clientele, but they were a long way from the mansions of Basin Street.
The "parlor houses" of the early 1900s made a point of replicating the
comforts and manners of an upper-class parlor where well-to-do white
men could relax, tended by nice young women who behaved properly in
public, then could be taken upstairs at the gentlemen's whim and treated
as the gentlemen chose. The better houses made a significant part of their
income by selling alcohol, and the pianists were there to provide a pleasant atmosphere and keep the clients happy in the downtime. The longer
a customer stayed, the better, and some men treated the houses like private clubs, enjoying the convivial company and only indulging in more
intimate offerings when they happened to be in that mood. Rose Johnson, who preceded Morton as the regular pianist at Hilma Burt's house,
recalled that when a customer came in, he would be invited to seat himself in an armchair:

> They had something like velvet footstools, we called them, and the girls
> sit there and talk; if you don't like that girl, she'd leave, another girl come
> and talk. Piano player's playing, you're dancing and having a nice time. No
> vulgarity! If you curse, five dollar fine.[8]

The "you" in that reminiscence shifted from the gentleman who was
having a nice time to the woman who would be fined for cursing, and I
am not romanticizing that relationship. Along with the standard services,
customers in the more expensive houses could request live sex shows,
sometimes involving women having intercourse with animals or eating

feces—Morton told Lomax the "dung-cakes" were actually gingerbread mixed with limburger cheese but noted the cruelty of the performances.

Parlor house pianists sometimes sang dirty songs or accompanied clients who wanted to harmonize on dirty songs and women who sang to entertain and excite potential clients. But Morton's years in the District ended around 1910, and although blues became a national craze in the early teens, through the first decade of the century everyone recalled it as a rough style limited to the poorest and toughest Black venues. Morton may sometimes have sung "Winding Ball" for white customers, but would more often have entertained them with pop hits like "My Gal Sal," and perhaps some naughty parodies of those songs, and played blues for after-hours sessions and the sporting crowd.

There are multiple levels of historical silence at work here. Jazz and blues researchers have tended to ignore musicians who did not favor those styles, and rarely explored the more sedate or mainstream repertoires of musicians who are remembered as jazz or blues players, even when the musicians boasted of their ability to play society dance music, operatic overtures, and the latest sheet music hits. Writers and promoters routinely associated jazz with Storyville, though the bands known for playing that style rarely worked in the downtown District and the white men who patronized the Basin Street houses favored the styles white men liked in that era: waltzes, light ragtime, saloon sing-alongs, and sentimental parlor ballads. Rose Johnson recalled Lulu White majestically descending the stairs of her house each evening to the strains of "When the Moon Shines," a romantic waltz, and insisted that, although White herself was Black or Octoroon, "she didn't use Negro entertainers. She used strictly white entertainers, and it was Jimmy Williams and Kid Ross."[9] Morton mentioned Ross as an adept ragtime player, but the only other trace of Williams is an advertisement offering piano lessons, and it seems likely he played the standard pop and light classical fare of the time and would not have interested jazz researchers.[10]

Johnson complicated that recollection a bit, saying she and Morton occasionally played in White's establishment and White's favorite song was "Stackolee." But she remembered Morton as playing romantic pop songs—"Sugar Moon" and "Mandy Lane"—and those kinds of tunes were the typical parlor house fare across the country. George Morrison, who worked as house musician for a Denver madam named Mattie Silks in the early 1910s, described the repertoire as "kind of quiet," mentioning "Blue Bell Waltz," "Red Wing," and "Silver Threads Among the Gold," and singling out "The Darktown Strutters' Ball" as a rare jazz number.[11] Pianos were the standard sporting house instrument, and were rarely used by jazz or ragtime bands. Many people thought of the instrument as refined and feminine, and Pops Foster recalled jeering at male pianists: "We'd call them 'Sissies' or say 'Look at that faggot up there.' The band musicians thought piano was for women."[12]

That was not just a quirk of turn-of-the-century New Orleans: James Brown's trombonist and bandleader, Fred Wesley, recalled switching from piano to horn in the 1950s because he was being teased for playing a sissy instrument, and from Tony Jackson through Little Richard, James Booker, Billy Preston, myriad gospel stars, and—in a different but related setting—Elton John, the instrument continued to be associated with gay men. By the same token, Lil Hardin Armstrong, Lovie Austin, Mary Lou Williams, and virtually all the famous female jazz instrumentalists throughout the twentieth century were pianists. Morton mentioned this as a reason for specializing in rough lyrics: "When a man played piano, the stamp was on him for life—the femininity stamp. And I didn't want that on, so, of course, when I did start to playing, the songs were kind of smutty." Which brings us back to "Winding Ball."

UNWINDING THE BALL

Although its title phrase appeared in a few folklore collections, no one published or recorded the song variously called "Winding Ball," "Winding Boy," or "Winin' Boy" before Morton sang it at the Library of Congress. As word of the Library recordings circulated through the growing community of New Orleans jazz enthusiasts, he was prompted to record cleaned-up versions in solo sessions for a couple of small collector labels and in a band session for RCA Victor's Bluebird subsidiary, performed it on the *Chamber Music Society of Lower Basin Street* radio program, and, as other musicians followed suit, it became a trad jazz standard. But all of that happened after 1938; at the Library, Morton said it had been a big hit for him in his New Orleans youth, but "that's an unknown tune right now." He sang it as an example of the sort of disreputable material he had abandoned thirty years earlier, and if Lomax had not pressed him to sing some lowdown, uncensored blues, it would likely have remained unknown.

Since the song had been considered unprintable and unrecordable, there is no way to know how much of it originated with Morton. The stump and snake verses could have been his inventions or may have been sung all over the South. Another of his verses was documented elsewhere in varying forms; in 1948 Vance Randolph collected a couplet from "an elderly lady" in southwestern Missouri, presumably white, who said she had learned it around 1910:

> *Buy a dime's worth of butter, and a nickel's worth of lard,*
> *Keep your pussy greasy till his pecker gets hard.*[13]

Canfield's "Hesitation" verses from the 1920s included an urban variant:

> *A nickel's worth of cold cream, a dime's worth of lard,*
> *Vaseline your coozie till my cock gets hard.*[14]

In "Winding Ball," Morton sang this couplet with a significant change:

> *Dime's worth of beefsteak and a nickel's worth of lard.*
> *Get a dime's worth of beefsteak and a nickel's worth of lard.*
> *Yes, a dime's worth of beefsteak, nickel's worth of lard,*
> *I'll salivate your pussy till my peter get hard.*
> *I'm the winding boy, don't deny my name.*

Given the pronouns and what Morton was proposing, I would guess he sang this verse for women and expected them to appreciate the suggestion—a theme I will pick up in later chapters. For the moment, I want to stick with "Winding Ball," because that phrase has caused some confusion and suggests some interesting connections. The Library's file card for the song gives its title as "Windin' boy," corrected in pencil to "The winding boy," but in *Mister Jelly Roll*, Lomax wrote "Wining Boy" and explained—writing in Morton's voice—that when Hilma Burt's sporting house closed for the night Morton would drink up the leftover wine and "right there was where I got my new name—Wining Boy." A footnote specified that Morton preferred this term to "Winding," which had a sexual connotation, and Morton supported this derivation in a letter to Roy Carew by writing the title as "Wineing Boy"—a spelling he said was "figured out by the publicity men at RCA."[15]

The "wine" explanation went along with the cleaned-up lyrics Morton sang on commercial releases, but was an afterthought. Throughout the Library recordings, he clearly articulated his nickname as "Winding Ball" when he was speaking—in one instance pausing to correct himself from "Winin'" to "Winding"—though when he was singing he sometimes pronounced it more like "Winding Boy" or "Win'in' Boy." On his first commercial recording of the song, for the Jazz Man label in December 1938, he sang "Winin' Ball," clearly articulating the second word; the following September, recording with a band of New Orleans stalwarts, he seemed to make a decision in the studio, singing, "I'm the Winin'—" then pausing and singing "Boy" (Frederic Ramsey, who was taking notes during this session, initially wrote the title as "Whinin' Ball," then corrected it to "Boy"); and that December, recording for the General label, he consistently sang "Boy."[16]

The shifting pronunciations and explanations are a reminder that oral culture is essentially different from written or recorded culture and attempting to determine a "correct" name or lyric often obscures an overlapping range of meanings rather than producing reliable clarity. Numerous writers have suggested that Morton's "winding" or "win'in'" was the same word Afro-Caribbean English speakers use for the swiveling hip motion common in African dancing. In 1790 a British visitor to the West Indies was struck by the wild dances of enslaved Africans—which reminded him of "the amusements [of] the vulgar peasantry in Ireland"—and quoted a song with the lines, *"You no jig like a-me! You no twist like a-me . . . ! You no shake like a-me! You no wind like a-me!"*[17]

Kid Ory said Morton was known around the District as Winding Boy because "he used to wind when he walked, you know, like turning the corner. . . . The women liked that . . . Sharp walk, you know. Put the hat there, and had one suspender down."[18] Other people gave the term a more overtly sexual meaning. Wilson Jones used it as a euphemism for masturbation, singing that Staving Chain *"saved his money en he wind his hand."* Danny Barker explained the nickname as "a slang of the Tenderloin . . . a ladies' man who is boasting of his physical, masculine prowess in the bed. He's a winder. He's a grinder. He's a long-distance body soother." Johnny St. Cyr told Lomax the term was "a bit on the vulgar side . . . How could I put it? The guy's a good jazzer." A bit later he added, "Most of those guys around the District . . . they all were halfway pimps," and when Lomax suggested that was the implication of "winding," agreed: "That's what it was."[19]

Those explanations make sense as long as we're talking about Winding Boy, but what about "Winding Ball"? Morton clearly said his name that way in the Library, and Joseph "Fan" Bourgeau, who did odd jobs around the downtown District in the first decade of the twentieth century, responded to a question about Morton's nickname—which the interviewer pronounced "Windin' Boy"—by saying, "They called him the Winding Ball."[20]

Though "Winding" could refer to swiveling hips, the full phrase suggests an alternate lineage, reaching back to a lyric preserved by the Scottish poet Robert Burns. Burns was an amateur folklorist and some of his most popular poems were adapted from oral traditions. Since he was often the first person to preserve a verse in print, it is impossible to determine how much he gleaned from rural singers and how much he altered or invented; some of his poems include material he heard in the countryside, and some lyrics he preserved as folklore show signs of his creative and editorial hand. Many of those lyrics include explicit sexual encounters and, although he cleaned them up for publication, uncensored versions were published posthumously as *The Merry Muses of Caledonia*. He apparently sang or recited these verses at a men's club in Edinburgh, and they give a unique picture of eighteenth-century Scottish customs and humor—for example, a rhymed conversation among a group of maidens planning to weave a kilt for a young man from their pubic hairs and, if those were insufficient, with hair from their arses.

Burns limited the circulation of his naughtier lyrics to gentleman acquaintances, but many were from a woman's point of view and in other situations were presumably sung by and for women. One of the most popular, "Comin' Thro' the Rye," is a strong statement of female sexual independence: the singer declares that "*if a body kiss a body*" it is nobody's business but her own—and the *Merry Muses* version did not say "kiss." It portrayed a woman walking through the fields, finding "*a staun o' staunin graith*"—a stand of standing material, presumably attached to a man—and singing:

> *Gin a body meet a body,*
> *Comin' thro the grain;*
> *Gin a body fuck a body,*
> *Cunt's a body's ain.*

Other lyrics cloaked intimate details in rural metaphor. A song called "The Yellow, Yellow Yorlin" described a lad wandering the countryside "*in the flow'ry month of May*," meeting a "*pretty maid*," and telling her, "*I wad fain fin' your yellow, yellow yorlin.*" *Yorlin* is the Scottish name for the bird known elsewhere as a yellowhammer, and the tradition of using birds to represent female genitalia is ancient: a survey of classical Greek poetry turned up nightingale, swallow, and thrush in that role, along with fig, rose, hyacinth, a bushy thicket, and bird's and mouse's nests.[21] The metaphor could be tender, but the plot of Burns's lyric was not: The maid protested that she already had a man "*Wha has baith sheep an' cows, that's feedin' in the hows, / An a cock for my yellow yellow yorlin*"; the singer responded that he would pay her and her man need never know; she scolded him for the suggestion, saying she didn't want his money and her parents would be horrified; so he raped her—*"I took her by the waist, an' laid her down in haste,/ For a' her squakin' an' squalin'"*—with the result that *"the lassie soon grew tame, an' bade me come again / For to play wi' her yellow yellow yorlin."*[22]

Most of the songs in Burns's collection are known only from his manuscript, which was reprinted multiple times in the nineteenth century, often in surreptitious and unreliable editions, but "The Yellow, Yellow Yorlin" lived on in oral tradition, traveling south to England and overseas to the United States. In the process, people who had never heard of a yorlin changed that part of the lyric. A version recorded in New Hampshire referred to *"a bird I call my little yorkla harlin,"* but most singers changed the phrase to something that made sense to them, and by the late nineteenth century *"fin' your yellow yellow yorlin"* was generally sung as *"wind your little ball of yarn."*[23] That was a proverbial phrase: nineteenth-century newspapers have numerous references to people "winding up their little ball of yarn," meaning to finish a talk or task. There were also numerous references to the song: a piece about a sumptuous dinner given by members of the Crescent City Battalion of the Louisiana State Militia in 1879 described the soldiers exchanging jokes and songs, "among which we cannot help mentioning the 'Little Ball of Yarn,' which was up to the point and admirably rendered."[24]

This article did not quote any lyrics, nor does any source I have found from the next fifty years, and several writers described the lyrics as unprintable. John Lomax recalled that when he first became interested in cowboy singers in the 1890s, he "listened intently, but . . . never dared to write out the words of 'The Keyhole in the Door,' 'Winding Up Her Little Ball of Yarn . . . ' and other favorite songs current in Dodge City, the end of the cattle trail." In 1942, a survey of American popular music included the song in a discussion of tavern favorites of the 1870s but gave only the first two verses, explaining that the other three contained "the usual erotica" and "must be omitted and imagined." And Gates Thomas mentioned "The Little Ball of Yarn" and "Baldy"—likely a variant of "Old

Chisholm Trail"—as Black work songs, "widely distributed over Texas and, perhaps, the South . . . to which I can only refer, as their pornography is such an organic part of their structure that it cannot be excised without destroying the point of the songs."[25]

American variants of "The Little Ball of Yarn" often added verses in which the young man—or, more rarely, the young woman—contracted a venereal disease during the tryst. Most portrayed the sex as consensual, but some ended with the man in prison, and one singer introduced his version as "sung by a man on the scaffold as he was about to be hanged for a certain unmentionable crime."[26] In a nice example of how folk memory can work, although the yorlin was replaced with yarn, many versions continued to mention birds. A lyric transcribed in the 1950s from John "Kid" Mike, a Black singer and reciter in Philadelphia, began *"'Twas in the month of June / And the flowers were in bloom/ And the birds were sweetly singing on the farm,"* though by the end his protagonist had caught the clap, been arrested, and lamented, *"In a prison cell I sit / With my fingers dipping shit, / Just for wounding up a little ball of yarn."*[27] Jennie Devlin sang a version, apparently learned in the late nineteenth century, that somewhat softened Burns's plot and added an avian chorus:

> *I put my arms around her waist*
> *And I gently laid her down,*
> *Intending not to do her harm.*
> *And there to her surprise,*
> *I rode between her thighs,*
> *As I wound up the little ball of yarn.*
> > *The blackbird and the thrush,*
> > *They were looking down on us*
> > *As I wound up the little ball of yarn.*[28]

Other offshoots went fully avian: an Arkansas man recalled a scrap from the late nineteenth century in which *"The bluebird and the robin kept their ass a-bobbin' / Till they wound up the little ball of yarn,"*[29] and Newman Ivey White printed a lone verse from a Black Alabaman in 1915—there were apparently several more, but his informant only sent one—which reworked the key phrase:

> *An old hen sittin in the fodder stack*
> *A hawk flew down and pecked her in the back*
> *If you can't thread a needle come wind the ball.*
> *If you can't thread a needle come wind the ball.*

In the same area and period, another of White's informants heard a group of Black workers singing a version of "Alabama Bound" that ended with the line, *"I'm a winding ball, and don't deny my name."*[30]

The evolution from "The Yellow, Yellow Yorlin" to "Winding Ball" was obscured at every stage by censorship. Burns's lyric circulated only in underground volumes of erotica, Morton's song was not recorded until the late 1930s, and a complete lyric of "The Little Ball of Yarn" did not appear in any collection of folklore or erotic verse until the 1960s. The latter omission is particularly odd: an article in the *Kentucky Folklore Record* from 1958 referred to the song as something "which most collectors know but do not print," but by the 1920s far dirtier lyrics were being printed in anonymous collections like *Immortalia* and bowdlerized for publication in academic journals and songbooks. A version of the song was recorded in 1937 by a white country duo called the Southern Melody Boys as "Wind the Little Ball of Yarn" but seems to have attracted no notice, positive or negative—though it included a reference to *"walking through the rye"* that suggests Burns was still lurking in the folk memory.[31]

In 1934 the *Bangor Daily News* printed a note that "a correspondent wants to know if we know the old song about winding up a little ball of yarn," adding, "We remember hearing that song sung more than fifty years ago, but recall only a few of the words. If anybody can supply the words we'll be glad to print them." The following week they printed a three-verse version from a retired lumberman who remembered hearing it "in logging camps, and everywhere else," which ended with a warning to "ladies fair" that once again referenced birds:

Like the robin and the thrush,
Keep your head beneath the brush,
And your hand upon your little ball of yarn.[32]

It seems odd that the *Bangor Daily News* and the Montgomery Ward department store chain—which issued the Southern Melody Boys record—were comfortable with a lyric that folklorists considered unprintable, and suggests that other lyrics described that way may have been similarly mild. In any case, the song was rarely documented until the later twentieth century, and its British heritage led to it being classified as white folklore and excluded from discussions of Black culture. This kind of segregation remains common in folklore studies and, as with other forms of segregation, the separation is not equal: studies of white culture in the United States have always included ragtime, blues, jazz, rock 'n' roll, and more recently rap as popular elements, but the fact that Black Americans danced square dances and waltzes and sang "She'll Be Coming Round the Mountain" and "Danny Boy" is generally treated as irrelevant to their culture—or, if relevant, as evidence that they were subject to Euro-American cultural hegemony rather than because Afro-American culture is as broad and omnivorous as any on earth.

The Lomaxes preserved multiple African American variants of "Barbara Allen," and other British ballads can be found in Black tradition if one cares to search—but it requires some searching. In part that may reflect what people sang in their communities, but collectors significantly slanted the historical record. Men who recited "Stackolee," "Signifying Monkey," and "Shine and the *Titanic*" also tended to know versions of poems like "The Cremation of Sam McGee," "The Lure of the Tropics," and "The Face on the Barroom Floor," but even when folklorists mentioned this broader repertoire, they saw no reason to collect Black versions of the "book poems." An obscure article by a graduate student named Anthony Reynolds provides the only evidence of Black reciters reworking lines and stanzas in performances of those poems, just as Black musicians were reshaping Euro-American melodies into blues and jazz.[33]

Naughty lyrics seem to have been particularly popular across racial lines, and dirty songs from the British Isles continued to be sung and recited in Black communities well into the twentieth century. I mentioned Ralph Ellison's recollection of Harlem drunks singing "The Bastard King of England"; LaWanda Page recorded an exuberantly filthy version of the Scottish "Ball of Kirriemuir," declaiming it in the style of a Pentecostal preacher; and variants of "Our Goodman," a musical dispute between a drunken husband and his cheating wife that was already old in the 1700s, were recorded by the Texas guitarist Coley Jones and the Kansas City blues singer Lottie Kimbrough in the 1920s (as "Drunkard's Special" and "Cabbage Head Blues"), by the Carolina guitarist Blind Boy Fuller in the 1930s (as "Cat Man Blues"), by the Mississippi Delta harmonica master Rice "Sonny Boy Williamson" Miller in the 1950s (as "Wake Up Baby"), and by Professor Longhair and Rudy Ray Moore in the 1970s and Ruth Brown in the 1990s (as "Cabbage Head").[34]

DIDN'T HE RAMBLE

ANOTHER BRITISH BALLAD EVOLVED INTO THE QUINTESSENTIAL JAZZ funeral song. As Morton explained, bands would play slow, mournful tunes on the way to the cemetery, but after the burial they would strike up a hot ragtime march:

> *Didn't he ramble, he rambled,*
> *Rambled all around, in and out the town,*
> *Didn't he ramble, ramble,*
> *Rambled till the butchers cut him down.*

This song was originally about a mythic beast, the "Derby Ram," and although the earliest surviving text is from 1814, it was already described as an "old ballad" and some scholars believe it is a survival of pre-Christian British fertility rites.[35] In the United States, a popular story told of George Washington singing it for the children of Oliver

Ellsworth, the Chief Justice of the Supreme Court, and some versions included samples of the lyrics:

> *As I was going to Derby,*
> *Upon a market day,*
> *I spied the biggest ram, sir,*
> *That ever was fed upon hay.* . . .
>
> *The wool upon his back, sir,*
> *It reached to the sky,*
> *And eagles built their nests there,*
> *For I heard their young ones cry.* . . .
>
> *The butcher that cut his throat, sir,*
> *Was drowned in the blood,*
> *And the little boy who held the bowl,*
> *Was carried away in the flood.*[36]

The surviving nineteenth-century texts were mostly associated with nurseries or glee clubs and none include the "Didn't He Ramble" chorus—the standard refrain seems to have been a string of nonsense syllables, *"Tow de row de dow, / Tow de row de da"*—but oral variants celebrated aspects of the ram that were more relevant to springtime fertility festivals. The first unbowdlerized printing I've found is from 1904, when George Davis Chase, a professor of classical languages at Wesleyan University, responded to a question about "The Derby Ram" in a semischolarly journal, *Notes and Queries*, with a lyric "learnt by a Cape Cod sailor during the war of 1812–15, when it was common, and . . . taught to his nephew, of whom I had it." The first five verses matched the Washington version, but rather than ending with the flood of blood, it continued:

> *Now this old ram's pizzle, sir, measured forty yards and an ell,*
> *That was sent to Ireland to ring St. Patrick's bell.*

There was forty gentlemen of honor, sir, come to see this old ram's bones,
And forty ladies of honor went to see this old ram's stones.

The man that owned this ram, sir, was counted very rich,
But the one that made this song was a lying son of a bitch.[37]

These verses seem to have been common all over the United States, though the ram's pizzle—an archaic word for *penis*—was often bowdlerized to "tail." (In some versions the "tail" got snagged when the ram jumped a fence, and there are numerous jokes about male animals having similar mishaps.) In 1927, Gates Thomas printed a "Derby Ram" lyric collected from a Black Texan thirty years earlier, which had the same final verse, along with one that—at least as published by the Texas Folklore Society—used a nonce euphemism for testicles:

The habits of that ram
They hung upon the wall;
A couple o' gals came into the shop,
Says, "We never eats mutton a-tall!"

This version added verses about other animals, and Thomas signaled their bowdlerization by marking some words with an asterisk and providing a footnote: "Of course, the Negro does not use these terms, except in the hearing of respectable people, but obscenities."

Of all the animals in this world
I'd ruther be a boar;
I'd twist my tail into a knot
And eat* forevermore. . . .

Of all the animals in this world
I'd ruther be a coon;
I'd clam way up some sycamore tree
And grimace* at the moon.[38]

Each verse was followed by the "Didn't He Ramble" chorus, which was apparently common among Black singers and may have been their innovation, but did not appear in print until the naughty ballad was reworked as a ragtime hit. James Weldon Johnson, the author, statesman, and songwriter best known today as cowriter of "Lift Every Voice and Sing," wrote in his autobiography that ragtime "was originated by colored piano players in the questionable resorts of St. Louis, Memphis, and other Mississippi River towns . . . [who] often improvised crude and, at times, vulgar words to fit the music." Making an analogy to Topsy in *Uncle Tom's Cabin*, he wrote that these songs had no particular composers but "jes grew" in Black communities; in the 1890s, some were "slightly altered or changed" by white composers, producing national hits like "The Bully" and "A Hot Time in the Old Town Tonight"; Black songwriters followed suit; and in 1902 Johnson teamed up with his brother Rosamond and Bob Cole and "appropriated about the last one of the old 'jes' grew' songs":

It was a song which had been sung for years all through the South. The words were unprintable, but the tune was irresistible, and belonged to nobody. We took it, re-wrote the verses, telling an entirely different story from the original, left the chorus as it was, and published the song. . . . "Oh, Didn't He Ramble!"[39]

The Johnson-Cole reworking was published under the pseudonym Will Handy, with a cover drawing of a top-hatted white dandy and verses about a man named Buster Beebe, the "black sheep" of his family, who rambles through various misadventures. It was a ubiquitous hit, played by dance bands, recorded by early phonograph artists, used as a rallying song for political campaigns and college football teams, and harmonized in every saloon. In 1903, a story syndicated in dozens of newspapers had a father warning his sons, "Whenever I am out late at night and see men taking more of the sidewalk than they are entitled to they are always singing that song. Maybe there are sober men who sing it, but I have yet to find one"—and ended with him coming home drunk and joining the chorus.[40]

Zutty Singleton recalled that "Didn't he Ramble" entered the New Orleans parade repertoire as the theme of the Bull's Club, which marched with a live bull and sang "a hell of a lot of verses." He did not remember the exact words, but approximated, *"His nuts was hanging here, his butt was hanging there."*[41] This suggests an interaction of pop trend and oral tradition: bands added the ragtime hit to their repertoires and marchers sang along using the old "Derby Ram" lyrics. When the trumpeter Oscar "Papa" Celestin, born in 1884, recorded the song, he sang two ram verses, the second a clean counterpart to what Thomas and Singleton recalled:

> *His head was in the market,*
> *His feet was in the street,*
> *A lady come walking by and say,*
> *"Just look at the market meat."*[42]

HANDY, MORTON, AND "THE MEMPHIS BLUES"

CELESTIN'S RECORD CREDITED W. C. HANDY AS THE COMPOSER, A COMMON mistake since the original sheet music was credited to "Will Handy" and by the mid-1910s William Christopher Handy had become famous for reshaping Black folk material into popular hits. The ascription was doubly misleading, since Celestin's lyric was older than the Johnson-Cole version, but the introduction of print and recording added new layers to oral traditions: when vernacular folk songs were reworked into commercial hits, people often sang the hit versions with a mix of familiar old lyrics, creating blends that were simultaneously new and traditional, and further confused folklorists by describing the result as something they had learned from their grandparents.

That process also made for other complications: as professional songwriters reworked and copyrighted "jes grew" songs, material that had been common in Black communities—and in some cases had been associated with particular performers—became their legal property. Handy was hailed for pioneering a new style and putting blues on the national map but also denounced as a sharp businessman who made a career out of claiming songs he had not written. Morton took the latter stance and had particular reasons for his resentment.

Handy was born in 1873 and began touring in the 1890s as the musical director of Mahara's Colored Minstrels. He taught for a couple of years at the Alabama State Agricultural and Mechanical College for Negroes; led dance bands in Clarksdale, Mississippi, and later in Memphis; and became nationally famous in 1912 with the publication of "The Memphis Blues," a three-part rag with a distinctive sixteen-bar section sandwiched between two twelve-bar blues. It was originally published as an instrumental, but Handy's band was hired to play at campaign events for Edward "Boss" Crump, a Memphis politician who was running on a promise to crack down on vice, and since the middle strain was similar to a song about all the things "Mama don't allow," listeners began singing, *"Mr. Crump don't 'low no easy riders here."*[43]

Handy told that story in his autobiography, and later writers continued to describe the middle section of "Memphis Blues" as a variant of "Mama Don't Allow"—an attribution supported by reports from 1913 of a Memphis singer named Susie Johnson complaining about the theft of her song "Mamma Don't Allow No Easy Talking."[44] Handy sometimes claimed to have composed the "Mr. Crump" melody himself, but also traced it to an incident in the Mississippi Delta that changed the course of his career. His band was playing for a white dance in Cleveland, Mississippi, and partway through the evening a customer sent up a request for some of their "native music."

> This baffled me. The men in this group could not "fake" and "sell it" like minstrel men. They were all musicians who bowed strictly to the authority of printed notes. So we played for our anonymous fan an old-time Southern melody, a melody more sophisticated than native. A few moments later a second request came up. Would we object if a local colored band played a few dances?

Handy's men were happy to take a break, and the local group turned out to be a trio playing "a battered guitar, a mandolin and a worn-out bass." He described their appearance as ragged and unkempt, their playing as monotonous and repetitive, the "kind of stuff that has long been associated with cane rows and levee camps." So he was astonished when the audience showered them with more money than his orchestra was getting for the whole evening. At that moment, he recalled, "I saw the beauty of primitive music."[45]

Back in Clarksdale, Handy set to work: "Within a day or two I had orchestrated a number of local tunes, among them *The Last Shot Got Him*, *Your Clock Ain't Right*, and the distinctly Negroid *Make Me a Pallet on Your Floor*."[46] When they began featuring these songs, his band's popularity at local dances "increased by leaps and bounds" and they were also hired to play "in less respectable places," specifically Clarksdale's red light district, the New World. This section adjoined a Black residential neighborhood and Handy recalled that, although the clientele was strictly white, "the oldest and most respectable Negro families . . . were required to pass before the latticed houses of prostitution" on their way to church. He described the workers as "lush octoroons and quadroons from Louisiana [and] soft cream-colored fancy gals from Mississippi towns."

> These rouge-tinted girls, wearing silk stockings and short skirts, bobbing their soft hair and smoking cigarets . . . were among the best patrons the orchestra had. They employed us for big nights, occasions when social or political figures of importance were expected to dine and dance with their favorite creole belles. . . . The shuttered houses of the New World called for appropriate music. This led us to arrange and play tunes that had never been written down and seldom sung outside the environment of the oldest profession. Boogie-house music, it was called.[47]

Handy's memoir went through multiple revisions, and the published version left out a significant detail: the group that upstaged his band in Cleveland was led by a local player named Prince McCoy and the theme it played was *"I'm a winding ball and I don't deny my name."*[48] Stack Man-gam, who played clarinet in Handy's group, recalled that Handy "went back in the corner and took his pencil and a piece of paper and copied a part of what they were playing."[49] Handy confirmed that this was the melody he used for "The Memphis Blues," writing that a few months later he was surprised to receive a score from New York for a song called "I Ain't Gonna Let Nobody Steal My Bear," which had "the identical melody that Prince McCoy had played in Cleveland." Published in 1910 as "Oh, You Bear Cat Rag," this song used the "Winding Ball" melody for its third strain.[50]

By the time Handy wrote about hearing the song at a Delta dance, Morton had recorded it twice, but only as a piano solo and an instrumental duet with King Oliver, coupled with a twelve-bar section and titled "Tom Cat Blues"—and since "The Memphis Blues" had hit a dozen years before those 1924 recordings, anyone who connected the melodies would have assumed he was imitating Handy. He had long since quit singing anything like "Winding Ball," and only a few old-timers from the New Orleans tenderloin would have recalled it as his youthful theme. Nor is it clear how closely Prince McCoy's song resembled Morton's; if the lyrics were equally filthy, I would have expected Handy to comment on them, but perhaps he considered them beneath comment or too common to require any.

In any case, Handy was struck by the melody and recycled it as the sixteen-bar strain of "The Memphis Blues." The precise dating is unclear: his hit was published in 1912, and although he said he performed it for Crump's 1909 mayoral campaign, that doesn't match his recollection of getting "Bear Cat Rag" a few months after hearing McCoy, so he may have debuted it for Crump's reelection campaign in 1911. By that time Morton had been playing around Mississippi and it is possible McCoy could have learned "Winding Ball" from him, either directly or through other performers, or both of them could have picked it up from earlier singers. Morton never claimed to have originated the song, but did say he brought it to Memphis and was responsible for inspiring the central strain of Handy's hit, adding, "I also brought the last strain there too, that was Tony Jackson's strain, 'Whoa, Strumpets Whoa.'"[51]

That claim has generally been ignored or dismissed—I would have dismissed it myself if I hadn't stumbled across Handy's unpublished mention of "Winding Ball"—and since Morton's first recording of the lyric only appeared in 1939, there was no way Handy could have connected Prince McCoy's song to him. Those layers of ignorance are the backstory for an incident that still clouds Morton's reputation. In August 1938, *Down Beat* magazine published an open letter from him under the headline: "I Created Jazz in 1902, Not W. C. Handy."[52] The first half of that headline is regularly quoted as evidence of his absurd braggadocio, but should be understood in the context of the second: a recent episode of Robert Ripley's *Believe It or Not* radio show had authoritatively presented Handy as "the man who created the blues" and "The Memphis Blues" as "the first jazz song ever written in America."[53]

From the perspective of Ripley's audience, those claims were reasonable: "The Memphis Blues" sparked a national blues craze that evolved into the national jazz craze and introduced the music to a mass white audience.[54] But from Morton's perspective, Handy was being celebrated as the originator of blues and the first composer of jazz on the basis of a hit copied from his personal theme song. It is easy to understand why he was outraged and, since no one was aware of the connection, why his reaction was treated as ridiculous.

Morton's letter should also be understood in the context of his preparations for the Library of Congress project. A week before the Ripley show, the *Washington Daily News* had announced he would be making "a musical recording of the history of jazz."[55] He wrote that he was planning to ask older New Orleans musicians like John Robicheaux, Manuel Perez, and Armand Piron how long they had been playing blues and listed some early performers who were known for the style: "Happy Galloways played blues when I was a child. Peyton with his accordion orch, Tick Chambers orch, Bob Frank and his piccolo orch."[56] As for primacy in print, he wrote that "the first publication with a title 'blues'" was by Chris Smith, whose "The Blues (But I'm Too Blamed Mean to Cry)" appeared in January 1912, eight months before "The Memphis Blues."[57]

Some of Morton's arguments were more tendentious, and a few were simply silly. He wrote that Freddie Keppard led the first band to play orchestrated blues in Memphis, which may have been true, but also described Keppard, a powerhouse trumpeter whose style owed nothing to Morton, as his "protégé." Similarly, there was a solid basis for his opening claim that "New Orleans is the cradle of jazz," but none for finishing that sentence, "and I, myself, happened to be the creator in the year 1902."

Morton's friends were used to that kind of self-promotion. Pops Foster recalled, "If you'd listen to him talk long enough, he'd claim he invented the piano." Creole George Guesnon quoted him saying, "I don't care what you call it—swing, jazz, anything you want—that's just names they put to it, but it's all Jelly Roll," and added: "Boy, that was a vain cat."[58] But they also understood that he had been working for over thirty years as an entertainer and manager of bands, shows, and clubs, and recognized the braggadocio as a performance. Omer Simeon recalled:

> Everyone liked to pick arguments with him because they liked to hear
> him talk and argue. . . . He was always talking about New Orleans; about
> Buddy Bolden, Frankie Duson, Buddy Petit, Tony Jackson—he could take
> off their mannerisms on a job and he was always a comedian. It was hard
> to keep up with him—he could talk 24 hours in a row.[59]

Handy was a comparatively sedate figure, better known as a composer and publisher than as a performer, and by the late 1930s he was a respected elder statesman, the "Father of the Blues."[60] That title was a bit extreme, but he wore it with genteel dignity and few people seem to have noticed that his reply in the subsequent issue of *Down Beat* was as tendentiously self-promoting as Morton's attack. He wrote that his band was "a household word throughout the Southland because we could play this music which we now call jazz better than any competitor" and "because of a knowledge of Negro music and because of my exceptional ability to write down the things peculiar to him, I created a new style of music which we now know as the 'Blues.'" Neither of those claims stands much investigation, but he was on firmer ground when he shifted from artistic to legal issues, noting that he "had vision enough to copyright and publish all the music I wrote so I don't have to go around saying I made up this piece and that piece in such and such a year like Jelly Roll and then say somebody swiped it." [61]

Aside from their personal issues, the Morton-Handy exchange marked a fundamental shift in how music was produced and marketed. Morton had never paid much attention to copyrights or publishing; he always made the bulk of his living by performing, managing clubs and shows, and pursuing various sidelines that involved going places and dealing with people face to face. By 1938 most jazz musicians considered his music old-fashioned, but he remained a formidable pianist and his recordings from that period show a verve, energy, and imagination Handy never approached.

From Handy's perspective, that was beside the point. He was not a showy entertainer and, after being tricked out of the rights to "The Memphis Blues," formed a company called Pace and Handy (later Handy Brothers), which published his songs, along with the work of other composers in the commercial blues style. In 1926 he compiled *Blues: An Anthology,* the first serious collection of blues or jazz music, tracing the music's evolution from rural folk songs to the composed style he pioneered, and culminating with excerpts from George Gershwin's "Rhapsody in Blue" and "Concerto in F." By the 1930s he was no longer keeping up with current trends—he responded to Morton's claim that he couldn't play jazz by writing, "I am 65 years old and would not play it if I could"— and tended to be mentioned as a forefather and authority on Black folk traditions. When Alan Lomax interviewed him for the Library of Congress, two weeks before Morton's first session there, he answered a few questions about his own compositions but mostly spoke as an older folklorist to a young one, discussing and demonstrating material he had collected during his years in the field. Morton would respond to a question about work songs by improvising a blues about a "levee man"; Handy responded by demonstrating an unaccompanied field holler and described pre-blues traditions in terms Lomax's father might have used—while simultaneously framing himself as part of the folk community:

> We sang about steamboats, mean bosses, pretty women, stubborn mules, fast trains—everything; and called our songs by such names as "Joe Turner," "Stavin' Chain," "Stack O'Lee," "Lost John," "Allius Brown," and so forth. But the term "blues" was not used in those days.[62]

Handy described "The Memphis Blues" as the first modern blues song and took credit for elevating, popularizing, and naming the style, but in the role of a cultural spokesman. When Lomax asked, "Did you get the word 'blues' from some folk source?" he responded: "I rather think that I did; I've heard the word used by barroom pianists and vagrant guitarists several times." He framed himself as an intermediary between the anonymous oral tradition and the modern world, explaining: "I had to revise many of these folk versions so that they would be suitable for the requirements of this mechanical age."

As a songwriter and publisher, Handy understood that the center of the music business was shifting from live performances to mechanical reproduction. In the case of blues, that involved cleaning up some language, but more fundamentally it meant songs were ceasing to be understood as elements of shared culture, which varied according to the singer, the mood, and the situation, and were becoming discrete objects with set melodies and lyrics, documented on paper or phonograph recordings, which could be owned like a building or a business.

Blues was a particularly fluid form; singers routinely mixed and improvised verses, and there was no expectation that anyone would sing the same verses twice in the same order. Even when someone sang a specific blues, it was typically just defined by the first verse or two, with others added as needed. Most singers had favorite verses and tunes that might be thought of as their special songs, but a verse or tune that was associated with one singer in New Orleans might be associated with another in Dallas or St. Louis.

Printing, recording, and copyrighting did not end that process. When "Hesitation Blues" was published simultaneously by Pace and Handy in Memphis and Billy Smythe in Louisville, each recognized the other's right to claim a version of the song, and each acknowledged that their version was based on vernacular sources.[63] Morton denounced Handy for having "taken advantage of some unprotected material that sometimes floats around," but likewise adapted some unprotected tunes, and Handy was right that Morton had devoted less energy to securing copyrights and publishing contracts. Morton protested that "a copyright doesn't always prove the rightful owner to a piece of music," but in legal terms one can own a song without having created it, just as one can own a piece of land, can own the crops raised on that land by other people's labor—or, within the memories of many people still alive in the 1930s, could own the laborers themselves. The commercial history of blues is, to a great extent, a history of songwriters and publishers appropriating, domesticating, and enclosing "unprotected material," turning shared and shifting culture into defined products with specific owners.

Morton's *Down Beat* letter appeared at a moment when an audience of white listeners was giving new importance to jazz as both a commercial venture and a vital artistic form. Within a few years, critics and historians would hail him as a brilliant innovator and composer, while lamenting that he was "led by his musical and personal frustrations to exaggerate and embellish the truth as freely as the occasion seemed to demand."[64] Some entertainers echoed those criticisms or staked their own claims. Willie "The Lion" Smith, another famous talker and a foundational master of the New York stride piano style, contended that "the blues comes from the brickyards in Haverstraw, New York," and Wilbur Sweatman, a reed virtuoso who nurtured the early careers of Duke Ellington and Coleman Hawkins, kidded Morton, saying: "What do you mean by claiming you invented jazz in New Orleans? Don't you know that I originated jazz in the Ozarks of Missouri?"[65]

When Alan Lomax went to New Orleans in search of material to flesh out his Morton book, he found further claimants: Albert Glenny said he formed a band in the 1890s with a violin player named Charles Edgar, and "we started that jazz."[66] Alphonse Picou, born in 1878 and known for his virtuosic clarinet solo on "High Society," recalled:

> I used to play in a nightclub at Villere and Iberville and they had a colored woman working there, and she had a husband working on the railroad, putting up tracks, you know? And while working, he was singing these songs, and that's where the blues come from—the first blues. . . . We went to her house and I caught on to the melody and I wrote it down, from her voice, with my instrument . . . and that night we came and we played it. That was the first blues ever known. . . . We used to call it the "Coon Blues."[67]

The claims and counterclaims were themselves a kind of folklore, like the ballads of legendary gunfighters, railroad men, and lovers. As Morton traveled from the honky-tonks and tenderloins of the Gulf Coast to Memphis, Houston, Chicago, New York, and Los Angeles, renaming himself and pioneering new forms of composing and arranging, he was still the Winding Ball, spinning fabulous yarns. He exaggerated his own exploits, but was equally ready to vaunt the talents of others, and his tales of old New Orleans established an array of mythic figures, including the bad man Aaron Harris, the eight-fingered pianist Mamie Desdunes, the virtuoso entertainer Tony Jackson, and the powerhouse trumpeter later fans would hail as the true originator of jazz: Buddy Bolden.

~ four ~

Buddy Bolden's Blues

Morton followed his uncensored performance of "Winding Ball" with a routine called "The Animule Dance." Starting with a cheery chorus of scat syllables, he introduced a cast of animal characters including the tree-tall Mr. G. Raffee and the trunk-toting Mr. L. E. Phant. Then the party started:

> *The monkey hollered, "Run, I say!"*
> *Wildcat did the bombashay,*
> *Tiger did the mooche,*
> *And the elephant did that hootchy-ma-cootch.*
> *That panther did the eagle rock, and began to prance,*
> *Down in the jungle at the animule dance.*

The steps and gyrations listed in that lyric were popular innovations in Morton's youth—or rather, the names were. Most of the movements were far older, involving rocking and rotating hips, and are still common throughout most of Africa and the diaspora. In the 1910s they were adopted in modified versions by white dancers, but at the turn of the century they were rarely seen outside Black working-class communities. The vaudeville singer and songwriter Coot Grant, born in 1893 and raised around the honky-tonk her father ran in Birmingham, provided a typical list including the Fanny Bump, Buzzard Lope, Fish Tail, Eagle Rock, Itch, Shimmy, Squat, Grind, Mooche, Slow Drag ("that was very popular—hanging on each other just barely moving"), and the Funky Butt, which involved a kind of fashion display: "The women sometimes pulled up their dresses to show their pretty petticoats—fine linen with crocheted edges." A mill worker named Big Sue was particularly noted for this move: "People would yell 'Here come Big Sue! Do the funky butt, baby!' As soon as she got high and happy, that's what she'd do, pulling up her skirts and grinding her rear end like an alligator crawling up a bank."[1]

There was also a Funky Butt song, which Morton played after "The Animule Dance." He described it as "one of the earliest blues, no doubt the first blues that was the real deal—that is, a variation from the real barrelhouse blues."

The composer was Buddy Bolden, the most powerful trumpet player I've ever heard or ever was known. The name of this was named by some old honky-tonk people. While he played this, they sang a little theme to it . . .

I thought I heard Buddy Bolden say,
"Dirty, nasty, stinking butt, take it away . . .
Funky butt, stinky butt, take it away,"
And let Mister Bolden play.

Charles "Buddy" Bolden was born in 1877 and led a group at the turn of the century that was noted for its rough, rowdy style. Morton wrote that "Bolden was a blues and ragtime player, knew nothing of jazz,"[2] but the terminology was in flux and when the *Louisiana Weekly* published a series called "Excavating Local Jazz" in 1933, a local writer named E. Belfield Spriggins suggested that "jazz tunes in their original forms" appeared during the ragtime era, and "probably one of the earliest heard was one played by King Bolden's Band."

It seems that one night while playing at the Odd Fellows Hall, Perdido near Rampart St., it became very hot and stuffy in the place and a discussion arose among the members of Bolden's band about the foul air. The next day William Cornish, the trombonist with the band, composed a "tune" to be played by the band. The real words are unprintable but these will answer.

"Thought I heard old Bolden say
Rotten gut Rotten gut!
Take it away."

The rendition of this number became an overnight sensation and the reputation of Bolden's band became a household word with the patrons of the Odd Fellows Hall, Lincoln and Johnson Parks, and several other popular dance halls around the city.[3]

One of those venues was the Union Sons Hall, a couple of blocks from the Odd Fellows in the heart of the uptown tenderloin district, which became known as Funky Butt Hall. It is not clear when that name caught on, and although jazz historians tend to suggest the hall was named for the song, it could as easily have been named for the dance or the kind of people who frequented it.[4] Louis Armstrong recalled that when he was five years old he would hear bands playing out front to draw customers— he sometimes said he heard Bolden, but other times was unsure—and when the musicians moved inside, "we'd go look through the big cracks in the wall of the Funky Butt . . . and to a tune like 'The Bucket's Got a Hole in It,' some of them chicks would get way down, shake everything, slapping themselves on the cheek of their behind."[5]

The word *funk* has been documented from the early seventeenth century, when a colonist named William Capps wrote about the miserable conditions on a ship bringing him from England to Jamestown: "Betwixt decks there can hardlie a man fetch his breath by reason there ariseth such a funke in the night that it causes putrefaction of bloud."[6] It seems to have originally meant tobacco fumes; was extended to other pungent smells; and Frank Marshall Davis, born in 1905, wrote that in the Black parlance of his youth, "funky was not a way of playing jazz music but described the odor of unwashed genitalia."[7]

The trumpeter Lee Collins recalled that when he played the Red Onion saloon, an uptown honky-tonk across from the Union Railway Depot, it "was always packed with out-of-town women" and the band's drummer, Alfred Williams, would comment, "You can cut the funk in this place with a knife."[8] Collins didn't directly connect the women to the funk, but when Morton recorded Bolden's theme for a later album, the notes said its "sarcastic verses" were inspired by "some low-down girls . . . on a Mississippi River excursion boat" and "had to be modified somewhat for recording purposes."[9] Zora Neale Hurston further clarified the matter, recalling the song as a favorite during her childhood in Eatonville, Florida, which her playmates would sing when no adults were around:

Everybody sung and danced on it. And you'd hear Negro orchestras, the local orchestras, they often play it now, the tune. They don't sing the words, but the tune is one of the favorite dance tunes. . . .

Thought I heard somebody say,
"Your nasty butt, your stinky butt, take it away
Oh, your nasty butt, your stinky butt, take it away,
I do not want it in here."

Oh, I am so glad that the law is passed,
The women in Tampa got to wash they ass,
Oh, the women in Tampa got to wash they ass,
Oh, I do not want it in here.

Oh, thought I heard somebody shout,
Hoist up the window, let the stink go out . . . [10]

In the Library sessions, Morton just repeated a single verse with slight variations, but over the next year and a half he recorded more extensive versions of Bolden's theme, with a similar verse about opening a window to let the "bad air" or "foul air" out. The first was at a session for RCA Victor in September 1939, backed by a band of New Orleans players including Sidney Bechet and Zutty Singleton, and Frederic Ramsey noted that everyone was surprised when Morton took a vocal, since "it had been pretty generally agreed that he wouldn't run the chance of getting some fine music censored by singing the words." He sang different lyrics on each take—an ornate variant went *"I'll open up that beautiful little gorgeous window . . . let the breeze come out"*—and on the issued take the "butt" reference was softened to an ambiguous *"You nasty but you dirty . . ."*[11]

In December Morton recorded a solo version for General Records, released as "Buddy Bolden's Blues," and that became the standard title for later recordings. This time he clipped the chorus phrase to *"You're nasty, you're dirty,"* and added two more verses. One was about a local judge who was notorious for sentencing Black men accused of minor crimes to a month of menial labor:

> *Thought I heard Judge Fogarty say,*
> *"Thirty days in the market, take him away,*
> *Get him a good broom to sweep with, take him away."*
> *I thought I heard him say.*

The other name-checked a trombone player who worked in Bolden's group and eventually took it over:

> *Thought I heard Frankie Duson shout,*
> *"Gal, gimme that money, I'm gonna beat it out,*
> *I mean, gimme that money, like I explained you, I'm gonna beat it out."*
> *'Cause I thought I heard Frankie Duson say.*

Morton dated the song to "about 1902," but those verses must have come somewhat later, since John J. Fogarty only became a judge in 1904 and Duson seems to have joined Bolden in 1905. The earlier date may have been chosen to cement the song's local origin; as Morton explained, "Later on, the tune was, I guess I'd have to say stolen, by some author I don't know anything about—I don't remember his name—and published under the title of 'St. Louis Tickler.' But with all the proof in the world, this tune was wrote by Buddy Bolden."

That author was a white pianist named Theron C. Bennett, and "The St. Louis Tickle" was a four-part rag that used the "Funky Butt" theme as its second section. It was published in 1904, under the pseudonym Barney and Seymore, and named to capitalize on the World's Fair taking place in that city. A vocal version appeared the following year, edited down to two sections, and the chorus had a cleaned-up paraphrase of the lines Morton recalled: *"Won't you play that tune, I say, / Saint Louis Tickle, oh, take it away"*—but a lot of singers seem to have stuck with the "funky butt" lyrics. Some also simplified the tune: the melody Morton played and Bennett published had a circle-of-fifths turnaround at the end of each verse, typical of ragtime and early jazz, but Hurston stayed within the three-chord harmonic range favored by older rural musicians, and similar variants were collected from country fiddlers. John Hurt, born in 1903 in the rural Mississippi Delta, sang a version with a tune similar to Hurston's and verses that likewise put the focus on women:

> *You see that gal with the red dress on?*
> *She got funky butt, stinky butt, sure as you born*
> *Well, I don't like it nohow.*[12]

Willie Parker, a clarinetist and contemporary of Bolden's, suggested the song was well known around New Orleans but not associated with a particular musician: "All of 'em, different bands, they would play ratty tunes: 'Funky butt, funky butt, take it away.'"[13] Morton's lyrics were specifically local, but the song varied from region to region and could be tailored to fit other figures. In Texas, Pete Harris sang, *"Thought I heard Mister Amos say, 'Nasty butt, funky butt, take it away,'"* and Newman Ivey White printed a verse from Georgia that had a Judge Pequette in place of Judge Fogarty, with a note that he "heard this same tune and almost the same words around 1903, with ribald variations, as a Negro street song in Statesville, N.C." E. C. Perrow printed a version with Hurt's red-dress couplet and a note that he first heard it around 1908 and knew eight or ten more verses he would not include, and Vance Randolph collected several versions from white Missourians, including one with the lyric *"Fifteen nickels an' a rusty dime, / Will buy a little funky-butt any old time."*[14]

DIRTY DANCING AND NASTY TUNES

RANDOLPH'S COUPLET COMPLETES A CIRCLE OF CONNECTIONS: THE ASSOCIA-tion of smell and sex is ancient, as is the misogynist association of smell with female genitalia, female genitalia with female buttocks, and female buttocks with sex, in phrases like "getting some ass." The Missouri lyric is also a reminder that songs and sex alike crossed racial lines, though the interactions were poorly documented, routinely concealed or denied, and complicated in ways many people prefer to ignore. The tolerated tenderloins of the early twentieth century catered primarily to white men and often replicated patterns from slavery times, selling Black women's bodies for white men's pleasure, and many people continue to believe that mixing in the opposite direction was virtually unknown. But in 1876 Lafcadio Hearn wrote about "a house of ill fame" on the Cincinnati waterfront district, "kept by a white woman, Mary Pearl, who boards several unfortunate white girls," which was "a great resort for colored men," and when he visited "the most popular dance-house of the colored steamboatmen," noted that "one-fourth of the women present were white."

Music was provided by a string trio:

A well-dressed, neatly built mulatto picked the banjo, and a somewhat lighter colored musician led the music with a fiddle, which he played remarkably well and with great spirit. A short, stout negress, illy dressed, with a rather good-natured face and a bed shawl tied about her head, played the bass viol, and that with no inexperienced hand.[15]

I can easily imagine that band playing "Funky Butt" and sounding like
a precursor of Bolden's group. The generation that made the shift from
ragtime to jazz was full of people who started on stringed instruments
and switched to horns as fashions changed: violinists picked up clarinets;
guitar players picked up trumpets; bass players doubled on tuba. Some
audiences preferred string bands, especially for indoor events, and if a
string group got an outdoor gig it might add a couple of horns for volume. The higher-paid Black bands played for white dances, as well as for
upper-class Creoles and the light-skinned "Colored" elite, and since they
used written scores we have a fairly good sense of their sound and repertoire: a mix of European and Euro-American quadrilles, schottisches,
waltzes, polkas, mazurkas, marches, and, by the 1890s, some ragtime hits
by composers like Kerry Mills and Scott Joplin. But there were plenty
of other bands whose music we can only guess at; Morton's list of early
blues players in the *Down Beat* letter included Charles "Happy" Galloway, born in 1869 and variously remembered as playing guitar, bass, and
accordion, and William Henry Peyton, five years older and likewise an
accordionist.[16]

A surprising number of early jazzmen played accordion, including
Freddie Keppard, Albert Glenny, Big Eye Louis Nelson, John Robichaux,
and, by some accounts, Buddy Bolden. Most seem to have used diatonic
instruments, with two rows of buttons rather than a piano keyboard—the
style still favored by Louisiana Cajun and zydeco musicians—and this
provides a clue to their repertoire, since it would have limited them to
relatively simple harmonies. They could easily have played the Hurt or
Hurston versions of "Funky Butt," but would have found it more difficult
to play the circle-of-fifths turnaround Morton used, and impossible to
play the full, four-part arrangement of "St. Louis Tickle."[17]

Louis Jones, a friend and contemporary of Bolden's, recalled Peyton's
group as "something like a string band," and it seems to have included
accordion, guitar, and bass, supplemented at times with cornet, trombone, or clarinet.[18] Morton said Peyton worked in "low class dance halls,"
and Alphonse Picou told the Belgian writer Charles Goffin that he played
clarinet with Peyton at the Big 25, a notorious tenderloin honky-tonk,

and almost quit after the first day because the place was so rough—
in Goffin's French transcription, an *"ignoble coupe-gorge"* or vulgar
throat-cutting place—patronized by "bandits, roustabouts, drunks, and
assassins," with a sack hanging from the ceiling which *"toutes les chiennes
de la ville"*—all the bitches of the town—had to kick as an entry fee.[19]
Peyton's music was sometimes described as ragtime, but rougher than
what the society orchestras played, and Jones added: "He used to play the
blues, too, but he didn't become famous with the blues like Buddy Bolden
did."[20]

In this context, "blues" did not refer to a twelve- or eight-bar chord
sequence; it was a slow, sexy dance music with strong West African
inflections, which older players often traced to the singing of roustabouts, field hands, rural guitarists, or church congregations. Picou
said he composed the first blues by adapting a railroad work song; Papa
John Joseph talked about a musical "professor"—a common honorific
for bandleaders—named Joe Poché who listened to cane cutters whistling in the fields and arranged their tunes for violin.[21] Kid Ory recalled
Bolden adapting tunes and rhythms from "Holy Roller churches," and
Bill Matthews said, "On those old, slow, low down blues, he had a moan
in his cornet that went all through you, just like you were in church or
something."[22]

Blues was simultaneously a new style and deeply familiar. Richard M.
Jones recalled nights at the 28, across Franklin Street from the 25, where
gamblers played three-card monte and women did ham-kicks: "They
would hang up a ham, real high, and it was a contest for the women, to
see who could kick the ham, and whoever could kick the highest would
win." Some people recalled the point of these contests being that the
women wore split drawers, or none, and they were regularly mentioned
as a mark of the rougher joints. Jones continued:

> They wouldn't play anything else there but the blues ... [which was]
> always slow in those days, even in the cornfields. Some of the sinners
> would take it into the dance halls and put those words to it and dance to it,
> but the same tunes would be used in the cornfields, and if the person was

religious they would sing words about how tired they were or troubled in mind. . . . It was the real blues. Just a slow beat that came right out of the jungle."[23]

Black country folk brought their songs and rhythms to the city, and blues is typically linked to that transition, but the influences went in both directions. Urbanites adapted country sounds, rural musicians picked up the latest urban styles, and it is rarely possible to sort out exactly what came from where—nor do we have a clear sense of how either the rural or the rougher urban aggregations sounded in Bolden's time. Since rural musicians rarely used written arrangements, our first good evidence of their styles and repertoires comes from the 1920s, when folklorists and commercial companies began to make recordings, but that evidence is often misleading. Both the folklorists and the commercial scouts went to rural areas in search of sounds they could not find in the city, and they preserved thousands of recordings of country fiddlers, banjo pickers, guitarists, and singers, but brass instruments were considered essentially urban—you couldn't make a trumpet by stretching a coonskin over a barrel hoop and tacking some strings to it—so neither the scouts nor the folklorists bothered to record any rural brass bands.[24] As a result, although Black brass bands were popular all over the rural South, the first recordings are from 1954, when Frederic Ramsey produced an album featuring the Lapsey Band and the Laneville-Johnson Union Brass Band in western Alabama. Some of the musicians in those groups had been playing together since the early 1900s and presumably retained traits and tunes from their youth, but we cannot winnow those elements from what they picked up in the intervening half century, nor do we know how they may have resembled and differed from similar bands in Mississippi, Louisiana, Texas, or even in neighboring counties of Alabama.

The Lapsey and Laneville-Johnson bands played in only three keys and had a repertoire of spirituals for funerals and religious meetings and secular tunes for dances, including "Uncle Bud" and some titles that were common around the South: "Going Up the Country, Don't You Want to Go," "Mama, Don't You Tear My Clothes," "My Baby Gone and She

Won't Be Back No More," and "Wild About My Daddy."[25] Anyone familiar with early blues will recognize those phrases, but they would not necessarily have matched the same tunes from one group to another, nor would that have mattered, since band performances rarely included singing. Even in New Orleans, the piece popularized on records as "Tiger Rag" was often just called "Number 2," after its position in a band's repertoire list, or "Jack Carey," after a trumpeter who used it as his theme, and Baby Dodds said it was also known as "Meatball" and "Snotsy."[26]

Other aspects of the rural brass band tradition were preserved in interviews with a group of musicians active around the turn of the century in the country around Hempstead, Texas, northwest of Houston. Formed by a cornet player named George Punchard, who had been born in slavery, this band was popular enough to be invited to New Orleans to play a Mardi Gras dance "for colored" in 1907 or 1908, and Manuel Williams, who was born in 1887 and played alto horn, recalled:

> We played regular concerts of band music and we played hot music for dancing—made-up music, you know. One of our big pieces was "Whore Alice" and the white folks loved it, only we never let on what the name of it was. We'd made it up ourselves. Some of what we played was old cornfield blues from guitar players that we got onto the horns.

Other bandmembers said they only played "Whore Alice" after the white folks went home, to signal that the dance was now a Black event, and would shout the title in the breaks. The rest of their repertoire was a mix of Tin Pan Alley hits like "After the Ball" and "Long Way to Tipperary"; vernacular pieces, including "See See Rider," "Mama Don't Allow," "Alabama Bound," and "Hog-Eye"; and some titles unique to the local scene: "Brazos Shout," "Houston Women Don't Mean You No Good," and "Sister's Selling Jazz," of which trombonist Wesley Gage said, "The word 'jazz' meant either a piece of hot music or a piece of hot woman—you didn't use the word in public." He added that they also played "a lot of hot, choppy things you call ragtime, but only one I know that had a name was 'Stavin' Chain'; others were just 'Texas Rag,' 'Dallas Rag,' 'Galveston

Rag,' 'Railroad Rag'—but you couldn't keep them straight by them names."[27]

Hempstead is twenty miles from Navasota, where Mance Lipscomb began playing guitar with his fiddler father around 1910, and he played a similar mix of pop hits, early blues, and local or vernacular pieces, named and unnamed, including some he considered too dirty to record. Rowdy audiences demanded rowdy lyrics, and Buster Pickens, a barrelhouse pianist who grew up around the Hempstead bandmen, recalled a guitarist named Frank Watkins who ran a joint in "the bottoms" and "used to sing some terrible songs he made up himself: 'Women going around fucking for fish and bread,' and then one about, 'who say pussy don't stink is a goddamn liar.'"[28] The "fish and bread" lyric was recorded by various singers around the country; the stink lyric was not, but there is no reason to think it was unique to Watkins or Hempstead, and Lipscomb may well have sung both when he worked similar joints.

Those sorts of songs were common in many rural and working-class communities, though uncensored lyrics were rarely preserved before the era of 2 Live Crew and Lil Jon—and, in the past as in the present, their appeal was not limited to Black listeners. Pickens recalled the Sugar Foot Green troupe performing for mixed audiences—white in front, Black in the back—and supplementing their regular shows with an adults-only "Midnight Ramble" at which "They sang songs that had the worst words in them—like 'screw' and 'fuck'—they'd be all through those rotten songs."[29] Vance Randolph collected dozens of filthy tune names from white fiddlers who played for "frolics" in the Ozark region, including "Fucking in the Goober Patch," "Fucking in the Kitchen," "Poontang on the Levee," "Hog Eye Sally," "Josie Shook Her Panties Down," "Everybody Knows How Maggie Farts," "Tickle His Balls Maria," "Kiss My Ass Says Rosie," "No More Cock in Texas," "Slippery Ass Wiggle," "Hard Pecker Reel," "Pecker on a Pole," and "The Biggest Prick in Town." The last title was provided by a fiddler named A. L. Pierce, who first told Randolph that the piece had no name and only later grinned and produced it, and other tunes described as "nameless" may likewise have had names musicians preferred to keep private.[30]

The Ozark fiddlers also played "Pallet on the Floor," "Stagolee," and "Uncle Bud," as well as tunes whose titles were considered inoffensive in white society but would be avoided or changed in later years because they were blatantly racist. "Run, Nigger, Run" was common throughout the South and seems to have originated in Black culture as a warning against the "patrollers" who roamed plantation areas to enforce slave-time regulations, and other titles undoubtedly had similar sources, though in white culture they took on different meanings: "Nigger in the Pea Patch," "Nigger Stole a Pumpkin," "Devil Caught a Nigger," "Devil Take a Yaller Gal," and a piece called "Ku Klux over the Hill." Innocent-sounding titles could also have naughty or racist implications for insiders: "Rye Straw" was a polite shortening of "Dog Shit a Rye Straw," and a fiddler near Pine Bluff, Arkansas, explained that a perky tune called "The Hickory Hornpipe" went back to slavery times, when "if a nigger wench didn't behave, they just fanned her ass with a hickory" and she would "holler and dance mighty lively."[31]

Song titles might be private jokes among musicians, but Randolph also collected over a hundred filthy square-dance calls, from relatively cute couplets like *"Gent's prick forward and it's howdy-do, / Lady winks her twitchet with a how-are-you,"* to *"Ladies to the center, squat and piss, / Gents to the center and fuck your fist"* and *"Do-si-do and a rattlesnake pass, / Grease your pecker and stick it up her ass."* Wythe Bishop, his source for many of these calls, dated them to the early 1900s and explained that most dances in towns and settled areas were "pretty decent," but at backwoods affairs "some of them white-trash was plumb vulgar . . . I've saw dances where big fat country gals would hang every stitch of their clothes on a nail!"[32]

Randolph lived in the Ozarks for sixty years, danced at local frolics, and could talk with white fiddlers and callers as a member of their community. No other collector preserved a comparable range of material, and he only got the dirtier titles and calls after establishing relationships and going back to the same people time after time. If he had interviewed Black dance leaders, there is no reason to think they would have been similarly open with him, and there is no telling what a Black or female collector with similarly broad interests might have preserved. In any event, Randolph was a rarity: most folklorists, whatever their background or gender, were on a mission to preserve the wholesome, hardworking peasant cultures of earlier times, which they regularly contrasted with debased urban tastes and lifestyles. African American folklorists had additional reasons to highlight the virtuous aspects of their culture and traditions, since they were countering the racist stereotypes of Blackface minstrelsy. When John Wesley Work published *Folk Song of the American Negro* in 1915, he introduced it with a discussion of the wide range of themes and styles in West African music but included nothing but spirituals from the United States and decried "the paucity and utter worthlessness" of Black secular songs, writing: "So few and so inferior are these latter that we may justly state that the Negro Folk Music is wholly religious."[33]

Most collectors did not go that far, and some were attracted and amused by the rowdier aspects of Black folk culture. W. C. Handy wrote about a dance caller at a frolic in rural Mississippi "where the baddest of the bad were in command":

They danced the old square dances with one of their own calling the figures. . . . I can still hear his unusual voice. "Swing yo' partners . . . swing corners all . . . first lady on de head lead off to de right."

The first lady on the head did lead off all right, and she laughed out gaily as she did so. But her key was wrong. The crooner's eyes narrowed angrily, and his next call shocked us. "Swing on de corners . . . swing, you bitch!"

A big husky black glowered down. . . . "Look out there, nigger. That's my sister."

Rhythmically—and still in the key of G—the answer came, "Too late now. The bitch done swung . . . All promenade."[34]

Alec Robertson, a Mississippi fiddler born around the time of the Civil War, led a string band that at times included horns and recalled that some dance leaders would "say most anything, calling the figures, you know; get an old fellow halfway drunk, he wouldn't care what he's saying."[35] Rowdy calls were not limited to the rural South: James P. Johnson recalled his mother hosting square dances in New Brunswick, New Jersey, with calls including "Cows to the front, bulls stay back" and "Ladies, show your underwear," at which the women would hike their skirts and get prizes for the fancy ribbons or lace on their pantalettes and petticoats.[36]

Recalling one of his first trips north, Morton sang some verses of "The Dirty Dozen," a song that "would be played in the houses in Chicago where they didn't mind about the language":

> The gals would have their dress up, way up to their ass. Just shaking it, and breaking it. At that time they wore what you call—the ladies did—the split drawers. They'd just be shaking it down. And some guy plunking on the piano, some rough-looking guy, I wouldn't know who—they had several of 'em. . . . They'd sing all kinds of verses. Some of them meant something, some of them didn't have any rhymes, and some did. . . . The main theme was the mammy wouldn't wear no drawers. I thought it was a very disgusting mammy that wouldn't wear some underwear. . . .

> *Oh, you dirty motherfucker,*
> *You old cocksucker,*
> *You dirty son of a bitch.*
> *You're a bastard, you're everything,*
> *And your mammy don't wear no drawers. . . .*

> *Said, look out bitch, you make me mad,*
> *I'll tell you 'bout the puppies that your sister had,*
> *Oh, it was a fad.*
> *She fucked a hog, she fucked a dog,*
> *I know the dirty bitch would fuck a frog,*
> *'Cause your mammy don't wear no drawers.*

CHALLENGES AND CHANTS

MORTON ASSOCIATED THE "DIRTY DOZEN" WITH CHICAGO, BUT IF NEW Orleans musicians weren't singing the song, many enjoyed trading colorful family insults, rhymed and unrhymed. Danny Barker wrote that Bolden, Duson, and guitarist Lorenzo Staulz "had the reputation of being the nastiest talking men in the history of New Orleans. . . . When they arrived on the bandstand they greeted each other with such nasty talk as, 'Is your mother still in the District catchin' tricks?' 'They say your sister had a baby for a dog.' 'Don't worry about the rent, I saw your mother under the shack with the landlord.'"[37]

In oral culture, popular phrases routinely meld into song lyrics and vice versa. In 2007, Wynton Marsalis responded to an interviewer who was surprised by his rap track "Where Y'all At" by explaining that he had grown up with "the dozens . . . making up rhymes, just teasin', pickin' on people":

> That's a thing that we do in New Orleans all the time. We mainly do it on "Jock-A-Mo": *"My grandma and your grandma standing by the bayou, my grandma told your grandma gonna set your ass on fire. Hey now, hey now, iko iko ah nay. Jock-a-mo feena ah na hey, jock-a-mo feena nay."* *"See that woman standing by the truck, she can't drive but she sure can fuck."* Whatever. Just make up nasty shit to go with it.[38]

Marsalis was quoting the most widely known song of the Mardi Gras Indians, a tradition reaching back to the mid-1800s in which "tribes" of Black men roam New Orleans in ornately feathered and beaded costumes, dancing, drumming, singing, and challenging other tribes for control of the streets. Morton recalled the Indian ceremonies in his Library sessions and made the first recording of an Indian chant, "Tu-Way Pocky-Way." A dozen years later, Barker recorded band arrangements of four more chants, including the one Marsalis mentioned, which he titled "Chocko Mo Feendo Hey." In 1954, James "Sugar Boy" Crawford released a rocking version of this song as "Jock-A-Mo"; the Dixie Cups got a hit with it in 1965 as "Iko Iko";[39] and in 1976, an Indian group called the Wild Tchoupitoulas recorded a variant called "Brother John," which added a chanted introduction: *"Jock-a-mo-feena-hey, jock-a-mo-feena-hey, / Well, if you don't like what the big chief say, you just jock-a-mo-feena-hey."*

That evolution is an example of how recordings simultaneously document and reshape oral traditions. The musical battles between Black Indian tribes were part of a broader local tradition of symbolic battling, including "bucking" contests between brass bands. In the early 1900s it was common for bands to advertise an upcoming dance by playing through the streets on horse-drawn furniture wagons, and when two bands met, they would face off and buck, with the prospective audience acting as judges and flocking to the winners' gig. Barney Bigard, who was born in 1906 and studied with an array of older musicians, recalled that these contests sometimes involved explicit challenges:

> Whichever band had the nastiest lyrics would win. Like Ory had a tune to which the band sang "If you don't like the way I play, then kiss my funky ass." This went over big with all the whores and they would gather around the wagon. Another real foul-mouthed man was Frankie Dusen . . ."[40]

Everyone on the local scene remembered Ory's victory song, though most were coy about the particulars. The original transcript of Bigard's memoir had "fucking" rather than "funky," and other chroniclers recalled the tune by that title, but typically softened or glossed over the language for publication. Louis Armstrong, who got his first regular job with Ory's band, just wrote: "Kid Ory would play a little tune on his trombone that made the crowd go wild. . . . It was a cute little tune to celebrate the defeat of the enemy. I thought it screamingly funny and I think you would too."[41]

A variant of Ory's theme was published in 1917 as "Mamma's Baby Boy: A Jazz Song," credited to Armand Piron and Johnny St. Cyr, and St. Cyr said he first heard it sung by Lorenzo Staulz with lyrics that were "unprintable."[42] Morton's friend and partner Roy Carew described it as "a 'ratty' tune and recalled a musician being arrested for playing it at a

party. He gave the title as 'If You Don't Like the Way I Walk,'" a bowdlerization echoed in the title "All the Girls Like the Way I Walk," which
was known in Bolden's time as "All the Whores Like the Way I Ride"
or "the Way I Jazz"—or, presumably, rougher terms, depending on the
singer and venue.[43] Ory released his own bowdlerized version in 1945 as
"Do What Ory Say," substituting some pseudo-Indian patois for the final
line:

> *Do what Ory say,*
> *Why don't you do what Ory say . . . ?*
> *If you don't like the way I do,*
> *Just tee-no, fee-no, ha!*

Other bands imitated this version and it seems to have fed back into
the local street tradition, melding "tee-no, fee-no" with "jock-a-mo
fee-na," and giving the latter a new meaning. In 1991, Donald Harrison,
"Big Chief" of the Guardians of the Flame, explained that the lyrics of
most Indian chants were "a gumbo . . . a patois of Creole, African, and
whatever words you make up . . . [but] 'chock-a-ma-fee-na-hey' has a specific meaning . . . It means, 'kiss my fucking ass.'"[44]

Thus street culture was censored and renewed: Ory bowdlerized his
fight song with a string of Mardi Gras Indian syllables, his hometown
listeners knew the phrase he was concealing, later singers reworked his
band challenge as an Indian challenge, and a phrase that had been considered a meaningless gumbo or patois took on a specific meaning. The
odd part of this story is that, although most Mardi Gras Indian lyrics
have no clear etymology and some may derive from African languages,
"chock-a-ma-fee-na" is authentically Native American. A news story
from 1879 described Mardi Gras maskers parading in feathered head-
dresses, waving tomahawks, and chanting, "Chick-a-ma-feeno! Chick-a-
ma-feeno!" and although the marchers may have been Black or Creole,
the phrase was from a local Choctaw trade dialect: *achukma* (sometimes
spelled *tchikamá*, *tchoucouma*, or *chicamaw*), meaning "good," with the
intensifier *fena*, meaning "very good."[45] Over the decades that meaning

was forgotten, the phrase became open to reinterpretation, and by the time Harrison sang, *"Mardi Gras day, get the hell out the way, you can chock-a-ma-fee-na-hey,"* the Choctaw survival and Ory's bowdlerization had melded in a potent expression of Black Indian pride.

At parades and dances in the pre-microphone era, lyrics were often concocted and sung by marchers, dancers, or onlookers rather than by musicians or hired performers. W. C. Handy wrote that it was the crowds at election events who began singing the *"Mister Crump don't like it"* lyric to his "Memphis Blues"; Zutty Singleton recalled parading Bull's Club members popularizing the rough lyrics of "Didn't He Ramble"; and Morton said Bolden's theme acquired the "funky butt" lyrics from "honky-tonk people" who sang along when Bolden played it. George Guesnon recalled Punch Miller singing dirty "Uncle Bud" verses when the Jack Carey band played "Tiger Rag," but Miller credited the dancers:

People out in the audience started to singing while we're playing; we'd get to that last part . . . [and] all over the dance floor you could just hear them hollering:

Jack Carey had a daughter,
On the water,
Selling pork chops, two for a quarter.
Play Jack Carey! Play Jack Carey![46]

Before amplification became widely available, it was rare for brass band performances to include singing. Few people could project their voices over the horns, and at dances the band's job was to provide steady, exhilarating rhythms. Bandmembers might occasionally sing a brief chorus or tag: when Marsalis created a simulacrum of Bolden's music for the movie *Bolden*, the musicians chanted the title line of "All the Whores Go Crazy About the Way I Ride," and Bolden's men may have hollered that line, as the Hempstead bandmen shouted the title phrase of "Whore Alice." Bolden would sometimes tell his musicians to play so quietly that he could hear the dancers' shuffling feet, and it is possible that in those moments Staulz would have sung a dirty verse to "All the Whores." But it is equally possible that the title was an inside joke, shared by the musicians for their own amusement, or that it was a shifting title, used for various tunes over the years and expanded into a song if inspiration struck. Pops Foster described how musicians came up with impromptu lyrics at dances:

> When one of the bands would be playing and a good looking chick would come in the place, one of the guys would say, "Gee, I know she's got good bread." Then someone else would sing it and pretty soon the whole band would be romping along playing and singing, "Gee, I know she's got good bread." It meant she's got good pussy.[47]

If the band kept singing that chorus at other dates, the tune could get to be known as "She's Got Good Bread" and might keep that title even if later bands did not sing the phrase, or someone might add verses to be sung in quieter moments. Miller said neither he nor Staulz sang at dances, but when an interviewer pressed him about Staulz's reputation, he amended that recollection, saying Staulz "was very funny" and after a few drinks "he'd do them kind of things."[48] Barker wrote that Staulz "could tell a million jokes and rhyme up anything. If you gave him a name he would start rhyming. He could rhyme it decent or uncouth."[49]

IMPROVISING RHYMERS

IMPROVISING NAUGHTY OR SATIRICAL VERSES IS COMMON IN MANY AFRICAN cultures, and those traditions spread with the diaspora. In 1804 a traveler to the West Indies wrote, "The facility with which the negroes dress every occurrence in rhyme, and give it a metre, rude indeed, but well adapted to the purpose of raillery or sarcasm, is no slight proof of genius."[50] Another visitor described "individuals who resemble the *improvisatori*, or extempore bards, of Italy," writing that the various

African groups had particular tastes, the Ebo preferring "soft and lan-guishing" melodies while the "Koromantyn" (Akan) songs were "heroic and martial," but at "merry meetings and midnight festivals" these sing-ers performed "ballads of another kind":

> They give full scope to a talent of ridicule and derision, which is exercised not only against each other, but also, not unfrequently, at the expence of their owner or employer; but most part of their songs at these places are fraught with obscene ribaldry, and accompanied with dances in the high-est degree licentious and wanton.[51]

A visitor to a Maryland plantation wrote of an enslaved woman named Clotilda who could "make you rhymes all day long . . . [and] melodies as well as rhymes" and suggested that "under 'expanding circumstances' she might have been a genius." As in the islands, these compositions included mocking lyrics about local white folk, which "caused much amusement at the expense of each one of us who in turn became the subject of satire."[52]

With the rise of minstrel troupes and vaudeville, this tradition was updated for the stage. Arthur Wollidge, known as "the Original Rags," was famous in the 1910s for "extemporaneous rhyming on individuals he happens to see in the audience"; one reviewer wrote that he "created an uproar" and another that "one fears that he will not turn up with the correct rhyme owing to his rapidity, but he never fails."[53] Abbe Niles described Butler "String Beans" May making similarly impromptu sal-lies: "To an accompaniment of hisses . . . [he] would improvise verses to his own blues tunes throughout his turn at the old Monogram Theater (a standby of Chicago Negroes); his audience loved, but felt they should hate him, so they would pack the place night after night." On a less elevated plane, Ralph Ellison recalled a Harlem restaurant "where the singing waiters sang dirty songs and improvised lyrics as they dashed back and forth serving drinks."[54]

In Morton's youth, the most famous local rhymer was a bass player named George Jones. Pops Foster recalled:

He made more money than any musician around New Orleans and couldn't play a nickel's worth of bass. He worked the whorehouses, banquets, and parties. Everybody would hire him. If you were giving a party, you'd hire him and give him a list of the names of the people who were coming. When they'd walk in, he'd saw on his bass and make up a funny rhyme on their name. . . . Jelly did rhyming like George except Jelly put more music to it.[55]

Jones has been ignored by most jazz historians, but the older musicians all remembered him. Johnny St. Cyr said he was known as "George the Rhymer," and Kid Ory recalled him singing smutty songs and an epic version of "Little Liza Jane." Ory worked with Jones at Pete Lala's club and said the group included a guitarist and pianist, played from eight in the evening till four in the morning, and attracted the cream of the sporting crowd:

Racehorse people and all. Boy, he had a good spot there. . . . The girls would come there, after hustling on the street, you know. Down the block was the cribs, you see. They'd make a few dollars, then they'd close up and say, "I'm going cabareting awhile." They'd come in and pick up some guy and then go back.[56]

Eddie Dawson told William Russell that Jones used "an old, ragged, cracked up bass" strung with sash cord—"he didn't care, throwed it around any kind of way"—while Dawson played the real basslines. It was not superlative music, but Jones knew his business:

He was well liked. He could rhyme. See, like you're named Mr. Russell— somebody'd meet him in the back and tell him, "That man in there is named Mr. Russell, he's in the shoe business," or "he's in such and such a business," and he'd come on in and start to singing and playing and rhyme on you, and make all kind of rhymes on you. You wouldn't know how he got your name. . . . Well, after he rhymed so good on you, naturally you'd get your wallet out.[57]

Israel Gorman played clarinet with Jones for several years at Tom Anderson's saloon and said Jones mostly played guitar and they worked "from can't to cannot," sometimes starting as early as six in the evening and going till nine the next morning: "Just as long as the money was rolling in, you could make a tip." Jones would sing "low-down blues" and "smutty songs," and the musicians got a minimal salary, but the big money was from tips and the biggest tips came from his bespoke improvisations: "Give him a two, three-bar introduction and that guy gonna rhyme something about you. He just was fast like that."[58]

Virtuosic lyrical improvisation is at the heart of numerous African diaspora traditions, from Trinidadian calypso, Spanish-language *decimas*, and Brazilian *desafio* to the freestyling and battle-rhyming of modern rap. None of those traditions can be adequately preserved by documentation or recording, because their brilliance is inseparable from the immediacy of the moment and situation. This is obviously analogous to the instrumental improvisation of jazz, but jazz historians have tended to ignore the relationship of skilled wordplay to the development of that form. Western academic culture tends to regard speech and music as separate categories, artificially segregating repertoires and techniques that are heard and performed indivisibly not only in Africa, but in many European and Euro-American cultures. From Homeric epics to Mexican *corridos* and southwestern cowboy ballads, lyrics have been performed using a broad range of vocal, physical, and instrumental strategies depending on the artists and situations, and there are still plenty of styles that are not easily divisible into singing or speech, including rap, reggae toasting, jump-rope chants, and the rhythmic cadences of drill teams, marching soldiers, and southern preachers.

Rappers are often said to improvise lyrics the way jazz soloists improvise melodies, but in historical terms the evolution went the other way. There are few reports of virtuosic instrumental improvisers—soloists known for creating new variations at each performance—in early jazz. Many observers noted the spontaneity and energy of musicians who played without written music and created their own parts, and historians regularly quote the description of a New Orleans band in the 1890s that "often repeated the same selection, but never played it the same way twice."[59] But there is an essential difference between varying a tune or song from one performance to the next—which is standard and inevitable in vernacular cultures—and making a point of improvising new material in the moment. Louis Armstrong astonished some early peers by playing chorus after chorus on his cornet without repeating himself, and their astonishment is evidence that this was not yet a common practice. Armstrong's ability to spontaneously compose brilliant solos helped to establish improvisation as a hallmark of the jazz style, but he later said this reputation was to some extent illusory, since he retained and recycled favorite choruses:

> Even back in the old days it was like that—when everybody was supposed to be improvising. Who knows who's improvising . . . ? Once you got a certain solo that fit in the tune, and that's it, you keep it. Only vary it two or three notes every time you play it . . . There's always different people there every night, and they just want to be entertained.[60]

Dancers did not care if a musical passage was invented in the moment, as long as it sounded good and had a powerful rhythm, and as Armstrong noted, even dedicated listeners cannot tell if an instrumentalist is playing something recalled or prepared. But when a rhymer hit someone with a personalized verse, naming them and including details of their appearance, history, or behavior, they knew they were getting something special and tipped accordingly. By the 1920s virtuosic instrumental improvisation was increasingly becoming a hallmark of jazz, and by the 1950s it was a requirement—but that was later, when the music had developed a substantial audience that came to listen rather than dance.

BACK TO THE FUNK

WHEN BARKER DESCRIBED LORENZO STAULZ SPONTANEOUSLY RHYMING ON any subject, "decent or uncouth," he was quoting an old-timer named

Dude Bottley. Bottley was an ideal informant, since his brother Buddy Bartley—the spelling was typically variable—helped organize Bolden's dances at Lincoln Park, and he recalled Staulz improvising infinite verses to the "Funky Butt" theme:

> He could sing all day and all night if he wanted to, because he would sing about all the notoriety whores, pimps, madames, and even about the policeman at the door. . . . He would even sing about the Civil War; about how General Grant made Jeff Davis kiss his behind . . . One chorus I'll always remember was:

> *I thought I heer'd Abe Lincoln shout,*
> *"Rebels, close down them plantations and let all them niggers out . . .*
> *You gonna lose this war; git on your knees and pray!"*
> *That's the words I heer'd Mr. Lincoln say.*[61]

Barker was born in 1909, two years after Bolden was committed to the Louisiana State Insane Asylum, and was nurtured on those legends. His grandfather Isidore Barbarin was a well-known horn player, five years older than Bolden; his uncles Paul and Lucien Barbarin were drummers; and he began playing professionally in his early teens. He moved to New York around 1930, worked for many years in Cab Calloway's orchestra, and by the mid-1950s was also doing research for a book on New Orleans music. He published a first article about Bolden in 1965, with Bottley as his main informant—and here things get tricky, because Bottley was a fictional character, a colorful conduit for stories Barker had been hearing since his childhood.[62] When challenged, Barker granted that his articles included "a little monkeyshine," and the Bottley recollections should be read with that in mind, but he had deep roots in the local culture, and the recollections of nonfictional observers are not necessarily more reliable. Oral history is always evolving, and by the time anyone was interviewing Bolden's contemporaries, his legend had acquired the formulaic quality of folklore: Bill Matthews recalled that when Bolden played slow blues, "that boy could make the women jump out the window"; Richard M.

Jones described a night at Longshoremen's Hall when "the women were so crazy to get to Buddy Bolden, some of them jumped out of the window"; and Ed Garland provided a variant of the formula, saying, "The girls loved him . . . One night at Longshoremen's Hall, some of their boyfriends got angry and a fight started—almost a riot—Buddy jumped out the back window!"[63]

Bolden was also famous for his "harem" of female admirers: Sidney Bechet, who was ten years old when Bolden was sent to the asylum, recalled, "You was always hearing, for example, how he had three or four women living with him in the same house. He'd walk down the street and one woman, she'd have his trumpet, and another, she'd carry his watch, and another, she'd have his handkerchief, and maybe there'd be another one who wouldn't have nothing to carry, but she'd be there all the same hoping to carry something home."[64] In some recollections, Bolden's theme song was "If You Don't Shake," also known as "P.I.," a tenderloin term for pimp,[65] and Pops Foster said his bandmates had similar vocations:

> Frankie Duson was a slick guy with the girls. He was a tall good looking guy with straight hair and kind of dark. Out in the little country towns the straighter your hair was, the more the girls went for you. Every time Frankie would play out in the country he'd carry some girl back to New Orleans with him or have her follow him. . . . He'd let them stay with him till he got tired of them, then he'd send them home. . . . Lorenzo [Staulz] was so popular he'd have girls waiting outside his room for their turn to go in. . . . He ran a little pressing shop and had a couple of girls on the line for him all the time.[66]

Like gangsta rappers a century later, Bolden and his men were known for their flamboyant and dangerous lifestyles. Morton recalled their dances as famously violent, saying he was almost shot while attending one and "very often you could hear of killings on top of killings." Kid Ory recalled Funky Butt Hall as the toughest place he ever worked:

If you didn't have a razor or a gun, you couldn't get in there. There were fights going on while we were playing, in the hall, on the sidewalk. People would get killed. I only played there once. I said, "No more."[67]

Contemporaries often described Bolden's style as "dirt music," "stink music," or "ratty music" and used similar terms for his musicians and the crowds that flocked to his dances.[68] Foster said Duson and Staulz were "real ratty guys" and, in another foreshadowing of rap fashions, recalled that "they wore their braces down with their pants half falling down."[69]

The analogy to rap is relevant not only because it highlights the enduring popularity and influence of freestyle rhyming, but as a reminder of deeper cultural continuities. Jazz was often attacked in its early years as unmusical, antisocial noise and its devotees spent decades fighting for it to be recognized as a major art form, comparable to the most elevated European concert styles. The characterization of jazz as "Black classical music" or "American classical music" makes sense in terms of the music's complexity and the skill required to play it at a professional level, but has prompted many writers to downplay the extent to which both the music and its audience were originally associated not only with working-class Black communities but specifically with the rowdier and less respectable members of those communities: the hustlers, gamblers, roustabouts, and sex workers of the sporting world. Jazz expanded beyond that milieu in the 1920s as it was adopted by middle-class and upper-class consumers, and by the 1930s the lyrical traditions of its original performers and communities had been superseded by a repertoire of Broadway and Tin Pan Alley compositions and were largely forgotten. When the culture of street beats and improvisatory rhyming resurfaced spectacularly in the 1980s, many writers noted that rap had deep roots, but jazz critics and historians still tend to compare their favorite artists to classical composers and concert virtuosos rather than to Rakim or Snoop Dogg. So it is worth remembering that in cultural terms—in terms of the audience, the neighborhoods, and the attitudes of insiders and outsiders alike—a rap show in a Black neighborhood club is closer to a night at the Funky Butt than any jazz concert has been for almost a century, beset by the same stereotypes and dangers and the same appreciation of rough comedy and rhyming.

Barker provided a typically colorful description of Bolden's dances at Lincoln Park, writing that the band would start by playing pop tunes, waltzes, and ragtime compositions for the middle-class customers—the Black teachers, doctors, lawyers, merchants, and their families—who came in the afternoons and early evenings, then shift to a different repertoire for the "low-life" characters who came out later. The big night for that audience was Monday, when the tenderloin district was closed and "them pretty whores would come to the park all dressed up with their pimps and madames":

He'd play them low, lowdown-under blues and them whores would perform something terrible till they'd get out of hand, shaking down to the floor and dropping their drawers and teddies: that was a beautiful sight to see.

Around eleven o'clock the crowd would get heated up and Buddy would play such nice love songs—like:

If You Don't Like My Potatoes, Why Do You Dig So Deep
Your Mammy Don't Wear No Drawers, She Wears Six Bit Overalls
Stick It Where You Stuck It Last Night
Let Me Be Your Lil Dog Till Your Big Dog Comes
Don't Send Me No Roses 'Cause Shoes Is What I Need
Pretty Pretty Mama, Open Your Legs One More Time
All the Whores Like the Way I Ride
Melpomene Street Blues
The Bucket's Got a Hole In It
Make Me a Pallet on the Floor

Lots of folks would faint and pass out from the heat and the strong body odor, 'cause there wasn't many colored people who had bath tubs in those days. In fact, very few white folks owned one. Lots of times when the crowd would be jammed in front of Bolden he would stop blowing, take his hat and fan the air in front of him and holler loud:

"MY CHILLUN'S HERE. I KNOW IT 'CAUSE I CAN SMELL 'EM."

That used to tickle the crowd, and everybody would clap, scream, laugh and holler. I'm tellin' you when that odor used to rise it smelled like burnt onions and train smoke.[70]

Barker's vignette may have been inspired by the "Funky Butt" song, but the smell of a crowded dance hall in the days before showers or air conditioning was powerful and blues singers often found inspiration in earthy realities. The funky aspect of sex was a favorite theme, though most of the surviving examples come from a couple of decades later. Georgia Tom Dorsey and Jane Lucas recorded a duet in 1930 in which he came home late and she demanded, "What's that I smell?" and Walter Davis similarly accused his lady:

> *Your hair all wrinkled and you're full of sweat,*
> *Your underskirt is wringing wet,*
> *You been doing something wrong, doing something wrong,*
> *Been doing something, I can tell by the way you smell.*[71]

Bo Carter asked "What Kind of Scent Is This?" and Blind Boy Fuller specifically demanded, "What's That Smells Like Fish?" Buster Pickens sang a version of "The Ma Grinder," a Texas barrelhouse standard, with the lines *"Been doing something, mama, smell is all on your hands,"* and *"You got good business, the stink's all over town,"* and Roosevelt Sykes expanded on that theme, singing:

> *You go away, and you stays all day*
> *When you come back, you smellin' in a different way . . .*
> *We could smell that thing, oh we may could sell that thing.*[72]

Some songs approached the topic preventively. The St. Louis guitarist Charley Jordan hit in 1930 with "Keep It Clean," a double-entendre blues with the chorus:

> *Ride her over, give her a Coca-Cola,*
> *Lemon soda, saucer of ice cream,*
> *Take soap and water, for to keep it clean.*[73]

This song was so popular that Jordan followed with "Keep It Clean—No. 2," "Keep It Clean—No. 3," "It Ain't Clean (That Thing Ain't Clean)," and "Keep Your Yas Yas Clean." A Virginia guitarist named Luke Jordan recorded an earlier variant of this song as "Won't You Be Kind," with verses that sanitized some familiar rhymes, bowdlerizing Hurston's verse about the law being passed that *"the women in Tampa got to wash they ass"* to *"the uptown gals got to cut they own grass"* and singing:

> *Get a nickel worth of beefsteak, a dime worth of lard,*
> *I'm gon' watch that bricklayer carry that hod.*
>   *Won't you be kind, to your kitchen,*
>   *I mean your dining room, scrub out your pantry,*
>   *Won't you be kind, and keep your backyard clean.*[74]

Mance Lipscomb eventually recorded a couple of uncensored versions of this song, with a variant of one of Morton's favorite couplets, *"Mama, Mama, look at Sis, / She's in the backyard doing that unknowing twist,"* followed by a gender-balancing sequel:

> Turn around and said, look at the boy—they done talked about
>   his sister—say: *Mama, Mama, look at Bud.*
> What Bud done? Say:
> *He's in the backyard acting like a stud.*
> Why you say he acting like a stud? Say:
> *Pull his britches below his knees,*
> *And shaking his dick at who he please.*

Ferdinand Morton, the teenage pianist and singer known as Winding Ball, circa 1906. He worked along the Gulf Coast for a half dozen years before moving into theaters and acquiring a new nickname: Jelly Roll.

Emma Sears.

This clever girl has been justly termed the colored Carmencita, and the name has certainly not been misplaced. As a tamborine dancer she has no superior and very few equals. Tall, graceful, winning. What more can be said? Let me add: Gentlemen, a visit to New Orleans is incomplete if you fail to visit Lulu White's and ask to see Miss Sears dance, sing or play some of her own compositions on a Steinway Grand.

Corine Meyers.

The poet has said that there are others, lots of others, but there is only one Corine Meyers, and we do not stretch the point when we re-echo and say that this is true. She can sing a song and rob the canary of its sweet voice. She can perform on any musical instrument, and is a bosom friend in a short while.

Basin Street:

Top: A parlor at Hilma Burt's house, with a pianist who might be the young Winding Ball. The white male customers are faintly visible in the mirror, enjoying the display; the pianist sees nothing.

Bottom: Two of the "entertainers" in a booklet advertising Lulu White's Mahogany Hall, c. 1899. The women were all listed as "Octoroons"—not Black, but, despite appearances, definitely not white.

KIZER'S SALOON,

Julia and Rampart Streets, where more than One Hundred Negroes were arrested.

Marshall Kizer's Railroad Saloon (above) uptown in the Battlefield, 1908. Morton heard a lot of blues in the uptown honky-tonks, and mentioned Kizer's as notoriously tough: "It was really dangerous to anybody that would go in there that didn't know what it was all about."

Tony Jackson (right, standing) and friend. Morton recalled, "Tony was considered, among all who knew him, the greatest single-hand entertainer in the world."

Best Description of 'Staving Chain' Found at Lafayette, La.

Folk Song Curator Launches Search for Information About Mythical Character.

BY EDDIE GILMORE,
Associated Press Staff Writer.

WASHINGTON, July 2.—John A. Lomax, curator of folk songs for the Library of Congres, today launched a nation-wide search for information concerning "Staving Chain," a mythical American character.

Although songs and fables represent him as possessing the strength of a giant and the industry of a beaver, folk songs describe him primarily as a Casanova of the cotton fields.

"Never in all my days of folk song exploration," said Lomax, who

PAGE FOUR, COL. SIX.

The collectors:

Above: John Lomax with the railroad worker and singer Henry Truvillion, Wiergate, TX, c. 1940; an article about Lomax's search for the mythic Staving Chain.

Facing page: Alan Lomax trading songs with Sonny Terry and Brownie McGhee, Bess Lomax in foreground; John Lomax's handwritten transcript of "Dink's Blues," c. 1909, with that telltale word; Lomax typescript of Pete Harris's version of "Uncle Bud," with some telltale x's in place of that word.

Meetle was money I'd be a Millionaire (3)
Just as soon as the big boat git way round the curve
O Lordy the fuckin' old pilot lookin all round the world
My cheeks grindin' every hole but mine (3)

My man is a jockey & he learned me how to ride
An' he learned me how to cock 'it on the side

Uncle Bud

A version of this notorious lewd song obtained from Pete Harris
Richmond, Texas, May, 1934.

Uncle Bud got corn in the crib that's never been shucked,
Uncle Bud got gals that never been ~~fuckxtzx~~ touched.
Refrain:
Uncle Bud, Uncle Bud,
Uncle Bud, Uncle Bud, Uncle Bud.

Louisiana dance bands at the turn of the twentieth century:

Top, the city: Buddy Bolden (standing, second from left) and his New Orleans band.
Bottom, the country: Kid Ory (second from left) and his Woodland band.

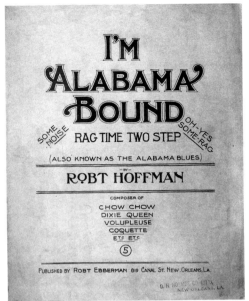

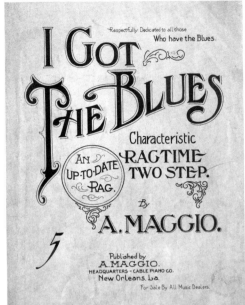

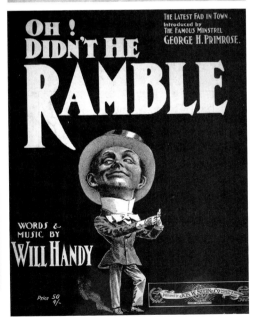

Ragtime intersects blues, 1908-09: "I'm Alabama Bound," a ragtime two step, a.k.a. "The Alabama Blues," and "I Got the Blues," the first published twelve-bar blues, advertised as "an Up-To-Date Rag."

Black culture marketed to the white middle class: the most popular blues song of the teens and a bawdy British ballad reworked as a ragtime hit and soon to be a New Orleans funeral standard.

Morton and Morton, Ferd and Rosa, as New Orleans Jelly Rolls and Ragtime Plano King, are meeting with great success at the Pekin, Dayton, O. Gordon and Graham and Baby Ethel are also cleaning up. Morton and Gordon think strongly of making up a good stock company.

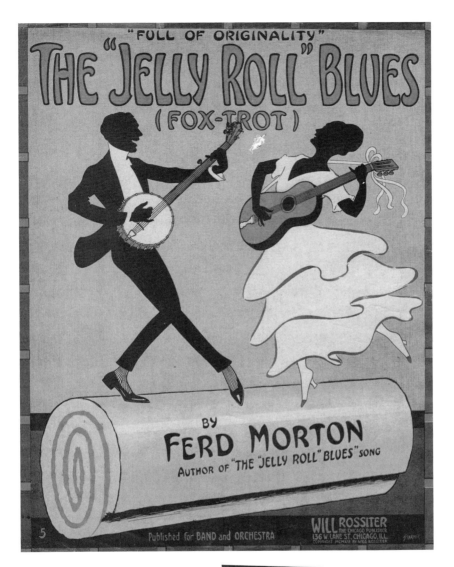

Morton on the road:

Facing page: With Rosa Brown as Morton and Morton, the "New Orleans Jelly Rolls," doing their comedy act c. 1914.

Above: In 1915, Morton's new theme song became his first published composition, with a minstrel banjo player on the cover.

Right: By 1924 Morton was done with blackface comedy, but record marketers were still working old stereotypes.

"JELLY ROLL" MORTON

Tickles the Ivories and HE'S RED HOT!

Uptown characters:
Young Louis Armstrong with his mother,
May Ann, and sister, Beatrice; Ann Cook,
a "barrelhousing woman" and fine
entertainer who could sing endless
verses of blues. In later years she declined
requests to talk about the old days and
sang only in church.

The Hegira of the Magdalenes

Three of the women driven by the police from the vice resorts. In the rear is a negro entertainer, who, likewise, felt the effect of the moral crusade. Below is one of the policemen enforcing blockade.

Closing the Red Light Districts (above): A 1917 article from San Francisco shows a scene repeated in New Orleans and across the country.

Morton and Ada "Bricktop" Smith (right), outside the Cadillac Cafe in Los Angeles, c. 1917.

"PROVE IT ON ME BLUES"

by "Ma" Rainey

What's all this? Scandal? Maybe so, but you wouldn't have thought it of "Ma" Rainey. But look at that cop watching her! What does it all mean? But "Ma" just sings "Prove It On Me" in this great new Paramount Blues No. 12668, with a bang-up accompaniment by the Tub Jug Washboard Band. Don't fail to get this record from your dealer, or send us the coupon.

"Prove It on Me" (top and rIght):
An ad for Ma Rainey's lesbian classic and
Gladys Bentley, the artist's obvious inspiration.

Lucille Bogan (above) recorded a matchless
repertoire of woman-centered sporting blues.

WOMAN KILLED.

Ella Speed Shot by Louis Martinez, Alias Martin.

The Deed Done in a Disreputable House.

Jealousy of His Octoroon Mistress the Cause.

Ballad singers, ballad heroes, ballad myths:

Top: Huddie "Lead Belly" Ledbetter, with Bunk Johnson and George Lewis.

Above: James "Iron Head" Baker, and a newspaper report of the murder of Ella Speed.

Facing page, clockwise from upper left: Frankie Baker, who inspired the "Frankie and Albert" ballad; a newspaper report on the trials of William Henry Harrison Duncan, hero of the "Duncan and Brady" ballad; a popular magazine cover from 1929, showing the mythic white "Frankie and Johnny"; sheet music for May Irwin's "Bully Song"—the original bully may have been a tough policeman, but for commercial purposes he became a razor-wielding Black man.

Jelly Roll Morton in 1939, and the cover of his first album, inspired by the Library of Congress recordings and adorned with a postcard of Basin Street, a *Blue Book*, and other souvenirs of the old Tenderloin District.

Each couplet was followed by a chorus:

> *You be kind to me, you be kind to me,*
> *I'll be good to you, I'll be good to you,*
> *Take soap and water, keep your boody clean.*

"Boody" has become a familiar term beyond African American communities, usually spelled "booty"—for example in the disco hit "Shake Your Booty"—and glossed as an archaic British term for buttocks, blended with the idea that female nether regions are illicit treasure. Lipscomb gave a different definition, saying it specifically meant "asshole" and explaining, "That's the stinkingest part you can find . . . That hole there never will be clean. You can wash it off; in an hour's time it's nasty again."[75]

Little Richard used the word with equal precision though more appreciation in the original lyric of his seminal rock 'n' roll hit:

> *Tutti frutti, good booty,*
> *If it don't fit, don't force it,*
> *You can grease it, make it easy . . .* [76]

That specificity, combined with Lipscomb's pronunciation, suggests an African etymology: the Manding and Bambara words for anus are *buudaa* or *boda*, preserved in Caribbean dialects as *boda, buda,* and *bonda*,[77] and although the overlap with English terms may have played a part in the word's wider assimilation, the use of "boody" (or "booty") for *ass* or *anus* was originally specific to Black culture and most likely survived as an intimate term passed from mothers to children in the advisory phrase that resurfaced as a rap theme in the 1980s: "Keep Your Booty Clean (Scrub That Butt)."[78]

Along with preserving a scrap of West African language, these songs reflect a more general aspect of the continent's culture. African singers frequently provide instruction or correction about societal and personal behavior, sometimes with didactic directness, sometimes with

friendly or insulting humor: a song that tells people to keep their boo-
dies clean implies that some people need to be told, and audiences can
laugh at or with them. Lipscomb explained his lyric by pointing out
that everyone has a funky butt, and blues audiences shared a similar
amusement at the funk of sex. When Bolden embraced that theme in his
signature song, he wasn't just joking about the hot, stuffy atmosphere;
he was signaling camaraderie with his most dedicated and generous
patrons, the women who underwrote the District's economy with their
hard, dirty, intimate labor.

~ five ~

Mamie's Blues

Women were standing in the doorways singing, or chanting some kind of blues, some very happy, some very sad, some with desire to end it all by poison, some planning a big outing, a dance or some other kind of enjoyment.

—Jelly Roll Morton[1]

Morton followed his tribute to Buddy Bolden with a pair of songs celebrating his own legend: "Mr. Jelly Lord"—"*He's simply royal at that old keyboard*"—and the "Original Jelly Roll Blues":

He's so tall, so chancy, he's the ladies' fancy.
Everybody knows him, certainly do adore him,
When you see him strolling, everybody opens up,
He's red hot stuff, friends, you can't get enough.[2]

He followed with a display of barrelhouse piano and a brief song
Lomax titled "Honky Tonk Blues," framed with a recollection of a couple of notorious saloons, Kizer's and Spano's, "terrible honky-tonks,
where occasionally it would be nothing for a man to be drug out there
dead. The place would be wide open just the same, no trouble happen-
ing. Ran twenty-four hours a day." Along with Funky Butt Hall, the
Red Onion, the Eagle, and dozens of places that were just known by the
names of their owners, those were familiar landmarks in the uptown
neighborhoods between Canal Street and the railroad depot at the
New Basin. Louis Armstrong spent much of his childhood in that area,
which he knew as "the Battlefield," and Manuel Manetta explained:
"Them fellows around there, they lived in jail. They did nothing but cut
and steal and shoot one another."[3]

Most of the neighborhood's bar owners were white—or, more specifically, Italian—but in 1908 Louisiana's Gay-Shattuck law mandated racial
segregation in establishments that sold alcohol, and many of them chose
to serve a Black clientele. Marshall A. Kizer had been a police detective
before he was dismissed for planning a diamond robbery, and he opened
his Railroad Saloon in 1907 while on trial, kept it running while he
served a six-month sentence, and made news the following year when a
policeman tried to arrest one of his female customers and, as they were
leaving, Kizer shouted, "Come on boys, I have him now," and "pounced
upon the officer," resulting in charges of resisting arrest, disturbing the
peace, and assault and battery.[4] His saloon was a regular target of police
raids, and in 1909 he left New Orleans and opened an unlicensed bar or
"blind tiger" for Black workers in the new sawmill town of Bogalusa,
where he was shot and killed in March 1910 by a manhunter from the
county farm, who beat him to the draw.[5]

If that sounds like a scene from a western, the Battlefield was similarly
romanticized in local lore—with the difference that the most notorious
characters tended to be Black and some of the most famous were women.
Newspapers carried regular reports of gun battles between Black desper-
adoes, along with stories of Italian "Black Hand" vendettas, sometimes
framed as semicomical anecdotes with stereotyped dialect. When George

"Boar Hog" Robertson killed Aaron Harris at the intersection of Franklin Street and Tulane Avenue, the *Daily Picayune* reported that policemen running from the station on the corner "found Robertson standing with smoking revolver still in his hand, while at his feet lay Harris, breathing heavily and bleeding from a bullet wound under his heart. 'I's waitn' to surrender, boss,' was Robertson's comment as he handed his revolver over to a detective."[6]

Armstrong started playing in local honky-tonks as a teenager and recalled that his most enthusiastic and supportive fans were prostitutes, who showed up when they finished work around four or five in the morning. He said most of them were nice young women, but some were "bad whores" with a "knife in their stockings, down their bosom. Those big bylow knives. Oh, yeah. Ann Cook and Mary Jack the Bear who lived in my neighborhood was the most promising ones."[7] Eddie Dawson and Lee Collins recalled the same two women, saying they "bummed" around the corner of Franklin and Gravier, and a newspaper story from 1912 mentions "a row among negresses at Gravier and Howard streets," two blocks from Franklin, resulting in the arrest of Mary Jack the Bear and a woman called Mary Meathouse.

Cook was a singer and made a record in 1927, "He's the Sweetest Black Man in Town" backed with "Mamma Cookie," in which she declared, *Barrelhousing now, been barrelhousing all my days.*"[8] Earl Humphrey, who played trombone at the session, described her as "one of them real outstanding barrelhouse, blues singers—you know, sang around home, but she hadn't never sang with a band—sang with piano players." He said she was used to keeping her own tempo and had trouble sticking to the larger group's arrangement. "She cussed us out a few times," but eventually someone came to the rescue: "Gave her a big shot, the man would, pep her up a little bit." The record was a moderate success and afterward she sometimes sang with Humphrey's band on jobs.[9]

Rose Johnson said she and her downtown friends didn't mix with the uptown crowd and preferred the Robichaux and Nickerson orchestras to the rougher bands and venues, but added, "them uptown Negroes could play some piano" and "we used to go up that way sometimes to see Ann Cook and that bunch . . . she was a great entertainer." Clarence Williams wrote that people would come from all over town to hear Cook at the Red Onion, noting that the club "was so named because it was not very large and it had no windows, and its strong aroma typified the red onion." It catered to the railroad and banana boat workers, and Cook "would sing according to the temperament and moods of the customers and could sing endless verses to one song."[10]

Danny Barker echoed Armstrong's recollection, saying Cook and a woman named Copper Wire were "the two roughest whores in the District" and "even the tough police don't fool with them," and Little Brother Montgomery said Cook killed a sailor at the Swing Club in Hattiesburg when he was playing there in the late 1930s.[11] Eddie Dawson seemed puzzled when an interviewer asked about her singing:

> All I knew of Ann Cook was up in the district. . . . After all they could get off a man, that's all they was after. Wasn't studying about no singing. . . . Women could play piano, too. Had talent, but they didn't convert it into nothing, you know, wasn't making no use of it. Could just do that ordinarily for pleasure; pastime, like that.[12]

It is easy to read Dawson's comments as dismissive, but sex work paid a lot better than music. Ada "Bricktop" Smith said she made twenty dollars a week as the featured singer in a Los Angeles nightclub and "that was quite a sum of money. It wasn't as much as a good prostitute made, but I still felt pretty proud." She was keeping company with a well-known pimp, and "that caused quite a stir in the sporting world. Pimps didn't usually take up with entertainers. . . . It was a comedown in life-style for Walter, and no woman was going to give him money while he was living with me."[13]

In the early twentieth century, sex work was a basic component of entertainment districts throughout the United States, supporting not only prostitutes, madams, and pimps, but a broader community of musicians, bartenders, cooks, waiters, maids, hotel managers, cabdrivers, and, at a slight remove, dressmakers, doctors, lawyers, grocers, laundries, and all sorts of other businesses. Henry Townsend recalled that the St. Louis red light district "supported the economy among the Black people pretty well, because it was a whole lot whites would come down and bring the money. And the money would stay in circulation for a while in the Black community until it had to go back out and be spent. . . . It was a great support. It meant something to everybody that was in that settlement."[14]

In New Orleans, the District also supported much of the white community. It attracted free-spending tourists, paid rent to landlords who lived elsewhere, and funneled money to nearby businesses: the *Blue Books* included advertisements from liquor companies, cigar manufacturers, jewelers, lawyers, physicians, and druggists. The sex workers made all of that possible, and if respectable folk looked down on them and insisted their business be restricted to particular areas, within those neighborhoods they were regarded as normal and valuable citizens. Armstrong maintained the attitude of his youth when he wrote, "If my mother was hustling, I could not say"—an emendation of his first draft, which read, "if my mother was selling fish"—and described his first wife, Daisy Parker, as "the prettiest and the bad'est whore in Gretna Louisiana . . . the Chick and the Apple of everybody's eyes."

Morton celebrated this spirit in a little chant:

When I get married!
Gonna marry a whore!
If I catch her fucking!
Know she done it before![15]

Armstrong added: "Those were my people my crowd and everything, and still are . . . Real people who never did tell me anything that wasn't right."[16]

Some sex workers increased their appeal with musical skills, and some female musicians picked up extra money doing sex work. Memphis Minnie was one of the finest guitarists and singers to record in the blues boom of the late 1920s, and peers remembered her working the streets before she began making records and continuing to turn tricks at the peak of her career.[17] The 1912 *Blue Book* lists a Rosie Johnson among the sex workers in a house on Bienville Street, and although the name was relatively common, other volumes list Pearl Wright and May Wilson, whom Johnson mentioned as popular local singers and musicians. Advertisements for the Basin Street houses sometimes highlighted the musical accomplishments of the "entertainers": Lulu White's Mahogany Hall souvenir book featured Corinne Meyer, who could "perform on any musical instrument" and "rob the canary of its sweet voice"; Irene Mantley, who played violin and mandolin; "Chippie" McKee, a pianist comparable to Paderewski; and Victoria Hall, who had "a form equal to Venus, a voice not unlike Patti." A 1906 *Blue Book* advertisement described Antonia P. Gonzales as "the only classical Singer and Female Cornetist in the Tenderloin," adding that her house was "the place . . . for rag-time singing and clever dancing" and "she has had offers after offers to leave her present vocation and take to the stage, but her vast business has kept her among her friends."[18]

Morton recalled that "the first blues I no doubt heard in my life" was played by Mamie Desdunes, a pianist and singer who lived near his godmother in Central City and was "good-natured, a fine dresser, and extremely popular with the sporting crowd."[19] Bunk Johnson said Desdunes was "a hustling woman; a blues-singing poor gal" who sang in the Battlefield dance halls and the top houses of prostitution—he mentioned Hattie Rogers's place in the uptown District and Lulu White's downtown—and Manuel Manetta recalled her running a house on Villere Street.[20]

Desdunes had lost the index and middle fingers of her right hand in a train accident and Morton described her as a talented but limited player, introducing the song he learned from her with the comment, "she hardly could play anything else more, but she really could play this number."[21] He demonstrated a spare, twelve-bar accompaniment with a gentle Caribbean lilt, and sang:

I stood on the corner, my feet was dripping wet,
Stood on the corner, my feet was dripping wet,
I asked every man I met.

Can't give me a dollar, give me a lousy dime,
You can't give me a dollar, give me a lousy dime,
Just to feed that hungry man of mine.

Mary Celina Desdunes was born in 1879 to Clementine Walker, the longtime mistress of Rudolphe Lucien Desdunes, a prominent member of the New Orleans Creole community. Her father was a leader of the Comité des Citoyens, which sponsored the civil rights actions that led to the *Plessy v. Ferguson* case; wrote a book-length celebration of Creole culture, *Nos Hommes et Notre Histoire*; and maintained an official family that included a son, Daniel, who became a nationally known musician, composer, and bandleader. It is not clear that Mamie had much, or any, contact with either of them, and if Morton had not credited her as an early influence we would be unlikely to know her name. Aside from the train accident in which she lost her fingers, her only mention in the local press was when she was acquitted of assault with a dangerous weapon in 1898. The 1900 census found her married to a man named George Degay, the 1908 city directory gave her profession as seamstress, and other documents listed her variably as Desdunes, Degay, or Dugue, the name on the certificate recording her death from tuberculosis in 1911.[22]

If Morton's re-creation was accurate, the song he called "Mamie's Blues" is one of the earliest surviving twelve-bar blues, and its lyrics suggest how that form overlapped and drew on other song forms. The Leighton brothers, a pair of white musicians who became famous for reworking vernacular Black material into pop hits, wrote that they hoboed to Butte, Montana, around the turn of the century and were hired to sing in a saloon with a pianist named Dell, "a mulatto girl, hollow-eyed, who turned her back on the throng at intervals to manipulate a hypodermic

syringe that flashed against the brown of her lean arm." After they had
done a few numbers, the boss asked Dell to sing one. She "struck a minor
chord and, in a husky soprano, wistful and pain-fraught, she voiced the
lament of the forsaken woman . . . "

> *I worked out in the rain, I worked out in the snow*
> *What all I done for that man nobody will ever know.*
> *He woke up one mornin' and skipped with all my dough.*
> *An' just said—Fare thee honey, fare thee well.*[23]

The Leightons' stereotyped recollection should be taken with some
grains of salt, since that verse was published in 1901 by John Queen in
a "coon song" that used the tag line for its title—but Queen was a central figure in a group of white songwriters who specialized in recycling
lyrics from Black tradition, and Dell's theme was common throughout
the Black South. When John Lomax recorded Dink's early blues on the
banks of the Brazos, she also provided a song with the tag line *"Fare
thee, honey, fare thee well,"* and the phrase was recycled in numerous blues
recordings of the twenties and thirties.[24]

Desdunes's theme also turned up in an early version of the gunfighter
ballad "Stackerlee," which Palmer Jones, a pianist and bandleader whose
wife Florence preceded Josephine Baker as the Black queen of Parisian
nightlife, wrote out for a customer during their French sojourn. He said
he had learned it in Memphis in 1903, and several verses described Stackerlee's "hustlin' women" responding to a plea for bail money:

> *Stack's street gals says, "It's too cold out here,*
> *The sidewalk's full of ice and sleet,*
> *Damned if we'll hustle to get him out,*
> *Up and down this damn cold street,*
> *Cause he's a good for nothing p.i., Stackerlee."*

Another woman was better situated but equally dismissive:

Stack's chippy girl in the parlor house
Says, "I've got a lot of ready dough,
But I've turned over a new leaf, boys and girls,
I keep no god damn pimps no more."

That left Stack's "old girl ... who'd been with him twenty years or more," and she hit the pavement:

She says, "John if you ain't got a dollar,
I'll take you on for a dime,
I've got to have some money
For that hungry pimp of mine."[25]

"Mamie's Blues" may have borrowed lines from laments like "Fare Thee Well" and ballads like "Stackerlee," or those songs may have absorbed verses from early blues. Whatever the paths of influence, the theme circulated widely. Perry Bradford, who composed and produced "Crazy Blues" for Mamie Smith in 1920, sparking the Race record boom, and shortly followed with a "Fare Thee Honey Blues," wrote that he hoboed into Chicago around 1908 and met "a very nice looking brown skin chick" outside the freight yards, who took him to a piano contest at a saloon in the Levee, the city's tenderloin district:

All the landladies and their stables were in full bloom; "High Yellows" and seal skin Browns with their "Birds of Paradise" feathers draped on down with diamonds that looked like electric lights.

Among the celebes of the Sporting Madams was Viney Fields and a sister of ebony hue known as Black Mag.

My little guide who evidently was a street walker but still hip to VIP's took me to two fine looking gals, one of whom was named Ann Brown. She took me to the man who ran the contest by the name of Charley Warfield, the writer of "Baby Won't You Please Come Home" and "I Ain't Got Nobody."

The competition was fierce and Bradford was not a virtuoso player, but "old 'Mojo' seemed to whisper in my ear, 'Sing and play your blues . . . ' I saw all the pimps with their gals and I remembered this verse":

> My gal walked the street in the rain and wet,
> This is what she said to every man she met.
> I don't want your nickel just give me a lousy dime,
> So I can feed this hungry pimp of mine.[26]

Bradford won the contest, Brown took him to a notorious Levee joint called Big Jim's Saloon, and he was hired to play and sing there for the next few months.

SINGERS AND SEX WORKERS

OTHER MUSICIANS SHARED SIMILAR STORIES OF BEING SPONSORED BY SEX workers, and mentioned blues as the style that drew the women's attention. Kid Ory wrote that when he was a young man living in the country west of New Orleans, he walked to a nearby sawmill town with his guitar, wandered into a bar, and "started in playing some blues. . . . Along came a nice brown-skinned gal. She walked right up to me and said, 'You must be a stranger in town.' I said, 'Yes, I am. I'm just scuffling, trying to make a living.' 'You're going to make one right here,' she told me." She turned out to be a local madam connected with the bar owner and arranged for him to play every Saturday night.[27]

Lee Collins told about arriving in Bloomington, Illinois, on his first trip out of New Orleans at age sixteen and being picked up on the street by a woman named Bessie who brought him to a dance. At first he couldn't get in because he was underage, but he snuck past the doorman and asked the musicians if he could play a tune. The cornet player handed him a horn, he "started driving down some mean old blues," the crowd went wild, and Bessie took him home and gave him money to buy new clothes. She was a "payday woman," earning her living by traveling to railroad camps on the days when laborers collected their salaries, and he stayed with her for three months before continuing his travels.[28]

Some people would have called Collins a pimp, and he might have claimed that title when he told the story to friends back home, but he had nothing to do with Bessie's business. She liked his music, took care of him for a while, and if he cared how she earned her money, it would have been because being kept by a sex worker was a status symbol. Armstrong wrote that he took up with a woman named Nootsy when he was fifteen, because "I would notice the youngsters whom I ran with, they all had a woman who were prostitutes. They did not get much money from them. But the notoriety among them were great."[29]

Pops Foster recalled:

All the musicians back in New Orleans wanted to be pimps. You had a lot of girls who went for you, and you'd put your girls to work on the line. . . . The girls back in those days liked to have a good-looking man they took care of. The girls gave you money, bought you clothes, and sent you out looking nice. If you mistreated your girl or she caught you talking to another girl, she'd get mad and call the cops and send you to jail. . . . Jelly always had two or three girls on the line for him, and that's where he got his diamond tooth.[30]

Some men encouraged or forced women to do sex work; some accepted that the women they were with did that work; some wished their lovers were in another line of business and urged them to get out of the game. A guitarist named Augustus Haggerty, recorded in a Texas prison, sang a blues in which he asked his lady *"not to sell it . . . not to give it away,"* and went on:

> *Pull off your little teddies, mama, hang 'em up on a rusty nail,*
> *Write a sign on your shimmy, mama, "No more cock for sale."*[31]

Outsiders tended to call all of those men pimps, just as they called any woman who had sex with a man other than her husband a whore, but the

sporting world had different standards and categories. When the sociologist E. Franklin Frazier quoted a Harlem sex worker referring to her
"man," he parenthetically added "[pimp]"—but a few paragraphs later
the woman specified that he was not "a real pimp," but just a man she kept
around because "you gotta have someone for protection when you ain't
working."[32]

In her history of Black sex workers in Chicago, Cynthia Blair writes
that there was a shift from the turn-of-the-century period "in which
the majority of black prostitutes worked in brothels . . . to a trade in
which most struggled to earn 'just one lousy dime' on the streets." In
that transition, the typical relationships shifted from women supporting
a sweet-back man who might be a lover or husband to being under the
"protection" of a pimp who might control and exploit them. The varied
reactions of the women in Palmer Jones's "Stackerlee" verses match that
evolution: Stack's "old girl" wanted to take care of him, while the younger
women were glad to be out from under his thumb. Of course, there
were exploitive relationships in earlier times as well, but Blair writes:
"Although nineteenth century commentaries on prostitution often noted
the presence of pimps, men's control of women's work pace, earnings, and
bodies did not emerge as an endemic feature of urban prostitution" until
the closing of the tenderloin districts, where women had mainly worked
in houses run by other women.[33]

Though it lacks Storyville's historic reputation, the Chicago Levee
was equally famous in its day, with its own celebrities and legends. Vina
Fields, whom Bradford mentioned as one of the "celebes" at the piano
contest, operated houses there for more than thirty years, bought a home
in a respectable neighborhood, supported her sisters in another state, and
sent her daughter to a convent school. The 1889 *Sporting and Club House
Directory*, which predated the Storyville *Blue Books* by a decade, listed
Fields in a brief section on "Colored Houses" and displayed the same
combination of racism and colorism that was standard in New Orleans,
saying she had two houses with "about twenty boarders, among whom
there are several blonds"—women who were considered Colored, but
looked white—and adding in italics: *"No colored men admitted."*[34]

Maggie "Black Mag" Douglas, the other celebe in Bradford's story, overtook Fields as the Levee's most famous Black madam in the early twentieth century, and an item in the society column of the *Broad Ax*, an African American weekly, mentioned her attendance at the annual Knights Templar ball, looking "very charming in her black skirt, white silk waist and her new Easter hat." Blair suggests this description was "sarcastic" but also that it indicated "the porous barriers separating respectable men and women from the disreputable elements of Chicago's black society."[35] As W. C. Handy noted in his recollection of Clarksdale's New World, vice districts were typically—and purposely—situated in or near Black neighborhoods, and residential segregation forced respectable Black families to live with neighbors whom even the poorest whites could potentially avoid. The dual results were, on the one hand, pervasive worries about young people being led astray—not only by predatory pimps and madams but by the attraction of fancy clothes and the seductive rhythms of jazz and blues—and on the other hand, inevitable overlaps and associations between the sporting and respectable worlds.

The *Broad Ax* regularly printed articles decrying immorality and sexual license, but the glowing description of "Miss Black Mag" was in its society gossip column, and if some readers took the tone as sarcastic, others presumably took it as a normal social note. We all read and listen from our own perspectives; if verses about walking the streets in rain, sleet, and snow for "a lousy dime" were taken by many people as warnings about the misery of sex work, a streetwalker might appreciate them for expressing how it felt to be out on a bad night, and a brothel worker might hear them as reminders of the superior comfort and status of parlor employment.

Blues lyrics have often been misunderstood—or at least differently understood—by outsiders, who hear sadness or desperation in lines the original audience would have greeted with laughter. This obviously reflects differences of race and culture, but there is a similar disconnect between outsiders and people in all kinds of tough situations—soldiers, nurses, coal miners, prisoners—who laugh at stories and songs about familiar mishaps, miseries, and horrors, bonding in a camaraderie of shared experience.

Willie Mae Brown, who worked as a singer and pianist on the Texas honky-tonk circuit in the 1930s, sounded nostalgic when she recalled the saloons and bordellos of Galveston, "a wide open hell town," and exuberantly described a police raid on a popular bawdy house:

We all of us went out the window, hand over feet, and down—splat!—into the mud and running off laughing, and carrying on. I never will forget us sitting there, slipping and sliding in that mud, the police pounding around with that "Hit the floor you whores" talk they used to shout out when they came raiding. See, the raid didn't mean nothing—it was just to put on a show.[36]

Her friend Andy Boy worked a similar story into song:

Now it's the 'fore-day in the morning when the shack got raided,
The women got scared, start to tipping under the bed
Policemen start to whipping all the darkies 'cross their head,
My gal got scared, said, "Don't kill Andy Boy dead."
I said, "Now, don't you worry, 'cause I ain't gonna be here long."[37]

Brown added:

There wasn't nothing you couldn't buy, nothing you couldn't sell down there. I hate to admit some of what I sold down there—but I was young, I was full of hell, and I did love that carrying on. I sold it back in those days—not often enough to be called a regular, but often enough to be called a whore. But you know, that's how the times was. It wasn't nothing terrible.[38]

Most of the sex workers, musicians, and hell-raisers were in their teens or twenties, and if outright prostitution was more common in those days than it would be later, in other ways the attitude was typical of urban youth. When I was a young barroom musician in the 1970s and

1980s, most of the people I knew were similarly cavalier about sex, sleeping with lots of people, often for reasons that were more complicated than mutual attraction. Few of us took cash, but we took meals, accommodations, and all sorts of other benefits.

In earlier times, respectable people tended to accept young men running around with prostitutes as "boys will be boys," while regarding any woman who had sex outside marriage as equivalent to a sex worker. A verse collected in Texas in 1891 went:

My old man's a railroad man, he works on Number Nine;
Gets his fifty dollars a month, and half that money's mine.
My old man's a railroad man, he works on Number Four;
He's a rustlin' son of a bitch, and I'm his dirty whore.[39]

This lyric does not suggest the woman was doing sex work; she was just shacked up and supported by a man without benefit of marriage. It is a modern innovation to limit the term *whore* to the women Brown called "regulars," and sex workers in the early twentieth century often expressed contempt for the amateurs or "charity girls" who would "offer themselves to strangers, not for money, but for presents, attention, and pleasure."[40] Zora Neale Hurston quoted a "jook woman" in Florida saying, "Who's a whore? Yeah I sleeps with my mens, but they pays me. I wouldn't be a fan-foot like you—just on the road somewhere . . . making paydays and don't git a thing for it but wet drawers."[41]

In the first decades after slavery, getting paid for what had previously been forced labor was a significant step forward, and attitudes to sex work often fell within that context. The history of Black sporting life and sporting women has been insightfully explored in recent years by Blair, Cheryl Hicks, LaShawn Harris, and Saidiya Hartman, among others, and Alecia Long and Emily Landau have examined the particular interplay of race and sex in Storyville. All note the oppressive conditions that pushed women into sex work but also insist that to understand those women and their world one has to begin by recognizing that many were making reasonable choices.

Race aside, there were few decent jobs available to young women at the turn of the twentieth century, especially outside the industrialized Northeast, and sex work was far more common and obvious than it would be in later years. Every city and town had well-known houses of prostitution, as well as hotels and "assignation houses" that functioned as sites for independent practitioners. Manhattan's Tenderloin covered the crosstown blocks west of Sixth Avenue from 14th to 42nd Streets, often with six or eight houses on a block, and was just the largest of several vice districts on the island.[42]

In Portland, Oregon, a survey of 547 hotels, apartment buildings, and lodging houses found that 194 accepted or ignored prostitution, 124 considered prostitutes good or preferable tenants, and 113 were "wholly given up to prostitution or assignation." The research was largely done by young women asking to rent a room and explaining that they expected to use it professionally, and landlords and landladies often responded by commending their honesty. Many of the householders were described as respectable and their tenants as a mix of working folk, "professional sporting women," and women who "work during the day and sport at night." In less reputable hotels the tenants might all be doing sex work, and the chambermaids might "also be used for sporting purposes" or work as "fill-in girls" on busy nights. Most of the women seem to have gone into the trade to cover basic living expenses, but one showed the investigators a carefully kept account book, explained that she was normally "a $2 girl" but gave discounts to patrons who came oftener than twice a week, and the report noted that she had a "considerable bank account," had recently bought some plots of real estate, and "in every way has a pretty good business head on her."

This survey barely mentioned race, but a final section suggested the particular hurdles faced by Black women: the authors wrote approvingly of a city program that offered single women instruction in typewriting and stenography, but added that some Black students had enrolled and, since "the demand for colored girls as stenographers . . . was absolutely nil," the directors had wisely advised them "to take up other vocations where there was a greater chance of success."[43]

Those vocations were presumably domestic: cooking, cleaning, laundry, and child care—all poorly paid and often requiring workers to live in their employers' homes, with no fixed hours or privacy. Given the choice between an attic or back room in a house full of white people who made constant demands—frequently including sexual demands which could not be resisted without endangering your job—or a brothel where the work was at least clearly defined and you had co-workers with whom you could socialize, commiserate, and go out partying, it is not surprising that some women preferred the latter option. Sex work was often unpleasant, but so was slaving over a washtub or a hot stove—and you could wear nice clothes, live in the most vibrant part of town, and make more in an hour than a domestic worker made in a week. If you worked in a parlor house, you also had more protection and potential access to powerful men who, if played adroitly, might guarantee bank loans or fund your own business ventures. As in other professions, the few who started as workers and ended up owning businesses were exceptional, but the possibility existed: when Willie Piazza died in 1932, her estate included a mansion on Basin Street, substantial amounts of cash and jewelry, and twenty-nine parcels of land.[44]

For most women, those advantages were more than balanced by the social stigma and constant humiliations of sex work, and romantic depictions of grand old bordellos ignore the exploitation and degradation basic to that business. George Guesnon described Ida Jackson, a prominent Black madam, as running a place that made Emma Johnson's Circus House—a white establishment notorious for presenting shows with women and animals—seem "like a Sunday church meeting when it came to dishing out the lowest forms of undiluted gutter filth." Jackson started at the turn of the century and was still operating a house on Conti Street in the 1920s, and a news story from 1904 told how she met a fifteen-year-old girl named Rosie Trater in Gulfport, Mississippi, "induced her to come to the city . . . to a den of infamy," kept "every cent of money she made," put her into debt by giving her a three-dollar secondhand coat and charging her to pay it off for eight dollars—and when Trater left after two weeks, had her arrested for stealing the coat.[45] Experiences varied from place to place and person to person, but when I was trying to identify brothels situated outside the New Orleans "restricted districts," one clue was newspaper reports of young women attempting or committing suicide.

For Black women, sex work also maintained and capitalized on white men's nostalgia for a time when Black bodies could be purchased outright. In the 1920s Vance Randolph collected several variants of the song Lead Belly popularized as "Green Corn," in which white singers gleefully evoked that past:

> *Green corn, green corn, don't you come a-nigh me,*
> *Yaller gal, yaller gal, fuck her every Friday.*

> *Yaller gal, yaller gal, layin' on her back,*
> *Massa took his tillywhacker, stuck it up her crack.*[46]

Black women still faced those situations and sometimes sang about them. Mattie Mae Thomas, imprisoned in Mississippi's Parchman Farm, recorded a verse that circulated throughout the region:

> *Mattie had a baby and he got blue eyes,*
> *Said, must be the captain, he keep hanging around.*

Another of Thomas's verses described the sporting life in terms that could be variously heard as criticism or approval:

> *She won't cook no breakfast, she won't wash no clothes.*
> *Say, that woman don't do nothing but walk the road.*

And she suggested how things might be different:

> *You keep on talking 'bout the dangerous blues.*
> *If I had me a pistol, I'd be dangerous too.*

Well, you may be a bully, say, but I don't know,
But I'll fix you so you won't give me no more trouble in the world, I
know.[47]

Morton's first album—a relatively rare form of packaging for nonclassical recordings, which were typically sold as individual 78s—appeared in 1939 as a commercial follow-up to the Library sessions and was titled *New Orleans Memories*. Its cover showed a nostalgic postcard of the Basin Street mansions, and the accompanying booklet was designed to look like a *Blue Book*, with notes by Charles Edward Smith recalling the glory days of "Storyville" and the "fabulous Sportin' houses with their mirror'd walls, grand pianos, and oddly assorted personnel."[48] The atmospheric touches were relevant to Morton's early career, but appealed specifically to white men, who could imagine themselves listening to his music while reclining in luxurious armchairs surrounded by compliant Creole belles.

That fantasy nurtured an essential anachronism: white jazz fans in 1939 were entranced by styles that Black musicians had played thirty years earlier and imagined themselves back in that time with the tastes of their own time, listening to low-down blues and hot jazz as they sipped champagne or bourbon cocktails in velvet-draped parlors. In reality, the well-heeled white men of the early 1900s tended to have similarly old-fashioned tastes, and Morton and Tony Jackson got those jobs because they could mix perky ragtime with light classical selections and romantic songs like "Sugar Moon" and "Pretty Baby." Morton mentioned "You're Welcome as the Flowers in May" and "Bird in a Gilded Cage" as typical numbers, saying, "Most everything was sentimental. They just had a few honky-tonk players around," and Clarence Williams said "there was no loud playing. . . . It was sweet, just like a hotel."[49]

Since later chroniclers had no interest in that kind of music, most of the pianists from that world have been forgotten. Rose Johnson is remembered only because she lived long enough to do an interview about her more famous contemporaries, and she mentioned several musicians who are otherwise unknown, like Osceola "Osie" Burke, who first

recommended her for a job in the District. Many Black parlor house pianists were women; white male customers were more comfortable with
them than with Black men, and an advertisement for a house pianist
in St. Louis specified "colored woman preferred."[50] A newspaper story
about Willie Piazza's house mentioned that her regular pianist was Lelia
Chapman, who also performed with Bush's Ragtime Opera Company
at Lincoln Park and was billed as "the Louisiana nightingale."[51] This
may have been the Leda Chapman who was recalled as a girlfriend of
Buddy Bolden's and left a gaudy police record, but the identification is far
from certain; Johnson mentioned another pianist named Pearl Wright
who "played beautifully," and I initially assumed she was the same Pearl
Wright who became Ethel Waters's accompanist in the 1920s, but they
seem to have been unrelated. Nor is there any reason to think Burke,
Chapman, or Wright were particularly adept at blues or jazz.

All the Basin Street pianists would have been aware of the music
played in Black honky-tonks a few blocks upriver, and some white clients presumably requested that sort of material, but it was not the norm.
Piazza's listing in the 1902 *Sporting Guide of the Tenderloin District of
New Orleans* described her house as "the place to hear all of the latest
jubilee songs," a standard term for African American vocal specialties—
which in that period could mean anything from spirituals to blackface
"coon songs"—but later guidebooks just described her workers as "culti-
vated entertainers" who "for singing and dancing . . . have no equal." The
vagueness of that description is significant: whether providing music, sex,
or both, the entertainers were there to please the customers and were
valued for their ability to conform to the tastes of whoever was paying.
Forty years later, at the height of the New Orleans jazz revival, Bunk
Johnson would say, "I've played music for white people all over the world
and many of my best friends are white. But there's always somebody
who'll come up and say to you, 'Hey, nigger, play this.'"[52]

By that time plenty of white men were asking for "Milenberg Joys"
or "When the Saints Go Marching In," but when musicians of Johnson's
and Morton's generation talked about their audiences in the first decade
of the century, virtually all of them remembered the hotter jazz styles as

being limited to Black venues and blues as particularly favored by Black sex workers, in the early-morning hours when they came out to party.

LEGENDARY LADIES

FOR THE ENTERTAINERS, BASIN STREET WAS A WORKPLACE, NOT A PLEASURE garden, and when they got nostalgic in later years, they tended to mention different venues and characters than are found in histories of Storyville. As George Guesnon put it:

> Most books mention only the big time, mostly white, landladies in the District. From my viewpoint, other than that they hired Negro musicians to work in their houses, they didn't really fit that life as did such big time Negro landladies and fast spending sporting women as the famous Miss Ready Money, Eloise Blankenstein, Effie Sweet Wine, Corinne Mantley, and Mary Porter, who owned a block-long string of hustling cribs with nearly a hundred girls working for her on day and night shifts.[53]

I have found no other mention of Effie Sweet Wine and very little about Mary Porter, but the other names on that list have interesting stories. Eloise Blankenstein and Louise Abadie ran a house on Gasquet (now Cleveland) Street and later at the corner of Gasquet and Villere, in the area between the downtown and uptown Districts, which served a well-heeled Black clientele. Leonard Bechet, who played some trombone but made his living as a dentist, described them as "people that was like Lulu White, but they had associate Negroes, y'understand? The better class of Negroes . . . those that could handle money."[54] Morton recalled their place as "a rendezvous for all the big sports," with beautiful furniture and a convivial company, often including musicians like Tony Jackson and J. Paul Wyer, the Pensacola Kid, a pool shark, bandleader, and multi-instrumentalist who worked for many years with W. C. Handy before moving to Argentina and leading a popular orchestra in Buenos Aires.[55]

Blankenstein was from Natchez, Mississippi, born in 1884 to a Black woman named Delia Redden and a white man named Fritz Blankenstein—the 1900 census listed her as Eloise Redden, but as an adult she used her father's name.[56] Abadie was six years younger, apparently a New Orleans native, and they were presumably a couple, since they were still together when Blankenstein died in Tucson, Arizona, in 1929. Their house was unlicensed and thoroughly illegal but never seems to have been raided or mentioned in newspaper reports—a testament to their propriety and business acumen—and remained off the white world's radar to the point that previous writers have confused it with an unrelated saloon called Abadie's in the Downtown district. It was a unique establishment where musicians like Morton, Jackson, and Wyer could relax and play for one another and an elite company of Black professional men, away from any whites or the rowdy atmosphere of the honky-tonks. Rose Johnson said she would sometimes stop by after she got off work on Basin Street and regarded the proprietors as close friends:

You hadn't been to town if you didn't go up to their house . . . Everything beautiful in there. Nothing cheap . . . cheapest drink that you could get in there would be a dollar for a small bottle of beer. The doctors, the lawyers, everybody first class catered to that place. And it was high class; no rough stuff in there whatever. They made the money and they knew how to treat people. . . .

Louise Abadie, that was the brownskin one—beautiful, she was. And Eloise Blankenstein, you couldn't tell her from white. . . . Nothing about Eloise looked like a colored woman. They went out to Lincoln Park one night and the policemens made her get out of there because they didn't want to believe that she was a Negress. . . .

Her daughter married this white man right there in Natchez; he was a well-to-do man, and they tell me when he married her, that the citizenry protested against him, and say he brought her back after the marriage ceremony and carried her in his mansion—his wife had died and he married Lizzie—and set on his front porch with a shotgun, ready for anybody come interfere with him. And I learned that she has children and she's in business down there, runs a big shoe store, swellest shoe store in Natchez.[57]

Whether fact or legend, those kinds of stories circulated in Black New Orleans alongside tales of tough characters like Aaron Harris— who, as it happened, is listed in the 1910 census around the corner from Blankenstein and Abadie at 235 Villere. Emile "Stale Bread" Lacoume (or Lacombe), the blind white musician whose Razzy Dazzy Spasm Band played for tips on the streets of Storyville, was living a few doors away, and Osceola Burke was across the street in a building that would be raided as a drug den three years later, nabbing Buddy Duplessis, whom Morton recalled as a "very gentlemanly" pimp.

It was a small world, with an astonishing range of characters. Around the block on South Robertson was the elegant home of Dr. Smith W. Green, Supreme Chancellor of the Knights of Pythias (Colored), who supervised the planning and construction of the seven-story Pythian Temple, described by the *Daily Picayune* as "the biggest business enterprise ever attempted by the colored race in the United States."[58] Located a block from Funky Butt Hall on the edge of the uptown District, the Pythian had a theater that presented local and visiting artists and a roof garden featuring the finest dance orchestras. Much of the entertainment was coordinated by Dr. Green's stepson and secretary, Jacques Brown, who lived in the doctor's home and played a central role in another local saga, since, along with his respectable career and family, he was involved with Corinne Mantley.

The 1910 census listed Mantley as a "boarder" in Lulu White's place, but Johnson recalled her as running a house on Bienville, in the heart of the downtown District, and said she and "Jakey" Brown were a well-known couple until a St. Louis madam named Betty Ray—who by some reports had employed Scott Joplin as her house pianist—came to town with a stunning staff and opened a place on Iberville. "She was a sensation," Johnson recalled. "She set the District on fire with them broads she brought down here. So Jakey went gunning for one of them, and Corinne got jealous and killed him."

The murder was widely covered in the local press, and although Brown was a prominent figure in the Black community, the stories all focused on Mantley. None mentioned that she lived in the tenderloin or did sex work; the hook was her poise and aplomb. She sent her maid to ask Brown to meet her on Canal Street, shot him five times, then coolly waited for the police and handed them a confession she had written that afternoon. According to the *Daily Picayune*, she was "absolutely calm and self-possessed and told the story with as much nonchalance as she would have told an ordinary tale," saying she had lived with Brown for six months and supported him in high style by pawning her jewelry and giving him all her earnings, "which she did not object to" until she learned he was giving the money to another woman.[59] It was a fine drama and even had a happy ending: when the case came to trial, eight jurors voted to acquit, she was released pending a retrial that never happened, and in 1917 she was listed as Piazza's partner on Basin Street.

While Blankenstein and Mantley were well-known local figures, Ready Money made news from coast to coast. Morton knew her and her longtime partner Bob Rowe as prominent New Orleans sports and met them again when he moved to California. He recalled that Rowe ran the gambling at the Big 25 and "had so many suits, no one knew how many," while she "made her money hustling and she was a grand thief. Could get in your pockets and you didn't know."

Ready Money seems to have been born in Indiana around 1875, and by the early 1890s was living in St. Louis, where she was associated with Bettie Ray and went by the name Mabel Tyler. In 1899 she and a female partner were detained in Kansas City with five trunks of clothing and jewelry valued at several thousand dollars, apparently the fruit of a robbery in New York. She gave her name as Mabel Wendell, and reporters described her as a striking redhead and "somewhat of a curiosity," writing that the women were picked up because "their stylish dress and conduct excited suspicion" but were released for lack of evidence and ordered to leave town.

Three years later, she was arrested in Portland, Oregon, for "consorting with vile persons, white and black in the scarlet section of the city."

By then she was known as Mabel Robbins, and in 1903 she was arrested in Hot Springs, Arkansas, as "a pickpocket and general thief." The following year, she and Rowe were arrested in New Orleans as "dangerous and suspicious characters," and their case became major news because the judge ruled that the charge—which had been a standard pretext for getting undesirables off the street—was too vague and they could not be convicted unless they were caught committing a crime. In 1905 she was arrested for robbing a man who entered her "dive" on Bienville Street, and there were further arrests over the next few years, including a couple in Memphis. None seems to have interfered with her business, since her house on Bienville was listed in the *Blue Books* from 1906 through 1912 and at some point she added a second place on Marais. Rowe is on the city records in both locations, and although everyone in the District recalled him as Black, he was listed in the voter rolls as white.

Danny Barker wrote a fanciful piece about the couple, calling them "the District's most famous Negro madame" and "the king of the Negro tenderloin," and telling how they organized a "Grand Ball and Soirée . . . for the aid and protection of sick, needy, helpless, disabled, aged and persecuted Sporting girls and Madames," collected a fortune in donations, then skipped to California with the proceeds.[60] There is no record of such a ball, but the 1920 census found Ready Money managing a rooming house in San Diego, with Rowe as one of her lodgers and both listed as white. Rowe was meanwhile being covered in local newspapers as a well-known Black racehorse owner, in partnership with Kid North, a retired boxer whom Morton recalled as running a small house of prostitution, playing "a little piano," and composing a prostitute's lament called "Tricks Ain't Walking No More," which was reworked as the popular "Someday Sweetheart."[61] Their most famous horse, Coffield, won races across the United States and was a favorite of Black bettors, and after Rowe died in 1925, Ready Money married a local businessman and parlayed the rooming house into the most popular Black hotel between Los Angeles and Tijuana, with a nightclub called the Creole Palace that featured dancers, singers, a full orchestra, and a staff of over sixty people. She was regularly covered in the Black press and maintained the hotel until 1956, along with a pool hall and, for a while, in a separate location, a bordello.[62]

I am telling these stories to give a sense of some people who were more central to the New Orleans sporting world than any musician but have been completely ignored by historians, and to present some women involved in sex work as notable individuals who exercised control over their lives and the people around them. If their environment was often exploitive and abusive, they were all the more celebrated for turning the tables on the exploiters and gaining a stature they could never have attained in the straight world.

When Morton described Ready Money as "a grand thief," he was expressing a viewpoint many Black people would have understood, even if they disapproved. Richard Wright wrote that as a young man he had "seen at close quarters the haughty white men who made the laws; I had seen how they acted, how they regarded black people, how they regarded me; and I no longer felt bound by the laws which white and black were supposed to obey in common. I was outside those laws; the white people had told me so."[63] A familiar blues lyric asked, "What you want with a woman, if she can't rob and steal?" and James P. Johnson explained: "A good girl was measured by how much money she could draw, and the best kind of sporting woman was a thieving woman who knew how to get into a man's pocket and get his bankroll."[64]

It was not just a matter of money; there was also the satisfaction of turning a profit from the racism that victimized them in other situations: A New York streetwalker told the Black sociologist E. Franklin Frazier, "We only turn tricks with ofays. They're quicker and they don't squawk out loud if you roll 'em. They know they're in Harlem."[65] A New Orleans crib worker told a white researcher how she would "throw" white men by sprinkling them with holy water:

Like you having intercourse with a woman—you *jazzing* a woman? And while you's *jazzing* this woman, some woman comes in the room and steals your money out of your pockets. Well, naturally, the first thing pop into your mind is the law. That's true. Then when you get up, you going to get the law. Someone throws the water on and let the water touches you. And when you go out, well, naturally, you say, "Well, I'm white and that's a nigger woman; I won't go back there with the law, because there would be too much publicity and scandal."[66]

Other women took pride in being able to get a man's roll without providing any sexual services. Bricktop spoke admiringly of "Tack Annie" Williams, who "was known up and down the East Coast" and would lure a man into an alley, "run her hands over him to get him excited, then at the crucial moment . . . skillfully lift his wallet—and make herself scarce." Alberta Hunter said Williams "could walk up to a man and tell him, 'Honey,' and come out with a suitcase if he had it in his pocket." Both described Williams as a friend and patron: Hunter said Williams would meet other thieving women after work at the club where she was singing and they always gave good tips; Bricktop boarded in Williams's house and told how the older woman protected her from a jealous rival.[67]

WORKING FOR THE WOMEN

MUSICIANS WHO WORKED AROUND NEW ORLEANS IN THE EARLY YEARS OF the twentieth century consistently recalled sporting women as their most generous and enthusiastic audience. Lee Collins described Monday nights at the resorts on Lake Pontchartrain, when the parlor houses were closed and Lulu White would come in with "all the girls that worked in her famous Mahogany Hall. We knew we stood to make a lot of money any night she would come to hear us play . . . because all the madams would vie with each other to see how much money they could spend in the different cabarets."[68]

In particular, everyone recalled the women's fondness for blues. Bunk Johnson said Tony Jackson and Albert Cahill were the best piano players in town, but Morton was more popular in the uptown honky tonks, "because he played the music the whores liked":

Tony was dicty. But Jelly would sit there and play that barrelhouse music all night—blues and such as that. . . . I was playing with Frankie Dusen's Eagle Band on Perdido Street and sometimes after I'd knock off at four in the morning Jelly would ask me to come and play with him. . . . He'd play and sing the blues till way up in the day and all them gals would holler, "Listen at Winding Boy!"[69]

Louis Armstrong described similar scenes, saying, "Around four or five in the morning, that's when all them whores would come into the tonk—big stockings full of dollars—and give us a tip to play the blues."[70] George Guesnon started playing in the District as a teenager with Kid Clayton's band, and said his earnings were twenty-four dollars a week, "plus what them whores was giving us; them bitches would ask you for a number: 'Play me the blues—God, damn!'"[71]

John Handy added further details:

When the girls come out of them cribs, they go home and take their bath and straighten theirself up and put on them clothes and came out there and just throw away some money. . . . It wasn't nothing for them to come up there and give you four or five dollars to play a number. . . . They didn't have anything particular; just like a lot of ragtime stuff, jump stuff—they didn't like nothing too slow, lessen it was the blues. Now, you could play the blues for them all night, they'd like that. . . . But nothing slow like "Stardust . . . " That was too slow; they didn't want that. But if you played a blues in that tempo, that's right down their alley.[72]

Handy said the pimps were equally generous, and many musicians recalled women urging their escorts—whether lovers or customers—to give substantial tips. But women seem to have been the dominant blues audience from the start and continued to be the main customers when the style began to be marketed on records. Angela Davis, Daphne Duvall Harrison, and numerous other writers have emphasized the extent to which early blues recordings not only featured female singers but appealed to Black, female listeners, expressing their experiences, worries, joys, and dreams.

I am focusing on the audience of female sex workers, in part because they tend to be ignored as consumers and also because at the turn of the century they were setting fashions for other young women. A popular rhyme collected throughout the country in multiple forms and from women and men, white and Black, went:

> *Here's to the girl with the white cravat,*
> *Silk shirtwaist and big white hat,*
> *Patent leather shoes and blue parasol,*
> *Poor little pussy pays for it all.*[73]

Parents, preachers, and other guardians of public morals lamented that decent young women were dressing and acting like whores, and if that charge tells us more about the elders' fears than about the youngsters' behavior, it was not altogether wrong. Along with clothing and manners, many young women enjoyed stories and songs of sporting life, which suggested new possibilities and expanding freedoms, even if they were careful to limit their enjoyment to giggles and a vicarious shiver.

By the same token, sex workers shared the tastes and dreams of other young women, yearning for true love, crying over sentimental songs, talking baby talk to puppies and kittens, and dutifully attending church on Sundays. If some adopted a "live fast, die young" attitude, others assumed the responsibilities of their respectable peers: Ethel Waters wrote that many of the women in her Philadelphia neighborhood did sex work, and "some supported whole families and kept at their trade for years to send their trick babies through college." She added that, although "no woman in my immediate family ever turned to prostitution . . . they never saw anything wrong in getting what presents they could from their men—shoes for themselves or for me, clothes, or money."[74] Her cousin Blanche did sex work and died from a combination of syphilis and drug use before turning twenty, but Waters wrote of Blanche with affection and did not moralize. She understood the pressures and temptations and recognized her luck in finding another way out.

Relatively few commercial blues records dealt directly with sex work, but the theme was more common in that style than in any other form of popular entertainment, and those few provide a unique view of and from the sporting world. Presumably there were many more lyrics that were not recorded, and some that do not immediately seem to be about that world had particular meanings for the sporting audience. Willie Cornish told interviewers that the songs he played most regularly with Buddy Bolden were "Careless Love" and "219 Blues." The first was a plaint of pregnancy and abandonment that many sex workers would have heard as a personal story; the second referred to a train, and when Morton made a second recording of "Mamie's Blues" for General Records a few months after the Library sessions, he began by singing its title verse:

> *Two-nineteen done took my baby away,*
> *Two-nineteen took my babe away,*
> *Two-seventeen bring her back someday.*

Lee Collins associated this verse with the rows of "little two-room cribs" that lined the back streets of the District:

The women sat or stood, calling out to men as they passed by. If the men didn't want to go in or hadn't made up their minds, the women would decide for them by dragging them in off the street. The girls, dressed in short gingham dresses and Chinese slippers, would walk down the streets singing "Stack o' Lee Blues" or "219 Done Took My Baby Away." For a fact, all those women could really moan the blues.[75]

Morton told Charles Edward Smith that the 219 and 217 were "two fast trains; the first took the gals out on the T&P R.R. (Texas and Pacific) to the sportin' houses on the Texas side of the circuit, Dallas, Texarkana, etc. The 217 on the S.P., through San Antonio and Houston brought them back to New Orleans."[76] I suspect that explanation was another of Morton's improvisations, since matching numbers were typically used for trains going back and forth on the same line and I have found no evidence of a 219 train to or from New Orleans in the relevant period. The lyric may have originated further north: by the early teens there was a 219 running from Memphis to Hot Springs, Arkansas, a resort famed for gambling and prostitution, which at times continued to Houston and Galveston; the return train was the 220, which would fit the meter of the verse; and there was also a 17 train known as the Hot Springs Special.[77] Whatever the geographical specifics, the verse was widely understood as the lament of a sporting woman or man whose lover was traveling for business.

Morton did not include the 219 verse in his first recording of "Mamie's Blues," and there is no reason to think it was originally part of Desdunes's song or that the "219 Blues" Cornish played with Bolden used the melody Morton learned from her. Louis Armstrong and Sidney Bechet recorded a "219 Blues" a few months after Morton's record was released and, although it was credited to Desdunes and used Morton's piano arrangement as a model, Armstrong's lyric followed the opening verse with another about trains and never mentioned streetwalking. Ten years later, George Lewis recorded a "219 Blues" that had a different melody, and his version may be closer to what Bolden played, or yet another variation on the theme, and when Collins remembered women singing *"219 done took my baby away,"* we have no way of knowing what tune they used or what the next line would have been.[78]

Oral culture is always evolving and recycling, and any popular phrase or concept could become a theme for multiple songs, so we need to be careful about assuming we know what someone performed because we recognize a familiar verse or title. The song Morton called "Tricks Ain't Walking No More" and credited to Kid North shared nothing but that phrase with the sixteen-bar blues called "Tricks Ain't Walking No More" recorded in 1930 by Lucille Bogan and shortly covered by Memphis Minnie, and neither resembled the comic vaudeville song recorded as "Tricks

Ain't Walking No More" in 1931 by a Louisville singer named Kid Coley, or the perky ragtime number recorded under that title in the mid-1930s by the Atlanta guitarists Buddy Moss and Curley Weaver. There was also a song copyrighted in 1919 as "Trix Ain't Walking No More" by Clarence Williams and the unrelated Spencer Williams—who was a nephew of Lulu White and recalled childhood visits to her mansion on Basin Street—but all that survives of it is the copyright registration, so it may have been a version of the song Morton sang or yet another contender.

Of all the songs recorded under that title, only Morton's used the obvious rhyme:

> Tricks ain't walking no more,
> Why, they're passing right by that whore . . .
> I never seen things so tight before,
> Because tricks ain't walking no more.

I assume that rhyme was sung in other versions and censored for publication and recording. Lucille Bogan had clean and dirty versions of some of her compositions—much like the album and "radio edit" versions of rap hits—and the fact that she recorded a relatively clean lyric for "Tricks" does not mean we know how she sang it in clubs. Some lines would likely have been the same or slightly altered; others may have explored themes that were not suitable for the phonograph market. What survives is a streetwalker's clear-eyed declaration of her plans in a falling economy:

> Times done got hard, money's done got sca'ce,
> Stealing and robbing is going to take place.
> Cause tricks ain't walking, tricks ain't walking no more.
> I said tricks ain't walking, tricks ain't walking no more.
> And I'm going to rob somebody if I don't make me some dough.[79]

Bogan recorded two versions of this song in 1930—the first guardedly titled "They Ain't Walking No More"—and its popularity was presumably linked to the onset of the Great Depression.[80] Earlier variations on the theme echoed Desdunes's lyric about a bad night: Ma Rainey's "Hustlin' Blues" began *"It's raining out here and tricks ain't walking tonight, / I'm going home, I know I've got to fight."* Further verses told about the man waiting for her, threatening, *"If you hit me tonight, let me tell you what I'm going to do. / I'm gonna take you to court and tell the judge on you,"* and she made good on that threat in the last verse, telling the judge, *"I'm tired of this life, that's why I brought him to you."*

That lyric reflected a complicated balance of powers. In tolerated districts like Storyville and the Levee, sex workers often developed working relationships with policemen—according to folk etymology, the term *tenderloin* was coined when a New York police captain celebrated his assignment to the brothel district, with its unique opportunities for graft, by saying, "I've been having chuck steak ever since I've been on the force . . . now I'm going to have a bit of tenderloin."[81] Those relationships were often extortionate, involving both monetary and sexual payments, but could provide a measure of protection from other men, whether pimps or customers. Morton told about living with a "sporting girl" named Stella Taylor in Pensacola, beating her up because he thought she was cheating on him, and having to leave town when she called the police—by no means the standard result of a domestic violence complaint, then or now, and suggesting Taylor had connections.

The term *sex work* is often treated as a euphemism, but blues lyrics on that subject almost always focused on economics and working conditions rather than sex. A popular verse compared wages in various regions and seems to have been sung interchangeably about workers in other professions. An itinerant longshoreman named Carolina Slim sang a version on the New Orleans waterfront:

> *De boys in Wisconsin dey tak dere time*
> *Dey go to wurk to mak eight an a dime*
> *De boys in Chicago dey git a draft*
> *Dey go to wurk to mak eight an a half*
> *De boys in New York dey ought to be rich*
> *Dey go to wurk to mak eight six bits*

De boys in New Leans dey ought to be dead
Dey go to wurk for fish an bread.[82]

"Fish and bread" seems to have been a proverbial phrase for subsistence wages, perhaps derived from the biblical scene in which Jesus fed five thousand followers with five loaves and two fishes. Mahalia Jackson recalled that she started out as a "fish and bread singer," working for whatever the Lord or a local congregation might provide, and in the verse about regional wage scales it was typically a punch line suggesting that the singer's town paid particularly poorly.[83] In St. Louis, the pianist and singer Rufus "Speckled Red" Perryman used it in his uncensored version of "The Dirty Dozen":

The women in New York, they're doing very well,
Way up in New York, women raise plenty hell.
Women in Chicago they're doing very fine,
Selling cock for nine dollars and a dime.
Women in Memphis, say they ought to get rich,
Down there selling cock for eight-six bits.
Saint Louis whores say they ought to be dead,
Up here selling cock for fish and bread.
    Now you're a hungry motherfucker, cocksucker
    Out in the alley, doing this, that, and the other,
    Just keep going, shave your black ass dry.[84]

I'll get back to that last phrase in a moment, but first want to round out the regional litany. Many coastal communities of the southeastern United States were in regular contact with the Bahamas and, presumably because the islands had less access to current recordings and radio, Bahamian singers often retained songs and verses that had ceased to be common on the mainland. Alan Lomax transcribed a graphic version of the "fish and bread" verse in Nassau around 1935, and I assume both the language and the added coda circulated more widely:

Miami girls done gone rich
Fucking round here for three and six.
Nassau girl ought to be dead
Fucking round here for fish and bread.
Bread half sour, fish half done.
Get them drunk, you will fuck them for fun.[85]

Lomax's transcript includes no information on the singer or reciter, and although I would guess this verse was collected from a man, it expressed a common viewpoint of female sex workers facing hard times and competition from "charity girls." Jazz musicians liked to talk about the prostitutes who fell for them and gave them money, but an uptown District worker named Lizzie Barnes laughed about women "breezing around in early morn with musicians who . . . 'aint had nothin' but a hard, stiff dick,'" adding: "I don't care what a man had—I sho wouldn't stay up all night and work all day the next day to git it."[86]

The "fish and bread" verses limned an unpleasant situation with bitter humor, and Bertha Idaho recorded a similarly ironic song about Pennsylvania Avenue, the main street of Baltimore's tenderloin district, where Billie Holiday ran errands for a madam named Alice Dean and got a musical education by listening to Louis Armstrong and Bessie Smith on the parlor phonograph. "I guess I'm not the only one who heard their first good jazz in a whorehouse," Holiday remembered. "In Baltimore, places like Alice Dean's were the only joints fancy enough to have a Victrola and for real enough to pick up on the best records."[87] Idaho ended her description of the local scene with some wry advice for potential johns:

If you want good loving and want it cheap,
Just drop around 'bout the middle of the week,
When the broads is broke and can't pay rent,
Get good loving, boys, for fifteen cents,
Say, you can get it every night on Pennsylvania Avenue.[88]

"Pennsylvania Avenue" was credited to a prolific songwriter named Tom Delaney, but that verse was another fragment of shared culture. John Lomax collected an unsympathetic variant from a man in a Texas prison:

> *If you wanter git some pussy in de middle o' de week.*
> *Go down to eight avenue an' sixteen street.*
> *You catch dem no-good whores down dere tryin' to scull dey rent*
> *You kin git some damn good cock fo' fifteen cent.* . . . [89]

Leroy Carr provided another variant of this verse on a rowdy record called "Papa Wants to Knock a Jug," shifting the venue to Ellsworth Street in Indianapolis, and Lil Johnson inserted it in her "New Shave 'Em Dry," substituting the northern boundary of the Chicago Levee:

> *If you want something good and want it cheap*
> *You can go down on Eighteenth Street.*
> *Step right in, with your money in your hand,*
> *You can get it any way you want it, Sam.*
> *Now, must I holler? No, I'm gonna shave 'em dry.* [90]

SHAVE 'EM DRY

The "shave 'em dry" tag line marks one of the most widespread congeries of dirty blues, including Speckled Red's uncensored "Dirty Dozen" and George Guesnon's half-dozen variant, "The Sixes," which mixed it with the tag of a popular Texas piece, "The Ma Grinder":

> *When I dream about those sixes, and those motherfucking eights,*
> *When I dream about your mammy on the moonlight waves,*
> *Aw, she's a dirty motherfucker, and a cheap cocksucker,*
> *And the bitch didn't wear no motherfucking drawers at all.*
> *Must I holler, ma grinder, you'd better shave 'em dry.* [91]

Ma Rainey recorded a relatively clean "Shave 'Em Dry" in 1924, which expressed a common viewpoint of the sporting world:

There's one thing I don't understand,
Why a good-looking woman likes a working man.
Hey-ey-hey, daddy let me shave 'em dry.

Rainey hollered "hey-ey-hey" rather than singing about hollering, but when Papa Charlie Jackson covered her version a few months later, he sang the standard line: *"Mama, can I holler, daddy wants to shave 'em dry."*

Little Brother Montgomery recorded an uncensored variant that began with a naughty children's chant:

Your mammy had a baby, she named the motherfucker Jim,
Throwed the granny-dodger in the pisspot, to see if he could swim,
Now, he's a dirty mother fo' you. Now, baby, must I holler,
Now, golly, must I holler, must I shave 'em dry?[92]

Walter Roland, who played piano on many of Lucille Bogan's records, reworked the theme as a picaresque ballad of life on the road:

I left Cincinnati, you know, with something on my mind,
Chancres on the head of my dick, with blue balls in my grind
When I hit Birmingham, you know, I was feeling awful funny,
Nest of crabs in my ass, and the whores had my money.
You know, all I could say, you know them bitches done shaved me
*   dry.*[93]

Blues historians and exegetists have suggested numerous definitions for "shave 'em dry," and the phrase was sung with varied intentions—or at times just used as an upbeat tag, like the alternate *"Must I holler, must I shake 'em on down."*[94] Roland's usage was documented as far back as 1620, when a glossary provided "to ridde him of his gold, to dry shave him."[95]

In a more literal application, it meant cutting someone with a straight razor, the standard weapon for Black street fighters: a normal shave required hot water and soap; the kind people provided in moments of anger did not. Sippie Wallace and Alberta Pryme recorded a song about a wild rent party, "Parlor Social Deluxe," with the rhyme *"Pistol Pete shot Razor Jim, Jim got mad and dry-shaved him,"* and Bogan finished her commercially issued record of "Shave 'Em Dry" with a similarly clear couplet: *"If you meet your man and he tell you a lie, / Just pull out your razor and shave him dry."*[96] In other contexts, the phrase had a sexual connotation. Big Bill Broonzy defined it as "makin' it with a woman; you ain't doin' nothin', just makin' it,"[97] and the image of cutting someone's flesh as a metaphor for vaginal intercourse has a long pedigree, reduced to its most basic misogyny in the slang term "gash" for vulva and reworked in blues lyrics like *"I ain't no butcher, no butcher's son / But I can do your cutting till the butcher comes"* and Charlie Patton's *"I cut my little women both night and day."*

Bogan recorded by far the most explicit "Shave 'Em Dry" song, apparently as a private treat for Art Satherley, the British record scout who was directing her 1933 recording session.[98] Released surreptitiously on several small party labels and usually titled "Shave Me Dry," it began with a classic couplet:

> *I got nipples on my titties, big as the end of my thumb,*
> *I got something between my legs'll make a dead man come.*
> *Oh daddy, baby, won't you shave 'em dry?*
> *Want you to grind me, baby, grind me until I cry.*

Bogan was born in Amory, Mississippi, in 1897, lived much of her life in Birmingham, and died in Los Angeles in 1948. She recorded over sixty sides between 1923 and 1935, often under the name Bessie Jackson, including two versions of "Tricks Ain't Walking No More" and several other songs from the point of view of a sex worker, among them a "Pay Roll Blues" about working the railroad camps. Her "War Time Man Blues" summed up a common sporting woman's attitude, *"A working man is my living, but a gambler is all I crave,"* and she suggested another common viewpoint in "B.D. Woman's Blues"—B.D. meaning bull-dagger, or lesbian—which began: *"Coming a time, B.D. women, they ain't going to need no men."* Some historians have concluded that she was a prostitute and a lesbian, which would not have been unusual in the blues world of her time—but markets are determined by audiences rather than performers, and her records about doing sex work sold well enough to be covered by multiple other singers and may just be evidence that she recognized a saleable persona and theme.

Bogan's uncensored "Shave Me Dry" was one of two explicit blues she recorded at that session. The other, which remained unissued and largely unknown until 2004, was titled "Till the Cows Come Home" and opened with a bizarre boast:

> *I got a man I love, got a man I like,*
> *Every time I fuck them mens*
> *I give 'em the doggone clap.*
> *Oh, baby, give 'em the doggone clap.*
> *But that's the kind of pussy that they really like.*

I can only guess where Bogan would have performed those songs or what sorts of audiences might have enjoyed them, and have no idea how much other material was tailored to those venues or how much of her career was devoted to that material. She had mild variants of some dirty verses, singing *"I boogied all night, all the night before, / When I woke up this morning, I wanna boogie some more"* on the commercially released "Alley Boogie," and *"I fucked all night, and all the night before, baby, / And I feel just like I want to fuck some more"* on "Shave Me Dry," and there is no way to tell which version came first, or whether both were circulating in Black clubs for years before she recorded them.

Bogan's explicit recordings were marked "test only," meaning they were not intended for release, and it is not clear how "Shave Me Dry" made its way onto the party record market. It was issued anonymously, probably sometime in the 1940s, paired on discs with naughty songs and comedy routines by white performers and presumably intended for white buyers—but it was unlike anything else on that market, and that tells us nothing about where or for whom she would have performed it live. Some of the verses were oft-repeated toasts, like the one Alan Lomax assigned to Honeyboy Edwards:

> *My back is made of whalebone;*
> *And my cock is made of brass;*
> *And my fucking is made for working men's two dollars,*
> *Great God, 'round to kiss my ass.*

Another twisted a familiar rhyme-game into a string of insults:

> *Your nuts hang down like a damn bell clapper,*
> *And your dick stands up like a steeple,*
> *Your goddam asshole stands open like a church door,*
> *And the crabs walks in like people.*

Those verses do not sound like they were invented to amuse white johns, and if others were less openly abusive, they all had a rough humor that could easily have been shared by a room of laughing, like-minded sporting folk:

> *A big sow gets fat from eating corn,*
> *And a pig gets fat from suckin',*
> *Reason you see this whore, fat like I am,*
> *Great God, I got fat from fucking.*

None of that is salacious in the dictionary sense of "arousing or appealing to sexual desire." It treats desire with familiarity and contempt, and men as potentially ugly, diseased, and ridiculous, reflecting a world where sex might be a pleasure but was also a commodity and a chore. That realism distinguishes the dirty blues of Bogan, Morton, and their peers from the double-entendre songs that were popular on commercial "Race records," and from all the other sex-centered songs, rhymes, and jokes that wink, giggle, and exaggerate male fantasies. Sometimes mournful, sometimes boisterous; sometimes angry, mocking, or outrageous; they preserve the voices and attitudes of a culture that is still largely ignored and despised, in all its rough and varied glory.

~ six ~

Pallet on the Floor

In **1980 an** Englishman named Laurie Wright published *Mr. Jelly Lord*, an annotated discography of Morton's recordings, and included partial transcripts of two unissued songs from the Library of Congress sessions: "Pallet on the Floor" and the fifty-nine-verse "Murder Ballad." The book was published by Wright's Storyville publishing company, an offshoot of his *Storyville* magazine—both devoted to traditional New Orleans jazz—but despite that bow to the old Red Light District, he prefaced the transcripts with a note of distaste and excuse:

> The lyrics on the following pages . . . are offered here as the valuable historical document which they undoubtably are and it may be that the language found in them may be offensive to some readers. I would emphasize once again that Morton was clearly uncomfortable in recalling a period of his life which he had left behind and that this material was recorded much against his wishes and at the instigation and insistence of Alan Lomax.

Earlier in the book, Wright cited Morton's friend and publisher Roy Carew saying Morton should "be remembered primarily for his music rather than for the lurid language and details of 'Storyville,'" which he had only discussed because Lomax "wished to document this period from a primary source."[1]

Lomax was on a mission to collect the vernacular music of cultures that were disappearing with the spread of industrialization and mass media, and to preserve and amplify the voices of communities that had been oppressed or ignored. He saw himself as a social crusader, working to overturn the conservative politics and societal strictures of his father's generation, but he shared his father's romanticism about rural traditions and the rough poetry of laboring men and women. He described Morton as "a Creole Benvenuto Cellini," a telling comparison since, along with being a brilliant sculptor of the Italian Renaissance, Cellini was a picaresque character who faced imprisonment and exile for his sexual and financial entanglements and was remembered as much for a scandalous memoir as for his art. Lomax regarded Morton as a similarly swashbuckling figure from a similarly colorful world, and along with documenting the evolution of jazz and blues, he was determined to preserve the sounds and speech of that world and its denizens, untrammeled by bourgeois propriety. When Morton talked about a District ruffian named Sheep Bite, a "big-mouth tough guy" who would "bluff you and then he would murder you if it was necessary," Lomax demanded specifics: "What would he say?"

"Oh," Morton responded, "I couldn't afford to say the words that he would say."

Lomax interrupted him, insisting: "Go ahead and say it."

Morton demurred: "Oh, there's a lady in the house and I couldn't afford to say—"

The unidentified lady made an unintelligible comment that presumably amounted to "Don't mind me," since Morton continued:

Must I say a word like that in front of the ladies? Well, I tell you: his chief words, when he'd walk into a gambling house, everybody would start quitting, say, "Cash in my checks there, I gotta go."

He'd say: "You motherfucker, you gonna play. Sheep Bite's here and I'm the baddest son of a bitch that ever moved."

Through the 1950s it was illegal to include words like "motherfucker" in any publication or recording sent through the mails or offered for public sale, with the result that they were rarely preserved. This has led some people to think those words were uncommon in daily speech, but a couple of Texas court transcripts from the late nineteenth century eloquently prove the opposite. Though they are the first documented examples of the word, one shows witnesses arguing about whether one man called another a "God damned lying, cow-thieving son-of-a-bitch" or a "God damned mother-fucking, bastardly son-of-a-bitch"—suggesting the common quality of all those terms—and the other preserves a ruling that the phrase "motherfucking son-of-a-bitch" was so formulaic that it should be understood as "merely an insult to defendant himself, and not in the nature of a slander or insult towards a female relation."[2]

That distinction mattered because Texas law lowered the charge from murder to manslaughter if a killer was defending the honor of a female relative, and such laws rested on the ancient idea that a woman's honor and virtue are family possessions. Though often framed as a defense of women, that concept was independent of a woman's own intentions or inclinations, not to mention her sexual desires—which, if she was virtuous, were unmentionable. Protecting a woman's honor could require chaperoning her, limiting her movements, or imprisoning her, and maintaining the family honor might require banishing or killing her if she failed by choice or chance to keep her virtue intact.

Morton's family was respectably middle class, and his younger sister, Frances Mouton, recalled that after he started playing in the District, "my grandmother wouldn't let him live with us. . . . She said that he couldn't play in these shady places and come on back where all the children were." Though he chose another path, he retained the standards of that background and, when Mouton visited him in Chicago, refused to let her visit the clubs where he played or socialize with any musicians. Instead, he asked Mayo Williams, a record company executive and graduate of Brown University, to give Mouton a tour of the city's museums and colleges. "He never took me out to a night place," she recalled. "He'd never bring any of his friends around. . . . He always wanted to treat me

like I was still sixteen years old; he just couldn't imagine that I was married and had a child." Their only evening excursion was to see King Oliver's band at the Plantation Club—an ironic choice since, like New York's
Cotton Club, it served a largely white clientele and blended the latest
musical styles with the minstrel stereotypes enshrined in its name. Mouton recalled the impressive décor, saying, "The whole place was covered
with artificial watermelons made out of tissue paper."[3]

Standards of respectability inevitably protect and elevate some people
and communities at the expense of others, and what is deemed proper in
one era is often considered reprehensible in another. At the Library of
Congress, Morton was caught between two standards: it was wrong to
use honky-tonk language in front of a proper young woman in Coolidge
Auditorium, and likewise wrong to refuse a request from the director of
an official government recording project. He navigated this problem in
various ways, sometimes cheerfully playing a reprobate role, sometimes
demurring, sometimes acceding under pressure. He made disparaging
remarks about many of the characters and places he described, and only
used rough language when quoting other people or performing songs
from the early period of his life. At Lomax's urging, he sang lyrics that
included words like "fuck" and "cunt," but carefully avoided saying the
n-word: recalling his stint at the Monarch Saloon, he said, "Bad Sam
was really the toughest"—and paused for more than a second before
continuing—"Negro in Memphis," and underlined the implied correction
by adding: "No doubt he's the toughest man around that whole section of
the world, colored or white."

Morton took obvious pleasure in recalling scenes of his youth, but
shaped his stories to suit the situation, and sometimes the results were
contradictory. Recalling one of his early friends and mentors, the pianist
Josky Adams, he said Adams had a young and beautiful sister whom he
dreamed of marrying and, although Adams played blues at home, "that
would be behind his sister's and mother's back." Then, as an example of
Adams's style, he sang a version of "See See Rider" with stock verses
about *"a mama that's gonna be good to me"* and *"a gal that works in the white
folks yard,"* ending with the one he had sung earlier about his *"sweet mama,*

[who] lives right back of the jail." Lomax tended to keep quiet when Morton was singing but spoke up in the middle of this verse, urging, "Take your time, Jelly—play it right," and instead of ending with the line about the woman selling cabbage, he sang, *"She's got a sign on her window, 'Good pussy for sale.'"*

Morton's first inclination might have been to censor that lyric and convey a sedate picture of the Adams home, but after singing the uncensored line he added: "I'm telling you, those guys used to do all that stuff, see, while the family's there, you know. They'd have a wonderful time."

Over the next several discs, Morton described the street life of his childhood and his youthful rambles around the South. He played hardly any music on those sides, and my sense is that he and Lomax agreed to devote the next session to songs from the same period. Lomax was particularly interested in narrative ballads and had prompted Morton with a mention of Stackolee, though after Morton responded with the short blues about Aaron Harris they went on to other subjects. Now, Lomax may have returned to that theme, requesting ballads of sporting life and emphasizing that he wanted the real honky-tonk versions, in the authentic language of that world. Morton may have been reluctant and Lomax may have insisted, arguing that the material should be preserved for scholars and would not be released to the public. There are no notes about those conversations, but some negotiation clearly took place, since up to that point Morton had been relatively circumspect and the following sides preserved his version of "The Dirty Dozen" and the two most extensive and sexually explicit blues ballads on record.

MAKE ME A PALLET

THE FIRST WAS MORTON'S VERSION OF "MAKE ME A PALLET ON THE Floor," which he introduced as "one of the early blues that was in New Orleans, I guess, many years before I was born." It may have been closer to his own age, but had spread across the South by the turn of the century, and other musicians similarly mentioned it as one of the first blues songs. Some considered it an earlier form and put it in a somewhat separate category: the Mississippi guitarist Sam Chatmon explained, "it's a blues type, but it ain't a blues."[4] However they characterized it, everyone recalled a version: Blind Boone published the first transcription of the tune in his 1909 "Southern Rag" medley; several people mentioned it as part of Buddy Bolden's repertoire; Kid Ory said he played it with his teen band before moving to New Orleans; and W. C. Handy, who recorded a version in 1917 and later recycled it as the main theme of his "Atlanta Blues," listed it among the folk songs he heard in the countryside around Clarksdale.[5]

The earliest printed evidence of the song seems to be from 1906, when a comedian and singer named Benny Jones, "the Texas Teaser," featured "Make Me a Pallet on the Floor" in his starring turn with the Dandy Dixie Minstrels[6]—but that identification may be misleading. Merline Johnson, "The Yas Yas Girl," recorded a "Pallet on the Floor" in 1937 that was an unrelated blues about looking through a keyhole at her cheating man, and several white singers and bands recorded variants of a song called "Make Me a Pallet on the Floor" or "Bed on the Floor," which was at best distantly related to the song that Morton, Chatmon, and other Black southerners recalled.[7] The phrase was something of a cliché: stories about destitute living conditions often described someone sleeping on a pallet on the floor, and a popular ditty about color hierarchies had the verse:

> *The white girl sleeps in a nice feather bed,*
> *The brown skin do de same.*
> *The black gal makes a pallet on de flo',*
> *But she's snoozing just the same.*[8]

The word "pallet" originally came from the French *paille*, for "straw," the standard stuffing for pallets in rural homes, but in urban areas it typically meant a pile of blankets or quilts. Morton described pallets as makeshift affairs:

For instance, you have company come to your home and you haven't enough beds for you and your company. So what you do, in order to get them to spend the night over, is to make yourself a pallet on the floor. . . . You'll say to your guests, "Well you can stay overnight. It's perfectly all right. You're my friend, and I think it's rather dangerous—" During that time there was a lot of kidnappers in New Orleans. . . . "So maybe you better stay overnight and sleep in my bed, and I'll make me a pallet on the floor."

Lomax suggested a more prurient narrative: "What about a woman, when she has a man in her bed and she doesn't want her husband to smell him when he comes home? Is that where it comes from, too?" Morton may have mentioned that possibility in an unrecorded conversation, or Lomax could have come across it elsewhere; in 1934, a Memphis writer named George W. Lee traced the "Pallet" song to section hands whose jobs required overnight travel, leaving their "kept women" alone at home:

The women who had sweeties on the side lived in constant fear of being discovered by these rough men of the railroad who they knew would not hesitate to kill them for trifling. These women had a superstition that, if their sweeties even touched the bunk on which they had extended favors to their regulars, it would be found out. This feeling found expression in the song, "Make Me a Pallet on the Floor."[9]

Whatever Lomax's source, Morton picked up the prompt:

Well, I tell you: when a woman has got a man and she don't want her husband to know anything about it, it is very often—it has been known, that from time and time again, that the hard-working men in New Orleans have searched the women's underwear for stains and spots and so forth and so on. And sometimes they searched the bed for stains and spots and so forth and so on. So in order to eliminate that, in that case, if they're sure that the gentleman is on the job, so they make a pallet on the floor in that case, also.[10]

He followed this discourse by playing a gentle descent to a subdominant chord and singing:

> *Make me a pallet on your floor,*
> *Make me a pallet on your floor,*
> *Make me a pallet, babe, on your floor,*
> *So your old man will never know.*

Those lines were standard throughout the South, but the rest of Morton's performance was a startling anomaly, lasting fifteen minutes and extending over sixteen verses. Judging by their varied quality, he was sometimes remembering old couplets, sometimes half remembering, and sometimes improvising. The plot was an afternoon tryst between a sporting man and a laborer's wife. *"Are you sure, sweet baby, your man is hard at work?"* the sport asks in the first verse, and admonishes: *"Don't you let that dirty, no-good, son-of-a-bitch shirk."* He straightforwardly explains, *"I want to pitch some peter with you today, / So with your man you will not stay."* But his interests are not limited to carnal pleasures; in the third verse he tells her, *"Baby, I need some money to get my suit out of pawn,"* and threatens: *"Bitch, if you don't give me some money to get my suit out of pawn, / You'll wish today that you never, never was born."*

Morton paused there, perhaps considering the song finished, but after a murmured exchange with Lomax he played a couple of instrumental choruses in a brighter tempo and got down to business: *"Come here, you sweet bitch, let me get in your drawers,"* he sang, adding, "I'm remembering them things now."

> *Come here, you sweet bitch, let me get in your drawers.*
> *Come here, you sweet bitch*—Gimme that pussy!—*let me get in your*
>   *drawers,*
> *I'm going to make you think you fucking with Santa Claus.*

The next verse followed this theme, beginning *"You got the best cunt I ever had—"* and when the following lines were cut off by the end of the side, he picked it up on the next disc, repeating the line three times and capping it with a wry twist: *"Maybe it was that all I got was always bad."*

Morton reprised the stump verse from "Winding Ball," then went back to mocking the absent workingman: *"If that man knew, babe, I have this big prick in you, / What do you think that dirty no-good son-of-a-bitch would do?"* Not that he was worried: *"I would tell him to kiss my fucking ass / Just as long as you kissing ass will last."*

Two verses asked, *"Don't you like the way I grind?"* with the second adding, *"If you do, baby, let me get a little from behind."*

The woman responded: *"You know I like your grinding, baby, from the way I wind,"* and *"That's the reason why I'm gonna let you get a little bit from behind."*

He suggested another position: *"Would you throw your legs way up in the air / So I can take this big prick and put every bit right there?"* In a variant of Lucille Bogan's nursery parody, he added: *"Throw your legs up like a great church steeple, / So I can think I'm fucking all the people."*

Morton interrupted the narrative a couple of times to comment appreciatively on the whiskey he was drinking, and finished with a pair of postcoital stanzas, the first just repeating, *"Baby, it's been a pleasure in me fucking you,"* and the second requesting *"Bring me a towel, bring it dripping wet,"* and providing a rhyming capper: *"You're the fuckingest bitch, yes, baby, I ever met."*

This performance is in many ways unique and suggests how much of the musical culture of Morton's youth has been obscured, ignored, and forgotten. Obscenity laws would have prevented anything like it from being issued in the teens or twenties, or for decades afterward, and, aside from the language, it is striking for its length and the way it traces a cohesive story. Other versions of the song, recorded by Mississippi John Hurt in 1928 as "Ain't No Tellin,'" by Willie Harris in 1930 as "Never Drive a Stranger from Your Door," by Sam Chatmon in 1936 as "If You Don't Want Me Please Don't Dog Me 'Round," and by other rural players in later years, were made up of loosely linked floating verses, and the pop variants published by W. C. Handy and recorded by vaudeville artists like Virginia Liston and Ethel Waters were similarly non-narrative.[11]

The only exception was a relatively brief version Chatmon performed in 1978, when Lomax visited him with a television crew, and it provides an interesting parallel to Morton's saga. Though less than three minutes long and lacking the graphic details, it likewise narrates a sexual encounter, starting with the verse advising a woman to make a pallet on the floor so her man won't know, then adding a common homily: *"Don't never drive a stranger from your door, / He may be your best friend, you don't know."* Getting personal, the singer advises her to *"take one pillow off your feather bed and put it under your loving daddy's head,"* then describes her visitor: *"He's a country man and he just done moved to town, / He done sold his cotton, now he is walking 'round."* This character was a long way from Morton's protagonist, and Chatmon finished with a verse calculated to get a laugh from both the sporting crowd and their victims:

> *Just make him down a pallet on your floor,*
> *Just make him down a pallet on your floor.*
> *Just make him down a pallet on your floor,*
> *And send him back to the field so he can raise some more.*[12]

Chatmon was born in 1897 and grew up in the country near Jackson, Mississippi, in an extended family of musicians who played at picnics and dances. His brothers made hundreds of commercial recordings in the early 1930s, most famously as the Mississippi Sheiks, and in 1969 he told an interviewer that his oldest sister, then age ninety-eight, was still playing guitar and singing "Pallet on the Floor."[13] No one interviewed or recorded any of the Chatmon women, so we have no way of knowing what lyrics she sang; she might just have strung together some unconnected verses; might have traded verses with Sam, turning the narrative into a dialogue; or might have reframed the narrative from a woman's point of view.

Like Morton, Chatmon described "Pallet on the Floor" as an old favorite, and their storylines reflected their experiences and audiences: Chatmon sang about a country boy in town with a load of cotton, Morton about an urban hustler seducing a workingman's wife; Chatmon sang in language that would be appropriate for rural picnics, Morton in the language of the tenderloins and honky-tonks. Both portrayed common scenes with down-to-earth realism: Chatmon's farmer might enjoy a moment of romance but was headed back to the fields; Morton's fancy man ended by asking for a towel to clean himself off.

The performances also took place in quite different situations: in 1938 Lomax was an enthusiastic twenty-three-year-old, newly installed at the Library of Congress, fascinated with Black and working-class culture, and eager to plumb and preserve the raw lyrics of the sporting world. Forty years later he was the dean of American folklorists, revisiting familiar regions with a television crew to capture traces of a vanished world on film. If he had asked Morton to sing a clean, three-minute version of "Pallet on the Floor," suitable for commercial release, Morton could undoubtedly have complied, though perhaps with a mix of floating verses rather than a cohesive story. If he had asked Chatmon for a graphic, honky-tonk version of the song, we might have some rural Mississippi verses as raw as anything Morton sang—Chatmon's 1936 recording of "Pallet" for a commercial company showed he had more than a passing knowledge of saloon fare, including a standard "Hesitation Blues" couplet, *"I ain't no milkman, and no milkman's son, / But I can churn your butter till your milkman come,"* and his brother, Bo Carter, was famous for testing the limits of double entendre on the Race record market.[14]

CONTEXTS, CORRECTIVES, AND THE MCKINNEY MANUSCRIPTS

LOMAX AND MORTON CLEARLY ENJOYED AND BENEFITED FROM THEIR SESsions together, but each at times found the other puzzling or annoying. Morton hoped Lomax would connect him to other white promoters and wrote numerous letters over the next two years expressing his interest and concern about potential radio and record work. His tone swung between optimism and irritation, sometimes inquiring solicitously about Lomax's health, sometimes worrying that Lomax was part of a

Communist conspiracy; enthusiastic when Lomax brought him to one of Lead Belly's sessions with the small Musicraft label and the owner seemed open to making an album with him, frustrated when his letters and calls went unanswered. "I wonder how Lomax think that I dont need money to live, just the same as anyone else," he wrote to Roy Carew in 1940. "I worked for months doing the (Archives) & it meant nothing to me financially."[15]

On the Library recordings, Morton generally sounds engaged and enthusiastic, with moments of hesitation when Lomax asks for material he considers inappropriate or beneath him, but he was a skilled entertainer and neither his enthusiasm nor his hesitations should necessarily be taken at face value. He had spent much of his youth performing for white men who came to the District for an exotic thrill, and at times Lomax's requests for salacious lyrics may have felt all too familiar. Nor was it just Lomax; in an irritated letter to Carew, Morton wrote that Charles Edward Smith wanted to call his General Records album *Sporting House & Naked Dance*, "titles taken from the story by Smith very much against my wishes," and although it was eventually released as *New Orleans Memories*, he can't have enjoyed seeing the cover and booklet adorned with touristic images of Basin Street and a Storyville *Blue Book*.

Later historians have tried to counter that sort of imagery, pointing out that bands rarely played in the downtown District and there was little direct connection between jazz and the sex trade. Some have criticized Lomax for pushing Morton to record dirty songs and dismissed the result as naughty entertainment for white johns, preserved against Morton's wishes and irrelevant to his importance as a composer and bandleader. Those arguments have some merit, but none of Morton's comments suggest the explicit material was created for white listeners and it is a unique body of work, very different from the double-entendre blues of the Race record market or the naughty poems and ballads circulated in under-the-counter pamphlets and popular at white men's clubs and smokers. His "Pallet on the Floor" had two active characters, and if the man was pressuring and coercing the woman, at times aggressively, it did not impose a male perspective: the situation was graphically realistic, and it is easy to imagine female listeners shaking their heads and murmuring, "Yeah, I've known men like that."

Sexually explicit entertainment is often euphemistically called "adult" but tends to be conspicuously adolescent, designed as much to assuage male fears as to satisfy male desires, and wildly unrealistic about female desires. There is an inevitable vulnerability in being naked with another person, and both men and women often feel pressured to perform in ways we don't fully understand or care to examine. Straight men, in particular, almost never discuss those pressures or any serious sexual issues, conceal our fears, and fill that space with dirty jokes and lyrics that tend to be cartoonish, defensive, and often slighting or hostile to women. This discomfort crosses racial, economic, and educational lines, but seems to have been almost entirely absent from the early, uncensored blues. Even at their most graphic or fantastic, they tend to place sex in the context of broader encounters, often laughing at its complications and absurdities, but not nervously giggling or treating it as a naughty secret. And, once again, I will suggest that is because the songs were largely performed by and for women.

Female viewpoints and sensibilities are evident even in some songs collected in all-male environments. In 1933 the Lomaxes recorded an unnamed man in Wiergate, Texas, a few miles from the Louisiana border, singing a chant used to keep workers moving in unison as they shifted railroad ties to straighten a track. It was heavy work but also delicate; the ties had to be moved just right, and Alan would later print a version with the leader calling, *"Light / Tech it / Barely / Stretch it / Light ... "*[16] The 1933 chant prefaced similar instructions with a homely analogy:

What did the old lady say when her cock got so'?
Goin' let you this time, but ain' gonna let you any mo'.
Jes' barely touch it—[17]

The last line was repeated as the workers slid iron bars under the edges of the ties and gently eased the rails into line, and there is similar humor in some of the ballads of John Henry, the "steel-driving man," and

songs about the spike-drivers who nailed the rails to the ties. In Mississippi, Mose Andrews sang, *"I got a ten-pound hammer, the women love to
hear it sound / They says, 'Come on, Moses, go and drive it on down,'"* and the
St. Louis guitarist Teddy Darby recorded a blues called "Spike Driver,"
which addressed a female audience:

> *I'm a real good spike driver, my spike it never bend,*
> *For I know how to hold my hammer and I drive the spike right in. . . .*

> *When I drive my spike in your fat pine and your rosum begin to run,*
> *And then I know by that my spike drive it is well done.*[18]

Most of the John Henry ballads—at least, those that survive—were
more subtle, but one collected in Philadelphia in the 1950s reframed the
protagonist as *"a good fucking man"* who promised, *"before he'd let a piece
of pussy go by, / He'd die with his dick in his hand,"* and Big Bill Broonzy
alluded to this reputation, singing: *"I ain't John Henry, I am just John Henry's friend, / Where he left off at, that's where I just began."*[19] The Lomaxes
collected a version of the standard railroad ballad in the 1930s that
underlined the sexual metaphor with a tender domestic vignette:

> *John Henry told little Mary,*
> *"Baby, have my supper cooked soon,*
> *I got a forty foot pole and it's got to be drove down*
> *I'm going to drive by the light of the moon. . . . "*

> *John Henry said to little Mary,*
> *"Baby, let's go to bed."*
> *Says, "Wait, John Henry, 'til I lay the baby down,*
> *And I'll shake it all around your head."*[20]

If more material had been collected from Black women, by Black
and female researchers, we would presumably have more verses like
that and a different view of what was sung in kitchens, fields, and

honky-tonks. There was a significant discrepancy between the modes
of collecting in white rural communities, where folklorists routinely
sought out female singers, and in Black communities, where the vast
majority of collecting was done from men. There were several reasons
for that imbalance: The Lomaxes pioneered the custom of recording
Black singers in southern prison camps, where the horrific conditions
preserved worksongs reaching back to slavery times and men could easily be assembled and were glad to take a break and sing for folklorists.
As a result, traditions that had flourished in a world where men and
women worked side by side were preserved as male culture, and also
subject to a heightened level of censorship, since wardens and guards
were always present and would have punished anyone who used obscenities or was too clear about the cruelties of plantation life. In other settings, Black singers had no reason to invite white strangers into their
homes or spend hours singing into a recording horn or microphone for
no pay and, for obvious reasons, they were particularly dubious about
white men seeking Black women.

An exceptional sheaf of lyrics collected by a Black researcher in the
1930s suggests how much was missed or altered in that process. Three
years before Morton made his recordings at the Library of Congress,
a young newspaper reporter named Robert McKinney started working
for the New Orleans office of the Federal Writers' Project of the Works
Progress Administration. The FWP was a Depression-era program
that paid writers to conduct interviews about local lore and lifestyles,
and produced guides to the geography, history, and culture of each state.
McKinney was a native New Orleanian, born in 1909, who began writing
as a student at Dillard and Xavier Universities and served as an editor
and columnist for the African American *Louisiana Weekly*. He worked for
the FWP from 1935 till the end of the decade, but quit writing in 1940,
died in 1948, and although several of his pieces were published without
credit in a popular compendium called *Gumbo Ya-Ya*, most of his work
has been ignored or forgotten—including a "private" file of blues and
rhymes collected in his home neighborhood and along the docks of the
Mississippi waterfront.[21]

McKinney grew up in the neighborhood now known as Black Pearl, in
the uptown triangle between the river and Audubon Park,[22] and most of
the lyrics in his private file were collected there, from people who lived
in a three- or four-block radius and had likely known him since childhood. They clearly trusted him, and the result is a unique and tantalizing
glimpse of the sort of material that might have been preserved if more
collectors had shared his combination of access and interest. Some of the
verses may have been composed in the neighborhood; some may have
been known across the South. None show any influence from commercial
blues recordings, and their resemblance to Morton's songs suggests they
were part of a deep and evolving tradition.

McKinney's informants included two women, Hazel Prosper and Ethel
Easter, both of whom lived in the neighborhood, though his notes listed
them as "contacted in a beer parlor on Jackson Ave & Willow St.," three
blocks from Morton's old "hang-out corner" at Jackson and South Robertson in Central City.[23] Neither was a professional performer, and their
contributions were presumably the sort of rhymes people traded to amuse
one another at parties and drinking sessions. Prosper had worked for
some years as an elementary school teacher, and her lyric provided an
instructively female perspective:

> *Love is sweet as butter,*
> *To keep a woman yo way ya got to suck her.*

> *When ya suck a woman an she begin to come*
> *Tickle her purry tongue wid ya tongue.*

> *An if a woman laks to fuck fast,*
> *Ya can git her yo way by lickin her ass.*

> *Dere is really an art in sucking*
> *De women lak it better den fuckin.*

Easter's contribution was even more woman-centered:

Bull daggers git me freakish
De lovely sweet bitches
Dey git mah legs in certain places
An keep mah ass timing lak a judge of de races
An when mah pussy starts to git hot
Dey shake dere ass until Ah fot
An all of a sudden Ah want to run
Till dey slap mah ass an Ah begin to come
De come starts running out lak paint
An after it's all out Ah want to faint
Den she tickles me under de arm and den in de face
An kisses me an reaches down an put mah purry tongue back in place.

The term "purry tongue" for *clitoris* was current throughout the South, sometimes as "purr tongue," but does not seem to have appeared in print until the 1960s, by which time it was shifting to "pearl tongue." None of those terms were printed in dictionaries or studies of Black slang or attracted any mainstream attention until Snoop Dogg used the latter term on *The Chronic*—a good example of oral culture surviving for generations without being noticed by researchers.[24] Some scholars have suggested that slang terms for the clitoris are "virtually nonexistent" and dubbed it "the great unmentionable," which is an exaggeration—a slang dictionary from the 1890s provides "button" and "little man in the boat" and Victorian pornographers produced numerous vignettes of clitoral stimulation—but compared to the dozens of documented terms for *penis* and *vulva*, the imbalance is striking.[25]

"Purry tongue" has an affectionate warmth and seems to have been popular in McKinney's community, since along with the verses from Prosper and Easter, it appears in a song from his most prolific informant, Jacob Beasley. Beasley was born around 1905 and likewise lived in Black Pearl, though McKinney's notes say he was "contacted by St. Andrew St. wharf" in the uptown dock area and worked as a longshoreman or roustabout.[26] He provided McKinney with a half-dozen songs—nearly half the private collection—including an eight-verse "Black Rider Blues" that ended:

Let's go to bed an let's turn de light low
Mama, let's go to bed and let's turn de light low
Ah'm gwine to play wid ya purry tongue until de damn thing grows,
Black rider, black rider, black rider.

This song also included a verse about lesbianism and cunnilingus:

Why is it Henrietta laks Geraldine so
Ah say, why is it Henrietta laks Geraldine so
Maybe she's sucking her black go go . . .

In another verse, Beasley asked his rider to *"Let me know quick . . . If Ah cant fuck you right Ah'll get my cousin Dick,"* which I suspect was a mistranscription of *"I'll get my cousin's dick,"* a positive spin on the disparaging phrase "I wouldn't fuck her with a borrowed dick,"[27] but I may be mistaken, since another verse likewise offered to bring in a ringer:

You can tak mah money an mah fuckin' strength too,
Black rider, you can tak mah money an mah fuckin' strength too
When de juice from mah prick is gone, Ah'm gwine hav mah friend
   bull dag you.

McKinney also collected a couple of lyrics from Beasley's brother Herb, including one about pimping life, which appeared somewhat amended in *Gumbo Ya-Ya*:

You boys got wimmen, but mine is a honey,
De rich white men give her her money.
An jest lak she gets it she gives it to me,
Dat's why Ah'm sailing lak a boat on de deep blue sea.
Ah got a pinch back coat coming
Ah'm gwine to walk down Rampart St. humming
An Ah want it very plain to see,
Dont want you black bastards talking to me.

Ah'm gwine to put on airs,
Lak de woman who makes her money hustling upstairs.[28]

The editors credited neither Beasley nor McKinney and omitted the verse's final couplet:

So all you black bastards can run up de street quick,
If you don't lak de way Ah'm doing you can suck mah prick.

McKinney wrote or co-wrote hundreds of articles for the FWP, including profiles of roustabouts, cane cutters, cooks, voodoo practitioners, preachers, junkies, and sex workers, which give a rich sense of their voices and sometimes of his interactions with them. His profile of a woman named Mary Davis, "a combination cook and maid in a white assignation house on Baronne Street," began with her declining his request for an interview, then agreeing he could buy her a drink in a nearby bar, dancing with him, and suggesting she was available for a more intimate encounter if he could come up with five dollars. Instead they retired to a back table, where she told him she was from St. Louis, "the blues town," and after he named some women he knew from that city's sporting world, recounted her early life in intimate detail. After a painful first experience with a man, she decided she preferred women, then found a degree of happiness with a man who used his tongue—echoing Prosper's rhyme, she explained, "Sucking was better than fucking anyday." She quickly added that, whatever the gender, she did not reciprocate: "I ain't touched nobody nowhere with these lips! They can touch me . . . but I aint going to touch them. I like Bull Dagging but no funny business."

McKinney does not seem to have taken notes during this conversation and there is no way to know how accurately he conveyed Davis's comments, but there was no reason for him to exaggerate the racier details or language, since they made his work unpublishable. He shaped the interview into a polished composition filling fifteen typed pages, but a penciled note from the editors served as its epitaph: "Not used—a little too bad—worthless if cleaned up."[29]

McKinney wrote over a hundred pieces for the FWP, of which only a small proportion dealt with the sporting world, but he was clearly interested in preserving material that other researchers overlooked or avoided. His profile of a seventy-six-year-old man named Samuel Jenkins included a story about a woman named Black Martha who danced the Eagle Rock and Belly Twister, and a song "everybody used to sing and dance" about her, beginning:

> Black Martha is cool and cold,
> Black Martha is cool and cold,
> Her skin is black but her butt is gold

Further verses described her charms as thrilling and curative—"*If you want to git well let her put her stuff on you*"—and the final verse portrayed an impromptu orgy:

> Went down to de pool room saw what the boys was doin'
> Went down to see what de boys was doin
> But Martha was wid 'em, and dey all was screwin'.[30]

McKinney collected dozens of pages of riverfront folklore, including a lexicon of roustabout slang, distinctive superstitions, and verses about hard work, low pay, shipwrecks, liquor, and gambling. A dock worker provided an apt counterpart to Morton's "Pallet on the Floor" vignette, saying he worked from dawn to dark and feared his woman would look elsewhere for satisfaction: "Dont dese pimps worry us? Dey dont hav nothing to do but dat. An longshoremen dont hav de kick in dere back to giv de wimmen what dey spects."[31] A couple of lyrics in the private file suggested workingmen were learning new tricks: Jacob Beasley sang, "*Ah'm gwine to grease mah prick with milk / If ya let me put it in, its gwine to feel lak silk*"—though he ended by pleading, "*Baby leave de white folks kitchen an hurry home / Cause if ya don't hurry baby, Ah'm gwine to fuck dis telephone.*"

Some men were also getting the message about oral sex; one whom McKinney identified only as "contacted on the river front . . . refused to give name," recited:

> Guess what mah gal tol me de other night in bed?
> Do you know dat hoe tol me to use mah head.
> Ah tol her, baby, Ah aint no cock sucker
> Den she whispered she knew black John Rucker.
> Den what did Ah do?
> You wouldn't want John Rucker foolin wid ya gal, would you?
> Oh, you sucked her pussy, did you?
> Man, Ah sucked dat pussy til it was blue.[32]

CALL OF THE FREAKS

McKinney's collection is a potent reminder that sexual choices and behaviors were as varied and complicated in the past as in the present, but not all the reminders are celebratory. Earl Easter, presumably the husband or brother of the woman who rhymed about how lesbians made her "freakish," sang a blues that began:

> Ah took a bull dagger down to the Country jail
> Her pussy tongue start jumping like a lizard on de rail
> Baby, her pussy jumped lak a lizard on de rail.

It continued, "You can tell a bull dagger by lookin her in de eyes / Just watch her gun at a woman's noble thighs"—McKinney's lexicon of riverfront slang gave the definition, "to gun a woman means to look at her"—then veered into a brutal byway of medical history: "If you got a bull dagger, please don't be surprise / Just tak de hoe'er to a doctor and hav her circum'sized." In the nineteenth century, some eminent practitioners of the new field of gynecology advocated curing women of masturbation,

nymphomania, and other forms of unsanctioned sexual pleasure by surgi-
cal clitoridectomy, and through the mid-twentieth century many believed
an unusually large clitoris was a sign of lesbianism, though disagreeing
about whether it was a cause or effect.[33] I have not found any evidence of
clitoridectomies being performed on Black lesbians, but it was common
for medical pioneers in the United States to test their more experimental
or outlandish ideas on Black men and women, and this verse suggests
that stories about this practice circulated in Black communities.

Before the spread of literacy and mass media, people got their news
and entertainment from friends and neighbors, as well as from newspapers, magazines, and eventually phonographs and radio. The lines
between folk and commercial culture were never fixed; professionals
drew on deep wells of community lore and nonprofessionals learned
songs and recitations from print and records to share at social gatherings. Professionals also had pieces they performed informally: Ruby
Walker, who toured as a member of Bessie Smith's troupe, recalled that
after work the entertainers would "go into anybody's room and wind up
in there getting drunk and saying toasts."[34] Much of that material would
have been closer to what McKinney collected in riverfront beer parlors
than to anything in their theater shows, and some party pieces were also
reworked, sanitized, and presented onstage or on records. In 1936 Peetie
Wheatstraw, "The Devil's Son-in-Law," recorded a blues that borrowed
lines from a popular toast about a woman demanding oral satisfaction:
"*The first woman I had made me get down on my knees, / And had the nerve
to ask me, ooh, well, well, if I liked limburger cheese.*" He apparently acquired
a taste for the practice, or at least recognized its commercial value, since
four years later he was singing, "*I want some seafood mama, and I don't
mean no turnip greens / I want some fish, ooh, well, baby, and you know just
what I mean.*"[35] A pop hit on the same theme, "Hold Tight! (Want Some
Seafood, Mama)," had recently been recorded by Sidney Bechet and covered by the Andrews Sisters and Fats Waller—an amusing example of
the complications of censorship, since it was widely banned, but many
listeners thought it was a cheery song about seafood and could not understand why the censors were concerned.[36]

In the early twentieth century, oral sex was classified by most medical authorities as a perversion, and by legal authorities as a form of sodomy. In 1926 the Dutch gynecologist Theodore van de Velde published a guide called *Ideal Marriage* in which he took a more positive view, suggesting husbands faced with inadequate vaginal lubrication could apply "the natural moisture of the salivary glands," using "the *kiss of genital stimulation* or *genital kiss*: by gentle and soothing caresses with lips and tongue." But a footnote explained that he did not use the term *cunnilingus*, because that referred "to pathological practices"—licking a woman's vulva for pleasure, rather than to make it receptive to a penis.[37]

Of course, what people said or wrote for public consumption did not necessarily reflect their private beliefs or behaviors. Early sex manuals tended to discuss cunnilingus more frequently than fellatio, since it served the legitimate purpose of lubrication—as Morton sang, *"I'll salivate your pussy till my pecker gets hard"*—but there is no reason to think it was more, or even equally common. The Storyville *Blue Books* include voluminous listings of "French" houses and it was common knowledge that many customers demanded that attention from sex workers.[38] Social strictures were complex and shifting: in an enthusiastically sex-positive memoir of the 1920s, Helen Lawrenson wrote that although several of her early lovers "made oral love to me . . . it never entered my head that I might be expected to reciprocate, nor, I believe, did it occur to the men." She was aware of fellatio only as "something degraded, indulged in by perverts and so out of the ordinary that prostitutes charged extra for it"—but after moving to New York City, she "gradually began to realize that this practice was evidently something men found especially pleasurable and any woman who wanted to be considered good in bed had better learn how to do it."[39]

Lawrenson was a leader of New York's most modern and sophisticated set, an editor of *Vanity Fair* and regular contributor to *Vogue*, and her earlier view may have been more typical of American attitudes, regardless of race or class. None of McKinney's lyrics mentioned fellatio, except in the dismissive suggestion that a singer's critics could "suck my prick," and the act is hardly ever mentioned in surviving blues or jazz songs. Bo

Carter sang, *"Draw my cigarette, baby, until you make my good ashes come,"* and Lucille Bogan suggested a reciprocal arrangement on one of her private recordings, singing, *"If you suck my pussy, baby, I'll suck your dick,"*[40] but the few other references are more aggressive than erotic. Morton's recollection of "The Dirty Dozen" includes the order *"Yes, you dirty bitch, suck my prick, oh, eat me up,"* but it is an aside rather than an integral part of the lyrics and he presented this song as an example of the extreme, "freakish" stuff he heard in Chicago's lowest dives.

In Black communities, "freakish" often meant homosexual, but, like *degenerate* or *pervert*—the common medical and academic terms—it was not limited to that meaning. When Ruby Walker talked about her taste for receiving oral sex, she said:

> I was like a freak; I used to like men to go down on me, you know? And I had got so bad that I couldn't come unless a man did that to me. You know, I was a freak for that . . . And that poor little boy in the boat had growed, from the men pulling on the little thing.

One of the most widespread toasts was known as "The Dance of the Freaks," "The Freaks' Ball," or "The Bulldaggers' Ball," and described a party-cum-orgy with a shifting panoply of characters including Frankenstein, Dracula, and the Wolf Man, along with Cocksucking Sammy, Shit-Eatin' Shorty, "Bull-Dagging Fanny and her gray-assed granny," "cunt-lappers," "asshole shellackers," "freaks who drank blood from a menstruating womb," and *"Little Mis Vi from the Windy City of Chi, / She had a dick so long she had to be circumcised."*[41] Gershon Legman traced this toast to Scottish sources, citing a seventeenth century ballad called "The Blythesome Wedding," with a guest-list including *"Happer-ars'd Nansie / and Fairie-fac'd Jeanie be name, / Gleed Katie and fat-lugged Lisie, / the Lass with the gauden wamb."*[42] Another Scottish song, "The Ball of Kirriemuir," spread throughout the English-speaking world and featured characters with more prosaic names, but detailed their actions more explicitly: *"Johnnie Gordon, he wis there, lang may he thrive, / For afore he bedded his widow wife he fucked ither five,"* and *"There was fucking*

*in the parlor and fucking in the ricks, / And you could not hear the music for
the swishing of the pricks.*"[43]

Songs about wild gatherings have presumably been sung for millennia,
in all sorts of cultures. A popular recitation called "The Hobo Convention" survives in bowdlerized form, with characters like "Boogie Sam and
Biff 'n' Bam, and a little punk from Q"; a New Orleans song, likely collected by McKinney, started with Winchester Fanny warning Automatic
Sue to back off or face "Shot Gun Sammy and his whole dern crew"; and
the Chicago songwriter Willie Dixon recalled that when he composed
his hit variant "Wang Dang Doodle" and brought it to Howlin' Wolf, the
Mississippi blues master initially rejected it as archaic: "He hated that
'Tell Automatic Slim and Razor-Toting Jim.' He'd say, 'Man, that's too
old-timey, sound like some old levee camp number.'"[44]

Though "The Freaks' Ball" was in a long tradition, most versions
included lines that parodied a ragtime-jazz hit from 1917, "The Darktown Strutters' Ball," which paid homage to Morton with a reference
to his "Jelly Roll Blues." It was common for jazz and cabaret singers to
perform filthy parodies of pop songs at private parties or the rowdier
nightclubs, and "Darktown Strutters" was a particular favorite. Louis
Armstrong recalled a typical version:

> *Dick Lickin Annie told Fast Fuckin Fanny,*
> *To come on down and get your God Dam Mammy*
> *Be ready one and all*
> *To wipe your black stinking ass around the hall*
> *Now they don't do nothing but fuck and fight*
> *Eat up Cunt until the broad day light*
> *Now when the band play Jelly Roll Blues*
> *Get up there and fuck anybody you choose.*
> *Tomorrow night at the Cheap Cock Suckers Ball.*[45]

The Tennessee fiddler Howard Armstrong (no relation to Louis) sang
an almost identical version; the jazz violinist Stuff Smith sang a variant
that began "*Gun-shooting Pete told Cock-sucking Sammy*" in which the band

played the "Bull Daggers' Blues" at the Motherfuckers' Ball; and in the early 1950s the Clovers vocal group recorded a party single called "The Rotten Cocksuckers' Ball," backed with a version of "The Derby Ram." Most pop parodies were quickly forgotten, and the enduring popularity of this one as both a song and the framework for a widespread toast raises the question of whether the ragtime hit may have been based on a preexisting model. "Didn't He Ramble" was far from the only pop composition that cleaned up a vernacular predecessor: Armand Piron took credit for composing "I Wish I Could Shimmy Like My Sister Kate" but readily admitted it was based on a song with lyrics that "were too dirty to say in polite company," often associated with Louis Armstrong and variously recalled as "Take Your Hands off of Katie's Ass" or "Take Your Finger out of Katie's Ass."[46]

Shelton Brooks, who composed "The Darktown Strutters' Ball," along with "Some of These Days," "I Wonder Where My Easy Rider's Gone," and numerous other hits, said it was based on an underworld ball in Chicago. He recalled "all the pimps and whores, strutting around everywhere, big ostrich plumes in their hats," and explained that his version "turns the pimps into the vaguer 'strutters' and the whole thing becomes more general and universal."[47] Brooks did not suggest there was anything "freakish" about this event, but in 1899 a book with the evocative title *Chicago: Satan's Sanctum* described "a series of annual balls held by the 'fruits' and the 'cabmen,' advertised by placards extensively all over the city," and featuring "a seething mass of human corruption":

> At these disreputable gatherings the pervert of the male persuasion displays his habits by aping everything feminine. In speech, walk, dress and adornment they are to all appearances women. . . . The acts are those mainly suggestive of indecency. . . . The convenient bar supplies the liquid excitement, and when the women arrivals from the bagnios swarm into the hall, led in many instances by the landlady, white or black, and the streets and saloons have contributed their quotas, the dance begins and holds on until the morning hours approach.[48]

Such reports were normally framed as judgmental and disparaging, but clearly intended to titillate, and their popularity is evidence that sexual mores at the turn of the century were more complex and less consistently policed than many chroniclers acknowledge. In his landmark history of urban man-with-man sex, George Chauncey wrote that "the most striking difference between the dominant sexual culture of the early twentieth century and that of our own era is the degree to which the earlier culture permitted men to engage in sexual relations with other men, often on a regular basis, without requiring them to regard themselves—or to be regarded by others—as gay." By the 1950s it was common to think of a man who had sex with men or a woman who had sex with women as homosexual, but in earlier periods that classification was made on the basis of how people identified and presented themselves. Sexual roles were not necessarily more fluid, but they were differently defined: in Chauncey's formulation, it was understood "that 'perverts' were naturally interested in sex with 'normal' men and women and that in certain circumstances 'normal' men . . . were entirely susceptible to the perverts' advances."[49] Bessie Smith sang that she couldn't stand *"a mannish-acting woman and a skipping, twisting, woman-acting man"* but was recalled as enjoying sex with both men and women, and several bluesmen conveyed their willingness to subsume heterosexual preferences, singing, *"Lord, if you can't send me no woman, please send me some sissy man."*[50] (My father, born in 1906, sang a ditty with similar sentiments: *"Tiddley-winks, young man, get a fuck if you can / If you can't get a woman, get a clean old man."*)

Vice investigators in the early twentieth century described female and male sex workers competing for the same customers. An agent in the Chicago Levee wrote about a man who responded to his query about meeting a woman by asking if he was "particular," and continuing: "Wouldn't a boy do . . . ? I have two others besides myself, and we'll entertain you better than any women would."[51] To the authorities, that was exactly the problem: a 1917 War Department report on the New Orleans Tenderloin District warned that "Negro fairies" constituted "a grave menace to the soldiers and sailors" who had frequently been seen going into alleys with "these creatures."[52]

Despite the wealth of writing about gay life in turn-of-the-century New York and Chicago, and numerous studies of Storyville, there has been virtually no research on male sex workers or gay life in New Orleans in that period. This omission seems to be a matter of chance—there are no studies because no one has happened to do one—since there was a flourishing gay male scene in the District and its environs. In 1913 the local press ran multiple stories about a murder involving "degenerates" who met in a club above the White Hope saloon at St. Louis and Liberty Streets. The victim was a fifteen-year-old named William Griffey, who had renamed himself Eva Tanguay after a current vaudeville star, and other club members had similarly feminine monikers: Eva's best friend was called Jennie, the club's rooms were managed by Robert "Tillie" Murphy, and there were two men known as Lillian Russell, after a popular actress. Reporters mentioned the members' powdered faces, rouged lips, "high-pitched" voices, and distinctive manners, one writing that they "have a vocabulary all their own, and only the partially initiated can understand them."[53] Some worked as female impersonators in cabarets; some presumably did sex work. By contrast, the men accused of murdering Griffey/Tanguay were described as decent young fellows from respectable families who "had gone for a bit of fun with two degenerates" that got out of hand—they thought it would be funny to throw the teenager in the Old Basin canal, and he drowned. None of the articles suggested these men were themselves degenerate, and the trial ended in a rapid and unanimous acquittal; one newspaper headlined its story "Pervert's Murder" and reported that "the only defense was testimony as to the character of the accused, which was very good."[54]

Though one article described the proprietor of the White Hope as "Robert Leslie, a mulatto, who was arrested some years ago for selling cocaine," most stories named him as Robert Lester and did not mention his race. The club members were apparently white, or at least accepted as white, but racial mixing seems to have been fairly common and casual in such venues, as it was among female sex workers. Chauncey noted that in many cases those were overlapping worlds, writing that "fairies"—a standard term of the period, which he maintained for gay men who presented

as effeminate—"congregated in many of the same locales" as female prostitutes; indulged in "forms of sexual behavior, particularly oral sex, which
many working class and middle-class women alike rejected"; and dressed
and behaved in ways that were "not so much an imitation of women as a
group but a provocative exaggeration of the appearance and demeanor
ascribed more specifically to prostitutes." He added that male customers
"seem to have regarded fairies in the same terms they regarded prostitutes . . . and to use them for sexual purposes in the same way they used
female prostitutes."[55] Morton similarly suggested a hierarchy determined
by economics rather than sexual preference, telling Lomax, "The less
fortunate pimps took on sissies."[56] This equation was made not only by
members of the sporting world but by white officialdom: in 1913 the New
Orleans police sought to limit the spread of prostitution in saloons by
banning women from being featured as singers, and included female
impersonators in the ban, leading a disgruntled bar owner to complain,
"It just seems that they shy from skirts."[57]

Kid Ory described his confusion when he first began playing at
Spano's saloon, in the uptown neighborhood near the Battlefield:

> Sometimes you'd find eight or a dozen men in there hustling as well as
> the women . . . there would be a great big argument; that's my man, let
> him alone; then you'd discover that that was supposed to be another man.
> I began wondering, what's going to happen around here; everyone is
> man and everyone is woman; who is really the man and who is really the
> woman. . . . you'd find a woman was fighting about another woman and a
> man about another man. . . . later someone explained to me that they were
> freakish people.[58]

Manuel Manetta recalled the Frenchman's saloon, one of Morton's
favorite hangouts, as a center for "them freaky people . . . Tony Jackson's
bunch":

> They all was cooks and everything like that, you know. They worked for
> the big white people. And they'd go there, and that's where they'd have

their pleasure. That was their headquarters. And they'd dress just like ladies."[59]

Morton described the Frenchman's as a late-night gathering spot where all the pianists went after they "got off from work in the sporting houses," and although he agreed that "Tony Jackson always frequented this place," he did not suggest it was a particular hangout for gay men. On the contrary, he said Jackson moved to Chicago because the local environment was constricting:

> There was much more money in New Orleans than there were in Chicago, but Tony Jackson liked the freedom that was there. Tony happened to be one of these gentlemens that's called—a lot of people call them a lady or sissy or something like that. But he was very good and very much admired.

Neither Alan Lomax nor William Russell, who interviewed Manetta, asked if Jackson had any songs that dealt with his sexuality or were tailored to "his crowd," nor did they show any interest in this aspect of local culture. Like everyone else, folklorists and historians are influenced by the pressures and prejudices of their cultures and times. When Griffey/Tanguay was murdered, the immediate police reaction was to raid the club above the White Hope and arrest all the men they found there as "dangerous and suspicious characters," keeping them in jail for several weeks while the accused murderers walked free.[60] Robert Leslie (or Lester) was charged with keeping a "disorderly house," and when he argued that the Restricted District was specifically zoned for such establishments, the judge responded that his place "was frequented by men whose actions were in the highest degree shocking to decency and morality" and it was possible for a house to be "disorderly" even by the standards of the District.[61]

Some subjects were likewise considered unsuitable for discussion and preservation even by folklorists who sought forbidden lore. Lomax was interested in sexual material and aware that some of the men who sang for him were familiar with homosexual practices—his father recorded Huddie "Lead Belly" Ledbetter singing a song learned from a fellow prisoner known as Dick Licker—but I am not aware of him ever asking about male-with-male sexual relationships or folklore. When Morton introduced a piece titled "Call of the Freaks" as a hit for the Panamanian bandleader Luis Russell, Lomax asked if Russell was a "fairy," but when Morton said no, he dropped the subject—though he can be heard laughing in the background as Morton continued:

> There were so many freaks in the city of New York that were so bold they would do anything for a dollar and a half. When he'd start to playing this thing, why, they would start walking. They all become to know the tune. They'd throw their hands way up high in the air and keep astride with the music, and walking.... They used to have a little verse in here that goes like this:

> *Stick out your can, here come the garbage man,*
> *Stick out your can, here come the garbage man,*
> (The freaks would be marching, I'm telling you!)
> *Stick out your can, here come the garbage man,*
> (They'd stick theirself out in the rear.)
> *Yes, stick out your can, here come the garbage man!*

"Call of the Freaks" was composed by Paul Barbarin, who played drums on the first recordings of the piece by Russell and King Oliver in 1929 and on a second version by Russell with a vocal trio singing the verse Morton recalled. The repeated phrase may have been his invention, a mocking catchphrase, or an in-group idiom in places like the Frenchman's and the White Hope. Whatever its source, the song was quickly picked up by other bands, including some white jazz groups, and even turned up as the theme of a Betty Boop cartoon, which included a "fairy" character, identified by his falsetto lisp and red necktie.[62]

In the late twenties and early thirties, reporters in urban areas noted a rage for cross-dressing entertainers, both male and female, and particularly

Black cross-dressers working for white or mixed audiences. Ralph Matthews of the Baltimore *Afro-American* dubbed this a "pansy craze," writing, "For years, the business of masquerading was confined to private 'drags' and annual pansy frolics and were the private affairs of the twilight men and their boy friends," but now, "night clubs have dragged this offensive procedure out in the open and freaks of every nature are turned loose on a defenseless public."[63] As usual, it is hard to tell how much of the phenomenon was a change in what people were doing and how much was a shift in what was chronicled in print. Along with the "fruits'" and sex workers' ball in 1890s Chicago, there were scattered reports of events in other cities and of saloons and dance halls where man-on-man and woman-on-woman sexual acts were mimed for ostensibly straight audiences.

The wave of anti-vice crusades that culminated with the imposition of Prohibition in 1920 was aimed at destroying this world, and to some extent it succeeded: the open prostitution districts that flourished through the early teens never reemerged, and much of this book is about culture that was driven underground and largely forgotten. But a report on New Orleans carnival paraders from 1940 described an ongoing tradition of "Western Girls," gay men who used female pronouns and marched as Mae West, Joan Crawford, Ginger Rogers, and Josephine Baker,[64] and Matthews's "pansy craze" performers similarly assumed pop-culture pseudonyms that recalled the earlier Eva Tanguay and Lillian Russells. The most famous was a singer named Walter Winston, "the Sepia Gloria Swanson," who was born in Atlanta in 1906 and thrilled Chicago and New York with an infinitely expandable ragtime-blues called "Hot Nuts." Recorded by Lil Johnson, Georgia White, and Stella Johnson in the mid-1930s, this remained a ubiquitous party song through the 1960s, when the most popular Black group on the southern fraternity circuit took it for a theme, calling themselves Doug Clark and the Hot Nuts. It used the obvious double entendre of the title phrase to frame a middle couplet that varied from verse to verse and often was aimed at audience members:

Selling nuts, hot nuts, anybody here want to buy my nuts?
Selling nuts, hot nuts, I've got nuts for sale.

You tell me that man's nuts is mighty small,
Best to have small nuts than have no nuts at all;
Selling nuts, hot nuts, you buy 'em from the peanut man.[65]

Some singers used more direct language or found other ways to skirt the obscenity laws. Stella Johnson, who worked at Chicago's Cozy Cabin Inn alongside Dick Barrow, "the Brown Mae West," recorded a version that finished each middle couplet with an unspoken rhyme:

When a pig gets warm it starts to grunt,
When these men get warm they start looking for—
Hot nuts, hot nuts, buy 'em from the peanut man.[66]

Another of Johnson's records, "Don't Come Over," gave the same elision a lesbian twist:

Your mammy and sister putting on a front,
And all the boys know they're crazy 'bout—
Don't come over to my flat, I have somebody home with me.

Those records were not secret, in-group folklore; they were on the new Decca label, home to Louis Armstrong, Bing Crosby, and Guy Lombardo, which pressed cut-rate discs for the booming post-Prohibition jukebox market. There is no way to know how closely the recordings represented what Johnson and cross-dressing entertainers like Barrow/West and Winston/Swanson sang in clubs, since their more explicit material would have been cleaned up for release. Gladys Bentley, a lesbian cabaret star who wore men's suits and worked alongside Winston/Swanson at New York's Clam House, was described in newspaper reviews as leading the patrons in singing "filthy" lyrics, including "a seemingly endless song in which every word known to vulgar profanity is used."[67] Bentley made a few blues recordings in the standard vaudeville style of the 1920s, with lyrics about her mistreating man, but as an FWP reporter named Wilbur Young wrote, "She did not specialize in the blues but leaned towards ad libbing lyrics of popular tunes. So adept was she at this art that she could take the most tender ballad and convert it into a new low with her filthy lyrics."[68] Bentley recorded some anonymous party records in the late 1930s, including a risqué parody of "Two Sleepy People" as "Two Freakish People"; two versions of a smoking-room classic, "Christopher Columbo," emphasizing shipboard buggery; and a version of "Dangerous Dan McGrew" that similarly ended with Dan *down on the floor with his asshole tore."*[69] This seems to have been a favorite theme; a later profile quoted her singing a parody of the sentimental 1919 pop hit "Alice Blue Gown" with the lines *"He shoved that big thing up my brown. / He tore it, I bore it, Lord, how I adored it."*[70]

Bentley was the most visible of a large pool of underground entertainers. A police report from 1912 described cross-dressing male performers who sang songs "obscene to the farther limit," did a dance that mimicked "the action of committing sodomy," and "laid on a table and imitated the sexual intercourse."[71] Those performers were white, and later stars like Bentley and the "sepia" cross-dressers tended to work in white or "black and tan" venues, which theoretically served both white and Black patrons but generally favored the former. Sex shows including man-on-man and woman-on-woman action were also popular in "buffet flats" catering to Black customers, but there is no way to know what special songs Tony Jackson might have sung for "his crowd," or the range of venues that might have welcomed that material.[72]

It is also unclear how theatrical cross-dressing was related to offstage sexual preferences. Charles Anderson, who premiered "St. Louis Blues" in Black vaudeville, often performed in a "mammy" costume, but also in male attire, and I have found nothing to suggest his act was sexualized or that he was considered part of a "pansy" or "fairy" scene. The one male blues star who obviously walked that line was Frankie "Half Pint" Jaxon, a diminutive comedian, singer, and nightclub MC who specialized in songs like "You Got to Wet It" and recorded a version of the popular "How Long Blues"—which normally began, *"How long, how long, has that evening train been gone?"*—in which he just ecstatically moaned, *"How long . . . Daddy, how loooong?"* in a feminine falsetto for two and a half minutes and faked an elaborate orgasm.[73]

Judging by the surviving evidence, blues singers rarely credited "sissies" with the kind of sexual power accorded to "bull-daggers"—though Ma Rainey recorded a variant of "Hesitation Blues" that may represent an otherwise suppressed viewpoint:

> *I dreamed last night I was far from harm,*
> *Woke and found my man in a sissy's arms.*
> > *Hello, Central, it's bout to run me wild*
> > *Can I get that number, or will I have to wait a while?*
>
> *Some are young, some are old,*
> *My man says sissies got good jelly roll . . .*
>
> *My man's got a sissy, his name is Miss Kate,*
> *He shook that thing like jelly on a plate . . .*
>
> *Now all the people ask me why I'm all alone,*
> *A sissy shook that thing and took my man from home.*[74]

Rainey also recorded the most explicit lesbian lyric to appear on a commercial disc, "Prove It on Me Blues"—as it happens, at the same 1928 session where she recorded "Hustlin' Blues." Though most historians remember only her version, this song was recorded in male and female variants, and the gender shift was accompanied by a significant shift in perspective. Rainey's lyric framed her as the protagonist, lamenting that her "gal" had gone, and continued:

> *I went out last night with a crowd of my friends,*
> *It must've been women, 'cause I don't like no men.*
> *It's true I wear a collar and a tie,*
> *Makes the wind blow all the while . . .*

Wear my clothes just like a [fan?]
Talk to the gals just like any old man
Cause they say I do it, ain't nobody caught me
Sure got to prove it on me.[75]

An advertisement for the record pictured her looking like Gladys Bentley's twin in a masculine jacket, vest, tie, hat, and a matching skirt, chatting with two slim flappers while a cop watched suspiciously from across the street. The label credited Rainey as composer, but a songwriter named Charles Booker copyrighted a piece called "They Say I Do It" in 1926 and a male-oriented version was recorded by an obscure singer named Sloppy Henry two months after Rainey's disc. While Rainey's lyric was framed as a personal statement, the male version was in the third person, with an opening verse about Mose, who *"powdered his nose and even wore ladies' hose,"* and Pete, who held hands with him *"till the neighbors, they begin to signify 'bout the birds that flock together."* The chorus was sung by the fictional Mose with sissy-man signifiers: *"It's true I use a powder puff and has a shiny face / I wears a red necktie 'cause I think it suits my taste. / I know my voice is tenor, I reduce myself with lace"*—but finished by indicating this identity was on the down-low: *"When you see me with the gang, you'll find me singing bass."*[76]

Both Rainey's and Henry's lyrics insisted that the evidence of freakishness fell short of proof, and their caginess is a fitting epitaph for this chapter. The lyrics I have quoted are mostly of doubtful provenance, filtered through singers' memories and what they chose to sing or say for researchers and record producers; through the choices, prejudices, and interpretations of collectors; and through my own choices and limitations. I assume some male blues singers had sex with men—there is no reason to think Tony Jackson was unique and, aside from personal tastes, that was a common occurrence in prison and hobo life, both standard elements of blues biographies—but such relationships were generally deprecated. The surviving songs and reminiscences suggest a more appreciative attitude to women going with women: famous madams were often said to prefer female partners, and the list of lesbian and bisexual blues queens is notably long and star-studded. Alberta Hunter and Ethel Waters were exclusively lesbian for most of their lives and maintained long-term relationships with women; Ma Rainey and Bessie Smith were reported to have appreciated both male and female lovers; and although some lyrics equated bull-daggers and fairies, we have numerous examples of women singing blues in the character of bull-daggers and virtually none of men singing in the character of fairies.[77] This reflected broader community views, but given the prevalence of man-on-man sex, I assume it also reflects gaps in the historical record. Mack McCormick accused folklorists of ignoring or censoring "the vast number of prison songs that graphically describe the enforced homosexuality of modern penal systems," mentioning "a version of *Stackolee* which describes a duel between two tough convicts over possession of a favorite punk."[78] The popular "Big Rock Candy Mountain" was originally about a hobo tempting a "punk" to join him on the road, and John Lomax collected a prison parody of a 1903 waltz hit, "Under the Anheuser Bush," about a tramp who was caught sodomizing a boy on a flatcar: *"When the train pulled into town / Eli had it up his brown / Up in his round-eyeser bush."*[79] If more collectors had asked about that kind of material or record producers had seen a market for it, we might have a quite different picture.

It may be significant that the "Anheuser Bush" parody and Bentley's "Alice Blue Gown" were naughty twists on popular waltzes and nothing like them survives in blues or jazz settings, but two examples are not a foundation for broad theories, and it is possible that Morton, Jackson, Lorenzo Staulz, Ann Cook, or Lucille Bogan sang similarly graphic verses about man-with-man action when the audience or situation was right. Much as I value Morton's Library sessions and McKinney's private files, their uniqueness is a reminder of how much has been lost, and I can only guess at how typical the surviving scraps may be, or how well they represent the lives of the people who sang and heard them. At best, they are windows on worlds we can never visit, fogged and scratched, but challenging us to look beyond the glass.

~ seven ~

The Murder Ballad

I **began this book** with Jelly Roll Morton's "Murder Ballad," a generic title for a performance that is simultaneously generic, unique, and something of a mystery. By far the longest narrative blues on record, it should be longer still: the recording starts at the end of an instrumental chorus, and the first verse picks up a story already in progress. We don't know how it began or how many verses Morton sang before Lomax started the machine—which in itself is puzzling, since it is the only performance that was treated so cavalierly. Perhaps Lomax and Morton were discussing what they would record next, Morton began demonstrating a narrative ballad in twelve-bar blues form, and Lomax decided to record it in midperformance—but if Lomax considered it important enough to preserve, why didn't he ask Morton to start again from the beginning? Perhaps it was a technical glitch; Lomax could have thought he was recording and, by the time he noticed there was a problem, did not want to break Morton's mood. Whatever the reason, that missing section is a reminder that neither of them was intent on preserving a full song. What they were preserving was a process: the way an experienced practitioner could weave an epic narrative.

Folklorists in the early twentieth century were fascinated by the improvisational facility of Black singers. White ballad singers were celebrated for their ability to recall lyrics learned and preserved over generations; their performances inevitably varied, but most did their best to repeat what they had heard from previous singers, and the results were valued as historical artifacts. Some Black singers did the same, but others were noted for their ability to extemporize verses to even the most familiar ballads. The Lomaxes wrote that Moses "Clear Rock" Platt, a seventy-year-old singer they recorded on a Texas prison farm in 1933, could spin infinite versions of "Barbara Allen," the most widespread British ballad, interspersing verses from other songs and making up new ones to suit his mood and imagination. Alan wrote in his first published paper that Platt "sang to Father Version A, and to me Version B, very much changed. When we wrote back for more, he sent us a new song, Version C. Only two weeks ago, when we visited him again, he sang us Version D."[1]

Some folklorists saw that sort of variation as a deficiency. They were looking for the earliest, purest form of each ballad, and many singers affirmed that ideal by saying they were singing exactly what they heard from their elders, with every name and turn of phrase intact. John Lomax pioneered a new sensibility when he argued that cowboy ballads, though recent creations, were as folklorically valid as the European epics of previous centuries, and he was similarly enthusiastic about Platt's creativity, writing: "Although ballad scholars will probably call him a poor informant . . . his claim to have 'composed' every song he sings is literally true, for he has no need for a set sequence of verses to be sung or even for a pattern to follow."[2] He suggested Platt was a sort of African American Homer, with a store of lyrics "equal in continuous length to the *Iliad*"[3]:

He did not sing any song through. Always I had to stop him and ask for another tune. Nor did he hesitate for a word. If he ever forgot (I could not discover), his quick invention supplied a word or line without a moment's hesitation and in the spirit and rhythm of the song he was singing.

He sang a new version of *The Old Chizzum Trail*, an endless ballad describing the experiences of a band of cowboys driving a herd of Texas longhorn cattle from Texas to Montana. One of his cowboys, riding an unruly horse, was thrown and left hanging on the limb of a tree along the trail. Clear-Rock sang four stanzas describing this incident and then ended his song.

"That's rather hard on that cowboy," I suggested, "to go on up the trail and leave him sprawling on a limb in what is doubtless an uncomfortable position."

"Lemme git him down, boss; I'll git him down!" And at once he sang in perfect tune:

Cowboy lyin' in a tree a-sprawlin',
Come a little wind an' down he come a-fallin'.
Coma ti-yi yippy, yippy yea, yippy yea . . . [4]

Though thrilled by Platt's limitless facility, the Lomaxes added that, along with "some wonderful verses . . . this improvisation, naturally produces some fearful things."[5] That was potentially a problem, since they not only wanted to preserve vanishing folklore but to make a broad public aware of its value. Their solution was to preserve their unedited fieldwork in archives, while publishing revisions and compilations that would excite the attention and admiration not only of scholars but of ordinary listeners and singers—as well as inspiring politicians and foundations to fund further collecting, preservation, and publication. In 1933 they secured a contract with the Macmillan company for an ambitious book of American folk songs and made an extensive trip around the South in search of Black singers to supplement the large body of material John and other researchers had collected from white informants.

The Lomaxes would work together off and on for the next ten years, but they were from different generations and held somewhat opposing views of their mission. John was a white southerner of an older generation, and if his political views were relatively liberal, his work as a folklorist was essentially conservative and apolitical. Alan, by contrast, was an enthusiastic leftist who saw the effort to document working-class history and culture as a way of giving voice to the voiceless. Each felt he had a special affinity with Black southerners and could understand them in deep and significant ways—even, given their oppressed state, in ways they might not understand themselves—but Alan also saw himself as a conduit for Black pride and protest. Along with those ideals and impulses, he was a bright eighteen-year-old making his first journey into a mysterious, fascinating world. He wrote glowingly about his first experiences recording Black rural singers, but also about his frustration at their hesitancy to perform "sinful" songs at collecting sessions and his eagerness to get to New Orleans, "where we knew vice of all sorts flourishes, and where, accordingly, we hoped to record the songs and ballads that the country Negro was so reluctant to sing for us." [6]

STACKOLEE

THAT SENTENCE FORESHADOWED THE RECORDINGS LOMAX MADE WITH Morton, but I was surprised when I first read it, because I thought of him as primarily interested in rural music, and of the Morton sessions as exceptional rather than fulfilling an early aim. The concept of "folk music" grew out of European notions of pastoral peasants preserving a purer, older culture that city dwellers had abandoned and forgotten, and the Lomaxes devoted the vast majority of their collecting to rural singers and musicians. Blues historians have generally followed the trail they blazed, tracing the music's evolution from field hollers and back-country guitarists to urban pianists and jazz bands, and most continue to describe rural artists as playing older, purer styles even when the players are clearly copying records from Chicago or Los Angeles.

Ballads had a special place in folklore scholarship, honored as deep expressions of national culture and history. Early collectors traveled to Appalachia in search of British ballads, on the logic that people isolated in mountain hamlets might preserve songs and lyrics that had been forgotten in their industrialized homeland, and tended to regard local compositions as feeble imitations of the classic form, like the "broadside ballads" composed and cheaply printed for sale by urban hacks. When John Lomax claimed the noble mantle of balladry for the cowboy and outlaw songs of the American West, that went along with a claim of native virtue, equating their free-living, pioneering spirit with lost ages of chivalric knights and gallant highlanders. When he expanded that interest to include the Black ballad tradition, he favored rural singers and tended to date the most popular and widespread examples to the 1870s or 1880s, placing them alongside the white ballads of Jesse James and Billy the Kid. The Lomaxes began their 1934 collection, *American Ballads and Folk-Songs*, with "John Henry," a heroic ballad that Alan framed as a declaration of racial equality with its ringing cry, "A man ain't nothin' but a man"—but which also promoted the value of traditional manly labor over mechanization.

The Lomaxes were part of a new generation of scholars who accepted recent songs from rural or working-class communities as extending a folk continuum. When John began collecting Black folklore in the 1910s, he asked newspaper readers to send him not only songs of the "cotton patch" but also versions of more recent ballads like "Stagalee" and "Frankie and Albert."[7] He referred to Stagalee as a "desperado" in the Wild West outlaw tradition and was far less interested in Black urbanites, but times were changing. As James Weldon Johnson wryly noted in the preface to his 1922 anthology, *American Negro Poetry*, "a Negro in a log cabin is more picturesque than a Negro in a Harlem flat, but the Negro in the Harlem flat is here, and he is but part of a group growing everywhere in the country, a group whose ideals are becoming increasingly more vital than those of the traditionally artistic group."[8] Alan was ripe for that message; he shared his father's interest in older traditions but was thrilled to discover songs that expressed the modern, vital voice of the urban proletariat.

When Alan asked Morton to "tell us about old Stagolee," he was revisiting a standard gambit from the 1933 trip. At one of their first stops, on a plantation near Huntsville, Texas, he started a song-collecting session by asking "if there was anyone present who could sing 'Stagolee,' the famous ballad of the Memphis bad man." A month later, after recording some track-lining chants outside Wiergate, Texas, he asked if the work leader knew any songs like "Stagolee." Finally, wandering the streets of New Orleans with a typewriter under his arm, he was drawn by the sound of a piano to "a dim-lit, dirty" barroom, and "for the hundredth time I asked the question: 'Do you know the song about that bad man, Stagolee?'"[9]

The Lomaxes' initial experience of New Orleans had been disappointing. They made a first excursion into the city's "dives and joints" accompanied by "a brace of city detectives to serve as a card of admittance and a guaranty that we were all right," with the result that each place emptied as they entered.[10] Alan made a second attempt on his own but wrote that when he met a guitarist named Billy Williams and asked for some "old-time Negro songs," Williams responded:

"I knows what you wants. You wants to make records of my singin' an' play 'em over de radio en so nobody will ever wanter hear me play again 'cause den ev'body'll know de songs dat I knows an' den where am I at? Des' like you says, dey ain' many of us folks what knows de ole songs lef', an' dat's what makes me my livin'. Dat's de way I sees it—a cole cash proposition . . . Every minute I picks de geetar, every note I sings, is wuth money to me. How much do I git?"

Lomax described this attitude as "calculating," apparently seeing no parallel to his father's efforts to get more funding from the Library of Congress and their recently signed contract with Macmillan. As for his choice to present Williams's speech in stereotyped minstrel dialect, it fit the standard practice of many writers on vernacular culture—including many Black writers—but also suggests the gap between his dream of serving as a conduit for the voice of the Black proletariat and his ability to shake off the prejudices of his time and background. Black urbanites did not treat him with the deference of their country cousins, and although in theory he might admire their refusal to kowtow to white folks, he did not enjoy being personally snubbed or stymied. To make matters worse, he had been suffering from an intermittent fever and persistent cough, his father was hospitalized with malaria, he was on his own in a strange city, and he felt increasingly stuck and frustrated. As he wrote in a letter:

> I haven't heard a nigger sing all week. I've ransacked the town, scoured the barrel-houses, the redlight district, the French Quarter, the steamboat docks, the Creole section, and always there's a singer and always she's just around the corner, just stepped across the street, or, if I find him, just too busy.[11]

That was his mood when he made another foray into a Black neighborhood, asked the barroom piano player about Stagolee, and finally got the response he had been looking for: "Wid a little mo' gin in me, I kin remember ev'ything that Stack did and make up some mo'." Lomax gave the pianist's name as Sullivan Rock—official records have Rocks, but Professor Longhair, who credited him as a primary influence, likewise called him Rock[12]—and wrote that he seemed a bit puzzled, saying: "But what you want to hear dat song fer?" Lomax indicated the typewriter, saying he was collecting "old-timey songs" and "I want to put you down on record."

"Well, dat's diffunt," Rock responded. "You makes a recort and we splits de profit." He called for the bartender to bring another bottle on Lomax's tab, and, after passing it to "two of his favorite girl friends," began to sing:

> *Way down in New Orleans, called de Lyon club*
> *Every step you walkin' you walkin' in Billy Lyon blood.*

Over the next few hours, as they drifted from the original bar to an after-hours joint and a private home where they could continue at leisure, Rock provided Lomax with an epic narrative in which Billy Lyon won Stackerlee's Stetson hat in a cotch game, Stack went home and got his gun, came back and shot Lyon, was hunted down and shot by Police Chief

Maloney, survived to be sentenced to the Angola penitentiary, escaped and was recaptured, survived an execution by hanging but was shot again by Maloney, was buried with an expensive funeral, and finally *"took his big pistol an put [it] on de shelf / Took de pitch fork fum de devil say, 'I'm put in charge of Hell myself.'"*

At least, that is what is preserved in the earliest typescript of Rock's ballad. When Lomax wrote about their meeting a few months later, he credited Rock with some verses from that version along with some he had transcribed from another New Orleanian named Alexander Wells and a couple he and his father got from Ivory Joe Hunter, an eighteen-year-old pianist they met in Wiergate. He wrote that Rock sang forty-one verses, but his original transcripts included thirty-two from Rock, thirty-five from Wells, ten from Hunter, and sixteen from a New Orleans singer named Alexander Lyons, and the larger number instead fit the compilation the Lomaxes published the following year in *American Ballads and Folk Songs*. He was fairly open about this process, explaining that the book did not have space for more than one or two versions of each song, so, for example, he gathered all the versions of "John Henry" he could find and "spent a delightful week making a composite."[13] That was a common practice among ballad scholars: responsible collectors kept transcripts of each version they heard but compiled their own "jury texts" for publication, on the logic that oral tradition-bearers had done the same for generations, every collected version was only what one singer sang in one instance, and the demands of print publication were better served by presenting an edited ideal.

Ignoring broader issues of race and power, that approach was a reasonable extension of the oral tradition. If Lomax had asked Rock or Wells to spend a week going over versions of "Stackolee" and compiling an ideal text, and had provided a reasonable stipend for the work, they presumably would have come up with something different than what they sang for him in New Orleans and it would probably have been longer and more logically ordered than either's impromptu performance. However, no one was going to make such an offer to Rock or Wells, and along with assembling composite texts, Lomax exercised his creativity in ways that underlined that discrepancy. An introductory note to "Stagolee" reshaped the singers' identities to suggest a typical range of informants: it identified Hunter as "Ivy Joe White, barrel-house pianist extraordinary"; placed Wells in the Louisiana State Prison at Angola, though the field notes gave his location as New Orleans; and described Rock as a "rounder and roustabout on the docks of New Orleans," though nothing in Rock's biography suggests he was a dockworker and at the time Alan had lamented that "the river packets are gone and with them the singing roustabouts."[14]

Those kinds of discrepancies and stereotyping were not unique to the Lomaxes; many song compilers played far looser with their ascriptions and painted more stereotyped or demeaning pictures of their sources. I can trace the Lomaxes' choices and alterations because they were unusually scrupulous, preserving their original fieldwork, letters, and drafts and making all of that material available to later researchers. Nor is my point simply that collectors had access to power and funding their sources lacked. That was true, but the basic concept of *folklore* required that singers and songs be understood as representing larger communities and bodies of knowledge. The Lomaxes had only a few months to prepare a collection of American folk songs and wanted to give a broad sense of Black southern culture, so their notes on "Stagolee" combined the names of some specific singers with backgrounds that suggested the range of men who performed the song—a sleight of hand that made sense if one thought of the singers as archetypes rather than individuals.

I owe a huge debt to the Lomaxes, and to Alan in particular, but we cannot understand his career and the process through which he collected, preserved, and published an astonishing wealth of material without recognizing that his first work as a folklorist was a project in which a white teenager was given exceptional responsibility for presenting the vernacular culture of the Black South and the results were flavored by his enthusiasms, his prejudices, and, at times, his fantasies. He described his meeting with Rock as the culmination of a nighttime odyssey through the bowels of Black New Orleans, first "in the company of a pimp" who hustled him for drink money, then on his own, passing the dead body of a fifteen-year-old boy who had been stabbed with an ice pick, watching two men fight over a girl, and eventually trailing Rock through a succession of low dives, until "by three-thirty I had written down all the boy knew about Stack Lee." Rock was twenty-one, three years older than Lomax, but few white readers would have found anything problematic about that sentence.

The Lomaxes could assume most of their readers would be white, and although they consistently framed "Stagolee" as a Black outlaw ballad, by the 1930s it was also well known in white society. In 1905 a white actress named Allie Spooner featured it in her performances of "illustrated songs," and a version with many of the standard verses was published in 1910 as "Stack-O-Lee (A True Story from Life)," credited to the bizarrely named Three White Kuhns, a trio of German American brothers from Nebraska, who modestly claimed only to have "re-written" the words and music. It was recorded multiple times as a serio-comic pop song, and naughtier variants were current in men's clubs and college fraternities, with salacious lyrics about pimping and whores. A seventeen-verse version in *Immortalia*, an anonymous collection from 1927, included the familiar *"She got a nice clean crib down behind the jail. / She hung a sign upon her door, 'Fresh fish for sale,'"* with the tag line, *"She'd get the dough for Stackolee!"* That verse had obvious connections to Black tradition, but not specifically to the Stackolee ballad, and a man named Bill Nice described hearing a dirty version of the song from a "hill-billy sort of person" he met in 1913–1914 while touring with a Wild West show and suggested, "the smutty lines may have been introduced to make it appeal to a rough crowd." Palmer Jones sang a version he dated to Memphis in 1903 that referred to the hero as *"that hip-shakin back-breakin sweet-fuckin papa Stackerlee,"* but the surviving typescript is a copy of the handwritten text he gave a fan in Paris a quarter century later, with some added verses from the white pianist Les Copeland, and that line may have been added as spice for white expatriates.[15]

Cecil Brown wrote that his uncles in South Carolina recited "rhymed, obscene praise of Stagolee's badness" in the 1950s, and the raw language and aggressive posturing of the Stackolee toasts have often been cited as presaging gangsta rap. The earliest surviving toast texts are from the 1940s and avoid outright obscenities, but I assume Brown was right when he suggested they were "heavily censored." One of the couplets Alexander Wells sang for Alan Lomax went, *"Stagolee tol' Mrs. Billy, 'Ef you don't b'lieve your man is dead / Come to de barroom, see de hole I shot in his head,"* and he may well have softened the second line, which in later toasts tended to be phrased, *"Go down there and count them holes in his motherfucking head."*[16] When I suggest the Stackolee ballad may have been dirtied up for white consumption, I am not ignoring the possibility that there were equally dirty versions circulating in Black culture—but in the absence of evidence, I don't want to take that for granted. The analogy to rap is a reminder that sex and violence have often been marketed to white audiences with stereotyped images of savage Blackness, and Black communities have always enjoyed a wide and evolving range of musical styles, using varied language and suiting varied tastes.

As far as I know, none of the many Black versions of "Barbara Allen" included any rough words, and there is no reason to assume the early Black murder ballads used rawer language than white murder ballads. "Stack Lee" Shelton shot William Lyons in a St. Louis saloon on Christmas morning in 1895, when Ferdinand Morton was five years old, Mamie Desdunes was fifteen, and Buddy Bolden had not yet formed a band. Blues and jazz were on the horizon, but Black music was changing rapidly and virtually everyone described both styles as emerging over the next few years and drawing on an infinite range of previous music, from cornfield hollers to cotillions. Lyrics were influenced by a similarly wide range of sources, from the deepest African and European traditions to the popular story-poems of Rudyard Kipling, Robert W. Service, and their myriad imitators.

The earliest surviving lyric of "Stackolee" is from 1897, when the *Kansas City Star* ran an article about the songs of prisoners in the city jail. It was sung to a melody the writer found "peculiarly touching," and included some details that would remain standard, like Shelton's Stetson hat and a bullet going through Lyons and breaking a looking glass, along with a suggestion of police corruption and some characters who disappeared in later versions: Shelton's lawyer, Nat Dryden, and a witness or accomplice named Charlie Mann.

Along with some songs heard from white prisoners, the article included three other ballads from Black singers, two of which were about local cases and had lines redolent of Victorian magazine poetry, portraying a pair of condemned men *"Thinking of their sad fate / While the hours are passing, / Fleeting one by one"* and describing a man named Phil Martin falling through the hangman's trap *"like an arrow from a bow."* That style of composition seems to have largely disappeared from Black urban culture in the early twentieth century—or at least was ignored by folklorists and recording companies—but the moralizing chorus of the Martin ballad turned up thirty years later on a record by a local blues singer named Lottie Kimbrough: *"Boys, O boys, take my advice, / Quit your gamblin' an' a shootin' dice / From bad company you must shun / From policemen you must run."*[17]

DUNCAN AND BRADY

FOLKLORISTS HAVE OFTEN TRIED TO DISTINGUISH AUTHENTIC ORAL CULture from material learned from print sources or modeled on literary styles, and that distinction may be useful in some contexts, but it obscures deep overlaps and connections. Black schoolchildren memorized and performed the same poems white children learned, along with the works of Black literary poets like Paul Laurence Dunbar—in a regionally relevant example, Chuck Berry's brother was named after Dunbar, and Berry sometimes ended his rock 'n' roll concerts by reciting "Even This Shall Pass Away," a dolorous homily composed by a white poet named Theodore Tilton in the 1860s, which he recalled his father declaiming in his St. Louis youth.[18] As with Morton's performance of Verdi, the exceptional thing about this recitation is not that Berry knew the poem and regarded it as part of his heritage—there were plenty of Black people who played classical music and recited literary verse—but that it was preserved.

The *Kansas City Star* article coupled "Stackolee" with "another song from the St. Louis prisons that is a favorite," quoting four verses and noting that the full ballad included "more than a dozen" and was set to "such a slow-going time that it takes a negro about half an hour to sing it through."[19] Usually remembered as "Duncan and Brady," this song was collected from numerous singers in later years, and told about the shooting of an Irish immigrant policeman named James Brady by a Black man named William Henry Harrison Duncan, which made news from coast to coast in 1890 and led to several years of high-profile trials, retrials, and appeals. It described the key event succinctly:

Brady walked up to the bar,
Showed Duncan his shinin' star,
Says to Duncan, "You're under arrest;"
Duncan put a hole in Brady's breast.

Like Stack Lee, the Duncan portrayed in ballads was a fast-shooting desperado, so I was surprised to find a front-page drawing and article in the *St. Louis Post-Dispatch* following his execution that showed him lying in state and described him in quite different terms:

Duncan was one of the most popular colored men in St. Louis. He was a sport, a jolly fellow, a swell dresser, a ladies' favorite, but, above all, he was a magnificent singer. . . . They all say there never was a colored basso like him in town and few in the country who could outclass him.[20]

Friends recalled him winning a competition against the bass vocalist of the McCabe and Young minstrel troupe, singing the spiritual "Brother Daniel," and Henry Massey, a fellow bass and the colored lightweight boxing champion of Missouri, said Duncan performed for several years as a member of the popular Climax Quartette and his favorite song was "The Old Sexton," a deep-voiced specialty composed in 1841 by the British baritone Henry Russell. Massey was a tough guy outside the ring, arrested in 1889 after bashing Lee Shelton with a brick, and killed in 1895 by Nelson Casey, whose wife was a stepdaughter of Billy Lyons.[21] It was a small world, brutally segregated and often violent, but although the songs that made it enduringly famous tend to be associated with rural blues singers, Duncan's story is a reminder that rough characters and milieus do not always prefer or produce the art we might expect. The week after Duncan's execution, Massey provided the *Post-Dispatch* with a sixteen-verse poem that his friend had apparently composed and smuggled out of the death cell, titled "Harry Duncan's Misfortune" and detailing the writer's trials and tribulations. It began:

> *Kind friends, I have something to tell you.*
> *Pay attention, one and all,*
> *While I tell you all what happened*
> *Since the night I met my downfall.*

And ended:

> *Now, friends, I could not be guilty*
> *Of such a beastly crime,*
> *And though some may believe me guilty*
> *The truth will come out in time.*[22]

There was a long tradition in Britain and the United States of first-person lyrics ascribed to condemned men and women and supposedly written on the eve of their execution. This one may legitimately have been written by Duncan, but most were commercial "broadside ballads," composed by itinerant bards and sold at fairs, in stationer's shops and stalls, and on the street. At the turn of the twentieth century, this trade was common in Black communities: Newman Ivey White wrote of "those half-folk composers, the 'ballet' writers, who come into printing offices with doggerel verses penciled on ruled tablet paper and, paying cash and often giving no name, order printed broadsides, which are sung and sold wherever there is a gathering of Negroes."[23]

Some broadsheet lyrics were religious or romantic, some were composed about current news events, and White was not the only person to suggest that such single-sheet compositions were a source of songs that survived in oral tradition. In 1942, when Frankie Baker brought a defamation suit against Universal Studios for a film based on "Frankie and Johnny"—another St. Louis story, inspired by her shooting of Allen Britt in 1899—Nathan B. Young, a lawyer who doubled as unofficial historian of the local Black community, testified that the song was originally the work of a "barroom poet" named Bill Dooley who "improvised ballads on current news events" and would "sell his compositions on the streets of St. Louis at 10 cents a copy."[24]

No one has found any broadsheet originals for the St. Louis murder ballads, but they could easily have been lost; the city had two Black newspapers by the 1890s, the *Palladium* and the *American Eagle*—the former with a staff poet who chronicled local happenings—and the earliest surviving copy of either is from the 1900s.[25] If St. Louis was a center for topical broadsides, that could explain why it was the source of the three most popular Black murder ballads—"Stackolee," "Duncan and Brady," and "Frankie and Johnny"—as well as the ballad of Ollie Jackson, which was collected in Indiana, Virginia, and Mississippi and had a moralizing chorus, *"When you lose your money, learn to lose,"* that turned up in some versions of "Stackolee."[26] If those songs were originally composed for sale as broadsides, they presumably would have been phrased in the relatively sedate language of commercial publication rather than the raw speech of saloons, work gangs, and prisons.

Since I have devoted much of this book to recovering raw songs and language, it would be easy to read that last sentence as a value judgment, juxtaposing the true voice of the Black underclass with the stifled and censored language of print—but Duncan's story complicates that framing. His lawyer, Walter M. Farmer, was the first Black graduate of Washington University Law School and one of the organizers of a Negro Day of Prayer against lynching, and he made the Duncan case something of a cause célèbre. Frederick Douglass had made a widely publicized statement that "other men besides Anarchists can be goaded into making and throwing bombs," and when the *Post-Dispatch* asked Farmer what he thought of this, he responded that he did not "believe in dynamite or in any form of lawlessness or exercise of criminal force," but added:

> Patience has its limits, and it may be that the patience of the negro race in America has become exhausted at last. . . . When a race is subjected to such outlawry . . . what can be the final logical outcome of such a situation except that, finally despairing of protection under the law, the race so oppressed takes the law into its own hands? [27]

The article did not mention Duncan, but local readers would have been aware that Farmer had recently won a new trial for a Black man convicted of shooting a white police officer, and over the next year he took the case to the Missouri Supreme Court, becoming the first Black lawyer to argue before that body, and made a further appeal to a justice of the US Supreme Court. Community leaders formed a Duncan Relief Fund Association and in June 1894, with his execution looming, newspapers reported that the judge who tried his case had written to the governor expressing "the gravest kind of doubt about his guilt" and an appeal for clemency had been "signed by hundreds of reputable citizens." [28] There was credible evidence that the actual shooter was Charles Starkes, who owned the saloon where the killing occurred, and even reports that Starkes, who died shortly before Duncan was executed, had made a deathbed confession.

In an earlier defense, Farmer argued that one of Brady's fellow officers, John Gaffney, had been harassing customers outside the saloon, Duncan entered the bar to avoid a confrontation, Brady pursued him, and Duncan shot in self-defense. There was a long history of police harassment in the neighborhood, and Duncan's brother Luther, who owned a barbershop next to Starkes's place, had also been involved and may have cracked Gaffney's head with a pool cue. The *St. Louis Republic* headlined its story "A Bloody Battle: Desperate Affray Between Police and Negroes," and soon Black carousers were confronting police patrols with a mocking ditty:

Officer Brady is dead and gone,
Officer Gaffney has lost his gun,
We will now have lots of fun,
In Charley Stark's saloon.

Or, in some versions:

Brady's dead and Gaffney's down,
We'll get busy in this town.
Chase the policemen off the beat,
Chase the white folks off the street.

This verse was sometimes capped with a hearty chorus of "Ta-ra-ra boom-de-ay," and Starkes provided an additional layer of satire when he was arrested for singing it and claimed the officers were mistaken and he had actually been singing "John Brown's Body."[29]

BABE AND THE BULLY

W. C. Handy arrived in St. Louis with a vocal quartet in 1893, spent several months working odd jobs and sleeping on the cobblestones of the levee, and recalled "Brady, He's Dead and Gone" as one of a pair of songs that "grew out of the brutality of the police" in nearby Black neighborhoods. Historians have generally assumed this was a version of the "Duncan and Brady" ballad, since most were unaware of the anti-police street chant, and they may have been similarly misled about the other song, which Handy recalled as "Looking for the Bully."[30] This has generally been treated as an early sighting of the song published in 1895 as "The New Bully" and remembered as "Bully of the Town," but there were other bully songs and Handy was not the only person who mentioned a variant being sung as a protest against police brutality. In 1910 a St. Louis detective recalled that Brady's killing inspired "a negro comedian" to write a song called "A Bully Gone to Rest" and "it came to be dangerous for a negro to sing that song, or even to whistle the tune, when a policeman was within hearing."[31]

"The New Bully" was also published as "May Irwin's Bully Song" in honor of the white "coon shouter" who made it famous, and Handy and James Weldon Johnson both cited it as one of the hits by white songwriters that inspired them to adapt Black folk material.[32] A San Francisco newspaper columnist and horse-racing expert named Charles Trevathan was usually credited as the song's "originator if not the author," and he was open about the process of creation, saying he was visiting his family home in Tennessee and "heard a negro boy humming . . . a sort of improvised melody such as you have often heard negroes sing if you have ever been South," with the lyric:

> *When you see me comin' hist your windows high,*
> *When you see me goin' hang your heads and sigh.*
> *For dar's only one boss Bully an' you bet dat's me.*[33]

Back in San Francisco, he said that he hummed this verse to his frequent companion, a mandolin-playing "colored boy" named Cooley, who helped him shape it into an organized twelve-bar melody; added a chorus by "ragging" the tune of a sentimental British song, "The Maid of Athens"; and brought the result to a comedian named Ferris Harman, who performed it, apparently in blackface, in a burlesque adaptation of *Robinson Crusoe*.[34] In some tellings Irwin was passing through town and heard it; in others Trevathan sent it to her in New York or taught it to her on a train. Either way, she inserted it into her new play, *The Widow Jones*, and it became an international hit.

Cooley seems to have been a real person but also functioned as an archetype. Like the "negro ostler" who provided Thomas Rice with the tune and dance steps of "Jim Crow" in the 1820s, the "little colored boy" who was rumored to be feeding ragtime tunes to Irving Berlin in the 1910s, and inumerable unnamed men and women cited by song collectors over the years, he served as a stand-in for a generalized Black folk culture.[35] Some early articles portrayed him as a skilled musician who polished Trevathan's raw gleanings for public performance, but later writers typically described him as "a young negro boy" who would pick up ditties "in the more disreputable resorts of his race . . . and play them over to his employer, who would transcribe them and rewrite the words in order to suit them to polite ears."[36]

The "Bully" character likewise shifted to fit familiar stereotypes. Handy recalled him as a brutal white cop—policemen were often called "bulls"—but the cover illustration for Irwin's hit showed a Black ruffian wielding a razor, and most of its Tin Pan Alley sequels followed suit. As the song fed back into oral tradition, the anonymous Bully merged with real-life figures: Lee Shelton shot Billy Lyons just as the song was taking off, and lines from it were recycled in versions of the "Stackolee" ballad, sometimes making Stack the tough bully, sometimes merging Billy with Bully as his nemesis. Further afield, Huddie "Lead Belly" Ledbetter sang a ballad about the 1894 murder of Ella Speed in New Orleans with a verse in which the police went *"Lookin' for that bully, but he couldn't be found"*; the Lomaxes recorded a prisoner in the Tennessee State Penitentiary singing about an 1897 murder with the opening line *"Louis Collins was a bully in the town"*; and a 1927 recording by Henry "Ragtime Texas" Thomas blended a ballad about an 1899 murder by a man named Bob McKinney with some bully verses to the tune of "Make Me a Pallet on the Floor."

That list highlights a curious fact. Virtually all the Black murder ballads that were widely sung in later years date from the 1890s, and the most popular ones survived in versions that used variants of the twelve-bar form popularized by "The Bully": a rhyming couplet followed by a repeated tag line. This form was already around—the song Trevathan recalled hearing in Tennessee used it—but became far more popular over the next decade and has been cited as an immediate precursor and model for the twelve-bar blues, which likewise has two matching lines and a culminating third. In that formulation, Morton's "Murder Ballad" can be seen as a missing link, a late example of the Black ballad form and an early example of the new blues.

In a pattern that would become increasingly familiar, ballads that were falling out of fashion in Black communities by the twentieth century remained popular with white singers as nostalgic artifacts of the "naughty nineties." With the closing of the old vice districts and the passage of Prohibition, the 1890s were increasingly recalled as a wild, free, and joyously decadent time, and writers regularly traced ragtime's birth to the dives of San Francisco's Barbary Coast and the brothels of St. Louis—an origin myth presaging the later association of jazz with Storyville. A story from 1906 told how Irwin heard "The Bully" while "slumming" in San Francisco, "the 'Moulin Rouge' of America," with lyrics that "were decidedly risque and not fit for publication"; made a deal with "the negro composer, who also officiated at the piano . . . [and] the New Bully revised, and made chaste, was given to the world."[37] In an alternate version, Trevathan heard the song performed with "unmentionable words" in "Babe Connors' resort . . . that infamous St. Louis bordello where the redoubtable Mama Lou nightly regaled a tough throng with her raucous singing"; hesitated to sing it for Irwin because the words "weren't fit for the ears of a lady"; but eventually "filtered the muck out of the 'lyrics'," and a hit was born.[38]

Like Cooley, Connor and Mama Lou were real people who became mythic stand-ins for the Black roots of white favorites. An article from 1899 traced the "veritable volley of rag time and other oddities of negro composition and phraseology" to "a pretty Creole woman in St. Louis called 'Babe' Connors, who keeps a little café and music hall" where "the river boatmen and colored sports of the whole South and West," gathered around the piano and entertained one another with "the whole musical product of darkeydom below Mason and Dixon's line."[39]

In reality, Sarah "Babe" Connor's establishment was a three-story building known as the Castle, with crystal chandeliers, fashionable bedroom and parlor suites, and five "elegant" pianos—and, like the Basin Street mansions and Vina Fields's place in Chicago, served a strictly white clientele.[40] An article from 1894 reported that "the mahogany-colored proprietress and her coterie of saffron-hued cyprians make night hideous in their revels, and in the broad glare of the day display themselves at the windows . . . and the nightly debauches are beyond the power of description."[41] The house pianists included Tom Turpin, whose "Harlem Rag" was the first published ragtime piece by a Black composer, and some recollections included women dancing without undergarments on a mirrored floor, but the most memorable entertainer was Mama Lou, a stout, dark-skinned woman who performed in stereotyped "mammy" garb, with a calico dress, gingham apron, and a bandana on her head, singing lyrics that were notably obscene.[42]

Connor was apparently born in or near Nashville in 1857 and was running a brothel in St. Louis by the 1880s. When she died in 1899 an obituary in the *Post-Dispatch* painted her as a secret saint who helped the needy and sent two nieces to be educated in a convent, but other stories were less complimentary: in 1886 she was arrested during a visit to Nashville for "attempting to abduct Rebecca McGregor (colored) for the purpose of leading a sinful life," with the additional accusation that McGregor had brought a charge of rape against two local men and the abduction was "to prevent her appearance as a witness"; and in 1892 she was ejected from the St. Louis railroad depot for attempting to prevent the departure of an eighteen-year-old woman she called her "niece," who denied the relationship and was trying to escape a "life of shame."[43] Louise "Mama Lou" Rogers was born in St. Louis in 1862, worked with Connor throughout the 1890s, and took over the business for a few years after Connor's death, then opened her own establishment, where an article from 1912 described her inviting investigators into the parlor and singing several songs.[44]

The song first and most frequently associated with Connor and Rogers was "Ta-ra-ra Boom-de-ay," an emblematic hit of the naughty nineties that was typically performed with winking lyrics and a high kick or rump bump to accent the *"boom."* Though it lacked the rhythmic or melodic elements usually associated with Black styles and some writers traced it to European sources, most early reports suggested it "originated in a questionable colored resort in New Orleans"; was an old plantation melody that had "been heard for many years in the dance-houses of New Orleans, Mobile, [and] Covington, Ky"; or even came from the Kru people of West Africa, who "were magnificent sailors" and sang it as a hauling shanty, whence it reached the docks of New Orleans, Mahogany Hall on Basin Street, and eventually "a negress in St. Louis."[45] W. C. Handy wrote that it was "credited to a white composer who some years later told me that he had first gotten it from a colored piano player and drummer in the red light district in St. Louis," adding: "Possibly it was false pride that years ago restrained Negro composers of ability to write down such ditties."[46]

By the turn of the century plenty of Black composers were reworking vernacular melodies into popular hits, and some of the most expert were based in St. Louis, including Turpin, Louis Chauvin, Joe Jordan, and Scott Joplin. All of those men played in brothels, and according to one writer, "you could hear Joplin's latest compositions at Babe Connors' before he had set them down on paper"[47]—though I would suggest the main link between Joplin and Connor is the "you" of that sentence, which invited white readers to imagine themselves hearing a legendary Black musician in a legendary site of white male pleasure.

The legend of Connor and Mama Lou expanded over time: in the 1890s they were named as sources of "Ta-ra-ra Boom-de-ay"; by the turn of the century Connor's establishment was recalled as the birthplace of "A Hot Time in the Old Town Tonight"; and by the 1940s it was common to read that Trevathan first heard "The Bully" there.[48] A reminiscence from 1937 described the pianist Ignace Paderewski visiting the Castle and credited Mama Lou with being "among the first people to sing 'Frankie and Johnny' for entertainment," adding that there was "a tradition that [the ballad] originated in Babe Conners though of course it gathered innumerable stanzas elsewhere," and in 1942 Nathan Young testified that after Bill Dooley composed the lyric, it was set to music and played by pianists at Connor's place.[49]

FRANKIE AND ALBERT

THE STORIES ABOUT PEOPLE SINGING "FRANKIE AND JOHNNY" AT BABE Connor's are a reminder that we should be wary of nostalgic memories, since Connor died in August 1899, two months before Frankie Baker shot

Allen Britt—and a reminder of how much writing about Black music in this period is about songs and situations that interested white people.[50] "Frankie and Johnny" is a good example, since it was about a shooting in the Black sporting world and has often been grouped with other Black murder ballads but seems to have been far more popular with white singers and audiences, often in versions that cast the protagonists as white.

Frankie Baker was born in St. Louis around 1876 and told an interviewer in the 1930s that she began doing sex work in her teens after a messy romantic episode: she fell for a man who turned out to be a pimp, which she learned when his regular "sportin' girl" slashed her in the face, leaving a permanent scar.[51] A brief article from 1896 mentioned her fracturing the skull of a woman named Donnie Foster in a quarrel over a man.[52] Three years later she was living with Allen Britt, a sixteen-year-old piano player, whom one of their neighbors, Richard Clay, recalled as "Albert" and described as "wise for his years but not old enough to be level with any woman. Frankie was ready money. She bought him everything he wanted . . . Then while she was waiting on company he would be out playing around."[53] One of Britt's playmates was an eighteen-year-old sex worker named Alice Pryor, and another neighbor, Mariah Jones, testified that she saw them dancing at a place called the Lone Star Club, adding that they were "very fine waltzers" and she had never seen Baker waltz.[54]

On the fatal night, Baker had finished work and was sleeping in the front room of the apartment she shared with Britt and a streetwalker named Pansy Marvin. Britt came in late and angrily asked what she was doing in that room rather than their bedroom. She said she was sick and needed more air. Then, in her words:

> Allen walked around to the bed and started to cut me like this, twice. I asked him, say are you trying to get me hurt? I don't want to hurt you and I don't want you to hurt me. Best place for you to go is to your mother.
>
> He stood there and cursed me and said he wasn't going any place. I said, "I am boss here, I pay the rent and I have to protect myself." He run his hand in his pocket, his side pocket, opened his knife and started around to this side to cut me.

I was standing here, pillow lays this way, just run my hand under the pillow and shot him and he says, "Oh, you have me." Didn't shoot but one time, standing by the bed.[55]

The killing was ruled a justifiable homicide, and three decades later Baker recalled:

I felt terrible, of course, but I simply had protected myself. I had nothing to cry about. I didn't feel smart about it, either. . . . You know, I was afraid of Albert. He beat me unmercifully a few nights before the big-blow-off. My eye was festered and sore from that lacin' when I went before Judge Clark. He noticed it, too. . . . The judge even gave me back my gun. Don't know what I did with it. Guess I pawned it or gave it away. Everybody carried a gun in those days."[56]

In contrast to the Duncan and Shelton cases, Baker's was barely mentioned in the local press. Presumably it was bigger news in the Black sporting world and some women admired her for standing up to the man who beat and cheated on her. An upstairs neighbor, Tillie Griffin, recalled that no one in the neighborhood thought less of her for it: "Frankie wasn't convicted. And nobody wanted to be fussy about being social with her if she wasn't convicted."

Clay said the ballad was composed shortly after the shooting and "was sung all around town, in the social clubs and on the street."[57] Griffin said she first heard it "about three months after the trouble" and the dead man's name was changed to Johnny because Britt's family "raised a racket"—which Britt's father confirmed, saying he prevented someone from singing it after the funeral.[58] All those recollections were recorded thirty years later, by which time the song was known throughout the country as "Frankie and Albert," "Frankie and Johnny," and a raft of other names: the earliest documented version, collected in the first decade of the twentieth century, was set in Atlanta, began *Lilly was a good girl—ev'ybody knows . . . ,*" and told about her shooting a man named Paul or Pauly; a verse heard in Auburn, Alabama, around 1915 told how "*Susie went down to de barroom, called for a bottle of beer"*; and a version from West Virginia in 1918 began *"Maggie was a lady, a money-making girl,"* and called her lover Walter.[59] Carl Sandburg regularly sang the ballad at public appearances and published five versions in his *American Songbag*, in which women named Frankie, Sadie, and Josie killed men named Albert, Johnny, and Henry Brown.[60] And a singer in Durham, North Carolina, sang, *"Amy was a good woman,"* and described Albert cheating on her *"wid a woman what had blue eyes"*—an interesting twist, obscured by the transcriber's note that other stanzas "cannot be written."[61]

No other ballad circulated with such a variety of names, and many researchers have concluded that Baker's story was grafted onto an earlier family of songs.[62] That would explain why the lyrics bear little relation to the facts of her case: Baker shot Britt at home, in self-defense, and was quickly acquitted, but the song's heroine goes looking for her man, finds him with another woman, shoots him out of jealousy, and in most versions is convicted and executed. It seems unlikely that a song composed in the wake of the killing would have the facts that far wrong, and likely that the surviving versions merged her ballad with other sagas of romantic betrayal and revenge. Most versions included a moralizing tag line, *"He was her man, but he done her wrong,"* but others had *"It's one more rounder gone"* or *"It's all she's got done gone,"* which were also used in a ballad about Delia Green, a young woman murdered in Savannah, Georgia, the year after Baker's affray.[63] A white Kentucky singer named Emry Arthur recorded a long version called "Frankie Baker" in 1929 with a third tag line, *"He didn't come home,"* echoing a song collected from white Tennessee mountain folk in 1905 and recorded by Mississippi John Hurt, about a killer going out looking for his or her lover, and asking at the end of each verse, *"My darlin' baby, why don't yer come home?"*[64]

The shift from "Frankie and Albert" to "Frankie and Johnny" was cemented in white culture when the Leighton Brothers published a tongue-in-cheek adaptation in 1912, adding a catchy ragtime chorus and omitting any racial references, and it became an international hit— the first recording was made that year in London.[65] Most singers continued to use the *"He done her wrong"* tag, but the pop version probably helped shift the mood of the song to rollicking comedy, often spiced with references to Frankie's profession. In 1930 the cartoonist John Held Jr. published an illustrated *Saga of Frankie and Johnny*, with the descriptive verse:

> *Frankie worked down in a crib house,*
> *Worked there without any drawers.*
> *She gave all her money to Johnny*
> *Who spent it on parlor house whores.*

Held's drawings portrayed the characters as white, but he recalled learning the song in his Salt Lake City youth "from a colored piano player, who was called 'Professor' in a parlor house," and that sort of provenance was often provided as a seal of authenticity for naughty white variants.[66] Robert Winslow Gordon's "Inferno" collection included a version from a chapbook of dirty songs current among young men in Berkeley, California, in which Frankie lamented that the funeral procession was *"taking my Johnnie to the cemetery / And they'll never bring his penis back. / Best part of the man / That was doin' me wrong,"* with a note that it was learned "from a man that has played in cafes, and . . . said that is universal among the negroes," and another informant supplied a version supposedly heard "in hop joints up and down the coast . . . mostly sang by colored people and much loved by them as their idea of romance."[67] Vance Randolph provided a backdated version of this provenance, writing that the song had been popular since the 1870s, "in bawdy-houses and at stag dinners, particularly in the south, wherever Negro women served as entertainers. This sort of show consisted mostly of nude dancing and slapstick burlesque, but somewhere in every performance was a yaller gal who could sing about 'Little Frankie,' and how she killed her man when he 'went an' done her wrong.'"[68]

Like "Hesitation Blues," the Frankie ballad was a popular saloon sing-along, with patrons interpolating their own verses and harmonizing on the tag. A New York columnist noted that it was "still a favorite of the speakeasy backroom" in the Prohibition era, writing: "No one seems to know just how many verses there are to the jovial and ribald ditty. But one singer in West 48th street is able to sing 137 verses. And that, no matter how sloshed you are, is almost enough."[69] There were reports of epic versions that traced the protagonists' courtship, marriage, and domestic life before getting to the killing, and continued with verses about Johnny (or Albert) slowly dying in the hospital, Frankie's life in prison, and her eventual execution, funeral, and burial.[70]

Palmer Jones provided a long "Frankie and Albert" lyric along with his version of "Stackolee," saying he learned it from Frankie Baker herself in Omaha in 1908—a claim supported by later evidence that Baker moved there shortly after the killing. Alan Lomax included this version in *Folk Songs of North America*, noting the exceptional provenance but not that Jones had provided it to a white admirer in Paris in the 1920s and it had gone through at least three other white intermediaries before reaching him.[71] Lomax acknowledged the ballad's popularity with white singers, crediting the Leightons with changing the hero's name to Johnny "in the jazzy variant that became a favourite American college song" and writing that Missouri's "relatively relaxed racial attitudes . . . brought about frequent contacts between whites and Negroes in sporting-house areas, and thus a number of Missouri Negro ragtime songs (*Bill Bailey, Ta-ra-ra-boom-de-ay, Frankie*, etc.) became known to the whole country." He suggested that this gave middle-class singers "the thrill of vicarious participation in the sexually uninhibited and violent life of the demi-monde" and also served as an outlet for societal anger: "Feminine listeners revenged themselves through little Frankie on a predominantly patriarchal society which treated them as second-class citizens and disapproved of their erotic life," while for Black listeners the ballad "touched upon even more painful social problems," the hostile sexual relationships endemic in a community suffering from pervasive unemployment.[72]

A quarter century earlier, the Lomaxes printed two versions of "Frankie and Albert" without the social theorizing, describing it as a recent ballad that had already been collected in hundreds of variants. A footnote credited one of the texts to "Texas sources" and the other to "Lead Belly, 'King of twelve-string guitar players of the world,' Angola,

Louisiana"—though another note described the latter as "a composite of stanzas obtained from Connecticut, North Carolina, Mississippi, Illinois, Tennessee, and Texas," and none of its verses were from the brief version they recorded in 1933 from Huddie Ledbetter, a prisoner in the Angola State Penitentiary.[73]

Ledbetter was the Lomaxes' most famous "discovery." He was released from prison the following year, wrote to John Lomax requesting a job, traveled north as Lomax's chauffeur and song demonstrator at academic lectures, and went on to make dozens of recordings under their supervision. This relationship was complicated and exploitative, but all three found ways to benefit from it.[74] One of the earliest and most ambitious projects was a combined biography and folklore study, *Negro Folk Songs as Sung by Lead Belly*, which began with a chapter Alan compiled from interviews and titled "Lead Belly Tells His Story"—an initial effort at the sort of oral history he refined in *Mister Jelly Roll*.

Lomax transcribed Ledbetter's speech in a mix of standard English and phonetically spelled Black dialect, and a footnote explained that this was intentional, since "sometimes Lead Belly spoke in dialect, sometimes he didn't," and his speech "changed noticeably during the six months of travel with us"—a reminder that, as the Lomaxes studied him, he was simultaneously studying them and their world.[75] The book presented Ledbetter as a traditional folksinger and its cover photograph showed him sitting on a pile of sacks in bare feet and overalls, though friends remember him wearing fashionable suits and flourishing a gold-headed cane, and he was a versatile entertainer who sang everything from traditional field hollers to blues, cowboy songs, and pop hits.[76] Margaret Coleman, the mother of his first daughter, wrote that by his teens he was already popular at "all the big parties and dances" around the Caddo Lake region, on the Texas-Louisiana border, and "the white people with stores and drug stores asked Hudie to play Saturday nights at their places."[77] He was also playing in the red light district of Shreveport and recalled that period with a familiar verse: "*I got a woman living on the back side of jail, / Makes an honest living, boys, by the working of her tail.*"[78] He left that area in his late teens, roamed for a while—including, in one anecdote, a trip to New Orleans during which he heard Morton playing in a Rampart Street saloon—then settled in Dallas, where he put together a group of musicians that worked for "rich white folks." When he was arrested and imprisoned, he quickly made a reputation as "camp entertainer," playing guitar and leading an eight-piece band that performed for white visitors, including the governor of Texas, who brought guests to hear him and eventually gave him a pardon. John Lomax wrote that on their college tours Ledbetter had to be dissuaded from mixing pop and jazz songs with the folkloric material and "never failed to delight his audience when he 'passed his hat' at the end of his program. Then he always became the smiling cajoling Southern darky minstrel extracting nickels from his 'White folks.'"[79]

Black entertainers were keenly aware of the limitations of that stereotype, but also of its commercial appeal. In the 1940s, when Ledbetter was teamed with Josh White for a residency at the Village Vanguard, Pete Seeger overheard White threatening to quit if Ledbetter didn't stop clowning, and Ledbetter responding, "Come on, Josh—make a fool of yourself once in a while and take the white folks' money."[80] That history necessarily affected what white folklorists heard from Black singers, and when Ledbetter teamed up with the Lomaxes he astutely tailored his performances to the new situation, learning and reworking songs to satisfy them and their audience. He found that many white northerners had trouble understanding him when he sang, so he added spoken passages to draw them into the stories, turning "Goodnight, Irene" into an extended set piece about a rural courtship and expanding "Frankie and Albert" into a domestic drama that lasted nine minutes on record and almost twice that in concert. He omitted the ballad's naughtier elements, portraying Frankie as a decent woman who "was working in the white folks' kitchen," and explained that the bartender told her about Albert's cheating because "you take a white man, he gonna tell you the truth." It was a brilliantly calibrated performance, which listeners could simultaneously appreciate as authentic Black folklore and enjoy as an entertaining twist on a familiar favorite, gratifying new tastes and old fantasies.[81]

A HOUSE IN NEW ORLEANS

THE RELATIONSHIP OF COMMUNITY FOLKLORE TO COMMERCIAL ENTERTAIN-
ment, like the relationship of oral and print traditions, was often circular.
When John Lomax began collecting cowboy songs in the first decade of
the twentieth century, one of his most treasured discoveries was sung by
a Black saloonkeeper who had worked as a cow camp cook. In a story that
echoed his memory of Dink, he recalled this man responding to his first
approach by saying, "I'se too drunk to sing today. Come back tomorrow,"
but later singing several songs, one of which he titled "A Home on the
Range." He included it in his first book, *Cowboy Songs and Other Frontier
Ballads*, which appeared in 1910, and in the revised 1938 edition wrote
that although it attracted little attention at the time, it was later published by two sheet music companies, became "the most popular song on
the air," and was recirculated by cowboys who had learned it from the
book and other publications.[82] The song's commercial success led to a
court battle over its authorship, which established that a version had been
published in sheet music in 1904, four years before Lomax collected it,
and the lyrics had been printed in a small-town Kansas newspaper in the
1870s as "My Western Home"—but Lomax continued to believe it had
originated as a vernacular folk song.[83]

Another Lomax discovery has spawned similar confusion. When
I first heard Morton's "Murder Ballad," its theme and some lyrics
reminded me of "House of the Rising Sun," which I knew from recordings by Ledbetter and Josh White and thought of as a traditional blues
that had been popularized by urban folksingers and made into an international hit by the Animals. The Lomaxes suggested an earlier version
of that lineage in 1941, when they published the song in *Our Singing
Country*: Alan had collected versions from several white singers in the
Kentucky mountains, but they included it in a section devoted to Black
"Hollers and Blues," with a note that although they had heard it only from
southern whites, they believed it to be "fairly old as blues tunes go" and
"a few of the hot jazzmen who were in the business before the war have a
distant singing acquaintance with this song." I suspect that means Alan

sang it for some old New Orleans musicians who said it sounded vaguely familiar, and he definitely taught it to White and Ledbetter and spread the idea that it originated in Black tradition.[84]

The Lomaxes also suggested an alternate lineage, writing that "'Rising Sun,' as a name for a bawdy house, occurs in a number of unprintable songs of English origin." They provided no examples, and although there were numerous Rising Sun hotels, pubs, and saloons on both sides of the Atlantic, the only English song that mentions one of them was recorded by Alan in 1953. The singer was a Norfolk farmworker named Harry Cox, who was born in 1885 and had a large repertoire of old ballads, one of which began *"If you go to Lowestoft and ask for the Hole in the Wall, / There you'll find Polly Armstrong, she ain't got a hole at all."* At least, that was what he sang on the recording, but after he finished, Alan prompted, "There's another way to begin that song, isn't there, Harry?" and Cox recited an alternate couplet: *"If you go to Lowes and ask for the Rising Sun / There you'll find two old whores and my old woman's one."* Cox had a reputation for disliking modern music and that couplet may have been centuries old, but by 1953 he could have heard "House of the Rising Sun" from Josh White on the BBC or any number of young singers in folk clubs, and been giving the folklorists what they wanted.[85]

The song seems to have been circulating in the United States by the early twentieth century, at times with "unprintable" lyrics that provide an alternate view of the New Orleans sporting world. One of Vance Randolph's informants recalled miners in Joplin, Missouri, singing a version as early as 1905 that went:

> *There is a house in New Orleans, they call it the Rising Sun,*
> *An' when you want your pecker spoilt, that's where you get it done.*
>
> *They drink all day an' fuck all night, until your money's gone;*
> *They kick your ass out in the street, when the second shift comes on.*

Other singers were more circumspect but mentioned "nasty" lyrics they did not remember or care to sing; one woman declined to sing all the verses she knew but supplied one about *"the red light out in front, / An' the pictures on the wall / An' yellow gals dressed in purple shoes / Without no clothes at all."* [86] Some set the events in other locations—a version from Tennessee recalled *"a girl in Baxter Springs, they call her the Rising Sun"* [87]—but as a notorious center of debauchery, New Orleans was a logical site for the story of a woman trapped into sex work or a man "spoilt" while sampling her wares. The song was performed from both viewpoints, and one of Morton's "Murder Ballad" verses echoed its standard ending:

> *Ask my sister, please don't be like me,*
> *Ask my sister, please don't be like me,*
> *It's better to've had the things you don't want and go free.*

When I first heard that verse, I connected it to *"Tell my baby sister not to do as I have done / But shun that house in New Orleans they call the Rising Sun,"* and wondered if the familiar song might likewise have been, in some performances, a half-hour epic. On further thought, this seems unlikely: it was never framed as an extended narrative and seems to have come from a different area and tradition, collected from white singers in mountain regions with relatively small Black populations and portraying New Orleans as a faraway site of sin and misery. The only trace of it in Louisiana was a verse collected by WPA workers in the north of the state: *"My mother was a sweeper, she wore her blue jeans, / My father was a gambler, and he died in Noo'r'leens."* [88] But this was likewise sung by rural white folk and pictured New Orleans as the logical destination for a doomed sinner.

ELLA SPEED

CONSIDERING THE CITY'S REPUTATION, IT IS ODD THAT NEW ORLEANS WAS not a more popular source of murder ballads. Some later versions of "Stackolee" placed the killing there, but the only well-known song commemorating a local murder was "Ella Speed," which was collected from multiple Texas singers—among them Mance Lipscomb, whose version concluded: *"The last words I heard Ella say, 'Tell my sisters don't do like me. / That is fall in love with everyone, with everyone that you see.'"* The Texas versions tended to relocate the events to that state: Ledbetter told the Lomaxes that Speed was killed outside the railroad depot in Dallas shortly before he moved there. In fact, like the St. Louis ballads, the song dated from the 1890s: on September 3, 1894, newspapers reported that a white bartender, Louis "Bull" Martin, had shot and killed "his octoroon mistress," Ella Speed, in a "disreputable house" on Custom House Street.[89] The murder and trial were covered in detail, and the *New Orleans Item* condemned Martin for his "shameful association with the woman," while also criticizing the racial bias in local courts, predicting he would get off because he was white and she was a colored sex worker, though "were the murderer in this instance a negro and his victim a white woman, no matter how degraded . . . threats of a lynching party would be heard."[90] As it happened, Martin was convicted and sentenced to twenty-five years in prison, was pardoned in 1900, married a white sex worker, and, in a poetic coda, made news again in 1911 when he threatened to "do again what he did a long time ago" and she shot him.[91]

The earliest surviving version of the Ella Speed ballad was collected by John Lomax in 1908 or 1909—there are two typescripts, one with the earlier date and a note that it was sung by Dink on the Brazos River and the other more credibly crediting an unnamed "Negro girl" at Prairie View Normal College.[92] The Lomaxes later collected versions from other Texas singers, including Ledbetter, Wallace "Staving Chain" Chains, and Homer "Tricky Sam" Roberson, and Carl Sandburg printed a version from a college student who learned it while riding on top of a boxcar in Turkey, from a man from New Orleans who said he heard it from a hobo who learned it in Memphis "from a negro just arriving from Galveston." In that odyssey the heroine's name had shifted to "Alice B.," and in another wink to Dink, the lyric began and ended with the narrator *"goin' out west, down on the Rio Grande, singin' fare-thee, O my honey, fare-thee-well."*[93]

Some of the Texas versions of "Ella Speed" shared lines and verses with the "Stackolee" and "Frankie" ballads, but where the latter songs used twelve-bar, three-chord melodies that presaged the standard blues form, it had a more harmonically varied melody based on a circle of fifths and was apparently descended from a jaunty New Orleans ragtime song that was simplified as it moved west. Rose Johnson played the New Orleans version during an interview about her days as a house pianist on Basin Street, but the piano drowned out her vocal and the only surviving lyric comes from Edmond "Doc" Souchon, a white guitarist born in 1897 who played with various local groups including his own Six and Seven Eighths String Band, and recorded two versions in the 1950s. He performed it as rowdy comedy, with a cautionary chorus:

> *Come all you pretty girls and take heed,*
> *Don't you die the death of Ella Speed.*
> *You may be running around, and having you a lot of fun,*
> *Some man gonna shoot you down just like Martin done.*[94]

Souchon introduced the song as "a story of old Storyville . . . similar to 'Frankie and Johnny,'" but my sense is that it followed a different path, beginning as a ragtime-pop composition played to entertain white listeners, and only later being absorbed into the vernacular Black ballad tradition. Given the period and setting, I assume Morton would have been familiar with it and perhaps included it in his early repertoire, but Lomax had only heard "Ella Speed" from Texas guitar players and had no reason to associate it with New Orleans. So instead Lomax asked about "Stackolee" and Morton responded with the improvised blues about Aaron Harris, and somehow, at a later session, produced the epic twelve-bar "Murder Ballad."

MORTON'S MURDER BALLAD

PERHAPS I'M BEING UNFAIR AND LOMAX DID ASK MORTON ABOUT "ELLA Speed." We have eight hours of recordings and a few pages of additional notes from their sessions, but they were planning the project for months, continued to discuss it as they went along, and must have considered numerous songs that did not make the final cut and themes that were not pursued.[95] Some of those conversations were recorded and others can be assumed: the session with "Pallet on the Floor" and "The Murder Ballad" was followed by thirteen discs of Morton's piano compositions, with no conversation, and it seems safe to conclude that, after giving Lomax a chance "to see how much folklore Jelly Roll had in him," Morton was making sure the project included his essential works.[96]

I am sorry those discs don't have some commentary, exploring the background of the pieces and Morton's compositional process, but it is easy to understand why he wanted to record them and why Lomax did not pursue that discussion. Lomax was not interested in jazz or ragtime, and a note he scribbled on the session notes for "The Pearls," one of Morton's instrumental masterpieces, was typical: "technically proficient and cold . . . brilliance but little heart or passion."

By contrast, "The Murder Ballad" cries out for explanation. No one but Lomax would have been likely to record a half-hour, fifty-nine-verse African American narrative ballad in that period, and he could not have done it if they had not been at the Library of Congress, with access to plenty of blank discs—but why from Morton? It was not at all the kind of song he was known for performing, and granting that the Lomaxes did not have the resources to record similarly long performances from Iron Head Baker or Clear Rock Platt in the Texas prison farms, they had virtually infinite access to Ledbetter, a famously adept rhymer and improviser, and limited his longest recorded ballads to less than ten minutes, or what they could fit on the two sides of a 78-rpm disc.

Morton's performance took up seven sides, and Lomax not only recorded it but pushed him to keep going: by the end of the sixth side, the story was almost over, with the heroine saying *"there's nothing else for me to do"* and bidding *"Good-bye to the world, because I know I'm gone."* Morton rushed those last lines, trying to finish the verse, but the disc ran out before he could provide a rhyming close. Since Lomax had not bothered to record the song's beginning, he could have considered that sufficient and moved on to other material, but instead he turned the disc over and

Morton completed the interrupted verse, played a piano interlude, then sang seven more verses in which the heroine meditated on her impending death, asking her fellow sinners to pray for her and lamenting that she wouldn't be buried with her family but just put *"in a box in the prison yard, / Not even a tombstone or not even a card."* He provided an evocative ending, with her warning the other prisoners to be good girls, because *"that's the only way you gonna wear your diamonds and pearls,"* but most of this disc sounds as if he was filling space.

My sense is that Lomax chose to record that seventh disc, not because the song seemed incomplete but to see how Morton would improvise another four minutes of material. That fits what we hear on the record and makes sense as a folkloric experiment—but it still begs the question of why or how Morton came to be performing a long-form narrative ballad in the first place. Perhaps they had been planning something like this from the outset; Lomax could have mentioned the ballads Platt and Baker sang, and Morton might have said he could do things like that. Maybe it happened more spontaneously, with Lomax commenting on the length of "Pallet on the Floor" and Morton saying that was nothing, he could sing songs that lasted an hour and told someone's whole life story. Lomax was fascinated by the ballad-making process but wrote nothing about this performance, either at the time or in later years. He may have been disappointed in the result, which included some clumsy and repetitious verses, and dismissed it as a failed experiment; may have decided it wasn't worth pursuing because so many of the lyrics were unprintable; or may have meant to write about it but got caught up in other projects. As for Morton, he had no interest in this kind of material; he recorded some old blues styles at Lomax's request and later at the request of other white sponsors, but was trying to reestablish his reputation as a popular composer and bandleader. He also wanted to be recognized as an authority and a pioneer of early jazz, but a long doleful ballad was irrelevant to that mission and he must have been aware that he was out of practice and did not bring it off with the flair of his youth.

To me, the fact that neither Morton nor Lomax considered this performance noteworthy is one of the most interesting things about it. Although there is no other recording or mention of a half-hour narrative ballad in the standard twelve-bar blues form, Morton cannot have invented that combination in 1938 at the Library of Congress. I assume he had sung similar things in the past, and heard other people sing them, perhaps as a regular thing, perhaps as an occasional way of entertaining a quiet gathering on a slow night. As for Lomax, he had heard other Black singers improvise equally long ballads, and may just have thought of Morton's epic as a less canonical cousin of "Stackolee" and "Frankie." I would have expected him to be surprised that Morton could do something like this, and excited about the "lowdown" language and theme, but there is no reason he would have particularly noted the form. *Blues* had not yet been strictly defined, at least among folklorists; he and his father included "Betty and Dupree," the one widespread twelve-bar blues ballad, in the "Outlaws" section of *Our Singing Country* without distinguishing it as blues, and placed numerous songs using other forms in the "Blues" category.[97]

If it was common for singers to improvise epic twelve-bar ballads, I would guess their period of popularity was relatively brief, as older ballad traditions overlapped the new musical style in the early years of the twentieth century. That was when Morton was working the Gulf Coast honky-tonks and it makes sense that his generation of singers would have given their story-songs a modern twist. I doubt he could have come up with a version of "Barbara Allen," or would have wanted to, and he shrugged off Lomax's request for "Stackolee," which he might have considered only slightly less old-fashioned. In hindsight many of us hear the Black murder ballads of the 1890s as an early form of blues, but to musicians of his generation those songs must have sounded as dated as the rock 'n' roll "oldies" of the 1950s sounded to young Black dancers in the age of James Brown and Aretha Franklin.

The form of the older murder ballads was perfectly suited to barroom singing sessions: the story moved in quick, rhyming couplets and everyone could join in for the tag-lines, harmonizing *"He was her man but he done her wrong"* or *"He was a bad man, that mean old Stackolee."* By contrast, the twelve-bar blues is essentially a solo form; it is ideal for spontaneous improvisation, since the two repeated lines gave a singer time to come up with a rhyming third, and in the hands of a skilled practitioner the repetition creates a momentary suspense that the third line satisfies, but it does not encourage group participation. Nor is it well suited to narrative ballads; the repeated lines would make the story drag and the most popular blues verses are gems of concision, complete in themselves. Some blues specialists were known for their ability to formulate infinite verses, but their themes were as personal and varied as a barroom conversation, commenting on their romantic travails and conquests, expressing shifting emotions and opinions, and making comical or philosophical observations about their lives and the people around them. [98] There are a few examples of twelve-bar ballads, but all are relatively short and, aside from "Betty and Dupree," which was composed in the 1920s and recorded by several artists in the following decades, they were quickly forgotten.[99]

Morton's storyline—a jealous woman killing her rival and suffering the consequences—was classic ballad material, but it did not commemorate a famous incident or even provide the characters with names. It mixed older verses with stanzas improvised on the spot, and if he had recorded a second version or another singer had been inspired to follow his model, the result would undoubtedly have been quite different. In that sense it was not a set ballad, but a style of musical storytelling that blended the older narrative form with the conversational style of the jook joints and honky-tonks. Morton used some stock couplets—*"Policeman grabbed her and took her to jail / There was no one to go that poor gal's bail"*—but that verse was followed by an exchange that seems as unrehearsed as it is realistic:

> *She got in the jailhouse, they asked her: "What you there for?"*
> *Her inmates in the jailhouse: "What are you here for?"*
> *She said, "I killed that bitch, that's what I'm here for."*

Morton's language startles many modern listeners, because we are used to hearing the past through layers of nostalgia and prudery, but on repeated listenings those passages are less striking for the raw words than for the straightforward ways he used them and the viewpoints they reflected. His story was set in a familiar world and mostly told in the words of the female protagonist. Some verses have the immediacy of eyewitness reportage; others sound like old favorites he could have picked up from Ann Cook or one of her many blues-singing peers:

> *Time is coming that a woman don't need no man.*
> *Time is coming a woman won't need no man.*
> *You can get it all with your beautiful hand.*

Or:

> *Years and years, I could take a prick just like a mule.*
> *I could take a great big prick just like a great big mule.*
> *I found out, what a big damn fool.*

A vice commission report from the early 1910s described a New York club "well filled with both white and colored people," where two white women kicked so high that "their person could be seen" while the entertainers sang, *"There'll come a time when a whore won't need no man,"* and twenty years later Lucille Bogan sang about a coming time when a "B.D. woman" wouldn't need a man.[100] Those lyrics were about lesbianism rather than masturbation, but I assume Morton's *man/hand* rhyme had been around for a while, a female equivalent to Stavin' Chain's *"Couldn't get a woman, he'd fuck his fist,"* which similarly portrayed the other sex as generic and expendable. The *mule/fool* rhyme was likewise an old standard; a dirty ballad known as "The Jolly Tinker," which T. S. Eliot preserved from his St. Louis youth, had the verse *"Oh daughter, oh, daughter, I think you are a fool / To run against a man with a john like a mule."*[101] In this case, Morton provided a significant shift of perspective: "The Jolly Tinker" was about a man with a huge penis and a woman who wanted it but couldn't handle it, while his heroine was tired of penises, whatever their size, and wanted nothing more to do with them or the men attached to them.

Another verse from the same sequence sounds equally common:

> *She had a thing just the same as mine,*
> *She had a thing just the same as mine,*
> *We rubbed together, my, but it was fine.*

I have not found any other examples of this couplet, and when I checked with John Patrick, an assiduous bibliographer and compiler of dirty verses, he responded that it was not familiar and "lesbian sentiments in the bawdy tradition are extremely rare." But, as always, that is a description of what has been preserved, not of what people sang.[102] The "bawdy tradition" that survives in print and on record is overwhelmingly white and male, with few examples from Black culture, fewer from women, and virtually none from lesbians. The subject of lesbianism has historically been ignored or avoided by writers of all sorts, except in occasional articles for psychiatric journals—and, as it happens, an article by a psychologist working in a women's prison in the 1920s included a letter from a Black woman named Ocean to a white woman she addressed as "My dearest Wife Gloria," with the epigraph:

> *You can take my tie*
> *You can take my coller*
> *But I'll jazze you*
> *'Till you holler.*[103]

Those sentiments and relationships were common among sporting women, and it is easy to imagine Morton singing a long, sultry epic like "The Murder Ballad" to entertain an audience of tired sex workers in the early morning hours—exactly the setting older New Orleans musicians tended to associate with blues.

I don't know how closely Morton's recording matches the way he would have shaped this kind of performance thirty years earlier, or the ways other people shaped similar songs. It is a unique glimpse of the world in which he learned his trade, and that uniqueness is a reminder that most of what we know—or think we know—about that world is based on scraps and shadows, filtered through flawed processes of preservation, omission, and suppression. For us, this recording is a historical curiosity, but the early morning listeners at Blankenstein and Abadie's or the Frenchman's had grown up hearing long ballads and were surrounded by blues, and its story and language were the stuff of their everyday lives. Some might have been struck by the accuracy or humor of Morton's observations and his skill as a rhymer, but the voice of his female protagonist would have been familiar, whether going for her rival—*"I'd like to see someone stop me . . . this ain't no slavery time"*—or facing her fate with proverbial resignation: *"When I'm dead, dead way down in my grave, / No more good peter of that man I'll crave."*[104] Listening to it, I hear echoes of Mamie Desdunes, Ann Cook, and all the now-nameless singers recalled in old memoirs and interviews, some as exceptional artists, others just as working women who entertained themselves and their friends by moaning the blues. Few would have been likely to create such a long and involved narrative, but it is easy to imagine them weaving shorter performances from the threads those few wove into epics.

In that metaphor, Morton's recording is not a finished fabric; the makeshift and clumsy stanzas are a reminder that we are listening to a process of creation and re-creation, the act of composing rather than a fixed composition. If he had recorded other versions of this ballad, he might have traced the same story in a similar mix of lines and verses, or his inspiration might have led in other directions and we would call the result a different song.

LAST CALL

In the same years the Lomaxes were recording Black singers in the American South, a Harvard professor named Milman Parry recorded thousands of discs of Yugoslavian *guslari*, traditional minstrels who performed epic ballads that lasted many hours and extended to tens of thousands of lines. Parry died in 1935, but his work was carried on by his assistant, Albert B. Lord, and in a classic study, *The Singer of Tales*, Lord analyzed how different guslari, or the same *guslar* on different days, employed a shared repertoire of plots, verses, motifs, and formulas to recall and reconstitute ancient epics. He wrote that although a singer would say he was repeating a piece exactly as he had heard it, "In a very real sense every performance is a separate song; for every performance is unique."

> The singer of tales is at once the tradition and an individual creator. . . . he is forced by the rapidity of composition in performance to use these traditional elements . . . and yet he practices great freedom in his use of them because they are themselves flexible. His art consists not so much in learning through repetition the time-worn formulas as in the ability to compose and recompose the phrases for the idea of the moment.[105]

Parry and Lord were inspired by the question of how Homer and his followers in ancient Greece created and re-created the *Iliad* and *Odyssey*, but their observations are equally applicable to West African griots, saloon balladeers, or the infinite unknown bards who sang or recited epics of murders, disasters, and adventures from the tropics to the tundra. They found that successive recordings of any epic, even when made by the same person, varied significantly from one performance to the next, and some readers came away with the idea that the singers were mistaken or misleading when they claimed to be precisely recalling and repeating pieces that had been sung for centuries. But in oral traditions, repeating something exactly does not mean producing a stenographic copy; it means accurately replicating the experience, which involves both more and less than the words. In a homely example, it is what toddlers mean when they insist that a favorite bedtime story be told exactly the same way every time: no child will object if you vary the word order a bit or make some additional comments, but if Father Bear says "Who's been sitting in my chair" in a high, squeaky voice, that's simply wrong.

A more significant analogy is the way jazz musicians play standards: they know a song's defining melody and chord pattern, have played it

before and heard innumerable other artists play it, but every performance is unique. Some listeners may not even recognize it as a familiar
song, and if others say, "oh, that's the way Coleman Hawkins—or Charlie
Parker, or John Coltrane—played it," they are talking about style and
approach, and perhaps some familiar licks, but not suggesting that anyone is playing exactly the same notes in the same order. Morton was a
skilled jazz player, raconteur, and rhymer, and rather than those skills
being separate or even complementary, his Library recordings remind
us that what we choose to call *music* or *poetry, jazz* or *blues, ballads* or *rap*,
or *storytelling*, or *theater* can all be present in a single performance, in an
infinite continuum that draws on traditions from Africa, Europe, and all
around the world.

All of those traditions are precious and I am grateful that examples of them have been preserved, but also conscious of how easily
and frequently those examples are misunderstood. Pete Seeger wrote
that a printed or recorded folk song is like "a photograph of a bird in
mid-flight. . . . The bird was moving before the picture was taken and
continued flying afterward . . . [and] no one is so foolish as to think that
the picture *is* the bird."[106] We need to remember that discrepancy: when
Morton said he was singing Mamie Desdunes's blues, or any blues from
his youth, he was re-creating a lived experience, giving the people watching, listening, and interacting with him in a particular place and time a
sense of what it might have been like to be in other rooms, in other times.
Lomax preserved some wonderful snapshots of that process, but they are
only snapshots; Morton was showing birds on the wing.

Historians aspire to a similar aim: to select and order surviving material in a way that gives readers a sense of what it was like to experience
the past. That process inevitably requires a mix of research and imagination: if we want to understand the experience of a night at the Funky Butt
or a Gulf Coast honky-tonk in 1905, we may learn as much by spending
nights in modern rap or dance clubs as by reading old newspapers or
listening to scratchy discs—and every approach is inevitably both illumi-
nating and misleading. At best we can learn what other people have preserved, remembered, claimed, and imagined; filter that through our own

experiences and understandings in our evolving present; and imagine a reality that fits all of that and feels authentic—but we cannot guarantee that it will feel authentic to other people, who may imagine other realities, and all are re-creations and improvisations.

I began this book as an attempt to connect the music and world of Morton's youth to what I was hearing and experiencing in twenty-first-century Los Angeles. I wanted young rap fans to know that the tracks their parents and grandparents reviled had a deep history; that a century earlier, other young people had been similarly excited by music that reflected their world and was similarly disrespected. And I wanted to broaden my own understanding and the understanding of other fans of blues and jazz, getting a better sense of how those styles evolved and were experienced in their formative years and how that history has been preserved and obscured.

It was not an exercise in nostalgia. Much of the history in this book is painful or ugly, and much of the music reflected and reacted to that pain and ugliness. There are things I miss or regret about that vanished world, much I wish had been better preserved, and there were many moments when I envied the people who lived among musicians and songs I can only imagine and reconstruct from scraps and memories. But this book was also born of my excitement at the survival, evolution, and continued brilliance of the Black oral tradition; of seeing and hearing freestyle rhymers creating contemporary art using techniques and materials the folklorists of my youth believed were dying or dead, for audiences as young and rowdy as any that crowded the Funky Butt.

Again, that analogy is not nostalgic: the Funky Butt is remembered as a site of great music but was also despised and avoided by many people, and rap continues to express and reflect a lot of misery and anger. In the years since I began this project, the notion that "the past is not past" has gained fearsome resonance. The cliché that people who do not learn from history are doomed to repeat it is true up to a point, but the repetitions always have new characteristics, and people who have learned history are as subject to them as anyone else. As I was researching and writing, many of the voices and events felt startlingly contemporary, sometimes in ways that were far from pleasant.

Perhaps that is the point of this book. Nostalgia is a siren song, a censored and selected soundtrack to an illusory past. The reality, always, is that the past was wonderful, at times, for some people, and likewise dreadful. Some things were better, some were worse. Everything was different, and much remains the same. The more honestly we look back, and the more stories we preserve and tell, from more kinds of people with more varied experiences, the more power we have to make our own histories. That was a basic role of the old ballads: ensuring that people whose ancestors were ignored or disparaged in written records had a history. The sung histories were not more accurate than the book histories, but they were different and helped people shape a different conception of their past and, in that process, of their future. As I wrote at the outset, this is more a book of questions than of answers. It is a call to look again at the history we think we know, asking what is missing, and why, and how many voices we may still be able to hear if we make the effort to listen.

Acknowledgments

I MUST FIRST THANK ALL THE PEOPLE WHO COMPOSED AND PERFORMED the lyrics that are the core of this book and the communities that nurtured and inspired them, starting with Jelly Roll Morton and his contemporaries in New Orleans. When I could find their names, I have credited them; in many cases I could not, and I want to emphasize the importance both of their contribution and of their erasure. I must also thank all the people who collected and preserved those artists' lyrics and recollections; though I often disagreed with their choices, I could not have done this project without them and am deeply aware that many of them did difficult, painstaking, and inspiring work. I must single out John and Alan Lomax, who made this and many other books possible, not only by spending years collecting American folk songs but by preserving so much supporting material and making it available to other researchers.

As to all the people who helped me directly, I should have kept better lists and apologize to everyone whose name does not appear here. I must particularly thank Chris Smith, who provided advice and support at every stage of this project and whose meticulous fact-checking brought out a wealth of new information and saved me all kinds of embarrassment. Bruce Boyd Raeburn was a constant source of encouragement and an invaluable guide to old New Orleans. Eric McHenry became a friend and working partner for the ballad chapter, and I look forward to seeing the fruits of his further research. Matthew Barton, who has helped me immeasurably on previous projects, fielded numerous phone calls and once again cast his keen eye over the entire manuscript. Among many others, I am grateful to John Cowley, John Patrick, Todd Harvey, Bruce Jackson, Susan Davis, John Troutman, Lynn Abbott, David Evans, Diane Goldstein, Eric Seiferth, Melissa Weber, Elliott Hurwitt, Ted Anthony, Rich Remsberg, Sharon Wolff, Howard Rye, Preston Lauterbach, Bruce "Sunpie" Barnes, Clifford Ocheltree, Kip Lornell, Stefan Grossman, Glenn Hinson, Marcia Segal, Edward Meyer, Daniel Vernhettes, Matt Sakakeeny, Mark Wilson, Jared Snyder, Bill Edwards, Kim Vaz-Deville, Robert Eagle, Emily Landau, Eric McHenry, John Szwed, Ethan Leinwand, Seva Venet, Jari Honora, Stephen Winick, John McCusker, and Judith Legman. And I am infinitely grateful to the many librarians, archivists, and collectors who provided access and guidance for my searches over the many years this project was germinating and coming to fruition.

As ever, I'm grateful to my agent, Sarah Lazin, for finding this book a good home—two good homes, actually, but I had to pick one, and it has been a pleasure to work again with Ben Schafer, an old friend and veteran editor to whom I owe much of my career as an author. I appreciate the way Fred Francis shepherded the manuscript through to completion and graciously fielded my endless emails. And I'm infinitely grateful to Sandrine Sheon, who puts up with me, gives useful advice and consistent support, and, once again, designed the photo spread.

Photo and Image Credits

P.1: Photo of Ferdinand Morton ca. 1906, WRJC/HNOC, acquisition made possible by the Clarisse Claiborne Grima Fund, Acc. No. 92-48-L.73.

P.2: Photo of Hilma Burt's Mirror Ballroom, courtesy of the New Orleans Jazz Museum. Pages from New Mahogany Hall booklet, HNOC, Acc. No. 56-15.

P.3: Kizer's Saloon, from New Orleans *Times-Democrat*, March 16, 1908. Tony Jackson and friend, WRJC/HNOC, Acc. No. 92-48-L.242.

P.4: Henry Truvillion and John A. Lomax, 1940. Photo: Ruby T. Lomax, LOC, Prints & Photographs Division, Lomax Collection (LC-DIG-ppmsca-38771). Clipping from *Shreveport Journal*, July 2, 1936.

P.5: Alan Lomax with Sonny Terry and Brownie McGhee, Bess Lomax Hawes Collection, AFC 2014/008. Handwritten transcript of "Dink's Blues" from James Avery Lomax Family Papers, Dolph Briscoe Center for American History, UT, box 3D, folder 192. Typescript of "Uncle Bud" from Lomax song files, AFC.

P.6: Photo of Buddy Bolden band, date and photographer unknown. Photo of Kid Ory Woodland band, WRJC/HNOC, Acc. No. MSS 520.2303.

P.7: Sheet music covers.

P.8: Photo of Morton and Morton comedy act, WRJC/HNOC, Acc. No. MSS 508.72. Clipping from the *Indianapolis Freeman*, May 30, 1914.

P.9: "Jelly Roll Blues" sheet music. Rialto Music Shop advertisement from the *Chicago Defender*, June 14, 1924.

P.10: Louis Armstrong with his mother and sister, WRJC/HNOC, Acc. No. 92-48-L.280. Ann Cook, WRJC/HNOC, Acc. No.,92-48-L.276.

P.11: Advertisement for Jungle Inn, *Washington Times*, March 27, 1937. "Creators of Jazz and Swing," *Pittsburgh Courier*, April 2, 1938. "Winding Boy" recording card, AFC 1938/001. Headline from *Down Beat* 5(8), August 1938.

P.12: "Hegira of the Magdalenes," from the *San Francisco Bulletin*, February 15, 1917 (courtesy of Ivy Anderson and Devon Angus, who printed it in *Alice: Memoirs of a Barbary Coast Prostitute*. Berkeley, California: Heyday, 2016). Morton and Ada "Bricktop" Smith, Floyd Levin collection.

P.13: Ma Rainey, "Prove It on Me," Paramount Records advertisement, *Chicago Defender*, September 22, 1928. Photo of Gladys Bentley, reprinted in *Ebony*, August 1952. Lucille Bogan, photographer and source unknown.

P.14: Photo of Bunk Johnson, Huddie "Lead Belly" Ledbetter, and George Lewis, Stuyvesant Casino, New York, ca. June 1946, by William P. Gottlieb. William P. Gottlieb Collection, LOC (http://www.loc.gov/item/gottlieb.04541). Photo of James "Iron Head" Baker, Sugar Land, Texas, June 1934, by Alan Lomax. Lomax Collection, AFC (http://www.loc.gov/item/2007660010). Headline and drawing of Ella Speed, New Orleans *Times-Democrat*, September 4, 1894.

P.15: Photo of Frankie Baker, photographer and source unknown, originally published in the *St. Louis Post-Dispatch*, February 13, 1942. Article on Harry Duncan from the *St. Louis Globe-Democrat*, March 13, 1894. *Smokehouse Monthly* and "Bully Song" covers.

P.16: Jelly Roll Morton at the RCA/Bluebird recording session, 1939, photographer unknown. Cover of *New Orleans Memories*, General Records 78 album, 1940.

Selected Bibliography

(Works cited multiple times or providing significant background.)

Abbott, Lynn, and Doug Seroff. *The Original Blues: The Emergence of the Blues in African American Vaudeville.* Jackson: University Press of Mississippi, 2017.

———. *Ragged but Right: Black Traveling Shows, "Coon Songs," and the Dark Pathway to Blues and Jazz.* Jackson: University Press of Mississippi, 2007.

———. "'They Cert'ly Sound Good to Me': Sheet Music, Southern Vaudeville, and the Commercial Ascendancy of the Blues." *American Music* 14(4), Winter 1996.

Abrahams, Roger D. *Deep Down in the Jungle: Negro Narrative Folklore from the Streets of Philadelphia.* 1963. New York: Aldine, 1981.

Abrahams, Roger D., and John F. Szwed, eds. *After Africa: Extracts from British Travel Accounts and Journals of the Seventeenth, Eighteenth, and Nineteenth Centuries Concerning the Slaves, Their Manners, and Customs in the British West Indies.* New Haven, CT: Yale University Press, 1983.

Anonymous [A Gentleman About Town]. *Immortalia: An Anthology of American Ballads, Sailors' Songs, Cowboy Songs, College Songs, Parodies, Limericks, and Other Humorous Verses and Doggerel.* N.p., 1927.

Anthony, Ted. *Chasing the Rising Sun: The Journey of an American Song.* New York: Simon & Schuster, 2007.

Armstrong, Louis. *Louis Armstrong, in His Own Words.* Edited by Thomas Brothers. New York: Oxford University Press, 1999.

———. *Satchmo: My Life in New Orleans.* New York: Prentice-Hall, 1954.

Barker, Danny. *Buddy Bolden and the Last Days of Storyville.* New York: Continuum, 2001.

Bechet, Sidney. *Treat It Gentle.* New York: Hill & Wang, 1960.

Blair, Cynthia M. *I've Got to Make My Livin': Black Women's Sex Work in Turn-of-the-Century Chicago.* Chicago: University of Chicago Press, 2010.

Bricktop (Ada Smith Ducongé), with James Haskins. *Bricktop.* New York: Atheneum, 1983.

Brothers, Thomas. *Louis Armstrong's New Orleans.* New York: Norton, 2006.

Brown, Cecil. *Stagolee Shot Billy*. Cambridge, MA: Harvard University Press, 2003.

Burns, Robert. *The Merry Muses of Caledonia*. 1800[?]. Edited by Gershon Legman. New Hyde Park, NY: University Books, 1965.

Charters, Samuel B. *Jazz New Orleans 1885–1963: An Index to the Negro Musicians of New Orleans*. New York: Oak, 1963.

Chauncey, George. *Gay New York: Gender, Urban Culture, and the Making of the Gay Male World, 1890–1940*. New York: Basic Books, 1994.

Cockrell, Dale. *Everybody's Doin' It: Sex, Music, and Dance in New York, 1840–1917*. New York: Norton, 2019.

Collins, Lee, with Mary Collins. *Oh, Didn't He Ramble*. Urbana: University of Illinois Press, 1989.

Cox, John Harrington. *Folk-Songs of the South*. Cambridge, MA: Harvard University Press, 1925.

Cray, Ed. *The Erotic Muse: American Bawdy Songs*. Urbana: University of Illinois Press, 1992.

David, John Russell. "Tragedy in Ragtime: Black Folktales from St. Louis." PhD diss., Saint Louis University, 1976.

Davin, Tom. "Conversations with James P. Johnson," *Jazz Review* 2(5–8), 3(3), Jun–Sep 1959, Mar–Apr 1960.

Davis, Frank Marshall. *Livin' the Blues: Memoirs of a Black Journalist and Poet*. Madison: University of Wisconsin Press, 2003.

Foster, George "Pops," with Tom Stoddard. *Pops Foster: The Autobiography of a New Orleans Jazzman*. Berkeley: University of California Press, 1971.

Gilbert, Douglas. *Lost Chords: The Diverting Story of American Popular Songs*. Garden City, NJ: Doubleday, 1942.

Gilfoyle, Timothy J. *City of Eros: New York City, Prostitution, and the Commercialization of Sex, 1790–1920*. New York: Norton, 1992.

Goffin, Robert. *La Nouvelle-Orléans: Capitale du Jazz*. New York: La Maison Française, 1946.

Gushee, Lawrence. "The Nineteenth-Century Origins of Jazz." *Black Music Research Journal* 14(1), 1994.

Gwaltney, John Langston. *Drylongso: A Self-Portrait of Black America*. New York: Random House, 1980.

Handy, W. C., ed. *Blues: An Anthology*. New York: Albert & Charles Boni, 1926.

———. *Father of the Blues*. New York: Macmillan, 1941.

Hanley, Peter. "Portraits from Jelly Roll's New Orleans." http://www.doctorjazz.co.uk /portnewor.html, accessed August 8, 2023.

Hartman, Saidiya. *Wayward Lives, Beautiful Experiments: Intimate Histories of Riotous Black Girls, Troublesome Women, and Queer Radicals*. New York: Norton, 2019.

Hobson, Vic. *Creating Jazz Counterpoint: New Orleans, Barbershop Harmony, and the Blues*. Jackson: University Press of Mississippi, 2014.

Hugill, Stanley J. (Long John Silver). "Sailing Ship Shanties." Unpublished manuscript, 1956. https://archive.org/details/1956sailingshipshantieslongjohnsilver, accessed August 8, 2023.

Hurston, Zora Neale. *Folklore, Memoirs, and Other Writings*. New York: Library of America, 1995.

Huston, John. *Frankie and Johnny*. New York: Albert & Charles Boni, 1930.

Jackson, Bruce. *Get Your Ass in the Water and Swim Like Me: African American Narrative Poetry from Oral Tradition.* 1974. New York: Routledge, 2004.

Johnson, Guy B. "Double Meaning in the Popular Negro Blues." *Journal of Abnormal and Social Psychology,* 22(1), April 1927.

Johnson, James Weldon. *The Book of American Negro Poetry.* New York: Harcourt, Brace, 1922.

Landau, Emily Epstein. *Spectacular Wickedness: Sex, Race, and Memory in Storyville, New Orleans.* Baton Rouge: Louisiana State University Press, 2013.

Legman, Gershon. *The Horn Book: Studies in Erotic Folklore and Bibliography.* New Hyde Park, NY: University Books, 1964.

Levine, Lawrence W. *Black Culture and Black Consciousness: Afro-American Folk Thought from Slavery to Freedom.* New York: Oxford University Press, 2007.

Lipscomb, Mance, as told to Glen Alyn. *I Say Me for a Parable: The Oral Autobiography of Mance Lipscomb, Texas Bluesman.* New York: Norton, 1993.

Lomax, Alan. *Mister Jelly Roll:The Fortunes of Jelly Roll Morton, New Orleans Creole and "Inventor of Jazz."* New York: Duell, Sloan and Pearce, 1950.

———. *The Folk Songs of North America.* Garden City, NY: Doubleday, 1960.

———. *The Land Where the Blues Began.* New York: Pantheon, 1993.

———. "'Sinful' Songs of the Southern Negro: Experiences Collecting Secular Folk-Music." *Southwest Review* 19(2), January 1934.

Lomax, John A. *Adventures of a Ballad Hunter.* 1947. New York: Hafner, 1971.

———. *Cowboy Songs and Other Frontier Ballads.* 1910. New York: Sturgis & Walton, 1915.

———. "Self-pity in Negro Folk-Songs." *The Nation* 105(2719), August 9, 1917.

Lomax, John A., and Alan Lomax. *American Ballads and Folk Songs.* New York: Macmillan, 1934.

———. *Negro Folk Songs as Sung by Lead Belly.* New York: Macmillan, 1936.

———. *Our Singing Country: A Second Volume of American Ballads and Folk Songs.* New York: Macmillan, 1941.

Long, Alecia P. *The Great Southern Babylon: Sex, Race, and Respectability in New Orleans, 1865–1920.* Baton Rouge: Louisiana State University Press, 2004.

Lord, Albert B. *The Singer of Tales.* Cambridge, MA: Harvard University Press, 1960.

Marquis, Donald M. *In Search of Buddy Bolden: First Man of Jazz.* Baton Rouge: Louisiana State University Press, 2005.

Martin, Sidney. "Black Diamond Express to Hell!" *Down Beat* 5(6), June 1938.

McCusker, John. *Creole Trombone: Kid Ory and the Early Years of Jazz.* Jackson: University Press of Mississippi, 2012.

Meryman, Richard. *Louis Armstrong—a Self-Portrait.* New York: Eakins, 1971.

Muir, Peter C. *Long Lost Blues: Popular Blues in America, 1850–1920.* Urbana: University of Illinois Press, 2010.

Newman, Katharine D. *Never Without a Song: The Years and Songs of Jennie Devlin 1865–1952.* Urbana: University of Illinois Press, 1995.

Odum, Howard W. "Folk-song and Folk-poetry as Found in the Secular Songs of the Southern Negroes." *Journal of American Folk-Lore* 24(93), July–September 1911.

Oliver, Paul. *Screening the Blues: Aspects of the Blues Tradition.* New York: Oak, 1970.

Oliver, Paul, and Mack McCormick. *The Blues Come to Texas*. Edited by Alan Govenar. College Station: Texas A&M University Press, 2019.

Perrow, E. C. "Songs and Rhymes from the South." *Journal of American Folklore* 25(96), April–June 1912; 26(100), April–June 1913; 28(108), April–June 1915.

Phillips, Harold. "Jelly Roll Charts Jazz." *Washington Daily News*, March 19, 1938.

Ramsey, Frederic, Jr. "Victor Recording Session of Jelly Roll Morton and His New Orleans Jazzmen." Typescript notes, HNOC.

Ramsey, Frederic, Jr., and Charles Edward Smith, eds. *Jazzmen*. New York: Harcourt, Brace, 1939.

Randolph, Vance. *Roll Me in Your Arms: "Unprintable" Ozark Folksongs and Folklore*, vol. 1. Edited by Gershon Legman. Fayetteville: University of Arkansas Press, 1992.

———. *Blow the Candle Out: "Unprintable" Ozark Folksongs and Folklore*, vol. 2. Edited by Gershon Legman. Fayetteville: University of Arkansas Press, 1992.

Reich, Howard, and William Gaines. *Jelly's Blues: The Life, Music, and Redemption of Jelly Roll Morton*. Cambridge, MA: Da Capo, 2003.

Roberts, Roderick J., Jr. "Negro Folklore in a Southwestern Industrial School." Master's thesis, Indiana University, 1965.

Russell, William (Bill). *New Orleans Style*. New Orleans: Jazzology, 1994.

———, ed. *Oh, Mister Jelly: A Jelly Roll Morton Scrapbook*. Copenhagen: JazzMedia, 1999.

Sandburg, Carl. *The American Songbag*. New York: Harcourt, Brace, 1927.

Saxon, Lyle, Edward Dreyer, and Robert Tallant. *Gumbo Ya-Ya*. Boston: Houghton Mifflin, 1945.

Schuller, Gunther. *Early Jazz: Its Roots and Musical Development*. New York: Oxford University Press, 1968.

Shapiro, Nat, and Nat Hentoff, eds. *Hear Me Talkin' to Ya: The Story of Jazz by the Men Who Made It*. New York: Rinehart, 1955.

Snyder, Jared. "'Garde ici et 'garde lá-bas: Creole Accordion in Louisiana." In *The Accordion in the Americas: Klezmer, Polka, Tango, Zydeco, and More*, edited by Helena Simonett. Urbana: University of Illinois Press, 2012.

Spencer, Scott B. *The Ballad Collectors of North America: How Gathering Folksongs Transformed Academic Thought and American Identity*. Lanham, MD: Scarecrow Press, 2011.

Szwed, John. *Alan Lomax: The Man Who Recorded the World*. New York: Penguin, 2010.

Talley, Thomas W. *Negro Folk Rhymes: Wise and Otherwise*. New York: Macmillan, 1922.

Taylor, Frank C., with Gerald Cook. *Alberta Hunter: A Celebration in Blues*. New York: McGraw-Hill, 1987.

Thomas, Gates. "South Texas Negro Work-Songs: Collected and Uncollected." *Publications of the Texas Folklore Society* 5, 1926.

Tucker, Sherrie. "A Feminist Perspective on New Orleans Jazzwomen." Center for Research, University of Kansas, 2004.

Vernhettes, Dan, with Bo Lindström. *Jazz Puzzles*, vol. 1. Saint-Étienne, France: JazzEdit, 2012.

Wald, Elijah. *How the Beatles Destroyed Rock 'n' Roll: An Alternative History of American Popular Music*. Oxford, UK: Oxford University Press, 2009.

Waters, Ethel, with Charles Samuels. *His Eye Is on the Sparrow.* Garden City, NY: Doubleday, 1951.

White, Newman I. *American Negro Folk-Songs.* Cambridge, MA: Harvard University Press, 1928.

Williams, Martin, ed. *Jazz Panorama.* New York: Collier, 1964.

Wolfe, Charles, and Kip Lornell. *The Life and Legend of Leadbelly.* New York: HarperCollins, 1992.

Wright, Laurie, *Mr. Jelly Lord.* Chigwell, England: Storyville, 1980.

Notes

ABBREVIATIONS:

AFC: American Folklife Center, Library of Congress
FWP: Federal Writers' Project
HJA: Hogan Jazz Archive
HNOC: Historic New Orleans Collection
LOC: Library of Congress
UT: University of Texas at Austin
WRJC: William Russell Jazz Collection

A Note on Language, Offensive and Otherwise

1. In Britain, G. F. Northall wrote in 1892 that "the *labia minora* are still termed 'cockles' in vulgar parlance" (*English Folk-Rhymes*, London: Kegan Paul, Trench, Trübner, 156), a usage hiding in the lyric about the pretty Dublin girl selling "cockles and mussels" and dying of a fever; in Black US speech, John Langston Gwaltney (*Drylongso*, 73) quotes a woman using *cockle-upwards* to mean "topsy-turvy."

Introduction

1. A typescript of Morton's unissued lyrics was available at the Library of Congress by the 1970s, but few people knew of its existence, and Oliver's 1968 essay in *Screening the Blues* (170) and Wright's 1980 discography, *Mr. Jelly Lord* (90), list the seven discs that comprise "The Murder Ballad" with separate titles and no indication that they make up a single song. One of the dirty takes of "Winin' Boy" was released on *Copulatin' Blues* (Stash LP 101) in 1976. Rounder Records issued the other "unprintable" sides in 1993 as

part of a four-CD "complete" series that omitted Morton's spoken sections, and the full LOC sessions as a box set in 2005.

2. Martin Richardson, "Negro Songs and Amusements," FWP, Jacksonville, Florida, 5–6.

3. Michel-Rolph Trouillot, *Silencing the Past: Power and the Production of History* (Boston: Beacon Press, 1995), 26, 29.

4. Cecil Sharp, *English Folk-Song: Some Conclusions* (London: Simpkin, 1907), 102–103.

5. Lomax, *Cowboy Songs*, n.p. The pop songwriters Frank and Burt Leighton wrote that they adapted hits like "Frankie and Johnny" from songs whose "most pungent verses were marred, according to accepted standards, by phrases of medieval frankness," adding: "What our old ballads have lost in passing into print, these songs retained" ("Origin of 'Blues' (or Jazz)," *Variety*, January 6, 1922, 27.)

6. Alain Locke, *The Negro and His Music* (1936; repr., Port Washington, NY: Kennikat, 1968), 87.

7. Howard Odum, *Social and Mental Traits of the Negro* (New York: Columbia University Press, 1910), 165–167. Newman Ivey White (*American Negro Folk-Songs*, 312) wrote that a quarter to a third of the lyrics he could have collected about women were "unprintable, as crude and filthy as brutal tastes could make them."

8. Lomax, *Adventures*, 35.

9. Lomax, *Adventures*, 37.

10. The year is not certain, but Lomax placed it as 1908–1909; his correspondence confirms that he was collecting African American songs in the Brazos River bottoms area by 1908 and acquired an Edison recorder around that time, and he quoted one of Dink's verses in a newspaper appeal printed as "Negro Folk-Songs," *Donaldsonville (LA) Chief*, May 25, 1912, 1.

11. Lomax, *Adventures*, 272–275. Lomax wrote that Dink said she was from Yazoo City, Mississippi, and in the mid-1940s he inquired about her there and was told she had died and was buried on "a nearby tree-clad hill."

12. Lomax, "Self-pity in Negro Folk-Songs," 143.

13. Sleepy Geoff Carruthers, "An Interview with Alan Lomax," *WKCR* radio bulletin, June 1988, 7–8. Alan similarly wrote that a naughty version of "Pullin' the Skiff" was actually collected by his assistant, Margaret Wormley, because the "little girls at the Friars Pt. wouldn't sing for me." (Mississippi notebook, 1941, Lomax collection, AFC.)

14. Handwritten transcript and typescript in James Avery Lomax Family Papers, Dolph Briscoe Center for American History, UT, box 3D, folder 192. Lomax's typescript has a note to "repeat the first line of each verse," with ditto marks for the third line of verses that repeated that line thrice; his handwritten text has a parenthetic "(3)" after those lines.

15. In another example, the Lomaxes transcribed a song from K. C. Gallaway and Tud Odum in Wiergate, Texas, ca. July 11, 1933, with no dirty verses but the lines "Goodbye, every fuckin' body, I'm goin' home, / I'm goin home, oh lord, I'm goin home" (Lomax papers, UT, box 3D, folder 185).

16. Lomax, "Self-pity in Negro Folk-Songs," 143.

17. Davin, "Conversations," 3(3), 13.

18. Mary Wheeler, *Steamboatin' Days: Folk Songs of the River Packet Era* (1944; repr., Freeport, NY: Books for Libraries, 1969), 98, 67.

19. Arvella Gray, Chicago, November 10, 1962, recorded by Donald M. Winkelman, Archives of Traditional Music, Indiana University, ATL 2435-F 285.

20. Luke Jordan, "If I Call You, Mama," Victor 23400, November 19, 1929; Robert Johnson, "32-20 Blues," Vocalion 03445, November 26, 1936. Johnson's record is a remake of Skip James's "22-20 Blues" from 1930, which referred to "the doctors in Wisconsin," presumably because that was where James made the recording.

21. Johnson, "Double Meaning," 19.

22. Samuel C. Adams, "Changing Negro Life in the Delta," in *Lost Delta Found: Recovering the Fisk University-Library of Congress Coahoma County Study, 1941–1942*, ed. Robert Gordon and Bruce Nemerov (Nashville, TN: Vanderbilt University, 2005), 289.

23. Gwaltney, *Drylongso*, 31.

24. Chris Smith (personal communication, December 6, 2022) notes Howard Odum's misinterpretation of a verse in "Casey Jones": *"Went on down to the depot track, / Beggin' my honey to take me back, / She turn 'round some two or three times: / 'Take you back when you learn to grind.'"* Odum explained this was "intended to portray the scene after the wreck, when the fireman . . . was out of a job," and apparently no one corrected him, since he published the verse and comment in 1911 ("Folk-song and Folk-poetry," 352) and repeated it in 1925 (Odum and Johnson, *The Negro and His Songs* [1925]. Hatboro, Pennsylvania: Folklore Associates, 1964, 207–208).

25. Lomax and Lomax, *Our Singing Country*, 244.

26. Lomax, *Cowboy Songs*, 1911, 70–71.

27. Annie G. Gilchrist, "Sailors' Songs," *Journal of the Folk-Song Society* 2(9), 1906, 249.

28. Frank T. Bullen and W. F. Arnold, *Songs of Sea Labour (Chanties)*. London: Orpheus Music, 1914, vi–vii.

29. Richard Runciman Terry, *The Shanty Book, Part 1: Sailor Shanties*. London: Curwen, 1921, xi, xiv.

30. Douglas Morgan (a pseudonym for John D. MacDonald) published a book of "unexpurgated sea chanties" (*What Do You Do with a Drunken Sailor* [Pomfret, CT: Swordsmith, 2022]), but they were mostly collected in the late twentieth century, and although some use explicit language, the version of "Hog-Eye Man" is thoroughly bowdlerized.

31. Hugill correspondence and notes to unexpurgated shanty collection, at https:// archive.org/details/1956sailingshipshantieslongjohnsilver. Hugill did not always avoid the subject of anal sex; this manuscript includes notes to a shanty called: "Timme Arse-ole, Bung-o-lero."

32. Hugill, "Sailing Ship Shanties"; manuscript in the Legman collection at the Kinsey Institute, reprinted in Jessica Floyd, "Jib-booms, Barrels, and Dead-eyes: Singing Sex in Sea Chanteys," PhD diss., University of Maryland, 2017, 326, 310. Hugill's "Hog-Eye Man" text has the comparable verse: *He came to the shack where Jinny she did dwell, / As soon as he saw her he tried to ring her bell . . . / She was too late to hide her snatch, / An' the hog-eye nigger jammed a bale down the hatch.*

33. Levine, *Black Culture*, 15, citing William Cullen Bryant, "A Tour in the Old South," (Prose Writings of William Cullen Bryant, Parke Godwin, ed. New York: Appleton, 1884, vol. VI, 32) who dated this lyric to 1843.

34. Solomon Northup, *Twelve Years a Slave* (Auburn, NY: Derby and Miller, 1853), 219–220.

35. Hugill, "Sailing Ship Shanties." He gives the lyric *"wid a hard-on on."* W. B. Whall printed a "Hog-Eye" lyric from San Francisco, dated to 1849–1850, writing that mining materials were shipped inland on barges called "hog-eyes" and "The derivation of the name is unknown to me." (*Ships, Sea Songs and Shanties* [Glasgow: James Brown & Son], 1913, 118.)

36. Septimus Winner, *Winner's Collection of Music for the Violin* (Philadelphia: Davis, 1853); B. B. Barker, "Farming in the Monte," *Los Angeles Star,* December 8, 1855, 3.

37. *Raleigh (NC) Sentinel,* March 18, 1868, 2; "A Disgraceful Exhibition," *Daily North Carolinian* (Fayetteville, NC), March 17, 1868, 3. The association of this song with abolitionists had more general currency; the first surviving example of the standard shanty chorus is in a scurrilous satire: "Lincoln's 'Hog Eye' Dream," *Shreveport (LA) Semi-Weekly News,* June 3, 1862, 4.

38. Elí de Gortari, *Silabario de palabrejas* (Ciudad de Mexico: Plaza y Valdes, 1988, 512), with the gloss "Se dice particularmente del culo del puto."

39. Ernest Hemingway, *A Moveable Feast* (New York: Scribner, 1964), 19. Hemingway's terms are echoed in a toast, "The Ball of the Freaks": *"Her action was like a flash, her cunt opened like a gash, / And her brown-eye lost all its feeling"* (Dennis Wepman et al., *The Life: The Lore and Folk Poetry of the Black Hustler* [Philadelphia: University of Pennsylvania Press, 1976], 111); Bruce Jackson recorded a poem from Kenny "Midge" Grenert in the Indiana State Prison about a man arrested for anal intercourse with a boy and still dreaming of "that round brown eye" (Bruce Jackson collection, Archives of Traditional Music, Indiana University, recorded in Indiana State prison, 1962, ATL 62-011 F, tape 24).

40. For example, *"Here's to the girl that dresses in black, / Always looks neat and never looks slack, / When she kisses she kisses so sweet, / That she makes things stand that have no feet."* (Anonymous typescript, March 2, 1906, http://www.horntip.com/html/books _&_MSS/1900s/1905-1907_bawdy_manuscript_from_ny_state_(MS)/index.htm.)

41. Gates Thomas ("South Texas Negro Work-Songs," 166) quoted a common verse from a Black singer, *"Said the ole rooster to the hen, 'You ain't laid an aig in God knows when,' / Said the ole hen to the rooster, 'You don't call aroun' any more, like you use'ter,'"* with a note that it "represents the Negro's re-synthesis of a pornographic barroom ballad that was current (usually on the cards of whiskey-drummers) about the turn of the century."

42. Texas Alexander, "Boe Hog Blues," OKeh 8563, recorded March 10, 1928. *Noodle* as a metaphor for buttocks may come from the German *knödel,* for "dumpling."

43. Geeshie Wiley, "Skinny Leg Blues," Paramount 12951, ca. March 1930.

44. John Jeremiah Sullivan, "The Ballad of Geeshie and Elvie," *New York Times Magazine,* April 13, 2014, https://www.nytimes.com/interactive/2014/04/13 /magazine/blues.html.

45. Thornton and Lillie Mae Wiley are listed as husband and wife in the 1930 census, but his death certificate listed him as single and her as Scott, her birth name, so they may not have been legally married.

46. *National Register Evaluation of Sewerage Pumping Station B New Orleans Louisiana,* U.S. Army Corps of Engineers, 1992, https://apps.dtic.mil/sti/pdfs/ADA 259636.pdf, 18. In 1910 only a fifth of the city's buildings were connected to sewer lines.

47. Speckled Red recalled that in sawmill, turpentine, and levee camps, they would have a "big house . . . where they have some fun when they come in at night . . . In those days and in them places you could say some of them smelly words and don't think nothing of it" (Paul Oliver, *Conversation with the Blues* [1965; repr., Cambridge, UK: Cambridge University Press, 1997], 65). Alan Lomax asked the Scottish singer Davie Stewart, "Did they have any songs that were, er, not quite proper, not quite— That you wouldn't be able to sing on the air? Wouldn't be able to sing on the radio; the words a little bit off color . . . ?" Stewart responded, "Dirty ones . . . ? I've lots of dirty songs myself." ("Interview with Davie Stewart About Bawdy Songs," December 1, 1957, https://archive.culturalequity.org/node/57751.)

48. Armstrong, *Louis Armstrong*, 120; Foster and Stoddard, *Pops Foster*, 29. New Orleans newspapers occasionally used the term *Storyville*, but more often referred to the *Tenderloin*, the *Red Light District*, or the *Restricted District*. The earliest surviving guidebook to the District, published ca. 1900 and archived at HNOC, is titled *Blue Book: Tenderloin '400,'* satirizing the "Blue Book" of New York's "400" high-society families, and included "all the sporting houses in the tenderloin district, both Storyville and Anderson County [an area on the river side of Basin Street]." The uptown District covered four blocks between Gravier and Perdido; some recent historians call it "Black Storyville," but this name has no historical basis.

49. Hurston, *Dust Tracks on a Road* [1942]; "Characteristics of Negro Expression [1934]," in *Folklore, Memoirs*, 692, 840.

50. Davin, "Conversations," 2(5), 16; Willie the Lion Smith with George Hoefer, *Music on My Mind* (London: MacGibbon & Kee, 1965), 53.

51. Russell, *Oh, Mister Jelly*, 444.

52. Bechet, *Treat It Gentle*, 3.

53. Angela Y. Davis, *Blues Legacies and Black Feminism: Gertrude "Ma" Rainey, Bessie Smith, and Billie Holiday* (New York: Vintage Books, 1999), xvii, 3–4.

Chapter One

1. Morton LOC recordings.

2. Morton generally said he was born in 1885, and some later documents give that year. Sam Davis, apparently born on October 8, 1885, said he and Morton "were carried at the same time," and Joseph "Fan" Bourgeau said Morton was already playing in the District when he began working there in 1903 (John G. Heinz, "Sam Davis," in Russell, *Oh, Mister Jelly*, 331; Joseph "Fan" Bourgeau, interview, HNOC). Lawrence Gushee argued for the 1890 date based on a baptismal record, and it is supported by multiple interviews with Morton's contemporaries and internal evidence from Morton's recollections and publications, few of which include any references to events or music before about 1907. I lean toward the later date but remain agnostic.

3. Richard M. Jones, interview, HNOC, mss. 519, Jazzmen folder 29.

4. Jelly Roll Morton, "Jelly Roll Says He Was First to Play Jazz," *Down Beat* 5(9), September 1938, 4.

5. Manuel Manetta, interview and clarinet lesson, June 20, 1958, HNOC.

6. Goffin, *La Nouvelle-Orléans*, 72.

7. Lomax notes, LOC, Rounder box set booklet, 186. Presumably Morton substituted "gals" for "whores."

8. Lucille Bogan also used a version of this line in her 1935 "Shave 'Em Dry": *"All of you cack women, you better put on the walk / 'Cause I'm gonna get drunk and do my dirty talk."* "Cack" was slang for *proper* or *snooty*.

9. Will Shade, "The Dirty Dozens," *Beale St. Mess Around*, Rounder LP 2006, 1975.

10. Mance Lipscomb, "You Be Kind to Me," *The Unexpurgated Folk Songs of Men*, LP issued by Mack McCormick, copyright 1960.

11. "Federal Writers' Project: Slave Narrative Project, Vol. 16, Texas, Part 2, Easter-King," https://www.loc.gov/item/mesn162, accessed August 8, 2023.

12. Brothers, *Louis Armstrong's New Orleans*, 135–136.

13. Examples include "I Have Got the Blues To Day!" (1850), "Oh, Ain't I Got the Blues!" (1871), "Oh Susie! Dis Coon Has Got the Blues" (1897), and "I've Got de Blues" (1901), which is noteworthy because eleven years later its composer, Chris Smith, published "The Blues (But I'm Too Blamed Mean to Cry)," which Morton recalled as the first real blues to appear in sheet music. In fact, it was predated by "I Got the Blues," a twelve-bar instrumental published in 1908 by a New Orleans pianist, Antonio Maggio, which shares the melody W. C. Handy later used for "St. Louis Blues." This subject is explored at length in Muir, *Long Lost Blues*, 7–9, 117–120, 184–187. If we consider "Alabama Bound" a blues, it was also the first blues released on a record, by Prince's Band in 1910.

14. Mississippi John Hurt, "Pay Day," *Today* (Vanguard LP). Hurt recorded other versions with slightly different verses.

15. Weston A. Goodspeed, *Counties of LaGrange and Noble, Indiana: Historical and Biographical* (Chicago: Battey, 1882), vol. 1, 252.

16. Victoria Spivey, "Blood Hound Blues," Bluebird B8619, 1929.

17. The cover title is "Strains from the Flat Branch," but the first page of music omits the *the*, and the section was called Flat Branch, after a river that previously ran through it.

18. Véronique Hélénon, Thomas Klingler, and Bruce Sunpie Barnes helped with this transcription and translation. Notably, each used different orthographies: Hélénon, French from Martinique, wrote "Si vou vlé rinmin mwen [apré?] vou bô mwen dé troi foi." Klingler, who studies Louisiana Creole speech, followed the *Dictionary of Louisiana Creole*, which is based on Haitian Kreyòl: "si vou vlemèmwen mape vou bo mwe deu trwa fwa." I have used Barnes's spelling, because he provided the most complete translation.

19. The phrase *paix donc* in this lyric is often transcribed *payez donc*, but the former, meaning "be quiet" or "calm down," is a common phrase in Louisiana and fits the meaning (Thomas Klingler, personal communication, March 30, 2021).

20. Leonard Bechet translated *cancan* as "gossip," and *paix donc* as "shut up, don't tell me that" (https://archive.culturalequity.org/field-work/new-orleans-jazz-interviews -1949/leonard-bechet-449/interview-leonard-bechet-about-his-2). Alfred Delvau's *Dictionnaire de la Langue Verte: Argots Parisiens Comparés* (Paris: Dentu, 1866, 72) defined *cancan* first as "Médisance à l'usage des portières et des femmes de chambre," and secondly as a previously popular dance that had been supplanted by "d'autres danses aussi décolletées."

21. Roger Abrahams said none of the African diaspora communities he studied made strong distinctions between sung and recited rhymes; most verses could be performed either way. (Personal conversation, March 12, 2010.)

22. Lomax notes to Library of Congress sessions.

23. Louis Armstrong, interview by Bob Rusch, *Cadence* 12(1), January 1986, 12.

24. Lomax, *Mister Jelly Roll*, 4.

25. Lovie Austin, interview, April 25, 1969, HJA. Morton was writing musical arrangements by the 1920s, but several people remember him as a nonreader in earlier years, and he may have remained a "speller," able to read and write notes but not to play fluently from a score. The story about him reading upside down was from Jasper Taylor (Reich and Gaines, *Jelly's Blues*, 43).

26. Information on Morton's family names is from Peter Hanley, "Jelly Roll Morton: An Essay in Genealogy," 2002, http://www.doctorjazz.co.uk/genealogy.html, drawing on the work of Lawrence Gushee.

27. Frederick A. Ober, "A Search for the Border Ruffian," *Outing* 5(1), October 1884, 38.

28. "Federal Writers' Project: Slave Narrative Project, Vol. 16, Texas, Part 2, Easter-King." Elizabeth Kilham, a white schoolteacher who worked in Black southern schools after the Civil War, wrote, "it seemed as if they were desirous of exercising their new privileges in this as in everything else, and would take a new name whenever it suited them," and some of her students used "two or three names which they changed indiscriminately" ("Sketches in Color—Second," *Putnam's Magazine*, January 1870, 33).

29. Collins and Collins, *Oh, Didn't He Ramble*, 29; Marquis, *In Search of Buddy Bolden*, 52.

30. Davin, "Conversations," 2(5), 16; 2(6), 10.

31. Giles Oakley, *The Devil's Music: A History of the Blues* (New York: Harcourt Brace Jovanovich, 1976), 77; Jim O'Neal, "Little Brother Montgomery," *Living Blues* 43, Summer 1979, 19; Paul Oliver, *Conversation with the Blues* (1965; repr., Cambridge, UK: Cambridge University Press, 1997), 66–67. Montgomery mentions many of the same people in an interview with William Russell archived at HNOC.

32. Robert Shaw, taped interview by Tary Owens, tape 1, at UT archive.

33. The Lomax and Lomax listing exemplifies the vagaries of historical production: John Lomax wrote the name as Hunter on his original transcript of the lyric (Lomax papers, UT, box 3D, folder 185), and said it that way in the intro of the cylinder recording, but whoever transcribed it from his handwriting apparently misread it as White and some later scholars noted that Hunter's mother's maiden name was White and assumed he took this as a pseudonym.

34. Margaret McKee and Fred Chisenhall, *Beale Black & Blue: Life and Music on Black America's Main Street* (Baton Rouge: Louisiana State University, 1981), 176.

35. Alan Lomax notebook, Coahoma County, MS, 1941, AFC 2004/004, folder 07.02.08.

36. Lomax, *Land Where the Blues Began*, 397.

37. Lucille Bogan, "Shave Me Dry," ARC TO-1317, recorded July 19, 1933, surreptitiously issued on 78 party records as "Shave 'Em Dry." (Howard Rye, "The ARC TO-'Test Only' Series, Part 4," *Names & Numbers* 15, October 2000 , 19.)

38. Big Bill Broonzy, with Yannick Bruynoghe, *Big Bill Blues* (1957; repr., New York: Oak, 1964), 48.

39. Handy, *Father of the Blues*, 152.

40. Lawrence Gushee and Vic Hobson settled on 1910, since Morton told Lomax that he worked at the Savoy Theater in Memphis for Fred Barrasso, who opened the theater

that year. (Gushee, "A Preliminary Chronology of the Early Career of Ferd 'Jelly Roll' Morton," *American Music* 3(4), Winter 1985, 396; Hobson, "Reengaging Blues Narratives: Alan Lomax, Jelly Roll Morton and W. C. Handy," PhD diss., University of East Anglia, 2008, 127). In 1911 Morton traveled with William Benbow's vaudeville troupe, and a review mentions Rebecca Kinzey, the "Black Swan," singing "All That I Ask Is Love." (*Indianapolis Freeman*, July 22, 1911, 6.)

41. Dave Stuart, from interviews with Morton, in Russell, *Oh, Mister Jelly*, 132.

42. Rosalind "Rose" Johnson, interview by William Russell, February 23, 1970, taped, HNOC. Lilly Delk Christian, who met Morton in Chicago, also mentioned "Barbershop Chord" as one of his standard songs (Russell, *Oh, Mister Jelly*, 394).

43. Davin, "Conversations," 2(7), 15.

44. Alison Blaire, "I'm a Sweet Papa Pigmeat," in *Selections from the Gutter: Jazz Portraits from "The Jazz Record,"* ed. Art Hodes and Chadwick Hansen (Berkeley: University of California Press, 1977), 206.

45. Onah Spencer, "Jelly Would Flash That G-Note, Laugh in Your Face," *Down Beat* 8(15), August 1, 1941, 4. Elsewhere, Jones said the original Jelly Roll came from Kansas City and "Ferdinand Windenboy came along, took the name of Ferdinand Moten, called himself Jellyroll." (Richard M. Jones, interview, HNOC, mss 519, Jazzmen folder 29.)

46. Johnson, "Double Meaning," 13.

47. S. L. Jenkins, "Jenkins and Jenkins Having Success," *Indianapolis Freeman*, January 18, 1913, 6.

48. Abbott and Seroff, *Original Blues*, 105.

49. Phillips, "Jelly Roll Charts Jazz." Lomax recalled that Morton came to the Library with some friends, saying he wanted to "correct the history of jazz." Lomax telescoped the process, saying he was blown away when Morton played "the most beautiful 'Alabama Bound' I'd ever heard," ran upstairs to tell his supervisor he needed fifty blank discs, and "decided to do a full-scale interview" on the spot. (Jelly Roll Morton Symposium, transcript, Tulane University, May 7, 1982, 37, HJA.)

Chapter Two

1. Records show a Porter King in Mobile as a child in 1880, marrying in 1901, and working as a cabdriver in 1910, then moving to Chicago, working as a porter and laborer, and dying in 1946. Chris Smith provided these documents and noted that they do not mention him as a musician and this many not be the man Morton recalled.

2. Alan Lomax, quoted in Jelly Roll Morton Symposium, transcript, Tulane University, May 7, 1982, 37, HJA.

3. Gus Kahn's lyric to "Pretty Baby" was published by Jerome H. Remick in 1916. Jackson's original lyric was recalled by Morton and also performed by Glover Compton on a 1956 recording released as *Meet Glover Compton*, Windin' Ball CD 106, copyright 1999.

4. The categories and listing practices in these guidebooks varied over the years. The 1900 book had a separate section for a "Jew Colony" on Bienville, but most of the Jewish houses were outside the official district and are not included in later books, though some still distinguished individual Jewish workers.

5. "City Authorities in Conference; Dance Halls Are Closely Watched," *Times-Democrat* (New Orleans, LA), January 6, 1909, 5; "Barrel Houses Raided and One Negro Killed," *Times-Democrat* (New Orleans, LA), March 16, 1908, 5. M. A. Kizer's Railroad Saloon was at 762 Rampart St., on the corner of Julia. This is often listed as the Red Onion's address, and the New Orleans *Picayune* once referred to it as "Kizer's 'Red Onion' Saloon" (March 16, 1908), but other reports describe them as under separate ownership and place the Red Onion at 1113 Julia, between Rampart and Saratoga.

6. Foster and Stoddard, *Pops Foster*, 96.

7. Harris was killed on July 14, 1915, by which time Morton would have been unlikely to hear a local song about the event, if such a song existed.

8. The spring sessions were recorded on fifty-one 12-inch 78-rpm acetate discs. Most of the discs are not dated, but the last three sessions are dated more thoroughly and each preserved about an hour of material. The first session, on May 23, began with three dated discs and the conversation seems to continue directly from side to side for nineteen sides, totaling seventy-eight minutes. The first side after those begins a conversation about funeral music that leads into another cohesive series, and it seems likely that the thematic break marked a change of session. The final session, in December, was presumably in a different venue, since Morton had a guitar rather than a piano and Lomax recorded it on lacquered aluminum discs at 33⅓ rpm.

9. This was a common verse, often found outside the "Hesitation" context; for example, in several lyrics in White's *American Negro Folk-Songs* and a 1929 record by Sleepy John Estes, "Divin' Duck Blues." In the notes to Handy's *Blues: An Anthology*, Abbe Niles quoted it as typical of vernacular versions of "Hesitation," and Charlie Poole and the North Carolina Ramblers used it in 1930 for a recorded version issued as "If the River Was Whiskey."

10. *Indianapolis Freeman*, January 1 and July 29, 1916, in Abbott and Seroff, *Original Blues*, 172. Smith had been performing professionally for at least four years, but previous reviews did not mention her repertoire, except to call her a "coon shouter," the standard term for women, Black or white, who performed markedly Black material.

11. "Columbia Graphophone Co. to Make Records of W. C. Handy's Music," *Chicago Defender*, December 29, 1917, 11.

12. Handy, *Blues: An Anthology*, 42, 12.

13. Abbott and Seroff, "'They Cert'ly Sound Good to Me,'" 441–442, 453.

14. Handy's version was recorded in 1923 by Esther Bigeou, backed with his "Beale Street Blues"; Louis Armstrong, James P. Johnson, and a few other singers did it in later years; White (*American Negro Folk-Songs*, 325–326) reports a Black singer in Alabama singing two of Handy's verses, mixed with other verses, around 1915–1916, and a Texas prison inmate named Smith Casey retained the idea of singing about a phone call when he recorded an otherwise unrelated version in 1939. Most early recordings, whether by Black or white artists, credited Middleton and Smythe, and a few included their introductory section, but most just used the "Hesitation" framework, so it is hard to tell if they were following Middleton and Smythe or if that just became the standard credit.

15. George Blau, *Art Gillham: Waiting for Ships That Never Come In*, 2018, at https://archive.org/details/ArtGillham2818. The quotation is from Blau, not Gillham, but he was reporting Gillham's story of how the song was composed.

16. Art Gillham, "Hesitation Blues," Columbia 343-D, recorded February 25, 1925. The printed lyric was *I'll go down to the levee, take a rocking chair, / If the blues doesn't leave me, babe, I'll rock away from here.*

17. John Lomax, *Adventures*, 42; Guy Logsdon, *"The Whorehouse Bells Were Ringing" and Other Songs Cowboys Sing* (Urbana: University of Illinois Press, 1989), 64. The Lomaxes printed a version in *American Ballads and Folk Songs* (376) with a note that "there remain hundreds of unprintable stanzas," and their note to a comparably additive song from World War I, "Mademoiselle from Armentieres" (558), claimed, "There is in print a private, not mailable, collection of more than six hundred stanzas." The longest version I've found of the latter song, in the Canfield manuscript, has about sixty verses, so I'm guessing that number is exaggerated by a factor of ten, but I would love to be proved wrong.

18. Abbott and Seroff, "'They Cert'ly Sound Good to Me,'" 442.

19. Walter Kingsley, "Whence Comes Jass?" *Sun* (New York), August 5, 1917, 23.

20. Gilbert, *Lost Chords*, 240.

21. Bricktop, *Bricktop*, 29, 40, 41, 45.

22. Supreme Court of the State of New York, Appellate Division—Third Judicial Department, Petition of George E. Green . . . for an Order Revoking and Cancelling Liquor Tax Certificate . . . [of] John J. Reed, Albany, NY, January 4, 1916, 15, 17–18.

23. From John Cowley, who copied it in the Lomax song files in the AFC.

24. Hubert L. Canfield collection of dirty songs and rhymes, ca. 1925–1926, https://archive.org/details/1926canfieldcollection/page/n11/mode/2up.

25. Chris Smith found documentation for three men named Fred Fields in the Waco area, one white and two Black.

26. Robert Lockwood, interview by Bernard MacMahon, for the documentary series *American Epic*.

27. "He's Off to Germany—S'Long, Tom, S'Long!," *Enid (OK) Eagle*, April 21, 1918, 20.

28. Britt Craig, "Georgia Soldiers Sing Away Pain and Cares at Mobilization Camp," *Atlanta Constitution*, July 5, 1916, 5. He divides verse and chorus into four lines each.

29. Bessie Smith, "Foolish Man Blues," 1927; George Guesnon, taped interview, May 17, 1958, HNOC, MSS 530.3.25; Claude McKay, *Home to Harlem* (1928; repr., Boston: Northeastern University Press, 1987), 36.

30. Reminiscences from "Janice from NJ" and "Lori" at https://mudcat.org/thread.cfm?threadid=2219, June 13–14, 2004.

31. "The German Blues: It's Neutral," words by Bob Lurtey, music by L. E. Zoeller (Louisville, KY: L. E. Zoeller Music, 1916), https://digitalcollections.libraries.ua.edu/digital/collection/p17336coll5/id/10381.

32. Text from anonymous source, in Newman Ivey White, "Negro songs and folk-lore: with some songs, etc., of the southern whites, vol. 1, original mss from informants," unpublished manuscript, 1917, MS Am 2580, Houghton Library, Harvard University; also, with some words missing, in White, *American Negro Folk-Songs*, 398.

33. Papa Charlie Jackson, "Hot Papa Blues," 1925; Frankie "Half Pint" Jaxon, "It's Heated," 1929; Walter "Buddy Boy" Hawkins, "Voice Throwin' Blues," 1929; Bo Carter, "All Around Man," 1936; Charles "Cow Cow" Davenport, "I Ain't No Ice Man," 1938.

34. Rev. Gary Davis, *Blues & Ragtime*, Shanachie CD LC 5762, 1993; recorded at Michigan State University in 1968 (Stefan Grossman, personal communication, April 27, 2021).

35. Zora Neale Hurston, "Story in Harlem Slang," originally published in *American Mercury*, July 1942, in Alan Dundes, *Mother Wit from the Laughing Barrel: Readings in the Interpretation of Afro-American Folklore* (New York: Garland, 1981), 223.

36. I discuss the term *cake-eater* more thoroughly in Wald, *How the Beatles*, 61–64.

37. Sam Theard, "She's Givin' It Away," Brunswick 7073, 1929; verse collected "on the farm" by A. M. Kearly of Auburn, Alabama, in Newman Ivey White ms., Houghton Library, Harvard University; there are two versions of Bray's verse in the John Lomax papers at UT, boxes 3D-182 and 3D-192, and a similar verse without the rhyming tag line in his recording of "Trench Blues," October 17, 1934, AFC, AFS 000 92-A.

38. Rev. Gary Davis, *At Home and Church: 1962–1967*, Stefan Grossman's Guitar Workshop CD 130/1/2. This set also includes a version of "Little Boy Who Made Your Britches" with verses like *"Gal was out there chinquapin hunting / Stuck my peg in her, God knows she kept a-grunting."* In the interjection I quote, Davis may have meant "Hear what . . . " rather than "Here what . . . " and his listeners could have interpreted it either way.

39. Zora Neale Hurston, recorded by Stetson Kennedy, Jacksonville, Florida, 1939, Library of Congress, http://www.loc.gov/item/flwpa000 012/.

40. Lomax typescript, AFC, labeled "Vulgar song; Iron Head, James Baker, Central State Farm, Sugarland, Texas, June, 1933." Baker sang versions of all four stanzas I quote from Hurston; his original name and birth year are from his death certificate, provided by Chris Smith, along with the 1910 and 1920 censuses, which list him as Tom and James Barkley. Lomax recorded a similar version the following year from Pete Harris. The typescript dated to 1908 is from the Robert Winslow Gordon "Inferno" collection, AFC.

Thomas, "South Texas Negro Work Songs," 180; Frankie "Half Pint" Jaxon, "Let's Knock a Jug," Vocalion 1285, 1929. Jaxon also sings, *"Uncle Bud's got jugs ain't never been touched."* Other recordings include Leona Williams, "Uncle Bud (Bugle Blues)," Columbia A3736, 1923, and Tampa Red and Georgia Tom, "Uncle Bud (Dog-Gone Him)," Vocalion 1268, January 1929; Coot Grant and Socks Wilson did a version the following month as "Uncle Joe," Paramount 12833. The song was less common in white culture, but a cleaned-up "Uncle Bud (Tennessee Blues)" was recorded in 1922 by the Tampa Blue Jazz Band, a group of white players that backed Mamie Smith and other Black blueswomen on a couple of dozen recordings, and Gid Tanner and his Skillet-Lickers recorded an "Uncle Bud" song in 1926 to the tune of "Froggie Went a-Courting."

41. This chorus was in the 1908 typescript and recorded by James Brown and Rufus Bland for Carita Doggett Corse and Robert Cornwall, Kenansville, FL, July 1940, AFC, AFS 03900 A02.

42. George Guesnon interview by William Russell, September 18, 1959, HNOC.

43. Ralph Ellison, "Living with Music," in *Living with Music* (1955; repr., New York: Modern Library), 2001, 4; Richard Wright, *The Long Dream* (1958; repr., Chatham, NJ: Chatham Bookseller, 1969), 101. "The Bastard King of England" was a common barroom song, often attributed to Rudyard Kipling, with the chorus *"He was wild and wooly*

and full of fleas / And his terrible dong hung down to his knees / O! God save the bastard King of England." (Randolph, *Roll Me in Your Arms*, 506.)

44. Alan Lomax, 1941 field notes, Coahoma County, MS, AFC 2004-004, folder 07.03.15.

45. Lomax, AFC 1933/002, miscellaneous texts 1933–1934, folder 066.

46. Whistlin' Rufus, "Sweet Jelly Rollin'," Bluebird 5306, 1933. This artist's name was apparently John Henry Bridey, born in Georgia in 1889, 1890, or 1891, depending on whether one believes his World War II registration card, his World War I registration card, or his tombstone. (Information from Chris Smith.)

47. Al Bernard, "Stavin Change (The Meanest Man in New Orleans)," Joe Morris Music, 1923.

48. Mance Lipscomb, "Stavin Chain," *The Unexpurgated Folk Songs of Men*, LP issued by Mack McCormick, copyright 1960.

49. Lil Johnson, "Stavin' Chain (That Rockin' Swing)," recorded for Vocalion, 1937, but not issued on 78.

50. Lomax and Lomax, *Our Singing Country*, 305; Sigman Pyrd, "Folk-Lorist Decides S.A. Is Gold Mine," *San Antonio Light*, May 4, 1941, sec. 2, p. 6. Lomax recorded a cylinder labeled "Stavin' Chain" as early as 1908–1910, but it is no longer playable and that's all we know about it.

51. Homer "Tricky Sam" Roberson, "Stavin' Chain," first verse from LOC 210-A-1, recorded at the State Penitentiary, Huntsville, TX, April 1934; second verse from LOC 215-A-1, same location, November 21, 1934.

52. Lomax and Lomax, *Our Singing Country*, 305. The first two verses are from Roberson's April 1934 recording (LOC 210); another is from their recording of Wilson "Stavin' Chain" Jones; the rest are presumably from other singers and perhaps other songs.

53. Mack McCormick, notes to *The Unexpurgated Folk Songs of Men*, LP issued with no label name, 1960, 7. The verse is from the King James Bible, and I imagine adolescents giggling over the previous line: "thou shalt make staves of shittim wood."

54. Johnny Temple, "Stavin' Chain," Decca 7532, recorded April 22, 1938.

55. Blind Willie McTell, "Chainey"; Furry Lewis, "Kassie Jones, pt. 1"; Zora Neale Hurston, "Cock Robin," in *Collected Plays*. Rutgers University, 2008, 89.

56. Onah L. Spencer, "Boogie Piano Was Hot Stuff in 1904!" *Down Beat* 6(7), July 1939, 22. Jones told another version of this story in an interview summarized in HNOC, mss. 519, Jazzmen folder 29.

57. Johnny St. Cyr, interview by Alan Lomax, April 2, 1949, Association for Cultural Equity, recording T997R09.

58. Alan Lomax research notes, LOC box set, 179.

59. "Negro Kills Woman and Fatally Wounds Bystander," *Times-Democrat* (New Orleans, LA), December 6, 1907, 8; "A Suspected Negro," *Daily Picayune* (New Orleans, LA), June 27, 1908, 7; "Wrong Party Under Arrest," *Daily Picayune* (New Orleans, LA), July 1, 1908, 16.

60. Recording made April 23, 1939. Wallace Chains and Sylvester Jones agreed the former would be called "Big Stavin' Chain" and the latter "Little Stavin' Chain" or "Texas Stavin' Chain"—Chains was originally from New York. ("Ramsey State Farm 4/39," at https://archive.culturalequity.org/node/63086.)

61. Typescript of song performed by "Stavin' Chain II (Wilson Jones)," Lafayette, LA, June 1934, in Lomax papers, AFC.

Chapter Three

1. Theodore Dreiser, *Dawn: An Autobiography of Early Youth* (1931; repr., Santa Rosa, CA: Black Sparrow, 1998), 114, 172. John Jeremiah Sullivan suggests this woman was known as Sallie Davis and her original name was Annie Brace, Brice, or Swommer ("The Curses: Part II: The Curse of the Dreamer," *Sewanee Review*, 125[2], Spring 2017).

2. Supplied by John Cowley from the Lomax song files in the AFC. There were infinite variations of this verse; Robert Winslow Gordon's "Inferno" collection at the AFC includes one from a man who did time on a chain gang in Tennessee and remembered Black prisoners singing, *"I got a gal she live in Baltimore / She's high yellow / And there's c—t marked on her door."*

3. Newman, *Never Without a Song*, 102.

4. Chris Smith suggests this is a reference to Dr. William M. Shankle, a physician practicing in the Waco area in the first quarter of the twentieth century.

5. Lipscomb, *I Say Me for a Parable*, 131, and "Won't You Be Kind," *Unexpurgated Folk Songs of Men* LP.

6. In the first of his two Library performances of "Winding Boy," Morton sang the variant, *"I pulled that snake right from her big ass."*

7. Russell, *Oh, Mister Jelly*, 114, 119.

8. Rosalind "Rose" Johnson, interview by William Russell, February 20, 1970, tape, HNOC.

9. Rosalind "Rose" Johnson, interview by William Russell, February 20, 1970, tape, HNOC. Manuel Manetta and Kid Ory also claimed to have played for White, and it seems likely that Black players were sometimes brought in on busy nights or at a customer's request.

10. "Help Wanted," *New Orleans Item*, March 21, 1903, 7; this may be a different Jim Williams, but the date and address make sense.

11. Schuller, *Early Jazz*, 362.

12. Foster and Stoddard, *Pops Foster*, 99.

13. Randolph, *Blow the Candle Out*, 674.

14. Hubert L. Canfield, collection of dirty songs and rhymes ca. 1925–1926, https:// archive.org/details/1926canfieldcollection/page/n11/mode/2up.

15. Jelly Roll Morton, letter to Roy Carew, September 16, 1939, HNOC.

16. Jelly Roll Morton, recordings of "Winin' Boy Blues": Jazz Man 11, recorded December 1938; Bluebird B10429, recorded September 14, 1939; Ramsey, "Victor Recording Session"; General 4004, December 14, 1939.

17. J. B. Moreton, *Manners and Customs in the West India Islands* (London: Richardson, 1790), excerpted in Abrahams and Szwed, *After Africa*, 290–291.

18. Kid Ory, interview, April 20, 1957, HJA, https://musicrising.tulane.edu/listen /interviews/edward-kid-ory-1957-04-20/.

19. Typescript of song performed by "Stavin' Chain II (Wilson Jones)," Lafayette, LA, June 1934, in Lomax papers, AFC; Danny Barker, quoted in Russell, *Oh, Mister Jelly*, 98; Johnny St. Cyr, interview by Alan Lomax, April 2, 1949, Association for Cultural Equity, recording T997R02.

20. Joseph "Fan" Bourgeau, interview by William Russell, January 24, 1970, HNOC, http://hnoc.minisisinc.com/thnoc/catalog/3/11234.

21. Jeffrey Henderson, *The Maculate Muse* (New Haven, CT: Yale University Press, 1975), 46. *Yorlin* derives from *yowlering* or *yoldring*, meaning "yellow ring," so "yellow yellow yorlin" is triply redundant.

22. Burns, *Merry Muses*, 112, 39–41, 47–49.

23. The "yorkla harlin" verse is on a recording of Maynard Reynolds (b. 1883), made by Eloise Hubbard Linscott in Pittsburg, NH, September 28, 1946, AFC, afc1942002_sr069a. A variant in the Canfield collection further modified "ball of yarn," referring to "a gal that made my balls to yearn."

24. "The League Guards," *New Orleans Daily Democrat*, May 15, 1879, 8. This was an all-male affair, ending with a toast to "the ladies of Louisiana," who, in a period when ladies of the West and East were crusading for temperance and women's suffrage, "have no aspirations outside of the hearthstone, have no ambition but to educate their children in the ways of virtue and patriotism."

25. Lomax, *Adventures*, 32; Gilbert, *Lost Chords*, 74–75; Thomas, "South Texas Negro Work-Songs," 164. In 1884 a song called "Winding Up Her Little Ball of Yarn" was published in sheet music, inspired by the older song but with lyrics about a man falling in love with a lady he sees knitting.

26. Gordon, "Inferno" collection, quoting Lee Gotcher in Amos, CA, 1924. A variant collected in 1941 from a sixty-three-year-old female "camp entertainer" in Rhinelander, Wisconsin, starts from the male viewpoint but shifts in the second verse: "*I pulled up my clothes / And he pulled out his long hose / And he wound up my little ball of yarn.*" (Helene Stratman-Thomas Collection, University of Wisconsin-Madison, https://asset .library.wisc.edu/1711.dl/6RSN3U54BT5JI84/R/file-c5d5e.pdf#page=1.)

27. Roger Abrahams, "Negro Folklore from South Philadelphia, A Collection and Analysis," PhD diss, University of Pennsylvania, 1961, 251. Abrahams did his collecting around 1959–1960 and does not specify who sang this, but Cray (*Erotic Muse*, 93) credits it to Abrahams's prolific informant John H. "Kid" Mike.

28. Newman, *Never Without a Song*, 199.

29. Randolph, *Roll Me in Your Arms*, 101, collected in 1948 from Mr. F. H., Berryville, AR, who heard it in the 1880s. He also has a variant with donkeys: "*Says the jinny to the jack, / Just climb upon my back / An' hammer on my little ball of yarn.*"

30. White, *American Negro Folk-Songs*, 240, 307. Some minor differences in orthography and the mention of other verses are from White's papers at the Houghton Library, Harvard University (Am 2580). The Lomaxes borrowed verses from White's book for the version of "Alabama Bound" in the 1934 *American Ballads* (206–209), including "*I'm a windin' ball. / Great Godamighty, babe, / Don' deny my name.*"

31. Southern Melody Boys (Odus Maggard and Woodrow Roberts), "Wind the Little Ball of Yarn," Charlotte, NC, February 17, 1937, Bluebird B-7057 and Montgomery Ward M-7227.

32. L.T.S., "Ginger and Sweet of the Passing Show," *Bangor Daily News*, June 20, 1934, 18; June 27, 1934, 14. Randolph mentions a folk belief that if a woman threw a ball of yarn through a window she would see the image of her future husband, and suggests some "backwoods women use a little ball of yarn as a contraceptive" (*Roll Me in Your Arms*, 101–102).

33. Anthony M. Reynolds, "Urban Negro Toasts: A Hustler's View from L.A.," *Western Folklore* 33(4), October 1974, includes a variant of a cowboy lyric John Lomax recorded fifty years earlier, recited by a Black truck driver who also provided a variant of "The Face on the Barroom Floor." Roger Abrahams and Bruce Jackson told me they heard and ignored verses from Robert W. Service and other literary poets when they were collecting Black toasts.

34. Cray (*Erotic Muse*, 20) cites Joe Hickerson suggesting that if informants and collectors were not "handicapped by modesty," this might surpass "Barbara Allen" as the most widespread song in the English oral tradition.

35. Richard Clark, ed., *Words of the Most Favourite Pieces, Performed at the Glee Club, the Catch Club, and other Public Societies* (London: Philanthropic Society, 1814), 6. There is an earlier mention of a "tale . . . of the Derby Ram" in a letter from Henry Cantrell, Nunsfield, Derby, June 10, 1739, in *Notes and Queries*, February 24, 1917, 154.

36. "Gen. Washington in the Nursery," *Daily American* (Nashville, TN), April 2, 1876, 3.

37. *Notes and Queries*, 10th series, vol. 1, April 16, 1904, 306. Although no dirty versions were printed before the twentieth century, another correspondent wrote that the song was popular with Harvard students in the early 1860s and the lyrics "were decidedly coarse." (Charles Stratton, *Notes and Queries*, 12th series, vol. 3, May 1917, 309.)

38. Thomas, "South Texas Negro Work-Songs," 158–159. These verses were widely collected (for example, in Randolph, *Roll Me in Your Arms*, 376); the asterisked words are normally "fuck" in the first stanza and "jack off" in the second. *Habits* was not asterisked, but Thomas is the only source for the term and I am guessing he invented it. Uncensored recordings of "Didn't He Ramble" from Black singers include one from Pete Harris in Richmond, TX, in 1934 with the lyric *"That ram had full horns covered with brass, / One stuck out his forehead, the other stuck out of his ass."* (*Black Texicans*, Rounder CD1161-1821-2, 1999.) A variant often known as "Derbytown," which ends each verse with a missing but obvious obscenity, was recorded by the Black singers Old Ced Odom and Lil Hardaway in 1936 and the Clovers in the 1950s.

39. Johnson, *American Negro Poetry*, xi–xii. In *Uncle Tom's Cabin*, Topsy says, "I spect I grow'd. Don't think nobody never made me." By the 1880s this was being quoted as "I jes' growed," and by the 1910s as "jes grew."

40. "Hoist by His Own Petard," *Pine Bluff (AR) Daily Graphic*, March 12, 1903, 2.

41. Russell, *Oh, Mister Jelly*, 490.

42. Celestin's Tuxedo Jazz Band, "Oh, Didn't He Ramble," Bandwagon 78 RWP-11, 1950. Ira Cephas in Portsmouth, Ohio, sang two versions for Bruce Buckley in 1951 and 1952 (AFC 1958/005, reels 2 and 3), with the verse *"His head was in the market house / His nuts was in the street / Two pretty whores come walkin' by / Said, 'Ain't that sweet market meat."* Also *"The wool on the old ram's belly was eighteen inches thick / Took all the whores in Birmingham to find the head of his dick."* Will Starks, recorded by Alan Lomax in Clarksdale, Mississippi, on August 9, 1942, sang a variant of the latter verse and *"He rambled to his mama, say 'Mama, I wants to suck,' / Said, 'Get away from here, you rambling ram, cause I believe you wants to fuck'"* (https://archive.culturalequity.org/field-work /mississippi-delta-survey-1941-1942/clarksdale-842/didnt-he-ramble).

43. Handy, *Father of the Blues*, 93.

44. Abbott and Seroff, *Original Blues*, 153–154. The first mention of Johnson performing this song is from September 1912, the same month Handy's "Memphis Blues" was published, and it is not clear which came first.

45. Handy, *Father of the Blues*, 76–77.

46. Handy, *Father of the Blues*, 78. Mississippi John Hurt recorded "The Last Shot Got Him" in the 1960s, and Chris Smith and Cecil Mack published a cowboy-themed novelty with that title in 1912 that uses scraps of the same melody. Ki Ki Johnson recorded a song called "Lady, Your Clock Ain't Right" in 1928, but it does not sound like rural folklore.

47. Handy, *Father of the Blues*, 78–79.

48. "Fight It Out," the first surviving draft of Handy's memoir, archived in the Handy Home and Museum in Florence, Alabama, dated to 1935–1936 (Elliott Hurwitt, personal communication, January 26, 2021).

49. S. L. "Stack" Mangam, interview by Alan Lomax, ca. 1941–1942, typescript, Lomax papers, AFC 2004/004, folder 09.04.44.

50. "Oh, You Bear Cat Rag," words by William Tracy, music by Lewis F. Muir and Frederick Watson (New York: J. Fred Helf, 1910). Muir was a St. Louis pianist and composed "Play That Barbershop Chord."

51. Jelly Roll Morton, letter to Roy Carew, January 18, 1940, HNOC.

52. Jelly Roll Morton, "I Created Jazz in 1902, Not W. C. Handy," *Down Beat*, August 1938, 3.

53. Script of Ripley's *Believe It or Not*, March 26, 1938, in the Ripley Archive. Morton misremembered Ripley calling Handy "the originator of jazz, stomps and blues"; Ripley mentioned stomps only in reference to the Crump campaign, saying "The Memphis Blues" was "written for stumping, not stomping."

54. Blues hit nationally in 1912; the first printed mention of jazz as a musical style, in 1915, was headlined "Blues Is Jazz and Jazz Is Blues," and the first hit jazz recording was 1916's "Livery Stable Blues" (Wald, *How the Beatles*, 56–57).

55. Phillips, "Jelly Roll Charts Jazz."

56. These artists are normally called Tig Chambers, Bab Frank, and Happy Galloway.

57. Smith's song was not in a standard "folk" form and was ignored by historians until Peter Muir (*Long Lost Blues*, 7–9) noted its significance in 2010.

58. Foster and Stoddard, *Pops Foster*, 94; George Guesnon, interview by William Russell, June 21, 1958, HNOC. Two months earlier, *Down Beat* reported that Morton did not claim to have created swing or jazz: "Although he knows definitely that he picked it up when the music form hitched rides, all he claims is the first use of the word, 'stomp'" (Martin, "Black Diamond Express").

59. Omer Simeon, "Mostly About Morton," *Jazz Record* 37, October 1945, 5.

60. A 1917 article in the *Indianapolis Freeman* said Handy "ushered into musical composition a new FORM. A style to which no man can lay earlier claim—the BLUES style," and in 1919 the *Chicago Defender* called him "The Daddy of the Blues" (Abbott and Seroff, 'They Cert'ly Sound Good to Me,'" 422, 425). An announcement in the *Chicago Whip* (November 1920, 5) called him "Father of the Blues" as if it were a familiar phrase.

61. W. C. Handy, "I Would Not Play Jazz if I Could . . . ," *Down Beat* 5(9), September 1938, 5.

62. W. C. Handy, interview by Alan Lomax, May 9, 1938, AFC. Allius or Ollis Brown was a lawman in the country around Bessemer, Alabama, when Handy was living there in the early 1890s, and Handy recalled a song about him (Abbe Niles, introduction to Handy, *Blues: An Anthology*, 19). Two variants that did not name Brown were recorded in 1927, by the Birmingham harmonica player Ollis Martin as "Police and High Sheriff Come Ridin' Down" and as a square-dance instrumental by the (presumably white) Aiken County String Band as "High Sheriff," and Jesse Fuller recorded it in the mid-1950s as "Hangin' Round a Skin Game."

63. Abbe Niles (introduction to Handy, *Blues: An Anthology*, 42) wrote of the dual publication: "Neither song was stolen from the other, but the basis of the version here given was played and sung to Handy by a wandering musician who said he had it from a hymn (yet unidentified) . . . No doubt he visited Louisville as well."

64. Schuller, *Early Jazz*, 136.

65. Leonard Feather, *The Book of Jazz* (New York: Meridian, 1959), 27; Roy Carew, "Of This and That and Jelly Roll," *Jazz Journal* 10(12), December 1957.

66. Albert Glenny, interview by Alan Lomax, April 1949, https://archive.culturale quity.org/node/998. Leonard Bechet corrected Glenny, saying, "But they used to call it ragtime," and Glenny concurred: "Years ago, they didn't know no jazz, they used to call that a ragtime band."

67. Alphonse Picou, interview by Alan Lomax, April 3, 1949, recording archived at https://archive.culturalequity.org/node/61805.

Chapter Four

1. Marshall Stearns and Jean Stearns, *Jazz Dance: The Story of American Vernacular Dance* (New York: Macmillan, 1968), 24.

2. Jelly Roll Morton, letter to Rod Carew, June 22, 1938, HNOC. Leonard Bechet similarly said Bolden's band played ragtime and he credited Manuel Perez with leading the first jazz band (https://archive.culturalequity.org/field-work/new-orleans-jazz -interviews-1949/leonard-bechet-449/interview-leonard-bechet-about-early).

3. E. Belfield Spriggins, "Excavating Jazz," *Louisiana Weekly*, April 22, 1933, quoted in Lynn Abbott, "Remembering Mr. E. Belfield Spriggins: First Man of Jazzology," *78 Quarterly* 1(10), 1999, 14. Spriggins's bowdlerization of "funky butt" as "rotten gut" may have inspired the widespread belief that this song is about farting.

4. I have found no printed mention of Funky Butt Hall before the 1940s, but since the name was considered unprintable, that proves nothing.

5. Meryman, *Louis Armstrong*, 8. Armstrong sometimes said he heard Bolden play outside the hall, but here said, "If I ever heard Buddy Bolden play the cornet, I figure that's when."

6. *The Compact Edition of the Oxford English Dictionary*, vol. 1, 1096, dated to 1623. Earlier uses of *funk*, relating to sparks or smoke, are documented from the fourteenth century, including the obscure "That was not worth a fonk." Since the eighteenth century, the word has had other meanings, including "cowardice" and "depression."

7. Davis, *Livin' the Blues*, 36–37.

8. Collins and Collins, *Oh, Didn't He Ramble*, 62–63.

9. Charles Edward Smith, notes to Jelly Roll Morton, *New Orleans Memories*, General Records, 1940.

10. Zora Neale Hurston, "Tampa," recorded by Herbert Halpert, Jacksonville, Florida, 1939, downloaded from Florida State Archives, https://www.floridamemory.com/audio/hurston.php.

11. Jelly Roll Morton's New Orleans Jazzmen, "I Thought I Heard Buddy Bolden Say," Bluebird B-1043, 1939; Ramsey, "Victor Recording Session." I've corrected a typo, "ruin the chance," to "run the chance." Chris Smith notes Cow Cow Davenport's punning take-off on the window verses ("Mootch Piddle," Vocalion 1282, 1929): "Pull up the windows? No! Say you want some air? No, baby, we don't need no air. Without the windows down, there ain't no funk-tion!"

12. Mississippi John Hurt, LOC recording, July 1963.

13. Willie Parker interview, 7 Nov 1958, in HJA.

14. Handwritten ms., Eber Carle Perrow collection of Southern ballads, 1908–1909, Houghton Library, Harvard University; Randolph, *Roll Me in Your Arms*, 175–176; Pete Harris, "miscellaneous verses of reels . . . Richmond, Texas, May, 1934," typescript, supplied by John Cowley from Lomax papers, AFC; White, *American Negro Folk-Songs*, 279.

15. Lafcadio Hearn, "Levee Life," *Cincinnati Commercial*, March 17, 1876, quoted in *Lafcadio Hearn's America: Ethnographic Sketches and Editorials* (Lexington: University Press of Kentucky, 2002), 48, 51. The prohibitions against race-mixing were brutally unequal, but the realities were complex. When Alan Lomax suggested that relationships between Black men and white women were impossible in the South, Big Bill Broonzy responded, "More of it in the South than it is in the North. . . . There's women down there that's got Negroes and Negroes, and Negroes on top of Negroes" (https://archive.culturalequity.org/field-work/big-bill-broonzy-1952/paris-552/interview-big-bill-broonzy-about-black-men-and-white). See Martha Hodes, *White Women, Black Men: Illicit Sex in the Nineteenth-Century South* (New Haven, CT: Yale University Press, 1997.

16. Galloway's birthdate and instruments are given in Vernhettes and Lindström, *Jazz Puzzles*, 32; Peyton's birthdate is from Snyder, "'Garde ici et 'garde lá-bas," 68.

17. The two-row accordions that became standard in the southern United States have the rows tuned a fourth apart and can only play in two or three keys. There is another tuning system, in which the two rows are a half step apart, which is less suited to solo dance accompaniment but can play chromatic melodies, and it is possible Peyton had one of those, since Louis Nelson Delisle said he could not play Peyton's instrument. (Snyder, "'Garde ici et 'garde lá-bas," 71; Snyder, "Leadbelly and His Windjammer: Examining the African American Button Accordion Tradition," *American Music* 12(2), Summer 1994.)

18. Louis Jones, Hogan interview 19 Jan 1959; Vernhettes with Lindström, *Jazz Puzzles*, 32.

19. Goffin, *La Nouvelle-Orléans*, 126–127. I assume Goffin translated Picou's words, but it is possible that their interview was in French.

20. Louis Jones, interview, January 19, 1959, HJA.

21. Papa John Joseph, interview, November 26, 1958, HJA.

22. Edward "Kid" Ory, interview, April 20, 1957, HJA, in McCusker, *Creole Trombone*, 59–60; Marquis, *In Search of Buddy Bolden*, 100, quoting Bill Matthews, interview, May 10, 1959, HJA. Matthews's 1909 marriage certificate gave his age as twenty, and he also recalled Bolden playing waltzes.

23. Richard M. Jones interview, HNOC, mss. 519, Jazzmen folder 29. This is an undated typescript and the quotation seems to be a mix of Jones's words and the transcriber's paraphrase.

24. The Mississippi Delta blues guitarist Son House, born in 1902, recalled that his father and uncles had a brass band and "back in that time they didn't care for guitar much." (Interview by John Fahey, Barry Hansen, and Mark LeVine, in Venice, California, May 7, 1965. On file at the JEMF Archive, Chapel Hill, North Carolina.)

25. *Music from the South, Vol. 1: Country Brass Bands*, Folkways LP FA 2650, 1955. The Lapsey band's keys were E flat, B flat, and "the Spanish," described by a bandmember as "low music . . . you couldn't hardly hear 'em playing . . . that's Spanish . . . In E flat and B flat, that's up high . . . anybody can hear us, four an' five miles around."

26. Baby Dodds and Larry Gara, *Baby Dodds Story* (Baton Rouge: Louisiana State University, 1992), 14. Sam Charters (*Jazz New Orleans*, 24) wrote that Black musicians knew "Tiger Rag" as "Jack Carey" and white musicians called it "Nigger Number 2"— perhaps to distinguish it from another tune with that number. Other sources say it was generally known as "Number Two," and Johnny DeDroit and His New Orleans Jazz Orchestra recorded it in 1924 as "Number Two Blues."

27. Oliver and McCormick, *Blues Come to Texas*, 335–336.

28. Oliver and McCormick, *Blues Come to Texas*, 74.

29. Oliver and McCormick, *Blues Come to Texas*, 330.

30. Randolph, *Blow the Candle Out*, 758–759, 761. New Orleans musicians recalled that the tune published as "Milenberg Joys" had previously been known as "Pee Hole Blues" (Ramsey and Smith, *Jazzmen*, 32). Manuel Manetta recalled Bab Frank having a piece called "The Shit," adding, "Ladies come right up and ask for that" (interview, June 20, 1958, HNOC). Earl Humphrey recalled Chris Kelly's band playing a tune called "D.M.F." or "Dirty M.F." when they were tired and wanted to end a dance, because it always started fights (Karl Koenig, "Chris Kelly: Blues King of New Orleans Jazz," *The Second Line*, vol. 35, no. 4, Spring 1983, http://basinstreet.com/wp-content /uploads/2016/09/Jazz-Article3.pdf, 92).

31. Vance Randolph, "The Names of Ozark Fiddle Tunes," *Midwest Folklore* 4(2), Summer 1954, 82–86; Randolph, *Blow the Candle Out*, 759.

32. Randolph, *Blow the Candle Out*, 762–772.

33. John Wesley Work Jr., *Folk Song of the American Negro* (Nashville, TN: Press of Fisk University, 1915), 27.

34. W. C. Handy, *Father of the Blues*, 85, 207.

35. Alec Robertson, interview by Alan Lomax, Clarksdale,, Mississippi, July 28, 1942, https://archive.culturalequity.org/tapes/afs6641. Lomax wrote that Robertson was eighty-seven, and he may be the Alex Robertson listed in the 1900 census as being born in 1868.

36. Davin, "Conversations," 2(5), 15–16.

37. Barker, *Buddy Bolden*, 9.

38. Wynton Marsalis, interview by Bill Milkowski, *Jazz Times*, April 2007.

39. Barker's recordings of four Indian chants were apparently made between autumn 1950, when he moved to New York from Los Angeles, and autumn 1953 (Molly Reid Cleaver, personal communication, March 14, 2023). The issued records are mentioned in the *New Orleans Item*, February 14, 1954. Crawford's record is usually dated to

November 1953, but the first solid evidence of its release is a note in *Billboard*, March 6, 1954. Louis Dumaine released a record called "To-Wa-Bac-A-Wa" in 1927, but it is an instrumental version of the tune commonly known as "My Bucket's Got a Hole in It."

40. Barney Bigard with Barry Martyn, *With Louis and the Duke: The Autobiography of a Jazz Clarinetist* (Basingstoke, UK: Macmillan, 1987), 8.

41. Armstrong, *Satchmo*, 97–98. Charlie Lester quotes Bigard's original wording in "The New Negro of Jazz: New Orleans, Chicago, New York, the First Great Migration, & the Harlem Renaissance, 1890–1930" (PhD diss., University of Cincinnati, 2012, 66), citing a transcript archived in the HJA.

42. Staulz's draft record and most other sources spell his name this way, but the *Daily Picayune* (November 9, 1894) reported that "Lorenzo Stalls" had been charged with carrying a concealed weapon; Johnny St. Cyr said it should be spelled "Stawls" (interview, August 27, 1958, HJA); and Vernhettes and Lindström (*Jazz Puzzles*, 56) spell it "Staulze," tracing it to a German immigrant grandfather.

43. Roy Carew, "New Orleans Recollections," *Record Changer*, August 1943, 4; Carew, "Assorted Rags," *Record Changer*, February 1949, 6. Lee Collins recalled playing this tune at Funky Butt Hall with the "way I jazz" lyric, adding: "Of course, no one went to Funky Butt Hall but roustabouts, pimps, whores, and such." (Collins and Collins, *Oh, Didn't He Ramble*, 15.)

44. John Clark and Melissa San Roman, "'If You Don't Like What the Big Chief Say . . .': An Interview with Mr. Donald Harrison, Sr., Big Chief of the Guardians of the Flame," *Mesechabe: The Journal of Surregionalism* 8, Spring 1991.

45. Shane Lief and John McCusker, *Jockomo: The Native Roots of Mardi Gras Indians* (Jackson: University Press of Mississippi, 2019), 50, 75, 94–95, 136–137. The description of the paraders is from "Rex Has Come," *Daily Picayune* (New Orleans, LA), February 25, 1879. The first explicit mention of Black men masking as Indians is from 1895, but Lief and McCusker suggest the tradition was significantly older and the 1879 group was probably Black. Sugar Boy Crawford said he sang "Chock-A-Mo" and the record company misspelled it as "Jock-A-Mo."

46. Punch Miller, interview, April 9, 1957, HJA. William Russell told Guesnon that Miller wouldn't sing the "Tiger Rag" lyrics for him and asked if it was dirty; Guesnon said, "Sure, sure—it had some smut to it." (George Guesnon, interview, September 18, 1959, HNOC.)

47. Foster and Stoddard, *Pops Foster*, 56.

48. Punch Miller interview, April 9, 1957, HJA.

49. Barker, *Buddy Bolden*, 10.

50. Dena Epstein, *Sinful Tunes and Spirituals* (Urbana: University of Illinois Press, 1977), 187, quoting Clement Caines, *The History of the General Council and General Assembly of the Leeward Islands* (Basseterre, St. Christopher: R. Cable, 1804), 110–111.

51. Bryan Edwards, *The History, Civil and Commercial, of the British Colonies in the West Indies*, vol. 2, (Dublin: Luke White, 1793), excerpt in Abrahams and Szwed, *After Africa*, 292.

52. James Hungerford, *The Old Plantation* (New York: Harper, 1859), 100, 192.

53. "The Stage," *Indianapolis Freeman*, August 27, 1910, 5; "Original Rags," *Indianapolis Freeman*, February 14, 1914, 5.

54. Handy, *Blues: An Anthology*, 31; "Ralph Ellison's Territorial Vantage," interview, 1977–1978, in Ellison, *Living with Music*, 29.

55. Foster and Stoddard, *Pops Foster*, 96.

56. Kid Ory, interview, April 20, 1957, HJA.

57. Eddie Dawson, interview, June 28, 1961, HJA.

58. Israel Gorman, interview, October 21, 1959, HJA.

59. Oscar Monte Samuels, "New Orleans Makes a Claim," *Variety*, July 1, 1911, quoted in Gushee, "Nineteenth-Century Origins," 170. Gushee read this as evidence of early improvisation and was puzzled that "so much of the earliest jazz on phonograph records is so little improvised," but that discrepancy is an artifact of recording: the Original Dixieland Jass Band and their contemporaries were similarly described as playing anarchic music that was never the same twice, but because they were recorded, Gushee can hear how little of it was actually improvised.

60. Meryman, *Louis Armstrong*, 42–43.

61. Barker, *Buddy Bolden*, 22–23.

62. By 1955 Barker had "been collecting data and holding interviews for years" (Nat Hentoff, "Counterpoint," *Down Beat* 22(20), October 5, 1955, 65). He first published some Bottley recollections in the *Evergreen Review*, September 1965, and later explained to Alyn Shipton that this account was based on interviews and conversations with people who had seen or played with Bolden, plus "a little monkeyshine" (Barker, *Buddy Bolden*, ix).

63. Bill Matthews, interview May 10, 1959, HJA; Richard M. Jones, interview, HNOC mss. 519, Jazzmen folder 29; Vernhettes and Lindström, *Jazz Puzzles*, 31.

64. Bechet, *Treat It Gentle*, 83. Montudie Garland similarly recalled, "He'd have two or three with him at all times. One would carry his coat, another his horn" (Vernhettes and Lindström, *Jazz Puzzles*, 31).

65. Charters, *Jazz New Orleans*, 15a.

66. Foster and Stoddard, *Pops Foster*, 48–49, 89–90.

67. Russell, *New Orleans Style*, 176.

68. Shapiro and Hentoff, *Hear Me Talkin' to Ya*, 37; Foster and Stoddard, *Pops Foster*, 16; Manuel Manetta, interview, March 21, 1957, HJA. Robert McKinney spelled ratty as "raddy" in a 1940 piece quoting a New Orleans "baby doll" talking about "the way we used to walk down the street," which was excerpted in Saxon et al., *Gumbo Ya-Ya*, 9, and some later writers have used that spelling; in 1945, John Provenzano wrote of New Orleans music "good, bad and indifferent—jazz, fake, ragtime, raddy, and now called swing" ("Jazz Music of the Gay '90s," *Jazz Record* 36, September 1945, 11).

69. Russell, *New Orleans Style*, 104.

70. Barker, *Buddy Bolden*, 20–22. Other people mentioned "Pallet on the Floor" and "The Bucket's Got a Hole in It" among Bolden's regular numbers, and "All the Whores Like the Way I Ride" was recorded in later years by members of his band, but most of the titles in Barker's list are unsupported by other testimony and some may be his inventions. Several were common phrases that old-timers may have used for particular songs; "Don't Bring Me Posies (It's Shoesies That I Need)" was published in the 1920s and is presumably an anachronism, but could have been one of the numerous joke titles musicians used for generic blues or jam arrangements; Barker recorded a song called "Stick It Where You Stuck It Last Night" in 1992 that sounds

like something Bolden might have played but could also be something he composed after making this list.

71. Walter Davis, "I Can Tell by the Way You Smell," Bluebird B6059, 1935. In 1933 he and Roosevelt Sykes explored the same theme in "You Don't Smell Right," Bluebird B5324.

72. Buster Pickens, "The Ma Grinder No. 2," recorded by Mack McCormick, August 17, 1960; Roosevelt Sykes, as Dobby Bragg, "We Can Sell That Thing," Paramount 13004, 1930.

73. Charley Jordan, "Keep It Clean," Vocalion 1511, 1930.

74. Luke Jordan, "Won't You Be Kind?" Victor V38564, 1929.

75. Mance Lipscomb, recorded by Glen Alyn ca. 1970, http://glifos.lib .utexas.edu/index.php/Interviews_with_Mance_Lipscomb:Reel_2B, accessed May 25, 2011. Alyn printed an edited version of these lyrics and Lipscomb's explanation in Lipscomb, *I Say Me for a Parable*, 131–132. Lipscomb also recorded a version of this song on the LP *The Unexpurgated Folk Songs of Men*, 1960. Vance Randolph (*Roll Me in Your Arms*, 297) has a verse collected from a white Missourian in 1927 who described it as from Black tradition: "*I got another girl, she's lank and lean. / I like this girl because she keeps her boody clean.*"

76. Little Richard, in numerous interviews.

77. Philip Baker, "Assessing the African Contribution to French-Based Creoles," in *Africanisms in Afro-American Language Varieties*, ed. Salikoko S. Mufwene with Nancy Condon (Athens: University of Georgia Press, 1993), 142; Charles Bird et al., *An Ka Bamanankan Kalan: Introductory Bambara* (Bloomington: Indiana University Linguistics Club, 1977), 137; *Mandinka-English Dictionary* (Banjul, The Gambia: Peace Corps, 1995), 11, 133.

78. Super Sonic Sid, "Keep Your Booty Clean (Scrub That Butt)," Wrap/Ichiban Records 12-PO21, 1988.

Chapter Five

1. Jelly Roll Morton, written recollections given to Roy Carew, 1938; published in *Record Changer*, October 1944; in booklet to Morton, *Complete Library of Congress Recordings*, 53.

2. The sheet music for "Jelly Roll Blues" had no lyrics, and the lyric recorded by singers in the 1920s was unrelated to what Morton sang at the LOC, which may be a relic of his vaudeville act.

3. Manuel Manetta, interview, March 28, 1957, WRJC/HNOC, http://hnoc.mini sisinc.com/thnoc/catalog/3/10033.

4. "Kiser in Bad Again," *Times-Democrat* (New Orleans, LA), June 19, 1908, 15. The rest of the article spelled his name "Kizer."

5. "Marshall Kizer Meets His Death," *Daily Picayune* (New Orleans, LA), March 8, 1910, 7. A Blind Tiger was an establishment that sold alcoholic beverages in an area where such sales were prohibited.

6. "Negro Kills Enemy Who Threatened Him," *Daily Picayune* (New Orleans, LA), July 15, 1915, 12.

7. Meryman, *Louis Armstrong*, 19–20. Presumably "bylow" is Armstrong's idiosyncratic spelling of *Barlow knife*.

8. Ann Cook, "Mama Cookie," Victor 20579, 1927.

9. Alexander T. Wiatt, "An Interview with Earl Humphrey," *Jazz Report*, 5(6), 1966, 15.

10. Rosalind Johnson, interview, February 23, 1970, HNOC; Clarence Williams, *Boogie Woogie Blues Folio* (New York: Clarence Williams Music, 1940), 11.

11. Paige Van Vorst, "Little Brother Montgomery," *Jazzbeat* 19(1), 2007, 29.

12. Eddie Dawson, interview, April 5, 1972, HJA.

13. Bricktop, *Bricktop*, 65–66.

14. Henry Townsend, as told to Bill Greensmith, *A Blues Life* (Urbana: University of Illinois Press, 1999), 15.

15. Lomax notes, LOC, pdf file in Rounder box set, 191.

16. Brothers, *Louis Armstrong's New Orleans*, 34, 324; Armstrong, *Louis Armstrong, in His Own Words*, 124.

17. Honeyboy Edwards, Homesick James, and Hammie Nixon recalled Memphis Minnie doing sex work, Nixon describing a recording session where she suggested the male artists could use their earnings to buy some time with her. (Edwards in Lomax, Mississippi notebook, July 22, 1942, AFC; Lomax, *Land Where the Blues Began*, 402; James and Nixon in Paul Garon and Beth Garon, *Woman with Guitar: Memphis Minnie's Blues* [San Francisco: City Lights, 2014], 178.) The Garons write that some of Minnie's fans dismiss these stories, but the dismissal is not supported with evidence and reflects "middle class values" and "a violent antipathy to prostitutes [which] may contain truths about our attitudes toward women in general."

18. Storyville *Blue Books* are archived at HNOC, http://www.hnoc.org/virtual/story ville/blue-book. Pearl Wright is listed in 1905, May Wilson in 1906. There is also a May Wilson in a Mobile, Alabama, *Blue Book*, ca. 1912.

19. Jelly Roll Morton, "Mamie's Blues," on *New Orleans Memories*, General Records, 1940, and Charles Edward Smith, notes to this album.

20. Tucker, "Feminist Perspective," 240; Shapiro and Hentoff, *Hear Me Talkin' to Ya*, 7–8.

21. This comment is from Jelly Roll Morton, "Mamie's Blues," General Records, December 16, 1939.

22. Hanley, "Portraits from Jelly Roll's New Orleans"; "Girl Under the Wheels," *Daily Picayune* (New Orleans, LA), July 21, 1893, 6; "Criminal District Court," *Times-Picayune* (New Orleans, LA), September 22, 1898, 3.

23. Frank Leighton and Burt Leighton, "Origin of 'Blues' (or Jazz)," *Variety*, January 6, 1922, 27.

24. John Queen and Walter Wilson, *"Fare Thee, Honey, Fare Thee Well"*. (New York: Howley, Haviland & Dresser, 1901). Variants of this theme were recorded by Mamie Smith, the Mississippi singer Joe Callicott, and the Memphis Jug Band, among others; the Canadian patent office lists a "Fair Thee Well Blues" in 1927, credited to Thomas "Baby" Grice, whom Morton recalled as a prominent pianist in Mobile.

25. "Stackerlee," typescript, D. K. Wilgus Collection, UCLA Ethnomusicology Archive. Wilgus's source was Gershon Legman, who got it from a Parisian artist and bar owner named Hilaire Hiler. Legman variously wrote that Hiler's father got handwritten texts to this and "Frankie and Johnny" directly from Jones or from Les Copeland, a white ragtime pianist. Several verses are marked as Copeland's additions from

1928, implying that the others (including the ones I quote) were from Jones, but a note at the bottom says, "check with original hand-written version of Palmer Jones, 1903–1904," which I have not found. (Legman, "Who Owns Folklore?," *Western Folklore*, 21(1), January 1962, 2; Randolph, *Roll Me in Your Arms*, 480.) One of the Copeland verses refers to Stack's "old girl" as Nellie Sheldon—Stackolee's official name was Lee Shelton, and a version in the Robert Winslow Gordon collection at the AFC, sent in 1926 and dated to 1900–1901, has *"Go tell little Lilly Sheldon to get out on these icy blocks / And rustle for to get her man / Stackerlee some rocks."*

26. Perry Bradford, *Born with the Blues* (New York: Oak, 1965), 33–34. Bradford dated this trip to 1908 but wrote that it followed his tour with the New Orleans Minstrels; the *Indianapolis Freeman* reported he was leaving that troupe on October 17, 1903, and an article in the *Chicago Defender* of March 4, 1922, said he arrived in Chicago in 1906. Bradford's dates are generally unreliable; in the same book he gives his birth year as 1895, which would have made him thirteen in 1908; his World War I draft registration gives it as 1880, and the Atlanta city census of 1896 listed his age as sixteen. The 1900 census shows a Perry Bradford living in Chicago at 2400 Dearborn, a few blocks from Big Jim Colosimo's saloon.

27. Kid Ory, unpublished memoir, in McCusker, *Creole Trombone*, 49.

28. Collins and Collins, *Oh, Didn't He Ramble*, 19–20.

29. Brothers, *Louis Armstrong's New Orleans*, 199.

30. Foster and Stoddard, *Pops Foster*, 32–33.

31. Augustus Haggerty, State Penitentiary, Huntsville, TX, 1933 or 1934, typescript of lyric transcribed by John Lomax and Alan Lomax, AFC 1933/002, box 02, folder 025. Two other versions of this blues were recorded by the Lomaxes from Haggerty in Huntsville on November 20, 1934, as "I Met You Mama, 1929" and "When I First Met You, 1929."

32. E. Franklin Frazier, *The Negro Family in The United States* (Chicago: University of Chicago Press, 1939), 287–278.

33. Blair, *I've Got to Make My Livin'*, 10, 166.

34. *Sporting and Club House Directory* (Chicago: Ross & St. Clair, 1889), 38, quoted in Blair, *I've Got to Make My Livin'*, 63; information on Vina Fields is from Blair, *I've Got to Make My Livin'*, 123–124. Pamela Arcenault traces guidebooks for sex districts back to sixteenth-century Venice and lists examples from eighteenth-century London and nineteenth-century New York, Philadelphia, Milwaukee, Kansas City, Louisville, Los Angeles, and Colorado (*Guidebooks to Sin: The Blue Books of Storyville, New Orleans* [New Orleans: Historic New Orleans Collection, 2017], 32–33).

35. "Chips," *Broad Ax*, April 29, 1905, 4; Blair, *I've Got to Make My Livin'*, 186.

36. Oliver and McCormick, *Blues Come to Texas*, 138.

37. Andy Boy, "House Raid Blues," Bluebird B6858, 1937, apparently commemorating a raid on February 2, 1937, at a joint run by the wife of a man named Charlie Shiro, who is mentioned in a later verse (Chris Smith, personal communication, January 9, 2023).

38. Oliver and McCormick, *Blues Come to Texas*, 137.

39. Thomas, "South Texas Negro Work-Songs," 169.

40. Vice reformer George Kneeland, quoted in Kathy Peiss, "'Charity Girls' and City Pleasures: Historical Notes on Working-Class Sexuality, 1880–1920," in *Passion and*

Power: Sexuality in History, ed. Kathy Peiss and Christina Simmons (Philadelphia, PA: Temple University Press, 1989), 64.

41. Hurston, *Dust Tracks on a Road* [1942], in *Folklore, Memoirs*, 693. Regarding the varied implications of *whore*, a Louisiana court held that it was not slander to call a woman a whore if she "had carnal connection with a certain party" while unmarried, even if she later "married such party and has led a virtuous life ever since," but another held that a woman having sexual intercourse with her fiancé was not justification for calling her a whore, and a third specified that "not every act of illicit intercourse will justify calling a female a whore." (*Lawyers' Reports, Annotated, Book XXI* [Rochester, NY: Lawyers' Co-Operative, 1893], 506, notes to Louisiana Supreme Court case *Warner v. Clark*.)

42. Gilfoyle, *City of Eros*, 202.

43. Henry Russell Talbot et al., *Report of the Portland Vice Commission to the Mayor and City Council of the City of Portland, Oregon, January 1913* (Portland: np, 1913), 7, 15, 18, 24, 26, 197.

44. Long, *Great Southern Babylon*, 223. Katharine Bement Davis, superintendent of the New York Reformatory for Women at Bedford Hills, wrote that many women took up sex work because "compared with domestic service and factory work, prostitution . . . offered a better living" (Gilfoyle, *City of Eros*, 277); Maya Angelou wrote that in the sporting world, "smart women were prostitutes and stupid ones were waitresses" (Maya Angelou, *Gather Together in My Name* [New York: Bantam, 1975], 33). There were numerous cases of white men backing Black "landladies," an arrangement that could be highly profitable for both parties. Even before the Civil War, two free women of color, Fanny and Septimia Barnett, ran a bawdy house in Charlottesville, Virginia, for several decades and amassed substantial real estate holdings, in part with loans guaranteed by prominent local white men. (Kirt von Daacke, *Freedom Has a Face: Race, Identity, and Community in Jefferson's Virginia* [Charlottesville: University of Virginia Press, 2012], 139–169.)

45. "A Bad Woman," *Daily Picayune* (New Orleans, LA), December 22, 1904, 10. The judge dismissed the case and the *Picayune* suggested Jackson should be the person on trial.

46. Randolph, *Roll Me in Your Arms*, 313–314, sung by C.M., Joplin, Missouri, 1928, who said he heard it near Fort Smith, Arkansas, in the 1890s. Some verses collected from women made fun of beating the rape victims: *"Yaller gal, yaller gal, sleepin' in the grass / Massa wake her up with a hickory on her ass."*

47. Mattie Mae Thomas, recorded by Herbert Halpert at Parchman Farm, 1939, *Jailhouse Blues*, Rosetta Records LP 1316, 1987. A version transcribed from a woman in Parchman in 1935 is reprinted in Shobana Shankar, "Parchman Women Write the Blues? What Became of Black Women's Prison Music in Mississippi in the 1930s," *American Music* 31(2), Summer 2013, 194–195. The Lomax song files at the AFC have an uncredited "Danger Blues," apparently from the 1930s, with the verse about the blue-eyed baby, and they printed a "Tie Tamping Chant" credited to Rochelle Harris, whom they recorded in the Tennessee State Penitentiary in Nashville in 1933, with the variant *"Mary got a baby, an' I know it ain' mine, / I b'lieve it is de cap'n's 'cause he goes dere all de time"* (Lomax and Lomax, *American Ballads*, 18).

48. *New Orleans Memories*, General Records 4001-4005, 1940.

49. Shapiro and Hentoff, *Hear Me Talkin' to Ya*, 11; Lomax notes to the LOC box, 183. Roy Carew, a rare white listener who was already interested in jazz and blues, wrote that the music in the Arlington Annex on Basin Street seemed intended "to add to the 'genteel' atmosphere" and he did not remember "any playing there that had any claim to merit." ("New Orleans Recollections," *Record Changer*, September 1943, 3).

50. Rosalind Johnson, interview, February 23, 1970, HNOC; *St. Louis Globe-Democrat*, May 25, 1905, 10. The advertisement does not mention the nature of the establishment, but the address was 2626 Lucas, otherwise identified as Mama Lou's house.

51. Lelia Chapman was mentioned in a series of stories about an off-duty policeman who gave a group of women at Piazza's house some doped whiskey; for example, *New Orleans Item*, February 26, 1907. Marquis (*In Search of Buddy Bolden*, 45) mentions Leda Chapman's relationship with Bolden and documents her multiple arrests between 1900 and 1906. Abbott and Seroff (*Original Blues*, 39) cite Lelia's appearance at Lincoln Gardens and assume she is the same person as Leda; records for Lelia and Leda give roughly the same ages (twenty and eighteen, respectively, in 1900), and Emma Thornton appeared on the same show and was both a singer and an associate of Bolden's.

52. Shapiro and Hentoff, *Hear Me Talkin' to Ya*, 71.

53. Creole George Guesnon, in Russell, *Oh, Mister Jelly*, 107. Russell wrote "Corinne Medley," but Guesnon was clearly talking about Mantley. Sweetwine was a fairly common last name, but I haven't found an Effie or F. E. Sweetwine in any listings.

54. Leonard Bechet, interview by Alan Lomax, April 1949, Association for Cultural Equity, recording T994R02. Emily Landau, author of *Spectacular Wickedness*, writes: "The fact that there were high-class houses that catered to middle-class Black men is a fact worth emphasizing, because everything that I know that's been written about the area has neglected to consider even the possibility of such houses" (personal communication, August 30, 2021).

55. Lomax notes to the LOC sessions. Lomax transcribed the names as "Blackenstein" and "Aberdeen," a common New Orleans pronunciation of *Abadie*.

56. Blankenstein's parents are identified in her death certificate. The 1900 census lists her living in Natchez with her mother, Delia, age forty-five, and an older brother named Robert. The 1910 census has Fritz Blankenstein, grocery merchant, fifty-two, living with a white wife and three young daughters. Blankenstein and Abadie are listed in New Orleans in the 1910 census and the 1911 and 1912 city directories, then disappear from official records until Blankenstein's death in Tucson in 1929.

57. Rosalind Johnson, interview, February 23, 1970, HNOC.

58. "New Orleans Negroes Lead Their Race in Enterprise," *Daily Picayune* (New Orleans, LA), August 19, 1909, 5.

59. "Cold Murder," *Daily Picayune* (New Orleans, LA), November 8, 1913, 11.

60. Barker, *Buddy Bolden*, 53, 68–69, 77–90.

61. Morton claimed authorship of "Someday Sweetheart," published in 1919 and credited to John and Reb Spikes. He worked with the Spikes brothers in Oklahoma, was musical director for an amusement park they ran in Los Angeles, and shared credit with them for several songs, including "Wolverine Blues."

62. This section is based on numerous clippings from the *San Diego Union* and *Evening Tribune* and the African American *California Eagle*. Some hint at the bordello, which

is mentioned in Micheal Austin's "Harlem of the West: The Douglas Hotel and Creole Palace Nite Club," Master's thesis, University of San Diego, 1994.

63. Lovalerie King, *Race, Theft, and Ethics: Property Matters in African American Literature* (Baton Rouge: Louisiana State University Press, 2007), 38–39.

64. Gene Campbell, "Robbin' and Stealin' Blues," 1930; Bo Carter, "Old Devil," 1938; Davin, "Conversations," 2(5), 16.

65. E. Franklin Frazier, *The Negro Family in the United States* (Chicago: University of Chicago Press, 1939), 286–287, 288.

66. Harry Middleton Hyatt, *Hoodoo—Conjuration—Witchcraft—Rootwork*, vol. 2 (Washington, DC: American University Bookstore, 1970), 1681–1682. The woman amended her first mention of white men, saying, "white men or colored men—doesn't matter 'bout the nationality," but continued with specific reference to white customers.

67. Bricktop, *Bricktop*, 30–31; Taylor and Cook, *Alberta Hunter*, 29. King Oliver and Paul Barbarin honored Williams with a tune called "Tack Annie."

68. Collins and Collins, *Oh, Didn't He Ramble*, 24.

69. Lomax, *Mister Jelly Roll*, 104–105.

70. Meryman, *Louis Armstrong*, 19.

71. George Guesnon, interview by William Russell, September 18, 1959, HNOC.

72. John Handy, interviews, HJA, first section quoted in Karl Koenig, "Tango Belt," 184, https://basinstreet.com, accessed 2/11/2021; second from taped interview, December 1958. In another context, Alan Lomax quoted a singer of lumberjack songs, apparently in the northern United States, saying, "Nowadays the chippies like these old songs, just like the lumberjacks used to. They'll give me a dollar and a drink to sing it in those places where there ain't no decent girls" (Lomax, AFC 1933/002, box 03, folder 038).

73. Randolph, *Blow the Candle Out*, 725. This example was from a man in Pineville, Missouri, in 1927; another, from a woman in Noel, Missouri, referred to a "little brown spot" rather than a "poor little pussy." The Lomaxes preserved a variant from the Clement State Prison Farm in Texas, ca. 1933: *"Here's to the woman wears tailor-made clothes, / Spool heel slippers, polka dot hose, / Plumes on her hat twelve feet tall— / Her blessed little pussy gonna pay for it all."* (Lomax, AFC 1933/002, box 05, folder 050).

74. Waters, *His Eye Is on the Sparrow*, 17.

75. Collins and Collins, *Oh, Didn't He Ramble*, 64.

76. Charles Edward Smith, letter to William Russell, December 1939, quoted in Russell, *Oh, Mister Jelly*, 479.

77. Richard M. Jones was from southern Louisiana and his "Trouble in Mind" has the couplet *"I'm gonna lay my head on some lonesome railroad line / Let the 219 satisfy my mind."* Mooch Richardson, who seems to have been from the Memphis-Arkansas region, recorded a "T and T Blues" in 1928 with the line *"If I miss the 219, I'm sure gon' catch the Cannonball."*

78. The Armstrong-Bechet "219 Blues" was recorded for Decca in 1940; the George Lewis version, with a vocal by Elmer Talbert, was recorded in 1950 for Paradox. The Lewis version is musically similar to a version recorded by Lu Watters's band with Bunk Johnson in 1944, with a vocal by the white banjo player Clancy Hayes that mimics Morton's delivery on the General recording of "Mamie's Blues."

79. Lucille Bogan, "Tricks Ain't Walking No More," Brunswick 7186, 1930 (credited on other labels as Bessie Jackson).

80. Bogan recorded "They Ain't Walking No More" twice, but the first recording was not released and the second was presumably a retake.

81. This quotation is generally ascribed to New York police inspector Alexander S. Williams; the earliest source I find is "Of 'Fighting Alec'," *Daily Jeffersonian* (Cleveland, OH), August 23, 1894, 4, which dates it to his assuming command of the Eighth Precinct, on Prince Street in what is now SoHo, in 1876.

82. Robert McKinney, "Folklore on the Riverfront," unpublished manuscript, FWP, Northwestern State University, Natchitoches, LA, folder 53. Carolina Slim recited a toast he wrote to a woman who left him the day the *Titanic* sank in 1912, suggesting he was born in the 1890s or earlier.

83. Laurraine Goreau, *Just Mahalia, Baby: The Mahalia Jackson Story* (Gretna, LA: Pelican, 1975), 63, 83, 94.

84. Rufus "Speckled Red" Perryman, "The Dirtier Dozen," Delmark LP, 1956.

85. Lomax Collection, AFC 1933-001, box 10, folder 329. The John Lomax papers (UT, box 3D-202, folder 9) have a variant of this verse, apparently sent by someone in prison, with the lines *"Dese women 'roun' here mus' be fuckin' fo' fun / Dere meats all raw en' dere bread aint done,"* and a coda contrasting men in Cincinnati and Washington who *"live at ease"* and *"do as he please,"* while *"an Alabamy man will git on his knees / An' chew more cock dan a rat do cheese."*

86. Robert McKinney, "The History of the Baby Dolls," FWP, Northwestern State University, Natchitoches, LA, folder 423.

87. Billie Holiday with William Dufty, *Lady Sings the Blues* (Garden City, NY: Doubleday, 1956), 15–16.

88. Bertha Idaho, "Down on Pennsylvania Avenue," Columbia 14437-D, 1929. A rhyme titled "Whorehouse Chant" in the Canfield collection denounces this kind of chiseling: *"Chancres, blue-balls, crabs and lice, / I've had 'em all and some of 'em twice, / But the cock sucker who cuts a whore's price, / Is a son of a bitch, by Jesus Christ."*

89. Lomax papers, UT, box 3D-202. This is one of five poems and a list of monikers with no concrete provenance but apparently collected with other prison folklore in the 1930s.

90. Lil Johnson, "New Shave 'Em Dry," Vocalion 03428, 1936.

91. "Banjo lesson with George Guesnon," May 17, 1958, HNOC mss. 530.3.25. A popular Texas piano piece was called "The Ma Grinder," presumably a variant of *motherfucker*. Augustus Haggerty sang a blues with the line, *"Tell me Houston is a city and Galveston is a sea-port town / I'm going to move to San Antonio, stamp that big ma grinder down"* (Lomax papers, UT, box 3D-192). Guesnon wrote the phrase that way but sings it more like "moan grinder," which Sunpie Barnes defines as "Ol school word for whore . . . someone who sells sex to anyone who buys it, male, female, or in between. Like the organ grinder, the moan grinder will make it happen." (personal communication, July 12, 2021).

92. Little Brother Montgomery, "Shave 'Em Dry," *Deep South Piano*, Agram CD.

93. Walter Roland, "I'm Gonna Shave You Dry," ca. 1935, first issued on *Copulatin' Blues vol. 2*, Stash LP ST-122, 1984.

94. "Shake 'Em On Down" was recorded by Booker "Bukka" White in 1937, by Bo Carter and Big Bill Broonzy in 1938, and by Tommy McClennan and a Mississippi prison inmate named Lucille Walker in 1939.

95. Steve Calt, *Barrelhouse Words: A Blues Dialect Dictionary* (Urbana: University of Illinois Press, 2010), 213.

96. Lucille Bogan (as Bessie Jackson), "Shave 'Em Dry," Perfect 16972, 1935; Sippie Wallace, "Parlor Social Deluxe," OKeh 8232, 1925; Alberta Prime and Sonny Greer, "Parlor Social Deluxe," Blu-Disc T1007, 1924. (Prime [aka Pryme] is sometimes incorrectly identified as Alberta Hunter.)

97. Oliver, *Screening the Blues*, 225.

98. Bogan's obscene "Shave Me Dry" was listed in the ARC session log for July 19, 1933, as "test for A. E. Satherley" and numbered TO-1317, following "Till the Cows Come Home," which was TO-1316. Walter Roland played piano on this session and may have composed or co-composed the lyrics.

Chapter Six

1. Wright, *Mr. Jelly Lord*, 93, 195.

2. *M. H. Levy v. The State*, decided November 13, 1889, in *Texas Court of Appeals Reports: Cases Argued and Adjudged in the Court of Criminal Appeals of the State of Texas*, vol. 28 (1890), 206; *John H. Fitzpatrick v. The State*, decided January 13, 1897, in *Texas Criminal Reports: Cases Argued and Adjudged in the Court of Criminal Appeals of the State of Texas*, vol. 37 (1898), 21. These are the earliest English-language examples of *motherfucker*, but the insult was documented as μητροκοιτης (*mētrokoitēs*) in the writings of the Greek poet Hipponax in the fifth century BCE.

3. Frances Mouton Oliver, interview, May 10, 1969, HNOC, mss. 530.4.43.

4. Sam Chatmon, interview and performance, filmed by Alan Lomax, John Bishop, and Worth Long, Hollandale, Mississippi, August 1978, https://youtu.be/AkEhtf PN084, accessed October 13, 2021.

5. Handy's recording was released by Columbia Records in 1917 as "Sweet Child, introducing: 'Pallet on the Floor.'" "Sweet Child" was a pop song by Wallace Stovall and Billy V. Ewing; "Pallet" was credited to Pace and Handy.

6. Advertisement, *Washington Bee*, August 11, 1906, 8, and elsewhere. The Dandy Dixie Minstrels included dancers, musicians, jugglers, acrobats, and the Dixie College Rangers performing "a beautiful and harmonious blending of varsity class songs, patriotic airs, with the sweet old-time song of the south." Jones's other big number in that period was "If the Man in the Moon Were a Coon"; in 1909–1911 he was touring with Bob Cole and Rosamond Johnson in *The Red Moon*; and in 1913 the *Indianapolis Freeman* described him as an "eccentric dancer and singing comedian."

7. The Leake County Revelers recorded a fiddle tune for Columbia in 1928 titled "Make Me a Bed on the Floor," though they sang, "*Make me a pallet down on the floor.*" John Lomax printed a version of "Rye Whiskey" with the chorus "*O Baby, O Baby, I've told you before, / Do make me a pallet, I'll lie on the floor*" (Lomax, *Cowboy Songs*, 293–294); Howard Odum printed a lyric from a Black singer that began "*Make me a palat on de flo', / Make it in de kitchen behin' de do'*" ("Folk-song and Folk-poetry," 278–279).

8. H. A. Cherry, Lilesville, North Carolina, ca. 1924, in Newman Ivey White, ed., *The Frank C. Brown Collection of North Carolina Folklore*, vol. 3 (Durham, NC: Duke University Press, 1952), 546. White collected earlier variants of this verse in 1915–1919 (*American Negro Folk-Songs*, 317, 320).

9. George W. Lee, *Beale Street: Where the Blues Began* (New York: Ballou, 1934), 141.

10. Son Simms told Lomax (*Land Where the Blues Began*, 415): "That's how these women will do you, when you're off from home. They don't want to get the bed nasty with them and their kid man, so they put some old quilt down on the floor so they can do their business."

11. Hurt's and Chatmon's prewar recordings do not have the "Pallet on the Floor" verse, but both included it when they recorded the song in the 1960s and 1970s, and the earlier omission—like the alternate titles—was presumably intentional, so the recordings could be published as original compositions. Harris's recording includes the "Pallet on the Floor" verse, and other Mississippians of the same generation recorded versions of the song under the traditional title in later years.

12. Sam Chatmon, interview and performances, filmed by Alan Lomax, John Bishop, and Worth Long, Hollandale, Mississippi, August 1978, https://youtu.be /AkEhtfPN084, accessed October 13, 2021.

13. Sam Chatmon, interview by Lou Curtiss, 1969, quoted in *Khrome Kazoo* 13, 1970, https://blues-facts.proboards.com/thread/112/sam-chatmon. Bob Eagle identifies the sister as Gena Chatmon, and adds that Sam told him she was born in 1865 but the 1880 census listed her as seven years old (personal communication, October 13, 2021).

14. Chatmon Brothers (Lonnie and Sam), "If You Don't Want Me Please Don't Dog Me 'Round," Bluebird B6717, recorded October 15, 1936.

15. Jelly Roll Morton, letter to Roy Carew, September 29, 1940, HNOC, transcript in Russell, *Oh, Mister Jelly*, 269; parentheses in the original. In the summer of 1940 Morton attended meetings and saved flyers about Jewish and Communist influence in the entertainment business. His letter of June 8, 1940 (Russell, *Oh, Mister Jelly*, 248) warned that "the Jews are in a dominating position at this time, they are in control of the Union, radio stations, publishers, booking agents & etc. either Jews & Communists. . . . The Basin St. [radio] program happened to be controlled by this group . . . & it was told to me, my friend L. [presumably Lomax] is one. I always had a faint thought that he was."

16. Lomax, *Land Where the Blues Began*, 178–180. This version, ascribed to Houston Bacon, includes an "Uncle Bud" verse: *Uncle Bud got geese, Uncle Bud got ducks, / Uncle Bud got gals that really can fuck.*

17. "Tie Shuffling Song," transcribed by John or Alan Lomax from the singing of a section gang worker (perhaps Henry Truvillion) in Wiergate, Texas, June 1933, Lomax, AFC 1933/002, folder 073.

18. Mose Andrews, "Ten Pound Hammer," Decca 7338, March 30, 1937; Teddy Darby, "Spike Driver," Decca 7816, April 10, 1937. A spike-driving chant collected in 1933 took another comic tack, with the group chorusing *Driving hard—huh* to mark hammer strokes and punctuate the leader's commentary on a woman: *"hard to please, never done / Just one inch, was the bargain / Wants another, and another . . . / Wants a yard, foot ain't enough / Wants my hammer, handle too . . . "* (Louis W. Chappell, *John Henry: A Folk-Lore Study* [Jena, Germany: Frommannsche Verlag Walter Biedermann, 1933], 86–87.)

19. Lomax, *Land Where the Blues Began*, 442; Abrahams, *Deep Down*, 74–75. The toast was recited by John H. "Kid" Mike and may be a later parody of the familiar ballad, but early writers mentioned railroad workers using similarly explicit language.

20. Lomax, AFC 1933/002, miscellaneous texts, 1933–1934, folder 066.

21. Saxon et al., *Gumbo Ya-Ya*. McKinney is mentioned in the introduction as having collected much of the "Riverfront Lore," but not credited with the songs he collected or

with several sections he wrote, including two chapters, "Chimney Sweeper's Holiday" and "A Good Man Is Hard to Find," and the sections on the Zulus and Baby Dolls.

22. Black Pearl was previously known officially as Carrollton and unofficially by a name the local civil rights activist Lolis Elie discusses in a piece called "Niggertown Memories" (*Black River Journal* 1, 1977). Some older Black residents still use the latter name, with the implication that it was renamed Black Pearl to encourage white gentrification.

23. Hazel Prosper, born ca. 1900, is listed in city records as living two blocks from McKinney, worked as a schoolteacher, and their obituaries suggest they both attended St. Joan of Arc Catholic Church. I found no records for Ethel Easter, but one of McKinney's other informants, Earl Easter, lived two blocks from Prosper.

24. "Purry tongue" appears in a Black hobo toast dated to the 1930s (Anthony M. Reynolds, "Urban Negro Toasts: A Hustler's View from L.A.," *Western Folklore* 33(4), October 1974, 293). Frank Marshall Davis and Ray Charles recalled "purr tongue" from their Kansas and Florida youths (Davis, *Livin' the Blues*, 36; Ray Charles and David Ritz, *Brother Ray* [New York: Dial Press, 1978], 130). A "Freaks Ball" toast recorded from Elmer Lee Harvey in an Arizona youth facility in 1961 has "pearl tongue" (Archive of Traditional Music, Indiana University, Bloomington, ATL 5573, 061-41-F; Roberts, "Negro Folklore," 174); a transcription from 1965 has "pulltongue," but the transcriber says it could have been "pearl" (Jackson, *Get Your Ass in the Water*, 139, and personal communication, October 18, 2021), and that variant appears in poems by Quincy Troupe (*Watts Poets: A Book of New Poetry & Essays* [Los Angeles: House of Respect, 1968], 76) and Jayne Cortez ("Consultation," in *Scarifications* [New York: Bola Press], 1973), in one of Snoop Dogg's verses in "Bitches Ain't Shit" (*The Chronic*, 1992), and in some recent Black romance/porn novels, one of which also has "purr tongue."

25. Sallie Tisdale, *Talk Dirty to Me: An Intimate Philosophy of Sex* (New York: Doubleday, 1994), 240; Virginia Braun and Celia Kitzinger, "'Snatch,' 'Hole,' or 'Honey-Pot'? Semantic Categories and the Problem of Nonspecificity in Female Genital Slang," *Journal of Sex Research* 38(2), May 2001, 153; John S. Farmer and W. E. Henley, eds., *Slang and Its Analogues Past and Present*, vol. 4, printed for subscribers only, 1896, 278.

26. Jacob Beasley is listed in Black Pearl in the 1920, 1930, and 1940 censuses; in 1920 he was listed as fifteen years old, with his brother Herbert, thirteen; McKinney included a blues from Herbert in a manuscript on riverfront lore.

27. "I wouldn't touch her with a borrowed prick" was dated to the 1930s by Helen Lawrenson ("The First of the Big-Time Harlem Hustlers," *Esquire*, December 1, 1972, 296) and abbreviated by Ernest Hemingway as "Not with a borrowed" (*To Have and Have Not* [London: Jonathan Cape, 1937], 136).

28. Saxon et al., *Gumbo Ya-Ya*, 372.

29. Robert McKinney, "Mary Davis," UNC FWP papers, box 3709, folder 1024.

30. Robert McKinney, "Religion in de Dreams," interview with Samuel Jenkins, March 8, 1939, in UNC FWP papers, box 3709, folder 1023.

31. Robert McKinney, "Folklore on the Riverfront," FWP, Northwestern State University, Natchitoches, LA, folder 053.

32. This lyric may contain a bit of buried history: Preston Lauterbach's *Beale Street Dynasty: Sex, Song, and the Struggle for the Soul of Memphis* (New York: Norton, 2015, 35–36) includes a story from 1868 about a white named Mary Grady shooting a Black

woman, Isabella Walton, in a fit of jealousy over their mutual lover, a Black cabdriver named Jim Rucker. The case was sensationally covered in Memphis newspapers, and Rucker's sexual prowess may have inspired vernacular rhymers.

33. Isaac Baker Brown, a pioneering British gynecologist, recommended clitoridectomy as a cure for nymphomania, masturbation (which he termed "peripheral excitement"), menstrual cramps, epilepsy, depression, and hysteria. He was eventually discredited for performing the surgery without permission, but clitoridectomy was discussed as a cure/punishment for nymphomania and lesbianism well into the twentieth century. There were also numerous reports that Black women tended to have larger clitorises than white women—an obvious analogy to the male genital stereotype—and were prone to taking a male role in lesbian relationships. (Sarah B. Rodriguez, *Female Circumcision and Clitoridectomy in the United States: A History of a Medical Treatment* [Rochester, NY: University of Rochester Press, 2014], 11, 24, 49, 66.)

34. Ruby Walker, interview by Chris Albertson, on *Bessie Smith: Complete Recordings*, vol. 5, Columbia Legacy CD 57548, 1996. Walker was Bessie Smith's niece by marriage and recorded as Ruby Smith.

35. Peetie Wheatstraw, "The First Shall Be Last and the Last Shall Be First," Decca 78 7167, 1936; "I Want Some Sea Food," Decca 7657, 1939.

36. Eudora Welty wrote that the *Atlantic Monthly* would not let her quote the lyrics of "Hold Tight" in a short story, adding, "I never knew why." (Harriet Pollack, "Words Between Strangers; On Welty, Her Style, and Her Audience," in Albert J. Devlin, *Welty: A Life in Literature* [Jackson: University Press of Mississippi, 2007], 79–80.) Bechet claimed he composed the song in 1924 and Clarence Williams refused to publish it because it was obscene, but the vocals on his recording were by Edward Robinson and William Spottswood, and they were credited as composers on later recordings. (John Chilton, *Sidney Bechet: The Wizard of Jazz* [New York: Oxford University Press, 1987], 117.)

37. Alan Hunt and Bruce Curtis, "A Genealogy of the Genital Kiss: Oral Sex in the Twentieth Century," *Canadian Journal of Human Sexuality* 15(2), 2006, 75.

38. I am referring here to male customers, but Joan Nestle notes that lesbians also hired prostitutes and Mabel Hampton recalled a lesbian brothel in Harlem in the 1930s (Nestle, *A Restricted Country* [San Francisco, CA: Cleis Press, 2003], 166).

39. Helen Lawrenson, "How Now, Fellatio! Why Dost Thou Tarry?," *Esquire*, May 1, 1977; reworked in Lawrenson, *Whistling Girl* [Garden City, NY: Doubleday, 1978], 24.

40. Bo Carter, "Cigarette Blues," Bluebird 6295, February 20, 1936; Lucille Bogan, "Till the Cows Come Home," 1933, first issued in 2004. A few other early blues records have lines that can be interpreted as references to fellatio, but none are equally clear.

41. From variants in Abrahams, *Deep Down*, 168–169; and Jackson, *Get Your Ass in the Water*, 146–149.

42. *Watson's Choice Collection of Comic and Serious Scots Poems: The Three Parts, 1706, 1709, 1711, in One Volume* (Glasgow: Maurice Ogle, 1869), 9; Gershon Legman, "Bawdy Monologues and Rhymed Recitations," *Southern Folklore Quarterly* 40, 1976, 123.

43. The first couplet is from the earliest surviving text, titled "The Ball," in *Forbidden Fruit: A Collection of Popular Tales*, Scotland, ca. 1890s, 68; the second is from multiple sources and was reworked by LaWanda Page, who recited the poem as a mock sermon on *Watch It, Sucker!*, Laff LP A195, 1977.

44. George Milburn, ed., *The Hobo's Hornbook: A Repertory for a Gutter Jongleur* (New York: Ives Washburn, 1930), 26; Saxon et al., *Gumbo Ya-Ya*, 455; Willie Dixon with Don Snowden, *I Am the Blues: The Willie Dixon Story* (New York: Quartet, 1989), 88. Dixon performed and sold broadsides of another popular toast, "The Signifying Monkey," in his Vicksburg youth that used "all the bad terms and it was rough," then bowdlerized it, added a chorus, and made a hit recording with the Big Three Trio that was covered by Cab Calloway and Count Basie as "The Jungle King."

45. Armstrong, typescript joke book, Louis Armstrong House Museum Archive.

46. Armand Piron, quoted in Al Rose, *I Remember Jazz: Six Decades Among the Great Jazzmen* (Baton Rouge: Louisiana State University Press, 1987), 110; "Let's Keep the Record Straight," *Second Line*, July/August 1952, 13 (the anonymous author wrote that the title was unprintable "because it sounded like: 'Take Your Hands Off of Katie's Glass'"); Manuel Manetta and Kid Ory, interview, August 26, 1958, HJA; Manuel Manetta, interview, March 28, 1957, HJA (the transcript quotes Manetta recalling "Take Your Finger Out of Katie's Head," with a notation that "other sources mention a different orifice"). Armstrong may have varied the lyric; Johnny St. Cyr recalled him singing "Who Threw the Bricks on Katy's Head" and Kid Ory, though generally describing Armstrong's lyric as "too dirty" to perform, recorded a version that went, "Keep off Katie's head, I mean, get out Katie's bed" (Johnny St. Cyr, "Jazz As I Remember It," *Jazz Journal* 19(9 and 10), September and October 1966; Floyd Levin, *Classic Jazz: A Personal View of the Music and the Musicians* (Berkeley: University of California Press, 2000 , 69; *Kid Ory and Red Allen in Denmark*, Storyville CD 6038, 1998).

47. Shelton Brooks, filmed interview by Ian Whitcomb, 1972, from the collection of Will Friedwald; Whitcomb, "Shelton Brooks Is Alive and Strutting," *Los Angeles Times Calendar*, May 18, 1969, 12.

48. L. O. Curon, *Chicago: Satan's Sanctum* (Chicago: Phillips, 1899), 147. Curon may be a pseudonym, since I find no reference to him aside from this book.

49. Chauncey, *Gay New York*, 65, 147.

50. Bessie Smith, "Foolish Man Blues," 1927; Kokomo Arnold, "Sissy Man Blues," 1935, which was shortly covered by Josh White and by Connie McLean's Rhythm Boys.

51. Chad Heap, *Slumming: Sexual and Racial Encounters in American Nightlife, 1885–1940* (Chicago: University of Chicago Press, 2009), 263.

52. War Department Report, December 21, 1917, in Landau, *Spectacular Wickedness*, 191.

53. "Disappearance of Young Boy Believed Slain," *Times-Democrat* (New Orleans, LA), October 6, 1913, 2; "Basin Waters May Hide Boy's Murder," *Daily Picayune* (New Orleans, LA), October 6, 1913, 5; "Griffey Drowned; Two Are Arrested," *Daily Picayune* (New Orleans, LA), October 7, 1913, 5.

54. "Pervert's Murder," *Daily Picayune* (New Orleans, LA), March 31, 1914, 2.

55. Chauncey, *Gay New York*, 61.

56. Lomax notes, LOC, pdf file in Rounder box set, 178.

57. "Change Came Over Dance Hall World," *Daily Picayune* (New Orleans, LA), March 30, 1913, 28.

58. Kid Ory, "Storyville-Spano's," August 7, 1951, unpublished manuscript quoted in McCusker, *Creole Trombone*, 106–107.

59. Manuel Manetta, interview, December 27, 1968, WRJC/HNOC, http://hnoc.minisisinc.com/thnoc/catalog/3/1125.

60. This charge was later changed to "loitering and frequenting places where dangerous and suspicious characters gather" ("Faints on Trial as 'District' Habitue," *New Orleans Item*, October 18, 1913, 3).

61. *Daily Picayune* (New Orleans, LA), April 4, 1914, 5.

62. "Any Rags," Fleischer Studios Talkartoon, 1932. In 1897 Havelock Ellis quoted an American writing, "To wear a red necktie on the street is to invite remarks from newsboys and others . . . that have the practices of inverts for their theme. A friend told me once that when a group of street-boys caught sight of the red necktie he was wearing they sucked their fingers in imitation of fellatio." (St. Sukie de la Croix, *Chicago Whispers: A History of LGBT Chicago Before Stonewall* [Madison: University of Wisconsin Press, 2012], 24.) "Call of the Freaks," aka "Garbage Man Blues," was recorded by King Oliver, Luis Russell, Red Nichols, Milton Brown, and the Harlem Hamfats.

63. Ralph Matthews, "The Pansy Craze: Is It Entertainment or Just Plain Filth?," *Afro-American*, October 6, 1934, 7.

64. Robert McKinney, "Saint Joseph Night No. 2," 1940, FWP, Northwestern State University, Natchitoches, LA.

65. Lil Johnson, "Get 'Em from the Peanut Man (Hot Nuts)," recorded July 16, 1935.

66. Stella Johnson, "Hot Nuts Swing," Decca, 1936.

67. "New York Cops Hit Vulgar Dance in Cafes," *Chicago Defender*, March 17, 1934, 5. Phil Moore, who played piano for Bentley in Los Angeles, said she called wealthy white patrons, including the Duke and Duchess of Windsor, "whores and bitches . . . and they all just squirmed and snickered with perverse delight" ("Things I Forgot to Tell You," Phil Moore Collection, Indiana University Black Film Center/Archive).

68. Wilbur Young, "Negroes of New York/Sketches of Colorful Harlem Characters/Gladys Bentley," September 28, 1938, at https://digitalcollections.nypl.org/items/efed8640-5b2d-0133-8460-00505686d14e.

69. Thanks to Chris Smith for background and lyrical transcriptions of the Bentley party discs, recorded in Los Angeles ca. 1939–1940 and released anonymously on Bronze, Party Time, and her own Top Hat label.

70. Eric Garber, "Gladys Bentley: The Bulldagger Who Sang the Blues," *Outlook: National Lesbian and Gay Quarterly*, Spring 1988, 55. Bentley's repertoire was often drawn from white party material, and there is a virtually identical parody in *Mess Songs and Rhymes of the R.A.A.F.* [Royal Australian Air Force] *1939–1945*, apparently published by airmen in New Guinea.

71. Cockrell, *Everybody's Doin' It*, 123, 164–165.

72. Ruby Walker described a man-on-man show at a buffet flat in Chicago (*Bessie Smith: Complete Recordings*, vol. 5, Columbia Legacy CD 57548, 1996), and an investigator passing for Black in the Snug Café in Harlem in 1916 described a Black "lady entertainer" offering to take him to a buffet flat "where the women will dance naked for you and also show you how two women bulldike each other" (Cockrell, *Everybody's Doin' It*, 184–185).

73. Jaxon is frequently described as a queer blues singer, often sang female roles on records, and at times performed in drag, but he usually worked in male clothing

and in later years wrote boastfully about his multiple marriages and sexual prowess with women (Russ Shor, "Charlie Gaines," *Storyville* 68, December 1976–January 1977, 45–46; William H. Miller, "Great Little Guy: The Life and Times of Frankie "Half Pint" Jaxon," *Australian Jazz Quarterly* 3, Christmas 1946, 3–21).

74. Ma Rainey, "Sissy Blues," Paramount 12384-B, 1926. Some writers have credited this song to Thomas A. Dorsey, but the copyright and recording documents credit Rainey.

75. Ma Rainey, "Prove It on Me," Paramount 12668, recorded June 12, 1928.

76. Sloppy Henry, "Say I Do It," August 13, 1928. The *Pittsburgh Courier*, December 25, 1926, announced that "They Say I Do It" had been published by Chas H. Booker and recorded by Gussie Alexander, but not released (Chris Smith, Howard Rye, and Robert Ford, "Charles H. Booker: Music Furnished for All Occasions," *Names & Numbers* 100, January 2022).

77. Rainey and Smith are now frequently described as lesbian or bisexual, though some historians are dubious. The only evidence of Rainey's lesbianism seems to be her song lyrics, and although Ruby Walker gave a first-person account of sharing Smith's bed (*Bessie Smith: Complete Recordings*, vol. 5, Columbia Legacy CD 57548, 1996), Sara Grimes wrote that Walker was unreliable and other acquaintances of Smith's "dismissed rumors of bisexuality" (*Back Water Blues: In Search of Bessie Smith* [Amherst, MA: Rose Island, 2000], 242).

78. Mack McCormick, "The Damn Tinkers," *American Folk Music Occasional Number One*, 1964, 7.

79. Lomax papers, UT, box 3D, folder 182.

Chapter Seven

1. Alan Lomax, "'Sinful' Songs," 125.

2. "Barbara Allen (Bobby Allen)," typescript, AFC 1933/002, box 02, folder 024.

3. W. Prescott Webb similarly wrote of hearing a Black guitarist named Floyd Canada sing a blues with 160 rhymed couplets in Beeville, TX, in 1913–14, and referred to it as "The African Iliad." (W. Prescott Webb, "Notes on Folk-Lore of Texas" [*Journal of American Folklore*, 28(109), Jul–Sep 1915], 292–296).

4. John A. Lomax, "'Sinful Songs' of the Southern Negro," *Musical Quarterly* 20(2), April 1934; reprinted with minor alterations in *Adventures of a Ballad Hunter* (179–180). Alan recounted the same anecdote in his "'Sinful' Songs" (125–126).

5. "Barbara Allen (Bobby Allen)," typescript, AFC 1933/002, box 02, folder 024.

6. Alan Lomax, "'Sinful' Songs," 115.

7. "Negro Folk-Songs," *Donaldsonville (LA) Chief*, May 25, 1912, 1. John Lomax circulated this letter to newspapers around the South, requesting help from readers "who know such songs or know where they can be had."

8. Johnson, *American Negro Poetry*, xl.

9. Alan Lomax, "'Sinful' Songs," 106–107, 112, 118.

10. Alan Lomax, "'Sinful' Songs," 115.

11. Alan Lomax, New Orleans, July 28, 1933, in Lomax papers, UT, box 3D-192, folder 8. The Lomaxes' racial attitudes have been endlessly debated. In 1934, Lawrence Gellert wrote that they failed to find songs representing modern Black attitudes because they were "Good old Southern gentle folks with the good old Southern gentle folks'

attitude towards 'niggers'" ("Entertain Your Crowd," *New Masses*, November 20, 1934, 19). Lew Ney countered that John was "a southerner with all of a southerner's prejudices, but also with a southerner's peculiar sympathies toward Negro culture when the prejudices are left unaroused," and that Alan was a leftist whose "attitude toward the Negro is all anyone could wish" ("A Southerner's Prejudices," *New Masses*, December 11, 1934, 21).

12. Longhair recalled: "Sullivan Rock was my main person because he had the spirit and soul." (Bill Greensmith and Bez Turner, "Fess," *Blues Unlimited* 130, May–Aug 1978, 4. He is listed as Sullivan (or Selvin) Rocks in city directories, and signed his World War II draft card Sullivan Rocks.

13. Alan Lomax, remarks at the Fiftieth Anniversary Symposium for the Archive of American Folksong, Library of Congress, Washington, DC, November 16, 1978, in Matthew Barton, "The Lomaxes," in Spencer, *Ballad Collectors*, 153.

14. Lomax and Lomax, *American Ballads*, 93; Alan Lomax, card to Carl Engel, July 30, 1933. For the confusion surrounding Hunter's name, see Chapter 1, note **33**.

15. Anonymous, *Immortalia*, 34; Bill Nice, letters to Robert Gordon, December 14, 1923 and February 14, 1927, Gordon collection, numbers 462 and 2598, AFC; Palmer Jones, "Stackerlee," D. K. Wilgus Collection, UCLA Ethnomusicology Archive (see Chapter 5, note **25**).

16. Brown, *Stagolee Shot Billy*, 2, 8; Daryl Cumber Dance, *Shuckin' and Jivin': Folklore from Contemporary Black Americans* (Bloomington: Indiana University Press, 1978).

17. "The Songs of the Jails," *Kansas City Star*, March 14, 1897, 7; Lottie Kimbrough and Winston Holmes, "Don't Speak to Me," Gennett 6660, 1928. This article did not mention any dirty lyrics, but an article a month later suggested placing women in a separate wing to protect them from the men's "ribald songs and jests" ("Reforms at the Jail," *Kansas City Star*, April 16, 1897, 9).

18. Peter Guralnick, "Meeting Chuck Berry," http://www.peterguralnick.com/post /153471712891/meeting-chuck-berry, accessed August 12, 2023.

19. Vance Randolph noted a recollection of a Black singer singing "Duncan and Brady" for at least an hour without repeating a verse ("Unprintable" songs from the Ozarks manuscript collection, AFC 1989/016).

20. "Lay in State," *St. Louis Post-Dispatch*, July 29, 1894, 1.

21. *St. Louis Globe-Democrat*, May 7 1889, 3; "Slew a Prize Fighter," *St. Louis Post-Dispatch*, December 10, 1895, 1; "Too Much Murder," *St. Louis Post-Dispatch*, January 8, 1896, 3.

22. "Duncan's Last Lay," *St. Louis Post-Dispatch*, August 9, 1894, 3.

23. White, *American Negro Folk-songs*, 186.

24. "New Figure Brought into 'Frankie' Case," *St. Louis Post-Dispatch*, February 17, 1942, 11; "Folklore Expert Testifies Woman Is 'Frankie' of Ballad Fame," *St. Louis Globe-Democrat*, February 18, 1942, 9. Young's testimony was seconded by Baker's lawyer, Joseph McLemore; some articles gave the songwriter's name as Jim rather than Bill. Young's source was a policeman and reporter named Ira Cooper, who said Dooley later moved to Detroit and became a "slum preacher," and the US census listed William Dooley as a locksmith in St. Louis in 1910 and as a minister in Detroit in 1920.

25. The *Palladium* was published ca. 1884–1911 and a satirical piece in the *Post-Dispatch* (March 26, 1899, 34) includes a sample of its topical poetry, but the earliest surviving issues are from 1903; the *American Eagle* was published 1894–1907 and the only surviving

copy is from 1905. Numerous early collectors mention and quote from Black broadsides, but in years of searching archives I have found barely a half-dozen originals.

26. Ollie Jackson shot two men over a gambling dispute in 1901 in a saloon managed by William Curtis, who previously ran the bar where Lee Shelton killed Billy Lyons. Robert Winslow Gordon printed a version of the ballad as "Olive Jackson" (*Adventure*, July 30, 1924, 191–192); Alan Lomax recorded a version from Will Starks in Mississippi in 1942; and Furry Lewis's "Billy Lyons and Stack O'Lee" (Vocalion 1133, 1927) borrowed its chorus and some verses.

27. "Bombs for Redress," *St. Louis Post-Dispatch*, May 8, 1892, 17.

28. "Duncan's Last Hope," *St. Louis Globe-Democrat*, June 2, 1894, 8.

29. "Stark's Brutal Song," *St. Louis Post-Dispatch*, January 19, 1891, 5. Two policemen were mobbed at a dance where a woman sang this song at them ("Police Attacked," *St. Louis Post-Dispatch*, May 21, 1891, 4), and Keneth G. (Jock) Bellairs recalled police fighting with Black people who sang it ("Police Stories," *St. Louis Star*, October 11, 1923, 9).

30. Handy, *Father of the Blues*, 26–28.

31. William Desmond, "Cream Colored Station to Replace Old Bloody Third," *St. Louis Post-Dispatch*, October 9, 1910, 2B. Bellairs recalled "A Bully Has Gone to Rest" as "a victory song for Duncan" ("Police Stories," *St. Louis Star*, October 11, 1923, 9). A song called "Dere's a Bully Gone to Rest" was published in 1896 by Dryden and Mitchell, and the *Leavenworth (KS) Herald* (December 8, 1894, 3) mentioned a "rag" called "The Bully."

32. Handy, *Father of the Blues*, 118; Johnson, *American Negro Poetry*, xi.

33. "Wrote 'The New Bully,'" *Kansas City Star*, February 2, 1896, 7. Trevathan dated this to the summer of 1891; Gates Thomas ("South Texas Negro Work Songs," 168) included the same rhyming couplet in a Texas "levee song" dated to 1892.

34. "Who Really Wrote 'Dat New Bully'?" *San Francisco Examiner*, January 12, 1896, 36. Joseph Hirschbach claimed he adapted the song from "a raw melody" Trevathan hummed, and that John P. Wilson wrote the words, provoking a suit by Trevathan, who said Hirschbach's only contribution was a formal orchestration. The tune of the chorus was based on Henry Robinson Allen's setting of Lord Byron's poem "The Maid of Athens," and the *San Francisco Examiner* (December 29, 1895, 20) had a woman exclaiming, "The 'Maid of Athens' is the 'New Bully,'" provoking the query: "Does she wear bloomers?"

35. The *New York Times* (November 4, 1896) reported Cooley playing for May Irwin, and the *Kansas City Star* (February 14, 1897) said he had joined "Maisy Mayer's band of pickaninnies" in New York. Trevathan wrote a couple of short stories about "Mr. Wiley Carey of Tennessee and his colored servant, Cooley," for example "Cooley's Song," published in the *New York Journal* and widely reprinted in 1896.

36. "Rag-time," *Daily People* (New York), December 11, 1911, 3; James L. Ford, *Forty-odd Years in the Literary Shop* (New York: Dutton, 1921), 277.

37. "May Irwin Face, Laugh and Song Are Discussed," *Star-Gazette* (Elmira, NY), April 18, 1906, 6.

38. Maxwell F. Marcuse, *Tin Pan Alley in Gaslight* (Watkins Glen, NY: Century House, 1959), 177.

39. Versions of this piece appeared in the *Buffalo (NY) Review*, July 21, 1899, 4, and the *Spokane Chronicle*, July 22, 1899, 6.

40. Advertisement, *St. Louis Globe-Democrat*, November 25, 1906, 39.

41. *Reedy's Mirror* (St. Louis, MO), June 24, 1894, 4.

42. Many sources recycle Douglas Gilbert's description of Connor and Mama Lou (*Lost Chords*, 208–213), assembled ca. 1940 from the recollections of older St. Louisans.

43. "A Notorious Woman," *St. Louis Post-Dispatch*, August 6, 1899, 5; "Ejected from the Depot," *St. Louis Post-Dispatch*, December 8, 1892, 10; *St. Louis Globe-Democrat*, December 13, 1886, 2.

44. "Police Intimacy with Resort Keepers Shown," *St. Louis Star*, October 11, 1912, 6. Eric McHenry established Louise Rogers's identity from a death certificate and inquest (personal communication, June 2023).

45. *Brooklyn Citizen*, March 27, 1892, 6; "With Voice and Foot," *Chicago Tribune*, July 3, 1892, 15; "Ta-ra-ra Boom-de-ay," *News and Citizen* (Morrisville, VT), August 18, 1892, 1.

46. W. C. Handy, "A Panorama of Negro Music," in *Who Is Who in Music: 1941 Edition* (Chicago: Leo Stern, 1941), 566.

47. Ray Argyle, *Scott Joplin and the Age of Ragtime* (Jefferson, NC: McFarland, 2009), 53.

48. "'Babe' Connors Has Passed Away," *St. Louis Republic*, August 5, 1899, 7. A note from 1894 described May Irwin's "Mamie, Come Kiss Your Honey" as "one of Babe Conner's St. Louis plantation songs," implying that her house was already a familiar source before "The Bully" took off ("The Stage: Latest Gossip About Plays and Players," *Wheeling (WV) Register*, May 13, 1894, 6). "Hot Time in the Old Town" was elsewhere credited to Amanda "Mandy" Green, a hard-drinking, knife-wielding woman who "composed half a dozen negro songs" popular with after-hours crowds in Denver, Colorado ("'Hot Time' First Sung," *Kansas City Daily Journal*, August 24, 1898, 8).

49. Orrick Johns, *Time of Our Lives: The Story of My Father and Myself* (New York: Stackpole, 1937), 98; "Folklore Expert Testifies Woman Is 'Frankie' of Ballad Fame," *St. Louis Globe-Democrat*, February 18, 1942, 9.

50. By 1899 Connor had a second house called the Palace, which Mama Lou continued to run for a half-dozen years after Connor's death, and it is possible "Frankie and Albert" was performed there.

51. David, "Tragedy in Ragtime," 212, citing Dudley McClure, "The Real Story of Frankie and Johnny," *Daring Detective*, June 1935, 32. The 1900 census gives Baker's birth year as 1877.

52. "Was Jealous of Donnie Foster," *St. Louis Globe-Democrat*, January 30, 1896, 5.

53. Richard Clay, in Huston, *Frankie and Johnny*, 105, 109. Clay testified in the Baker suit that Baker and Britt were "just ordinary people, pretty well settled," but when Baker's lawyer asked him if she led "a lascivious life," he responded, "Well . . . she was a woman, just like the rest of them" ("Al's Friend Says Frankie Was Just an Ordinary Gal," *St. Louis Post-Dispatch*, October 21, 1939, 3; Ruth Moore, "It Was Song, Not Johnny, That Did Frankie Wrong, Witness Claims," *St. Louis Star-Times*, October 21, 1939, 9). Huston wrote that Allen Britt "liked to be called" Albert, but the earliest sources using that name are from the 1930s and may have been influenced by the ballad. The inquest and Britt's death certificate gave his age as sixteen; other sources say seventeen.

54. "Testifies 'Frankie' Ballad May Stem Back to Africa," *St. Louis Post-Dispatch*, February 18, 1942, 20.

55. "Frankie's Inquest Story in '99 to Be Used in Suit," *St. Louis Post-Dispatch*, October 16, 1939, 8, apparently quoting the coroner's inquest from October 20, 1899.

56. David, "Tragedy in Ragtime," 214–216, citing Dudley McClure, "The Real Story of Frankie and Johnny," *Daring Detective*, June 1935. I'm not clear whether the confusion of "Allen" and "Albert" was made by the speakers or the writers.

57. "Al's Friend Says Frankie Was Just an Ordinary Gal," *St. Louis Post-Dispatch*, 21 Oct 1939, 3.

58. "Frankie Was Christian, Says Targee St. Pal," *St. Louis Post-Dispatch*, October 28, 1939, 3; "Hearing Revives Classic Slaying," *Springfield (MO) Leader and Press*, October 29, 1939, 4. "Slain Johnny Had Fine Funeral but No White Horses," *St. Louis Star-Times*, November 11, 1939, 2; "'Johnnie' in Short Pants When Shot, Father Says," *St. Louis Post-Dispatch*, November 11, 1939, 3.

59. Odum, "Folk-song and Folk-poetry," 366–367; White, *American Negro Folk-Songs*, 214; John Harrington Cox, *Folk-Songs of the South* (Cambridge, MA: Harvard University Press, 1925), 218–219.

60. Sandburg, *American Songbag*, 75–86.

61. White, *American Negro Folk-Songs*, 214.

62. Numerous writers claimed to have heard "Frankie and Johnny" before 1899, and Alan Lomax (*Folk Songs of North America*, 558) suggested that "a number of Frankie-type ballads may have been composed by Negroes and whites . . . during this period, about a number of similar incidents."

63. The first surviving version of the Delia ballad was collected along with "Lilly" in Newton County, Georgia (Odum, "Folk-Song and Folk-Poetry," 353); John Garst published a study of the murder and songs, *Delia* (Northfield, MN: Loomis House, 2012).

64. Perrow, "Songs and Rhymes," 1915, 132; Mississippi John Hurt, "Hop Joint," *The Immortal Mississippi John Hurt*, Vanguard LP 79248, 1967.

65. Leighton Bros. and Ren Shields, "Frankie and Johnny or You'll Miss Me in the Days to Come," (New York: Tell Taylor, 1912); Gene Greene and Charley Straight, "Frankie and Johnny," Pathé 5370, recorded December 1912.

66. John Held, Jr., *The Saga of Frankie & Johnny* (1930; repr. New York: Potter, 1972), 6–8. The madam was Helen Blazes, who ran a house in Salt Lake City from 1892 to 1908.

67. Gordon, "Inferno" collection.

68. Belden Kittredge [Vance Randolph], *The Truth About Frankie and Johnny* (Girard, KS: Haldeman-Julius, 1945), 3. An article from 1870 describes a white-owned saloon in ⟩St. Louis where a sixteen-year-old Black woman named Hattie Terry, "having the reputation of being a prostitute," tended bar, served beer, "sang improper songs, and danced lewd dances" ("A Beer-Jerking Case," *Daily Missouri Republican* [St. Louis, MO], September 24, 1870, 2).

69. O. O. McIntire, "New York Day by Day," syndicated in *Joplin (MO) Globe*, June 8, 1929, 4.

70. A report from 1918 described a cowboy singing a fifteen-minute version of "Frankie" in an army camp ("With Songs of Prairie Trail 'Panhandle Shorty' Keeps Up Morale of Foot-Sore Rookies," *Daily Oklahoman* [Oklahoma City, OK], August 4, 1918, 13), and in 1914 a student at the Missouri School of Mines estimated that the full ballad comprised "two or three hundred stanzas," writing that he first heard "a rather obscene

version . . . popular among the underworld," and collected versions from mountain women, tramps and migrant workers, a fiddler, and a streetwalker who "sang some stanzas that were utterly sickening." (H. M. Belden, *Ballads and Songs Collected by the Missouri Folk-Lore Society* [Columbia: University of Missouri Press, 1940, 331–333], with additional information from Belden's report of communications from H. A. Chapman, 1914, in "Missouri Folk-Lore Society Ballads, Songs, Rimes, Games, Riddles, etc. Collected Between 1903 and 1917," Houghton Library, Harvard University [Am 2446], folder 65.)

71. Typescript sent by Gershon Legman to D. K. Wilgus in 1955, with handwritten annotations crediting some verses to Les Copeland, in Wilgus Folksong Collection, folder 181, Special Collections Library, Western Kentucky University. Legman wrote that he obtained Jones's texts thirdhand, as "an unexpurgated pencil manuscript . . . laboriously handwritten in 1927" (Legman, "Who Owns Folklore?" *Western Folklore* 21[1], January 1962, 2; Randolph, *Roll Me in Your Arms*, 480).

72. Lomax, *Folk Songs of North America*, 557–558, 570. Lomax wrote both that Jones learned the song from Baker in Omaha (558) and that it was "recorded in Kansas City by Palmer Jones" (559); and credited Legman as his source, but referred to Jones, who had died more than thirty years earlier as "my present informant."

73. Lomax and Lomax, *American Ballads*, xxvii, 103, 105.

74. After meeting Ledbetter in Angola, John Lomax wrote, "He sang us one song [presumably "Irene, Goodnight"] which I hope to copyright as soon as I get to Washington, and try to market in sheet form" (Lomax papers, UT, box 3D-192). The Lomaxes signed Ledbetter to an exclusive contract that split income from his concerts and recordings three ways and put their names as coauthors of his songs. Though some songs were adapted by all of them, others were recorded by Ledbetter without their input, and John Lomax also took a share of the tips Ledbetter collected during concerts for which they were already receiving a joint fee.

75. Lomax and Lomax, *Negro Folk Songs*, 3.

76. The Haitian dancer Josephine Premice remembered Ledbetter as always impeccably dressed, calling him "a peacock" (interview by author, 1995).

77. Margaret and Arthur Mae Coleman, letter to Alan Lomax, March 27, 1935, John A. Lomax and Alan Lomax papers, AFC 1933/001, box 13, folder 439.

78. Lead Belly, "Mr. Tom Hughes's Town," Louisiana State Penitentiary, Angola, LA, July 1, 1934.

79. Wolfe and Lornell, *Life and Legend*, 37, 85–86; Lomax and Lomax, *Negro Folk Songs*, x–xi, 7–9, 24–25, 52. Ledbetter recalled performing for Governor Pat Neff in the Sugarland, Texas, penitentiary, wearing a white suit and leading an eight-piece band. The Lomaxes mentioned a jazz orchestra in the Angola penitentiary and implied that Ledbetter worked with it, writing, "the boys played for Rotarian conventions and the like, and, when we came to Angola with our recording machines, he was in fine fettle."

80. Elijah Wald, *Josh White: Society Blues* (Amherst: University of Massachusetts Press), 2000 , 94.

81. Lead Belly, "Frankie and Albert," LOC recordings 127 and 148, 1935. Wolfe and Lornell (*Life and Legend*, 1992, 160–161) quote Alan Lomax describing Ledbetter's reworkings of his songs as "one of the most amazing things I've ever seen."

82. John A. Lomax and Alan Lomax, *Cowboy Songs and Other Frontier Ballads* (New York: Macmillan, 1938), xix, 424. John originally ascribed the song to the unnamed

cook, but later wrote that his lyric was "assembled from several sources"—whether because that was more accurate or to protect his claim to authorship.

83. Library of Congress, "Home on the Range," https://www.loc.gov/item/ihas .200196571, accessed August 12, 2023.

84. Lomax and Lomax, *Our Singing Country*, 368. Robert Winslow Gordon preserved the earliest known documentation of the song, in a letter from 1925 (AFC, Gordon collection, 925). The first recording was made by Clarence Ashley and Gwen Foster as "Rising Sun Blues" (Vocalion, 1933), and Alan Lomax recorded versions in Kentucky from Bert Martin, Henson Dawson, and Georgia Turner in 1937. Several nineteenth-century establishments in New Orleans used the Rising Sun name, as did many establishments elsewhere. Lomax consistently claimed that at least two British songs mentioned a bawdy house with that name, but I have only found the Cox recording.

85. Harry Cox, recorded by Alan Lomax, London, December 2, 1953, https://archive .culturalequity.org/field-work/england-and-wales-1951-1958/london-1253/she-was -rum-one. Josh White was featured on all three programs of the BBC in 1950–1951, and toured the UK regularly.

86. Randolph, *Roll Me in Your Arms*, 252.

87. Mellinger Edward Henry [sic], *Folk-Songs from the Southern Highlands* (New York: Augustin, 1938), 357–358, obtained as a "Song Ballet" from Ray Bohanan, Indian Gap, Sevier County, Tennessee, August 1929.

88. Saxton, *Gumbo Ya-Ya*, 442.

89. "Woman Killed," *Times-Democrat* (New Orleans, LA), September 4, 1894, 3; "Night of Revelry Ends in Murder," *Daily Picayune* (New Orleans, LA), September 4, 1894, 6.

90. "Martin's Murder," *New Orleans Item*, September 5, 1894, 8.

91. "Slayer of Husband Faints in Court," *New Orleans Item*, May 15, 1911, 3; "Mrs. Martin Acquitted," *Daily Picayune* (New Orleans, LA), May 27, 1911, 8.

92. Lomax papers, AFC.

93. Sandburg, *American Songbag*, 28.

94. Edmond "Doc" Souchon, "Ella Speed Blues," with Papa Laine's Children, Tempo 1268, 1952, and *Dr. Souchon Recalls Early New Orleans Minstrel Days and Blues*, Golden Crest LP 3065, 1959; Rosalind Johnson, interview, February 23, 1970, HNOC.

95. Among other unrealized plans, Morton said he was going to record a musical sermon, "The Black Diamond Express to Hell" (Phillips, "Jelly Roll Charts Jazz"; Martin, "Black Diamond Express").

96. Alan Lomax, remarks at Archive of Folk Song Fiftieth Anniversary Symposium, November 16, 1978, in Barton, "The Lomaxes," in Spencer, *Ballad Collectors*, 160.

97. Lomax and Lomax, *Our Singing Country*, 328–330, 366, 368, 371, 373. E. Simms Campbell wrote in 1939 that "the blues always consist of twelve bars" and most songs "termed blues" on radio programs were "merely bastard products" (Ramsey and Smith, eds., *Jazzmen*, 108), but at the time that was a rare and pedantic position. Newspapers routinely referred to any woman who specialized in mournful torch songs as a blues singer.

98. Though no recorded blues song lasts a half hour, Booker White, Lightning Hopkins, and other performers were known to keep playing and singing without a break for as long as their listeners were interested or the dancers kept dancing.

99. Frank Dupree or DuPre, a white man, was hanged in Atlanta in 1921 for killing a Pinkerton agent during a jewel robbery. A ballad about the event was recorded by several white singers in the 1920s, and Odum and Johnson printed two variants of another ballad in *Negro Workaday Songs* (55–59), which were not strict twelve-bar blues but included couplets that were standardized in that form by 1930 and recorded by several artists. The Lomaxes printed a twenty-three-verse version in *Our Singing Country* (328–330), with a note that Langston Hughes collected it in Cleveland in 1936.

100. Cockrell, *Everybody's Doin' It*, 171; Lucille Bogan, "B.D. Woman's Blues," ARC 5-12-58, 1935.

101. T. S. Eliot, *Inventions of the March Hare: Poems 1909–1917.* (San Diego: Harcourt Brace, 1996), 314. A full lyric of "The Jolly Tinker" appears in Anonymous, *Immortalia*, 91–92. Bessie Jones recited a verse that combined two of these themes: *"You son of a bitch, your dick is big as my wrist. Now, you go somewhere and fuck your fist, you big-dick son of a bitch"* (https://archive.culturalequity.org/field-work/bessie-jones-1961-1962/new-york-city-1061/toast-used-woman-insult-man).

102. John Patrick, personal communication, August 18, 2022.

103. Charles A. Ford, "Homosexual Practices of Institutionalized Females," *Journal of Abnormal and Social Psychology* 23(4), January 1929, 444–445. The letter continued in prose, but the final phrases rhymed: "if I were in cuba and you in spain the love I get for you will make a bool dog break his chain, and I don't care what you use to be but I know what you are to day if you love me or I love you what has the world to say."

104. For example: *"When I am dead and in my grave No more whisky will I crave"* (A saloonkeeper's epitaph, *Monumental News*, 14(4), April 1902, 260); *"When I am dead and in my grave No more pussy shall I crave"* (Cathy M. Orr and Michael J. Preston, *Urban Folklore from Colorado: Typescript Broadsides* (Ann Arbor, MI: Xerox University Microfilms, 1976).

105. Lord, *Singer of Tales*, 4–5.

106. Pete Seeger, *The Incompleat Folksinger* (New York: Simon & Schuster, 1972), 145.

Index